CW00820705

Scottish Housing in the Twentieth Century

SCOTTISH HOUSING IN THE TWENTIETH CENTURY

Edited by Richard Rodger

Leicester University Press
(a division of Pinter Publishers)
Leicester, London and New York

First published in Great Britain in 1989 by Leicester University Press
(a division of Pinter Publishers Ltd)

Editorial offices
Fielding Johnson Building, University of Leicester,
University Road, Leicester, LE1 7RH

Trade and other enquiries
25 Floral Street, London, WC2E 9DS

British Library Cataloguing in Publication Data
A CIP cataloguing record for this book is available
from the British Library
ISBN 0-7185-1278-2

Library of Congress Cataloging in Publication Data
A CIP record is available

Typeset by Acorn Bookwork, Salisbury, Wiltshire.
Printed and bound in Great Britain by Biddles Ltd of
Guildford and Kings Lynn

Contents

List of Figures

List of Tables

List of Contributors

Hunain Al-Qaddo is lecturer in Management at Basrah University, Iraq. His interests lie in the field of government and administration. His Ph.D thesis was concerned with the Scottish Special Housing Association, and his publications in the *Scottish Government Yearbook* and *Public Administration* also examine inter-departmental relations in Scotland.

Brian Elliott is visiting Associate Professor in Sociology at the University of British Columbia, Canada. He has co-authored two books with David McCrone on urban issues, and has co-edited *The Petite Bourgeoisie: Comparative Studies of an Uneasy Stratum* (1981) with Frank Bechhofer. He is editor of *Technology and Social Process* (1988).

Andrew Gibb is a Senior Lecturer in Geography and Director of the Applied Population Research Unit at the University of Glasgow. Publications include an urban biography, *Glasgow: the Making of a City*, and a wide range of papers on population and urban housing in the 19th century and post-1945.

David McCrone is Senior Lecturer in Sociology at Edinburgh University, and chairman of the Unit for the Study of Government in Scotland. His publications include, *The City: Patterns of Domination and Conflict* (1982); and *Property and Power in a City* (1989), both co-authored with Brian Elliott. He is editor of *Scottish Government Yearbook* (1983–89), and co-editor of *The Making of Scotland; Nation, Culture and Social Change* (1989).

Joseph Melling is Lecturer in Economic and Social History, University of Exeter. He has published widely in the areas of housing policy, tenants' struggles, labour history and business welfarism. He is presently working on a reinterpretation of labour in Scottish society, and the changing role of shop floor supervision in the decline of British Industry.

John Minett Managing Director Creative Holidays Ltd. and Oxford Workshops in Urban Design. He was previously Principal Lecturer in Planning History and Design Theory in the School of Planning at Oxford Polytechnic and has taught in U.S., Canada, Australia, Japan as well as many European countries. He has published many articles in magazines and newspapers relating theories of planning to practice in planning.

Nicholas Morgan is a lecturer in the Scottish History Department at Glasgow University, where he has special responsibility for the use of computers in teaching and research. His personal research includes a major computerised study of the housing market in late nineteenth and early twentieth century Glasgow, the building industry, and public and private housing in the inter-war years. Publications including a commissioned history of the National Housebuilding Council and a series of biographies of Scottish contractors and builders in the second volume of the *Dictionary of Scottish Business Biography*.

Richard Rodger has taught economic and social history at Liverpool and Leicester Universities, and during 1982–83 and 1986–87 held respectively Fulbright and Hall scholarships as a Visiting Professor of History at the University of Kansas. He is editor of the *Urban History Yearbook*, and his published research ranges extensively across the fields of urban, social and business history, and most recently included *Housing in Urban Britain 1780–1914: Class, Capitalism and Construction*.

David Whitham has worked on aspects of housing policy and practice in the Scottish Office and in an inner London borough. He has taught at Oxford Polytechnic, has published a number of articles and papers on housing and environmental matters and is now engaged in historical research on local government in Scotland.

1 Introduction

Richard Rodger

Housing and the contemporary context

Urban renewal in the 1980s has achieved a measure of popular appeal. Television programmes and newspaper features on the regeneration of the Scottish city, its inner core and the renewal of outlying council or 'peripheral' estates have so familiarised the public with the urgency and scale of contemporary Scottish housing problems that, paradoxically, there is a possibility that the housing issue will be demoted on the political agenda; familiarity may breed contempt for the housing question.

Media coverage has understandably focused on Glasgow, yet overexposure in one city should not distract attention from housing problems elsewhere in Scotland, nor should publicity be confused with achievement. Even more fundamental, the historical antecedents of existing problems, attempted solutions and the lessons of experience gained provide a crucial input to the comprehension of the nature of the contemporary problem and to the formulation of policy. Too often administrative reorganisation and the injection of cash have been deemed sufficient remedies to reverse Scottish housing problems; short-term policy expedients have predominated at the expense of analyses of the longer-term structure of the housing market.

Popular attention has also focused on the housing issue because the ideological shift associated with Conservative governments since 1979 enables local councils to sell public housing and therefore runs counter to the twentieth century Scottish housing experience in which the public provision of minimum standards of accommodation formed a central strand. In essence this has been a product of public expenditure constraints. Between 1970 and 1980 exchequer grants from London financed an average of 34 per cent of Scottish local authority housing—the peak in 1976–77 recorded 41 per cent financed in this way[1]—and in three successive years 1981–83, exchequer contributions to Scottish housing fell from 37 to 25 to 16 per cent and in 1986 to 7 per cent (see Figure 1.1).

Four possibilities followed from this abrupt change in housing finance: first, the shortfall could be recouped from increased rents and/or rates contributions; second, the volume of new council housebuilding could be restricted; thirdly, the size of the existing public sector housing stock could be reduced and its quality permitted to deteriorate; fourthly, other housing agencies—housing associations and private enterprise principally—could be encouraged

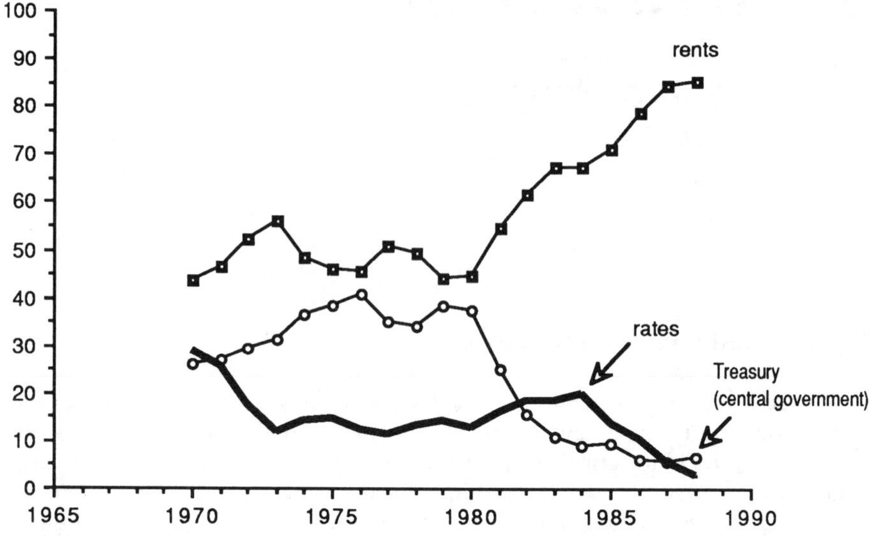

Figure 1.1 Sources of local authority revenue 1970–86

to replace public sector housing provision. The basis of media interest in Scottish housing largely revolved around the distributional impact of the four possibilities outlined, each of which was tried to varying degrees and with variable success. The impact of sudden directional changes of policy offered 'human interest' and sensationalism. Recent trends in Scottish housing shown in Figures 1.1 and 1.2 provide some of the empirical background to this popularisation of the housing issue.

Against a demographic background throughout the 1970s and 1980s in which new household formation averaging 0.9 per cent p.a. has been matched by similar increases in the Scottish housing stock, notable changes have taken place in other respects. In the three periods 1919–39, 1945–65 and 1966–76 Scottish council housebuilding (see figure 1.4) exceeded that of private enterprise by respectively 215, 632 and 265 per cent. Since 1967–70, when annual council building reached something of a plateau around 27,000 houses, a marked decline has taken place so that by 1979 it had declined to an annual level of about 5,000 houses. That trend has continued since. Private exceeded public housebuilding in 1978 for the first time since 1925 so that in the decade 1977–86 it had slumped to 32 per cent of private housebuilding. Significantly, but for a brief reversal in 1975, the pronounced downward path of public sector housebuilding since 1970 is not attributable to the ideology of the 'New Right' in the 1980s, but to longer-term factors affecting housing provision.

Demolitions have altered fundamentally too. In the mid-1980s the number of properties closed and demolished was only one tenth that of the annual average of 1955–75, and, in the face of significantly reduced levels of new housebuilding, it has been this reaction against demolition and a preference for refurbishment which has maintained the Scottish housing stock in rough numerically equivalence to the growth in households.

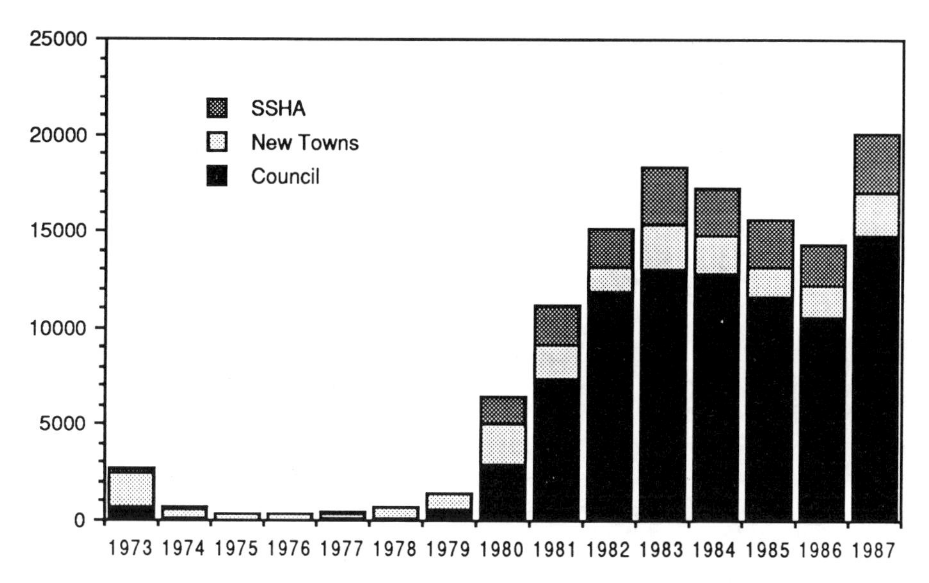

Figure 1.2 Public sector house sales 1973–86

Responses to public expenditure restrictions therefore comprised a rapid reduction of new building, and a switch towards the rehabilitation of the existing housing stock. But both strategies were implemented in Scotland before the Conservatives assumed power in 1979: refurbishment policies were in effect by 1974–5 and reductions to council housebuilding by 1970. These directional changes have been largely overlooked in the simplistic explanations offered by newspapers and television and attributed to ideologically inspired Thatcherite policies. In fact, much deeper, historical forces conditioned the response.

Sales of public housing, mostly by local authorities, to tenants at prices which were statutorily determined at least 30 per cent below market value represented another notable change of policy from 1979 and were more accurately attributable to an ideological shift (see Figure 1.2). But even this directional change had precedents[2] in the sale of houses to tenants by new town development corporations, and was partially conditioned by the same Treasury imposed controls on public expenditure in the attempt to contain the repair and maintenance elements of the housing expenditure accounts of local authorities.

Rate-capping prevented decreased central government housing finance being redirected at private property interests after 1984. Yet the burden of housing expenditure on the rates declined as much during the earlier Conservative administration of Heath as it did under Thatcher, and the proportion of housing finance raised from tenants' rents rose as rapidly during 1970–4 as it did in the years 1980–7 (Figure 1.1). Indeed real rents in Scotland increased more abruptly during the Heath period than at any other time (see Figure 1.3).

As the specific case of a rejuvenated Glasgow housing stock is paraded to

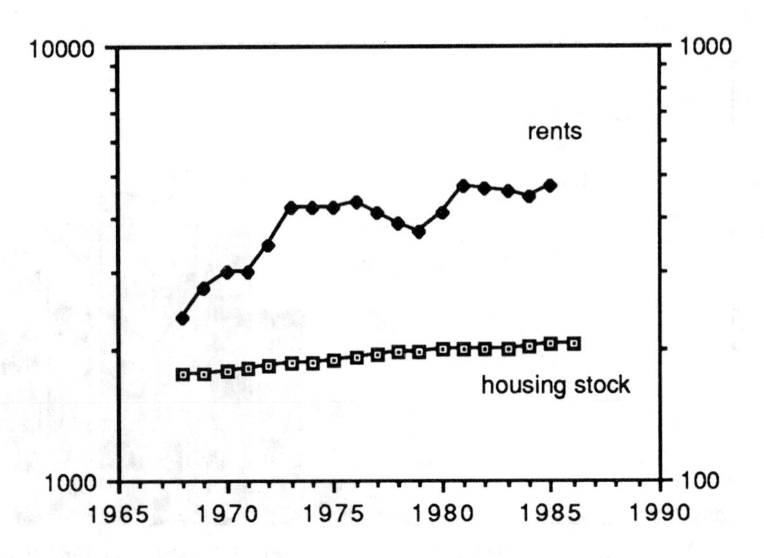

Figure 1.3 Council rents and the national housing stock

English councils as an exemplar of successful government housing policy in the 1980s, media attention both insufficiently acknowledges its own contribution to the hype and uncritically examines the historical path of housing provision in the twentieth century. In fact, the Glasgow East End Renewal project (GEAR) was launched in 1976 when the Labour Party controlled all three tiers of government—national, regional and district. Optimism and political alignment combined with a sceptism of central government involvement in local Scottish affairs to provide conditions which were ripe for some form of urban regeneration programme in Glasgow, and only riots in the major English conurbations in 1981 produced a commitment there to introduce more effective proposals for the reconstruction of inner city urban life.

Several aspects of current housing trends have attracted attention as innovative departures. Yet few policy ventures are taken without reference to earlier efforts, and fewer still represent adventurous departures since the political and economic implications of sudden directional lurches are considerable. It is the longer time scale, the historical dimension, which contributes significantly to an understanding of the background to current developments, and serves to redress accounts of the housing market which emphasise revised ideological stances and fail to take account of the complex, cumulative interplay of social, political, economic and wider cultural forces.

Continuity and change in Scottish housing: an historical perspective

The broad outline of Scottish housing is well known. A reliance on private enterprise construction overwhelmingly for rental purposes was the hallmark of housing provision prior to 1914. Alternative housing agencies—council and company housing, workmens' cooperative dwellings and philanthropic model houses—provided very limited additions to the housing stock, though for demonstration purposes were not unimportant. Municipal efforts were more of an environmental nature—water supply, drainage, street and building regulation, localised slum clearance, provision of parks, strategies designed to contain public health risks associated with extreme levels of urban overcrowding and less involved with direct building operations. Whether inevitable, or accelerated by wartime conditions, that pattern of private sector involvement was amended after 1919 when council housebuilding and management was ushered in, and within a few years were on a scale which far exceeded that of private housing provision. New designs, logistical considerations concerning housing production, and a new apparatus of administration and intergovernmental relations emerged, to each of which councils had to respond. That there were mistakes, failures and policy cul-de-sacs should come as no surprise in view of the rapidity of change in the inter-war period. Early subsidised council housebuilding was directed in the 1920s towards 'general needs' or quantitative additions to housing stocks. The focus shifted to qualitative improvements—slum clearance and 'decrowding' subsidies in the 1930s—but reverted to a numerical emphasis post-1945 when housing policy accorded priority to a massive expansion in the housing stock. This was the context in which extensive 'peripheral' council housing estates developed and, in the 1960s, coupled with trends in architecture, a new phase of high-rise council flats was built. Negative reactions to the social implications of such housing schemes produced a subsequent preference for the renovation of existing houses and a corresponding halt to demolition programmes, and more intimate housing arrangements, such as specific designs for special needs, notably the handicapped and elderly. Current emphases on council sales, diversified tenure, encouragement to housing associations and private builders are attempts to both reinforce and more finely tune this process.

The historical dimension offers a view of both continuity and of change as the balance of Scottish housing provision and its constituent elements has changed. Nowhere is this more evident than in the housebuilding industry. Before 1914, conforming to Glasgow building regulations, the model for many other Scottish authorities, added 40 per cent to building costs compared to the London building code, and even standardised Ministry designs for inter-war subsidised housing cost about 10 per cent more than for identical houses in England.[3] In the 1970s it was still strict, wide-ranging Scottish regulations affecting fire, safety, roof access, window hinges, chimney flues, ventilation traps on drains, minimum requirements for water storage, overflow pipes for sinks, baths and tanks which contributed to higher building costs than in England.[4] Notwithstanding the adoption in some quarters of new building materials after 1920, notably steel houses and poured concrete construction, the enduring conservatism of the majority of Scottish builders in relation to materials continued to add to building costs. Despite slightly higher brick prices in Scotland, their substitution by brick blocks remains least developed compared to the rest of Britain; only 12 per cent of houses in Scotland use this type of wall construction compared to between 40–57 per cent in the English regions south of the Tyne.

If relative building costs suggests a degree of historical continuity, this was not the case in relation to the structure of the industry. In contrast to the late nineteenth century, when the reliance on small builders in thirty Scottish burghs accounted for more than half the planning applications for houses, the concentration of output amongst Scottish building firms resulted in the ten largest firms in the 1960s producing 65–75 per cent of houses built. The two largest Scottish builders were responsible for one third of all Scottish housebuilding, and a single firm for one quarter of output in 1967 and 1968. Consequently 'Scottish builders have near monopolies in their own area', and the 'incidence of competition is slight compared with operations in England', where housebuilding firms in 1970 were only half the size of those in Scotland.[5] Though the trend towards a larger scale of operations was already underway before 1914, the extent to which structural change and operational scale were amended by the capitalisation associated with system of contracts for council housing in the inter-war and post-1945 periods, and the shift to multi-storey flats in the 1960s requires further investigation. But what has clearly altered since 1900 is the role of the small builder in Scotland.

Organisational structure may have changed, and system building may be more widely employed, but as with the building industry before 1914, lingering traditional practices increased Scottish building costs in the 1970s. For example, unlike English practice where windows are fitted as construction proceeds, in Scotland windows are commonly inserted after walls are built, necessitating expensive adjustments. The retention of the preference for suspended wood joist floors, and sarking or wooden boarding between rafters together added as much to building costs as all the additional materials costs combined.[6] Other criticisms of Scottish builders also have a historical echo. Inflexible site development, especially in relation to developing split level housing on hilly sites, or utilising oddly shaped plots, which, though difficult to quantify, applied in the 1870s and in the 1970s. And output per operative as measured by the number of completions per worker in the 1960s was 43 per cent lower than in English building. Low standards of bricklaying, covered internally by plastering and externally by roughcasting, caused defective wall alignments and expensive corrective work. Duplication by separate subcontractors in erecting scaffolding, lesser emphasis on brick blocks, thicker joinery, and other practices combined to lower productivity and to inflate costs, as did higher Scottish building wages. In addition, the structure of firms in the industry affected final pricing, where the concept of cost plus profit was often rejected in favour of what the market could bear. The inescapable conclusion of a report in 1970 targeted lower productivity and large scale builders' profits as important factors in the higher supply prices of Scottish housing in comparison to other regions of Britain.[7]

The level of legal fees associated with land transference in Scotland is another dimension in which continuity can be observed. The Royal Commission on Housing heard evidence in 1885 that 'the high cost of transfer of heritable property is generally regarded as a serious hardship by those dealing in such property and it has a material effect in increasing the cost of housing.[8] In 1970 the same view prevailed, with legal fees estimated to be 17–35 per cent above English charges.[9]

In the nineteenth century, supply prices for Scottish housing were above those in the rest of Britain. One indication of this was the fact that Scottish working class rents in 1908 were 19–26 per cent above levels in the midlands and north of England.[10] In broad terms this remains the situation according to a 1968 survey of one thousand housing estates throughout Britain. Compared at the regional level for identical specifications, the average selling price per square foot in Scotland was 16 per cent above Yorkshire, east midlands, and Northern Ireland prices, and 6–7 per cent above those in the north west, west midlands and south west England. Predictably, only in southeast England were average floor space costs higher (by 17 per cent) than in Scotland.[11]

The implications of higher supply prices on the quality of Scottish housing have long been compounded by weaker purchasing power north of the border. In the 1830s and 1840s Scottish wages were often 20–25 per cent adrift of pay in identical English trades; by the 1860s the differential had narrowed to 16–19 per cent and by the last quarter of the nineteenth century stood at between 9–13 per cent below pay in equivalent occupational grades in English and Welsh boroughs.[12] In specific areas of employment Scots were paid virtually as well as workers in the rest of the United Kingdom, but the pay differential remains a characteristic constraint on the Scottish consumer. For example, in the period 1919–39, 'income per head has been lower in Scotland, fluctuating between 87 and 96% of the United Kingdom average',[13] and in the years 1977–84 Scottish real incomes were only 96 per cent of the UK levels.[14] The long-run effects of historically weaker purchasing power on the suppression of living standards, and particularly on standards of affordable rented accommodation relative to the rest of the country, remains a key element in the quality of Scottish housing provision.

The continuing numerical importance of the older housing stock itself warrants further study. More than a quarter of Scottish housing was built before World War I; about one sixth of existing Scottish houses date from the years 1890–1918, roughly the same proportion as for the inter-war years, and slightly more than half the housing has been built since World War II. Of the privately rented accommodation, 68 per cent dates from before 1919, 17 per cent was built during the inter-war years, and only 7 per cent of post-1945 housing has been for private rental.[15] So two-thirds of privately rented accommodation is at least 70 years old, and since rehabilitation forms an important strand of current policy, knowledge of the life expectancy of Scottish housing, its character and cultural context is relevant to policy formulation (see Table 1.1).

Another important dimension of housing, its social significance, centres on the fact that it affects all family members. Accommodation represents the single most important item of personal expenditure, roughly equivalent to the amount spent on food, and proportionately is inversely related to income. Historically, working class households spent twice as much on housing as middle class families. Design, amenities and appliances affect daily household

Table 1.1 Age distribution of the Scottish housing stock in 1987

Period	No of houses (000s)	%
pre–1871	58	2.8
1871–90	170	8.2
1891–1918	318	15.3
1919–44	351	16.9
1945–70	761	36.6
1970–86	422	20.3

Source: Scottish Development Department, *Statistical Bulletin* (2) Housing Trends, 1987, Table 2.

relations and housing quality, most notably floor space, water supply and ventilation, has for long been closely allied with the incidence of disease and infant mortality, the physical development of children, and other indicators of the vitality of the population. Clearly factors other than housing quality are influential determinants—educational and occupational influences on demand for housing quality come immediately to mind—but it would be difficult to deny that they too were affected by the character and quantity of housing space.

Residential building continues to be a significant component of capital formation in Scotland, as elsewhere in the United Kingdom. During the 1970s and 1980s dwellings represented between 25–40 per cent of gross fixed capital formation in Scotland, levels similar to those a century before.[16] Not surprisingly, therefore, building and related construction workers, remain quantitatively important, accounting for 9 per cent of total employment, a little below levels achieved in the Victorian era, though clearly there are considerable implications for employment in the furniture and furnishings, consumer durables and the not unimportant Do-it-Yourself maintenance and repair trades. In terms of the production side of the Scottish economy housebuilding cannot be lightly disregarded.

Although Victorian slum clearance initiatives undertaken in the cities and major burghs of Scotland between 1866 and the 1880s provided a template for English authorities, relatively few additional properties were built on sites cleared of insanitary housing. Municipal housing expenditure was directed mainly at street widening, demolition, costs of compensation to landlords, and in a limited way to the construction of municipal lodging housing—seven were built in Glasgow in the 1870s. The Housing of the Working Classes Act 1890 permitted councils to themselves initiate new building proposals and in Scotland many burghs did so. Boosted by small loans from the Public Works Loan Board, Scottish municipalities had, by 1903, constructed 73 per cent more dwellings than all English and Welsh boroughs combined, London excluded.[17] By 1913, and mostly as a result of efforts over the preceding two

Table 1.2 Local authority housing in Scotland in 1913

Burgh	% of families in council houses	Families housed
Hamilton	0.31	23
Clydebank	0.35	26
Aberdeen	0.36	131
Bo'ness	0.47	10
Leith	0.47	84
Kilmarnock	0.77	58
Edinburgh	0.81	601
Glasgow	1.31	2,199
Perth	1.37	114
Greenock	1.40	214
Oban	2.07	24
Total	1.01	3,484

Source: Royal Commission on the Housing of the Industrial Population of Scotland Rural and Urban, *Report*, Cd. 8731, 1917, p. 387. The total for the 11 burghs accounted for all Scottish local authority housing in 1913.

decades, about 1 per cent of Scots were council tenants (see Table 1.2). In localised areas of Scottish burghs—Tynecastle and the Cowgate in Edinburgh, and the Townhead, Haghill and Stobcross districts of Glasgow—municipal housing had an impact on the local housing market, landlords' rental prospects, and the environment, and though this trend introduced uncertainties to the horizons of private sector housing and building interests, in 1914 it remained distant.

In 1913, about 1 per cent of families in the largest Scottish burghs were housed in municipal accommodation; by the 1980s more than 50 per cent of Scots lived in public housing. From 1919 the zeal of local authority building efforts transformed the nature of the Scottish housing market. Stimulated by a local political will and prompted by the introduction of Treasury, that is central rather than local government, subsidies for housing,[18] Scottish councils have only occasionally been surpassed by private sector housebuilding (1920; 1924–5; and since 1978) in the numbers of houses produced (see Figure 1.4).

This fundamental transition marks a central feature of Scottish housing in the twentieth century. It has brought public authorities into the arenas of production (as builders) and consumption (as landlords), and has drawn housing on to the political stage in contrast to its simpler status akin to other product markets in the nineteenth century. This transition of Scottish housing from the political wings to centre stage has not been even. In fact the volatility of council housebuilding in the inter-war years can be seen in Figure 1.4, where the successive stimuli of Treasury subsidies to local authorities contributed significantly to the ebb and flow of municipal housebuilding programmes. To a certain extent this was also reflected in private enterprise housebuilding, where a similar profile emerged, albeit with a dampened dynamic. After 1945, Scottish municipal and private enterprise built housing diverged markedly. In only twelve years between 1945 and 1986 has private sector building fallen in Scotland, and then often only by very small amounts. The long-term time trend has been very steadily upwards. By contrast, council housebuilding has fluctuated considerably, with falling levels of housing completions in 25 of 42 years. Though corporation building programmes between 1945–75 operated at levels higher than any of the inter-war years, output was significantly curtailed in the 1950s, and has again fallen almost uninterruptedly since 1970. Annual housing completions numbered 35,000 in 1970, declining to well below 5,000 houses in the 1980s. Conventional views about the predominance of council housing in Scotland must therefore be moderated by the historical ebb and flow in the pattern and composition of housebuilding in Scotland.

As such firm council commitment to housebuilding involved unprecedented capital resources, not only were new government departments formed, but they assumed responsibilities and functions which impinged acutely on local government autonomy. Designs, approvals and auditing interposed areas of overlapping responsibility. The historical legacy involved not only enduring tension between local authorities and the Scottish Office which invaded responsiblities beyond the housing arena, but more tangibly created a sizeable housing stock with considerable repair, maintenance, administration and replacement implications for councils. This radical route in housing provision by local authorities remains a central feature of contemporary Scottish urban life and the historical background to its development is itself worthy of a fuller examination.

An unusual reliance on public sector housing sets tenurial relations in

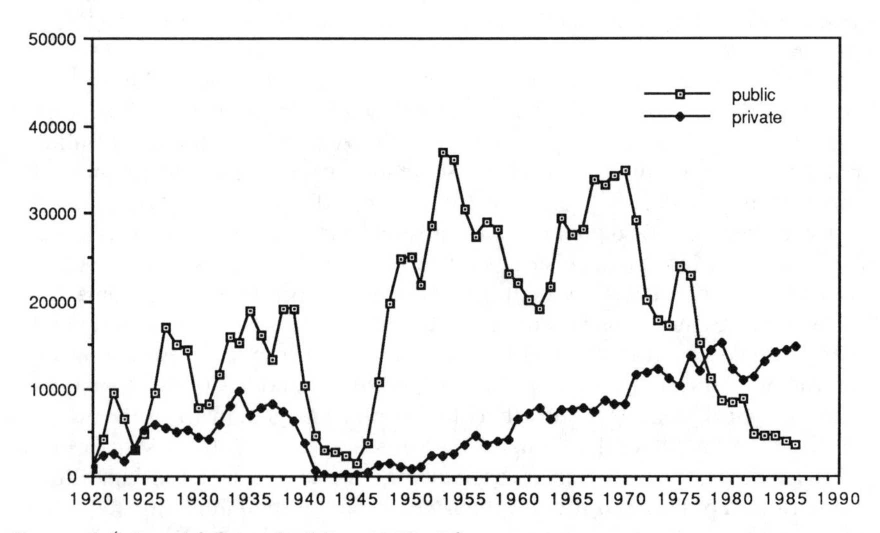

Figure 1.4 Scottish housebuilding 1920–86

Scotland apart from the rest of Britain. Approximately 50 per cent of the aggregate Scottish housing stock in 1986 was municipally owned. In individual Scottish burghs—Coatbridge, Irvine, Clydebank, Motherwell, Wishaw—more than 80 per cent of households lived in council-owned property; in Falkirk, Alloa, Airdrie, Greenock, Hamilton, Kilmarnock, Johnstone, Glenrothes and East Kilbride over 70 per cent of households lived in property rented from public authorities; and elsewhere, in Dundee, Glasgow, Paisley, Dunfermline, and Kirkcaldy, to name a few locations—more than 60 per cent of households were accommodated in council houses, a percentage double that of the British average (inflated by the inclusion of Scottish data) where 31 per cent of households lived in accommodation rented from councils and other public bodies.[19]

The prevalence of Scottish council housing is shown in Figure 1.5 where the proportion of housing tenanted from local authorities is shown for each of 150 Scottish burghs and an equivalent number of English and Welsh boroughs in 1981.[20] A consistently higher percentage of council-owned properties existed in Scotland, although there were always a few Scottish burghs—Blairgowrie, Troon, North Berwick, Giffnock, Bishopton, West Kilbride[21]— where owner occupancy predominated. Whereas the fifty English and Welsh boroughs with the greatest concentrations of council housing each owned at least 45 per cent of their stock, the same number of Scottish local authorities owned 70 per cent or more of the housing in the burgh. Even though the size of urban authorities was commonly smaller in Scottish burghs, the reliance on the council as housebuilder and landlord was typically twice that of English boroughs. For example, the first 100 municipalities represented in Figure 1.5 recorded English councils owning at least 30 per cent of the housing stock in their areas, while in Scotland the figure was at least 58 per cent.

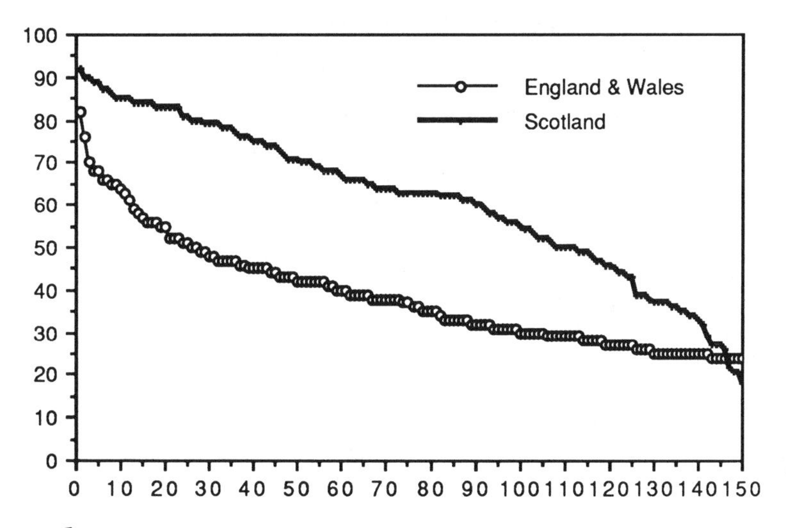

Figure 1.5 Comparative tenure 1981: percentage of public rented housing in urban areas

So the council as landlord is a distinctive feature of Scottish urban life. Many electors, many more than elsewhere in Great Britain, therefore have personal experience of the ongoing administrative performance of their local authority and there exists a Scottish tradition of radical tenant politics closely identified with rent strikers and red Clydeside, but in reality broader based, which has sustained landlord–tenant antagonisms irrespective of whether the landlord has been an individual or a council.

Procedures for allocating local authority housing to Scottish tenants have, according to one study, had a 'significant constraining effect on the mobility of labour'.[22] Notwithstanding the fact that the socio-economic composition of local authority tenants makes them less likely to be geographically mobile, qualification for good quality council housing on desirable estates according to the number of months which have elapsed since registering on the council's housing list has had a deterrent effect on the movement of households into certain local authority areas. Features inherent in the tenure itself rather than the personal or social characteristics of the households have acted as a limiting factor on labour mobility, and tenure has, therefore, partially reinforced structural economic problems by trapping families in areas of high unemployment.[23] Allocative mechanisms rely upon policies of grading council house applicants according to certain socio-economic characteristics.[24] So although council building policy may procure uniformly sound accommodation in terms of amenity and structural standards, allocative procedures have accentuated distinctions in the status of different estates, replicating nineteenth century residential segregation ranging across the spectrum from working class suburbs to slums, albeit in a changed spatial and architectural setting. By so doing, allocative policies have reinforced the social segregation of the city and thereby contributed to oppositional politics in the local council chamber.

Scottish tenure is distinctive but not confined to the numerical importance of council housing. Feuing, the terms under which property was transferred from a vendor (superior) to a buyer, had been a central feature of property development and building finance since before the Union in 1707. Land was sold outright in Scotland; the vendor ceded all rights over the property,[25] for which he received a lump sum for the sale and the right to exact an annual payment—the 'feu-duty'. This entitlement to a future annual income could be sold perhaps for twenty or thirty times its annual value,[26] or a bond raised on the security of future feu income. A small down payment on a piece of land could therefore be transformed into a considerable capital advance, and it was this access to finance which had encouraged many nineteenth century builders and estate developers to construct tenements. Intensive site development resulted from the very high value attributable to a site by the inherent legal rights to raise capital. Opportunities to sub-feu and thus 'farm' or inflate the value of land or to obtain occasional feudal payments on it further increased land prices in Scotland. It was land prices in conjunction with higher building costs, which caused rent controls in Scotland from 1915 to the 1960s to be maintained longer and regulated at levels considerably above provincial English boroughs and more in keeping with those of central London. The spatial pattern of Scottish Victorian housing, was therefore historically conditioned to a considerable extent by the nature of tenure, and provides an inheritance which contemporary policy cannot overlook.[27]

Architectural characteristics of a distinctively Scottish type leave an indelible mark on the most casual observer. Densely packed high rise tenement flats characterise the Scottish Victorian city, and are replicated in the smaller burghs of the urban hierarchy. Pebble-dashed or harled rendering typify inter-war council housing, and geometrically arranged groups of bungalows signify the Scottish owner-occupier equivalent of English semi-detached housing of the 1930s. Though council housing of the 1940s and 1950s also retained some distinctively Scottish characteristics, high rise council flats and more recently private housing has ceded certain elements of a distinctively Scottish design tradition which has been increasingly homogenised as national building and construction firms such as Barratt, Wimpey and Laing employ standardised designs and building methods. Bricks, colours, renderings, window styles and other details more in keeping with English urban design, and previously unknown, are now commonplace in Scotland.

Towards the end of the nineteenth century, the housing issue was capable of sustaining a coalition of previously under-represented political interests which in turn ultimately transformed housing itself into a class issue. More recent changes in the spatial arrangements of Scottish housing have had consequential effects on the basis of political organisation, as they have had on other community activities. Meetings in the street, drying green or in local halls were an important dimension in the process of sensitising public opinion until the 1930s. The density of dwellings contributed substantially to the success of such activity. The post-1945 proliferating peripheral estates divorced work and residence; the notorious lack of communal facilities inhibited the development of associational life, as did the trend to high rise council flats. Communality was increasingly replaced by individuality. Though political views are arguably as entrenched, they are based less on participatory politics at neighbourhood level, and in this way the leverage has reverted to the workplace and contributed to the exclusion of women who for long carried the political torch in central Scotland. Except over conservation areas, tree-planting/felling, suburban shopping malls, and similar areas of specific middle class interest, housing as a basis for women's participation in the political process fulfills a very different role to that of a century, or even fifty years ago.

Housing, if less a basis for political activism than formerly, was for long to the forefront of Scottish political consciousnesss. Twentieth century Scottish housing strategies—new towns, Scottish Special Housing Association accommodation for 'special' groups or areas, and particularly municipal housing—form part of a radical tradition of housing provision in Scotland in response to levels of acute deprivation in the standard of accommodation. Scottish municipalities formed the vanguard in housing initiatives which from the late nineteenth century successively, if only modestly successfully, embraced the demolition of insanitary properties, council housebuilding, and more recently high rise and refurbishment strategies. The sceptic might argue that such departures from the traditional provision of housing through market forces reflected the conspicuous failure of private enterprise in Scotland to build and manage sufficient housing consistent with the income levels of the working class. Alternatively, there is a more subtle, abstract argument that the civic gospel was firmly entrenched in Victorian and Edwardian Scotland, fostered by underlying principles of Presbyterianism and reinforced by a historical legacy which emphasised a closer relationship between church and state than was permissible in England.[28]

Criticisms of Scottish housing have proved remarkably consistent from one historical phase to the next: the destruction of neighbourhoods and resultant social havoc in communities; the inhumanity of tenement and council building as represented in their scale and monotony of design and colour; the insensitivity of housing management, both private and council; the destabilisation of local economies. Overcrowding has remained a consistent source of criticism. In addition, the complexity of bureaucracy had an intimidating effect upon tenants; the tension between central government objectives in Whitehall, those in the Scottish Office in Edinburgh, and the concerns of local councils created confusion, delay, frustration, and diffused the political will.[29] The ethos of housing policy was for long governed by the notion that quantitative provision was itself sufficient; little importance was attached to participation. Even when tenants were vociferous it served only to amend the particular form in which policy was imposed from above, and gave no great scope for participation in the initial decision making process. It was in part as a reaction to such criticisms that recent grassroots involvement, tenants' associations, smaller council housing management units, diverse tenure, and scope and responsibility for local initiatives were moulded together to form a more intimate, responsive approach to housing provision. Such initiatives were derived from the experience and appraisal of long term housing strategies; they were not an overnight ideological shift.

New contributions to housing history

This book attempts to provide a historical background to the nature and form of Scottish housing in the twentieth century. The contributors straddle various disciplines—town planning, sociology, social and economic history, public administration and geography—and curiously most are themselves Scottish by adoption rather than birth, which may add to their objectivity. All have previously published material on Scottish housing, and though the general line they adopt will be familiar to specialists, this collection groups together for the first time contributions which view Scottish housing over the course of the twentieth century and do so from varied standpoints. Contributors have attempted to provide something of a chronological or narrative account of central developments in their particular area of interest while at the same time offering an interpretative view, seeking where possible to identify the issues, problems and solutions, the conflicts and alliances which existed in the housing of the Scottish people. The contributions, though often based on a particular town or city, offer broadly conceived arguments of significance beyond the narrowly confined boundaries of the individual town. While not claiming to be entirely jargon-free zones, the authors have as far as possible avoided the highly technical aspects of the subject, presenting them in an accessible form.

Any consideration of twentieth century housing must take as its point of departure the nineteenth century legacy. This is provided in Rodger's chapter on 'Crisis and confrontation in Scottish housing 1880–1914 (Chapter 2) which establishes the problems facing builders, tenants, and local councils in the decades before World War I. Their disparate interests created a hiatus in housing and housebuilding. As a consequence of increased building costs, interruptions to building finance, local authority intervention both in housing byelaws and new construction, landlords' attempts to avoid empty properties yet retain paying tenants, and tenants' endeavours to obtain better value for money and improved terms on which flats were let, interest in the property sector diminished between 1900 and 1914. New construction was at unprecedentedly low levels—below even those of the depressed building years of the 1880s. In no small way this reflected disinterest in property, both as an investment and as a source of income for trusts, widows, and other small savers for whom tenements formerly represented a tangible and trustworthy outlet for their nest eggs. No longer did housing offer a dependable yearly income; the vagaries of the stock exchange were less daunting and advances to local borrowers appeared relatively attractive in view of the fall from investors' grace experienced by the property sector after 1900. Though standards of accommodation improved in aggregate, significant portions of the housing stock remained defective before 1914. This was crucial. Defective housing standards fundamentally affected the daily lives of half the urban population of Scotland in 1914; it had a particular impact on women and contributed to their early political awareness; and crucially, it produced spatial arrangements ie tenements unique to Scotland and which were difficult to reverse in the short term. Housing, like employment, became a terrain contested by the Scottish urban working class and an instrument in their politicisation.

This theme is developed by Melling, who by drawing on particular episodes such as Clydeside rent struggles, demonstrates the importance of tenants' movements to the emergence of Labour and to socialism in the west of Scotland. The delayed development and sectionalist nature of Scottish trade unionism enabled the inter-union trades councils to occupy a central place in labour and tenant politics after 1880, and stiffens the argument that a distinctive industrial structure contributed significantly to the social, political and cultural characteristics of the Clyde basin. Melling shows how the Labour Party harnessed and orchestrated early tenants' movements, how housing became a central electoral issue at the ward level before 1914, and examines the argument that landlords failed to develop a political identity capable of counteracting tenants' interests. Most important in the shaping of labour politics were the interlinking of housing issues and radical stances on suffragism and pacifism. In this respect it was women activists who were crucial in forging the political identity of Clydeside and Melling is careful not to exaggerate the contribution of official Labour Party figures. So, thus interpreted, wartime rent strikes were the catalyst for an intensification of existing class friction over workplace relations and employment terms. It was agitation surrounding housing conditions which initiated the radicalisation of Scottish politics and gave an impetus to wider working class movements—for example, the Cooperative, Unemployed Workers', and Communist movements of the inter-war years.

Housing became a live political issue at the beginning of the twentieth century. Superimposed on the politics of the labour market was the politics of the housing market; to the contested terrain of production was added that of consumption. It heralded the emergence of the consumer as an active political force and created conditions in which integrated strategies, for example, in town and country planning were more enthusiastically embraced in the 1920s.

Political realignment and emergent grassroots organisations characterised tenants' responses to early twentieth century housing issues. State responses are considered by David Whitham and John Minett in three separate, though closely related, phases of state sponsored building concerned with Greenock, Rosyth and Gretna. The eventual form of these projects provided design blueprints for subsequent town planning schemes, and particularly later council housing. But before they did the ambiguities of housing and town planning legislation produced confusion and delay over the provision of new housing schemes for munitions workers—the overlapping responsibilities of local authorities, the Local Government Board for Scotland (LGBS), Scottish Office and the Admiralty in London in particular led to tension between government agencies and frustration at the lack of progress.[30] Though there had been many council housing schemes before 1914, Rosyth marked a new departure, a central government sponsored and financed housing project in which garden city principles replaced traditional dependence on tenement style as a result of suspended local authority building byelaws. Whatever the baptismal problems associated with different administrative responsibilities, Whitham argues that the LGBS adopted a positive role, was instrumental in securing additional housing accommodation in various Scottish locations, and was influential at a national (British) level by virtue of the experience gained, through advice given to two important post-war national enquiries, and by the staffing and technical inputs to the newly formed central housing department at the Ministry of Health in London.

Complex and fractured administrative responsibility is a theme which runs through several of the chapters. Most conspicuously the pluralist structure of power was a formidable influence on new housing in Greenock and Rosyth. But Minett provides an intriguing account of the unified power and policy objectives together with the financial backing of central government during wartime which created Gretna. A rare glimpse of new town life and work is therefore available courtesy of Minett's research. The lifespan of Gretna was brief, however, and what is most instructive about the account of the death-throes and dismantling of Gretna, is the window it provides on planning thought at the end of World War I, and of the transience of planning ideals when confronted with conflicts between government departments, indecision at the War Office, infighting in the services as the navy and army sought to defend their own cordite supplies, and disinterest amongst local councils to takeover the plant and housing. If society learns by its failures, Gretna is instructive as a new town which failed.

Housing problems in 1914, though more general and intense than elsewhere, were not unique to Scotland. Clearly established housing needs existed in English boroughs too. But the events on the Clyde, and the Scottish experience of housebuilding for workers crucial to the war effort, coupled with a Royal Commission on working class housing in Scotland provided a degree of leverage on national policy formation in 1918. It has been claimed that state subsidised housing was not inevitable and that the property market could have recovered autonomously.[31] Certainly, the provision of housing could have embraced a wider range of alternatives—housing associations, garden city or public utility companies, cooperatives, company housing and other possibilities—but the cessation of residential building from 1915, and wartime restrictions on rents from that year too, fundamentally disturbed the housing market. To cumulative structural problems superimposed upon cyclical ones were added institutional factors which altered the shape of housing provision thereafter. The resurrection of the private housing market may have been possible in England and Wales, though even there such a contention takes little account of the regional pockets of extreme housing conditions. In Scotland in particular, the quantitative and qualitative shortfall in 1919 was of such proportions that suppliers, given labour and materials shortages, would have encountered formidable difficulties in producing sufficient new housing. Only a restructuring of priorities—to take account of training for building workers, new technological developments in construction and the manufacturing of materials—would have set the private sector afloat, and such interventionism was largely an anathema to governments of the 1920s where 'normalcy' and the restitution of market forces were paramount. Housing subsidies represented a lesser interventionist evil. Any lingering doubts were dispelled by the proclamation of 'homes for heroes' in 1919, now seen less as an electoral gimmick and more an expedient in the face of demobilisation, industrial militancy, a police strike, and the reverberations of bolshevism in Russia.[32] Lloyd George's strategy of buying off unrest by appealing to the material interests of consumers in the form of state funded improved housing 'Even if it cost a hundred million pounds', revised the structure of the housing market, and did so in a manner which proved irreversible except in the very long term.

How did local authorities cope with their new housing responsibilities? Without overturning estimates of the number of council houses built in the inter-war period, Morgan's account of Glasgow Corporation's efforts challenges the pessimistic notion that local authorities were sluggish in their response to subsidised housebuilding and management. Indeed, given formidable barriers, they appear to have responded enthusiastically and imaginatively to the new circumstances of the inter-war period. That Scottish council housebuilding did not achieve the annual production of houses sought is no condemnation of their efforts; indeed, given the difficulties encountered that local authorities built so many was almost miraculous. Morgan firmly rejects earlier interpretations of atrophy in inter-war Scottish housebuilding achievements. Not the least significant innovation was in the structure of the building industry where the previous reliance on small businesses receded as new corporate structures emerged based on single contractors. Morgan also introduces evidence to show how Glasgow Corporation itself had begun experiments into alternative building materials before 1918. It sought to diverge from conventional brick designs and commissioned or directly produced bricks, concrete and other materials from its own plants. Councils and private companies entered into the quest for new materials and designs and made substantial progress in this direction during the 1920s and 1930s.

Though considered from the standpoint of Glasgow Corporation the parallels in other parts of Scotland should not be overlooked. Corolite No-Fines and Duo-Slab produced respectively 50 and 1608 non-traditional houses for Edinburgh Corporation as early as 1923 and 1925; Tarran built 556 homes and in 1927 Boot and Sons added a further 500 steel houses for Dundee Corporation and two years later built 546 for Glasgow.[33] In Aberdeen, In-situ Concrete and Aberdeen Corporation Concrete at Tullos and Kairnhill provided council housing using new materials and designs, and timber was the basis of a later Corporation housing development at Auchinyell. The partnership between local authorities and private industry yielded several new designs, and experimentation with different materials added to the Scottish housing stock—about 6 per cent of new houses in the years of peak non-traditional building 1925–7 were made from steel.

A source of considerable tension inherited from the nineteenth century and a theme to which virtually all chapters make reference—namely the friction both between local and central government and within central government departments—concerned burghal autonomy in areas such as housing provision. Such testy 'inter-organisational relationships' blighted prompt execution of housebuilding; it had been a factor in early council housing, but grew in intensity as with the complexity of the state apparatus. Inter-organisational conflicts delayed the Greenock and Rosyth housing proposals before and during World War I, and as Gibb and Rodger and Al-Qaddo argue, also placed considerable difficulties in the way of housing provision by the Scottish Special Housing Association and Glasgow Corporation after World War II.

Whatever the ideological divisions of earlier periods, or indeed after World War II, Gibb shows how, for almost twenty years after 1945, there was a broad concensus in Scottish politics for an urgent expansion of the housing stock. Suburban 'greenfield' sites and then selective, intensive new town developments successively, though not always successfully, attempted to resolve the supply shortfall after 1945. Again the local–central clash emerged. The areas of contention mostly related to the level of planning—regional planning versus municipal—and the concession of a degree of administrative autonomy. The delicate trade-off concerning government grants to local authorities and political power associated with burgh revenues and population levels was balanced against the costs to municipal budgets of urban regeneration and social expenditure. Central government funds were not unconditional; a degree of participation in local decisions on housing and other matters was conceded by councils. Civic identity, autonomy and to some extent pride were negotiable in the face of housing and other centrally funded priorities. Overspill and new towns projects altered the established urban hierarchy, generating new economic and electoral power bases and diminishing existing ones. Many new council housing projects were driven by supply considerations—by the politicians' need for high completion rates and the technocrats dominance in matters relating to high rise designs, concrete construction and building methods. This supremacy of the suppliers paid little heed to the consumer, the occupant. The neutered tenants' movements associated in the nineteenth century with housing by private landlords were replaced in the twentieth century the emasculation of tenants' rights under council ownership. Bureaucracy had compartmentalised housing provision; individuals could only penetrate the maze of responsibilities with the greatest difficulty. To some extent, as Gibb shows, the variety of housing initiatives since the late 1970s represents a reaction to the impersonal and inefficient council housing provision of the 1950s and 1960s, and constitutes an attempt to offer choice and self-determination to the tenant. Most emphatic is Gibb's argument that the 1970s was 'a decade of radical departure', based jointly on the identification in 1969 of the opportunities for rehabilitation in the ancient Scottish tenement housing stock, and in 1972 with the reaffirmation of decentralisation associated with local government reorganisation. Power to the districts, claims Gibb, focused housing provision on the micro scale, stressing local qualitative and environmental considerations, and taking into account the views of occupants. Such principles therefore set the housing agenda. Conservative governments since 1979 have only accelerated the trend.

Second to Glasgow Corporation as builder and landlord is the Scottish Special Housing Association (SSHA), founded in 1937 as part of a regional economic policy to counter inter-war unemployment. Rodger and Al-Qaddo explore the early housing initiatives of the SSHA and illustrate how it has functioned in different ways to supplement general housebuilding programmes, to support economic development, to assist overspill housing, to accommodate the special needs of elderly and infirm, and lately, to refurbish inner city properties. Varied responsibilities have therefore given the SSHA an important rôle in Scottish housing since 1945. To achieve this the SSHA has proved an extremely adaptable organisation. In fact, the major thrust of the Rodger/Al-Qaddo chapter is to investigate the nature of the relationships between the SSHA, local authorities, the Scottish Office, and other administrative agencies. The durability of the SSHA is attributed to astute perceptions of changing housing needs and the identification of viable housing initiatives, to innovative technical developments and the expansion of professional services connected with housing, as well as access to policy formulation and implementation at the level of the Scottish Office. To a certain extent this last factor has also made the SSHA an agent of the Scottish Office in the attempt to implement the housing policy of a central government often at political odds with Labour councils in Scottish burghs. Nor has the SSHA been neutral in the ongoing tension between the Scottish Office in Edinburgh and Glasgow Corporation. For long anxious about the political autonomy of Glasgow, the Scottish Office has used various strategies to restrain the Glasgow power base in Scotland, ranging from the reorganisation of local government and the countervailing influence of Strathclyde region, to the impact on council revenues of rental levels and housing standards influenced by SSHA activities. To some extent the SSHA has therefore carved out its own niche, developing its technical expertise, expanding and redefining its housing rôle and, by virtue of its size and involvement with a complex web of local councils and official agencies making itself indispensable to the provision of Scottish housing. In this respect it has been a self-perpetuating quango, only to be undone with difficulty and the dedication of a keen political will.

Market forces and institutional intervention in the form of subsidised council housing were two directions from which private landlords' interests were squeezed. In 1989, only 6 per cent of the housing is owned by private landlords in contrast to their 90 per cent share in 1914. Yet, with 60 per cent of the British housing stock still rented in 1947, McCrone and Elliott show how resistant private landlords were to this assault. Nor was the decline linear. The inter-war period, contrary to general impressions, were years in which landlordism stubbornly resisted the immense upsurge in owner occupancy and council housebuilding. At the core of the apparent paradox is the persuasive argument that real rents rose in the inter-war years. In conditions of declining prices, rents fixed by rent control guidelines offered an economic 4–5 per cent return which compared favourably with other yields on capital, and with less risk to capital values than associated with stocks, commodities and other investment opportunities. Presumably the escalation of owner occupancy itself reflected just such an appraisal as individuals recognised that their personal participation in the property market made economic sense in terms of outlets for savings, low cost mortgages, and trends in house prices.

Against the national trend of decline in landlordism, McCrone and Elliott set the resistance of the local scale where specific areas of cities have continued to prove attractive to the private landlord. Their explanations for such revolve around the historical importance of the local investor, typically a petit bourgeoisie of shopkeepers and small businessmen, bolstered by a few doctors, lawyers and other professional interests. Destroy this social fabric of local investors, McCrone and Elliott contend, and along with it goes the destruction of the private landlord. So inner city commercial redevelopment, demolitions and overspill housing campaigns combine with other trends to undermine the environment in which this petit bourgeoisie functioned in the provision of rented accommodation. Attempts in the 1980s to revitalise the small business community and deregulate the rented sector are unlikely to prove successful in their efforts to reconstruct the private landlord, according to McCrone and Elliott, and they note that though recent Conservative government policies have contributed to some localised increases in rented accommodation, this has largely been in the hands of large corporate capital, and in any event, the aggregate position is still of significant decline in the number of private landlords which has fallen by 30 per cent between 1979 and 1987.

In surveying a century of property relations McCrone and Elliott synthesise many of the issues addressed by individual contributors. The socio-economic structure of a burgh is given a central position in the analysis, but not to the exclusion of cultural factors in the conduct and determination of social and political relations. Policies formulated at the national level were frequently amended in their execution by local interests—in the council chamber, in the community, and in specialist committees which considered housing matters. Indeed, from the late nineteenth century, the housing issue marked an important watershed since radical alternatives, oppositional politics, and resistance to the historical power of property were to a considerable degree associated with the rise of Labour politics in Scotland at both municipal and national levels. The politics of Scottish housing were a catalyst in that process, and if anything, the housing issue has become more pressing, more contested and politicised as the twentieth century proceeded. A contributory factor in that process has been the escalation of central and local conflicts of interest, so often considered a nineteenth century phenomenon, yet one which has proved equally 'if not more' pervasive in the twentieth century with the developing complexity of government and administration.

Conclusion

This book constitutes a stocktaking of recent scholarship in Scottish housing history. The contributors do not aim to chart a detailed route for future exploration yet their contributions do offer clear navigational aids for further research. Firstly, and most conspicuous, is the advantage of an interdisciplinary approach to a subject area which is transparently ranged across the social sciences. Secondly, another direction, implicitly urged, is to fuse locus and process, that is, to conduct housing studies at various levels in which the peculiarities of the urban location are not submerged by the power of macro scale forces. The interplay of local and national interests is a recurrent theme of several contributors, and without sufficient attention to their interaction the comprehension of the component parts is weaker. Thirdly, more diverse studies are required both in terms of urban scale and geographical location to offset the imbalance caused by undue concentration on Glasgow and Strathclyde. Fourthly, cyclical and structural components of the housing market require more careful separation in order to assess whether policy formulation and implementation address the real issues. Fifthly, the power of housing to drive the economic system has been underplayed in the past. No longer to be considered simply as a dependent variable, housing policies such as refurbishment have directly generated employment and enhanced the local economic climate, in contrast to an earlier preoccupation with employment creation as a pre-condition for environmental and housing improvement. Sixthly, a preoccupation with types of tenure—essentially between owner occupiers and tenants and between the suppliers of these, private enterprise and local authorities—deflects research from other important themes. Households, family and social relations, working class culture, community, local organisations, and political allegiance therefore are straitjacketed by being too closely identified with the nature of housing tenure. Finally, housing studies over-emphasise the supply side. Since the collection of statistics revolves around institutions and government agencies then the point of departure for housing studies is too frequently the housing stock, new building and other quantifiable variables rather than local income and employment conditions, community relations, neighbourhood issues and residents' reactions to housing provision. The twentieth century urban system therefore requires further study, particularly from a demand standpoint, and less reliance on government generated data.

Of course, more specific issues are also raised for future study. Did the subcontracting prevalent in the building industry before 1914 strengthen the position of large scale contractors in securing council housing contracts? Did this put local councils under their influence? Were small scale private builders inhibited and did this impede owner occupation in Scotland? Were councils any better as landlords than those in the private sector? How influential were individuals—not so much figureheads such as Lord Provosts, SSHA and New Town Development Corporation chairmen—but Scottish Development Department officials, and what was the impact of increasing reliance on surveyors, building engineers, architects, accountants and the professionalisation of housing supply? Was the changing occupational composition to local councils relevant to the decay of landlordism? Why was the politicisation of the housing issue particularly vigorous in Scotland?

To a degree, contributors address some of these issues, but there is need for much more research. Unlike current French and American research,[34] British historians have largely disregarded the experiential side of housing. Representational and psychological dimensions of the home have been mainly subsumed within class based explanations of housing differences or functional explanations of housing types. Did burglary constitute rape? Were trespassers defiling private space? How did residents respond to the monumentality of building? Personal interaction with the built environment therefore remains under-acknowledged in Britain; the impact of grey stone tenements is confined to the physical, to their effect on light and ventilation, to public health rather than to mental health. Put more specifically, did red sandstone materials in Glasgow brighten daily life in an otherwise drab urban landscape? Further attention could usefully be devoted to the interaction of resident and his/her home, and attention to the homogenisation of recent Scottish building design and encroachments on a national identity in this area might prove a useful point of departure.

If the contributions included here stimulate debate in any of these areas they will have served their purpose. And if they should advance a reliance on a historical dimension to assess and interpret the policies of today that in itself would be worthwhile.

Notes

1. Statistical material is derived from Scottish Development Department publications, *Annual Housing Returns* (–1977), and *Scottish Housing Statistics* (quarterly to

1983, annually 1983–) all published by HMSO. Some additional material has been supplied by the statistical department of the SDD, to whom I am indebted.

2. Though occupiers could borrow from local authorities under the Small Dwellings Acquisition Act 1899 to purchase the house in which they lived, in Scotland only in Bo'ness was it used. Bo'ness council built a tenement block of 8 two-apartment houses which it sold to workmen.
3. R Baird, 'Housing' in A K Cairncross (ed), *The Scottish Economy* 1954, 201; R G Rodger, 'The "Invisible Hand": market forces, housing and the urban form in Victorian cities', in D Fraser and A Sutcliffe (eds), *The Pursuit of Urban History* 1983, 204.
4. Scottish Development Department (Scottish Housing Advisory Committee), *The Cost of Private Housebuilding in Scotland* 1970, 18, pp.21–2.
5. Ibid., p.32.
6. Ibid., p.49.
7. Ibid.
8. Royal Commission on the Housing of the Working Classes, PP 1884–85 XXX, Evidence of Colville Q19085; Telfer Q19237.
9. Scottish Development Department, *The Cost of Private Housebuilding* p.12.
10. *Report of an Enquiry by the Board of Trade into Working Class Rents, Housing and Retail Prices, etc.*, Cd 3864, 1908, p.xxxviii; *Report of the Board of Trade Enquiry into Working Class Rents and Retail Prices*. Cd 6955, 1913 pp.xxxvi–xxxvii.
11. The percentage contribution of the constituent elements in higher Scottish building costs was as follows: materials (9.8), building regulations (19.1), traditional practices (13.0), earnings (14.0), legal fees (6.3) and profit and productivity elements together (35.1).
12. Enquiry by the Board of Trade into Working Class Rents, Housing and Retail Prices, 1908, op. cit. (note 10), p.xl.
13. A D Campbell, 'Changes in Scottish incomes, 1924–49', *Economic Journal* **65** 1955, pp.225–40; see also N K Buxton, 'Economic growth in Scotland between the wars: the role of production structure and rationalization', *Economic History Review* **33** 1980, pp.538–55.
14. Scottish Office, *Scottish Abstract of Statistics 1986* Edinburgh, p.143. This figure would be lower were the Scottish component removed from the UK data.
15. Ibid., p.59.
16. Ibid., p.143.
17. W Thompson, *The Housing Handbook* London, 1903, p.68.
18. Earlier subsidies were confined to English boroughs. See note 2 above.
19. Census 1981, *Key Statistics for Urban Areas* 1984, Table 4, pp.87–8.
20. Based on Census 1981, *Key Statistics* for Scotland, and for England and Wales.
21. Others included Strathaven, Prestwick, Newton Mearns, Ellon, Bishopriggs, Largs, Milngavie with a majority of properties owner-occupied.
22. G Robertson, 'Housing tenure and labour mobility in Scotland', Scottish Office, Economics and Statistics Unit, Discussion paper No 4, p.36.
23. J English, 'Housing allocation and a deprived Scottish estate', *Urban Studies* **13** 1976, pp.319–23.
24. Scottish Housing Advisory Committee, *Allocating Council Houses* Edinburgh 1967.
25. R G Rodger, 'The law and urban change: some nineteenth century Scottish evidence', *Urban History Yearbook* 1979, pp.77–91 explains that there were specific circumstances under which repossession was possible, or by which other residual rights, usually associated with levying further duties, were allowed.

26. Scottish Land Enquiry Committee, *Report* 1914, p.331 noted that with the diminishing attractiveness of property investment 1900–14 the capital value of feu duties had fallen from about 30 to 24 years purchase of the annual value.
27. R Rodger, 'The Victorian building industry and the housing of the Scottish working class' in M Doughty (ed), *Building the Industrial City* 1986, pp.172–4 expands these points.
28. C G Brown, *The Social History of Religion in Scotland since 1730* 1987 pp.6–14; S and O Checkland, *Industry and Ethos 1832–1914* 1984, chs 7, p.12.
29. T Hart, 'The comprehensive development area', Occasional Paper No 9, University of Glasgow Social and Economic Studies 1968.
30. These administrative tensions are more fully considered in S Gleave, 'The influence of the Garden City Movement in Fife 1914–23, with particular reference to Rosyth', unpublished MPhil thesis, St Andrews, 1987. The prevarication of various government departments and the impact of delay on workers' living conditions is admirably presented.
31. M J Daunton, *Hosue and Home in the Victorian City* 1983, pp.286–302.
32. M Swenarton, *Homes Fit for Heroes: The Politics and Architecture of Early State Housing in Britain* 1981, pp.77–87. On 3 March 1919 Lloyd George warned the Cabinet that in the face of considerable demobilisation the British government had promised social reform 'time and again, but little had been done. We must give them the conviction that this time we mean it, and we must give them that conviction quickly. Even if it cost a hundred million pounds, what was that compared to the stability of the State?' p.78.
33. Scottish Office, *A Guide to Non-Traditional Housing in Scotland* 1987.
34. See reports of such research initiatives in 'Conference reports', *Urban History Yearbook*, 1984, pp.92–3 and R Rodger, 'Built form and the cultural environment', *Planning History Bulletin* 9 1987, pp.8–13, which reviews a selection of approaches to the built environment from more than 125 papers presented at an international conference at the University of Kansas in November 1986.

2 Crisis and confrontation in Scottish housing 1880–1914

Richard Rodger

To an official enquiry, Scottish housing in 1885 presented no real cause for alarm. 'We have no great anxiety about the large towns' the Royal Commission on the Housing of the Working Classes complacently concluded.[1] The Commissioners validated their findings by quoting expert evidence, but deliberately took it out of context since it had been offered as an assessment of the sanitary inspectorate in the major burghs.[2] Despite this dubious practice in drafting the report, it was not wildly inconsistent with the tone of other witnesses, for if the Commissioners heard of various Scottish housing defects, these appeared of lesser proportions than in London. Not surprisingly, the recommendations of the Scottish report were conservatively confined to legislative consolidation regarding standardised building regulations, cheaper property transfer procedures including a reduction of stamp duty, and administrative reorganisation to spread the costs of bureaucracy amongst more ratepayers.[3] There was no hint of the confrontation ahead.

If, as one Edinburgh witness testified, there was no resentment or agitation amongst tenants living in insanitary conditions in 1885, matters had changed remarkably by the eve of World War I.[4] In October 1912, in response to public opinion, and more specifically to the representations of Scottish Miners' Federation leaders and MPs for mining constituencies,[5] the Secretary for Scotland, John Sinclair, after years of delaying tactics which included successive enquiries into housing conditions in mining communities throughout central Scotland,[6] was obliged to set up the most thorough investigation of general housing conditions ever undertaken in any part of the United Kingdom.[7]

What had happened in the intervening period? Put simply, there was a deepening concern from all quarters involved in housing about their own, often contradictory, interests. This was not confined to Scotland, and to some extent, Scottish housing was influenced by and contributed to a developing late-Victorian consciousness of urban living conditions. This 'hardening of opinion'[8] was fostered by articles in influential journals[9] and numerous widely distributed pamphlets, of which Octavia Hill's *Homes of the London Poor* (1883) and Andrew Mearns' *Bitter Cry of Outcast London* (1883) are the best known.[10] In Scotland, the celebrated status accorded to Medical Officers of Health such as Littlejohn in Edinburgh and Russell in Glasgow[11] projected housing and sanitary matters into local newspaper headlines through their reports, lectures and publications;[12] their grasp of the interconnections between housing conditions and environmental health was backed by meticulous statistical records, and combined with Russell's ability to ignite public opinion through lectures like 'Life in one room' (1888) and 'Uninhabitable houses' (1894), did more to educate Scottish public opinion than is normally recognised.[13] Raising public consciousness was the first step towards engaging the political will in relation to improved housing standards.

Scottish housing standards in 1914

If the Report of the Royal Commission in 1885 smacked of complacency no such impression permeated successive enquiries by the Presbytery of Glasgow; Dundee Social Union, Edinburgh Charity Organisation, Glasgow Municipal Commission, and the Liberal Party's Report into Scottish Land.[14] These atmospheric reports on housing conditions in the principal Scottish burghs were supplemented by the annual reports from government departments and supervisory agencies, including, for example, the Local Government Board for Scotland, Registrar General and the Scotch Education Department, by the investigations of statistical, literary and philosophical societies, and by concerned professional bodies of sanitary engineers, surveyors, and the medical fraternity.[15] Though some investigations were more partisan than others, each acknowledged progress in late-Victorian Scottish housing in certain respects—structural solidity, sanitary provisions, minimum street width and slum clearances. But such advances were far from universal. It was not until the 1880s that WCs were introduced to tenements as a matter of course; building codes were only applicable in a minority of burghs until the 1890s; and slum clearance programmes applied only to the cities and principal burghs—no more than ten burghs were affected in total.[16] And since there were problems of enforcement, lax drafting and jurisdictional disputes between regulatory authorities, these developments were of limited impact, and often only applied to new houses. Environmental improvements resulted less from deliberate municipal interventionism and more from four private decisions: firstly, qualitative improvements affordable by the middle class; secondly, their suburban aspirations which contributed to decongestion; thirdly, broader social trends evident from the 1880s towards smaller family size causing less pressure on housing space; and fourthly, transport and other commercial building which demolished the oldest areas of the urban core in their efforts to gain locational advantages for business purposes. There can be little doubt that from the 1880s the trend of Scottish housing quality was upwards.

The problem, the housing 'crisis', as contemporary reports acknowledged, was of low *absolute* Scottish housing standards. The trend of housing quality might be upward, but the point of departure was objectively minimal. No enquiry could resist the opportunity to shock readers, and atypical housing experiences have, therefore, to be set in this context of riveting readers' attention, a strategy in the larger campaign to influence public opinion on social issues. But the summary data offered by these investigations leaves little doubt as to the low general standard of housing in Scotland, a standard appreciably below that of English boroughs, and sufficiently disturbing to Scottish Office authorities as to vindicate tampering with measures of overcrowding in Scotland so as not to provide propaganda for advocates of municipal housing, subsidised building and social welfare reform.

Overcrowding, housing density, amenities such as water supply and room sizes, and the correlation between insanitary housing and both life expectancy and retarded physical development in children were among the features of late nineteenth century Scottish housing most frequently employed to convey the nature of daily life. The standard of more than 2 persons per room was generally used for statistical purposes as signifying overcrowded accommodation, yet with the exception of common lodging houses, local authority properties and 'ticketed houses' in Glasgow, no standard of overcrowding was applied to the overwhelming majority of Scottish houses until in 1903 the Burgh Police (Scotland) Act recommended cubic capacities for houses of up to three rooms. However, Table 1 shows just how common were such living conditions. In 1911, after some years of improvement, 45.1 per cent of the Scottish population and 47.6 per cent of the urban population, lived in overcrowded accommodation.[17] Between 60–9 per cent of residents in Airdrie, Govan, Motherwell, Barrhead, Clydebank, Port Glasgow and many other burghs in the Scottish central belt lived more than two per room, a degree of overcrowding ten times that of Manchester or Hull, and in the best-housed Scottish city, Edinburgh, the extent of overcrowding, approximately 33 per cent, was on a par with the worst housed areas of England on Tyneside and London's East End. As one report concluded, 'No person who has the welfare of the country at heart can regard them with indifference.'[18] Though the percentage of urban Scots living at a density of more than two per room had declined steadily between 1861 and 1911, the actual number doing so had risen from 1.7 million to 2.1 million (Appendix 2A).

In addition, the number of rooms per house or tenement flat gave cause for contemporary concern since this was an indicator both of the extent to which privacy could be ensured between parents and children, and of the degree to which the 'separation of the sexes' between the sons and daughters of a family was possible. So the fact that 56.8 per cent of the Scottish urban housing stock in 1911 had only one or two rooms distressed many who had concern for the morals of the nation. For example, the Edinburgh branch of the National Vigilance Association heard that 'housing conditions were so perfectly appalling . . . it was impossible to have the merest elements of decency.'[19] In crude numerical terms, 2.3 million Scots, equivalent to the total population of three Glasgows, lived in one and two roomed houses in 1911, a figure which had increased in every decade since the 1860s (Appendix 2C). Even though the percentage of one room houses had fallen steadily from 34 per cent to 13 per

Table 2.1 Overcrowded housing in Scottish burghs, 1911

	% of persons living more than		
	2 per room	3 per room	4 per room
Kilsyth	71.6	47.8	28.2
Coatbridge	71.2	45.0	23.7
Wishaw	70.1	45.1	24.2
Clydebank	69.0	38.2	14.8
Motherwell	68.1	40.3	19.2
Cowdenbeath	67.6	37.1	14.0
Port Glasgow	66.7	36.9	16.1
Hamilton	65.7	40.3	19.7
Airdrie	64.9	40.1	20.2
Barrhead	64.0	39.9	17.8
Govan	62.7	32.4	11.4
Renfrew	61.4	31.2	11.7
Johnstone	61.2	34.0	15.9
Pollokshaws	60.8	33.6	14.8
Tranent	59.8	31.4	11.7
Paisley	58.6	29.5	10.4
Bathgate	58.3	32.1	14.3
Denny	57.5	31.9	11.8
Greenock	56.7	28.9	11.6
Glasgow	55.7	27.9	10.7
Dumbarton	55.7	27.1	10.6
Kilmarnock	55.2	30.5	14.0
Rutherglen	54.4	29.6	12.5
Falkirk	53.3	26.2	9.5
Partick	49.7	24.3	9.4
Kirkcaldy	49.6	13.5	3.1
Dundee	48.2	20.0	6.1
Scottish burghs	**47.6**	**22.7**	**8.6**
Musselburgh	44.7	9.8	6.9
Leith	43.6	18.2	5.3
Dunfermline	39.2	14.8	4.2
Aberdeen	37.8	12.3	2.2
Arbroath	37.1	15.7	5.1
Galashiels	36.7	13.7	3.6
Stirling	35.8	14.8	4.8
Hawick	33.5	11.9	3.8
Edinburgh	32.6	12.7	4.1
Dumfries	30.9	8.4	2.1
Inverness	24.4	7.8	2.3

Source: Census of Scotland 1911, Report, *PP 1913 LXXX*, Table XLV.

cent (Appendix 2B) in the half century before World War I (two roomed houses remained fairly constant at about 37–40 per cent of the housing stock), the average house size remained far below the English standard. On the eve of World War I, 53.2 per cent of Scottish housing was of one and two roomed houses whereas the corresponding English figure was 7.1 per cent; and 45.1 per cent of Scots lived at a density of more than two persons per room which contrasted starkly with a figure of only 9.1 per cent for the English.[20]

Housing quality was often judged by the standard of amenities. Perhaps predictably, in a design almost universally based on block tenements, and where the predominance of one and two roomed units prevented specialised uses for rooms, facilities for the sole use of a tenant were by no means common. In Edinburgh and Glasgow respectively 29 per cent and 35 per cent of houses in 1914 had no separate WCs. Shared sinks were a feature in 8 per cent of the Edinburgh housing stock; 43 per cent of one roomed flats in the capital had shared sinks.[21] In the smaller burghs the percentages were often much higher. Sole use of cooking, washing and drying facilities characteristic of the overwhelming majority of English terraced houses, was not available to large numbers of urban Scots even in 1914. The impact of such communal facilities on daily domestic work routines was considerable. Rotas for the wash-house and drying green were inconvenient; cleanliness was hostage to the variable standards of residents; communal entrances to tenements hindered security, and were fouled by animals and humans alike. Each defect was a source of irritation amongst tenants. Daily domestic routines were made the more exacting by the absence of gas and hot water supplies and limited cooking facilities, delayed in their introduction to Scottish homes by the considerable installation costs of piping supplies to high rise dwellings. As more than half the Scottish urban population lived in one and two roomed flats the specialised use of rooms for cooking, eating, living, sleeping, and a front room for entertaining or family events in the manner available to most English terrace dwellers was impossible. Limited floor space used in a multi-purpose way meant frequent and laborious additional daily work for Scottish women. By definition, in four-storey tenements, three quarters of residents were not at ground level, and flights of stairs imposed additional physical strains on housewives in the conduct of normal daily chores.[22]

The impact of Scottish housing standards was most evident in the vital statistics of the burghs. Though affected by income levels and congenital factors, infant mortality in Edinburgh parishes with predominantly one and two roomed houses was six times higher in 1912 than in parishes where the housing was of four or more rooms. Comparable data for Glasgow in 1911 is shown in Table 2.2, but perhaps more revealing was the continuing adverse effect housing space on child mortality between ages one and five. As the Glasgow Medical Officer of Health, Dr Chalmers commented:

> The contrast in the rates at each age period associated with the house groups here shown is sufficiently striking, but . . . almost of equal significance is the rapid improvement in the rate ages 1–5 in three and four apartment houses.[23]

Thus although the death rate in four apartment houses was half that of one

Table 2.2 Infant and child mortality rates: Glasgow 1911

Size of House	Death rates (per 1,000) Under age 1	Aged 1 to 5	DR aged 1–5 as a % of DR < 1
1	210	41	19
2	164	30	18
3	129	18	14
4	103	11	10

Source: Scottish Land Enquiry Committee, *Report* 1914, p.371

room houses for infants,

> ... during the next four years of life the resistance of the child in the three and four apartment houses to fatal disease increases so rapidly, or the risks of contracting infectious disease are so diminished, that the death rate among children in three apartment houses to fatal disease increases so rapidly, or the risks of contracting that of one-apartment children.[24]

Whatever the trend of improvement, low housing standards were regarded as having a significant impact on child development. Most conspicuous was the correlation between the weight and stature of children and house size. In major studies[25] of the Scottish cities conducted between 1905 and 1907, larger, heavier children came from more spacious three and four roomed houses. More specifically, the incidence of rickets and other skeletal deformities (curved tibia, knock-knees, pigeon chests), valvular defects of the heart, various bronchial conditions, and many ear, nose and throat, as well as visual and glandular defects were most closely associated with children from smaller houses. It was from poorer housing and lower social status areas that heart disease amongst girls aged eleven to thirteen was most evident, and Dr Emily Thompson, alarmed that young girls' hearts should show such early 'signs of weakness and flabbiness, probably the result of underfeeding and overexertion', cautioned physical education instructors in Dundee that 'injury might be caused by the use of too heavy apparatus to girls whose hearts were enfeebled.'[26] It was a conclusion which 'merits grave consideration'.

Deficiencies in ventilation, lighting and sanitation, dampness and limited food preparation areas produced environmental conditions closely associated with the respiratory and intestinal diseases which were more prevalent in smaller houses. The list of diseases associated with such a hostile living environment were numerous; acquired deformities far outnumbered congenital ones. In Dundee, where the housing stock most closely resembled that of 'average' Scottish burghs (Table 1), 44 per cent of school children had impaired hearing, 48 per cent had a visual defect.[27] Enlarged tonsils and adenoidal conditions, eczema, impetigo, anaemia, bronchial catarrh, hypermetropia (long-sightedness due to underdevelopment of the eyeball) were common conditions and, though not exclusively attributable to housing conditions, the correlation was marked. Inescapably there were implications for national efficiency, pressure groups urging social welfare provisions, a medical lobby anxious to extend their influence into school medical inspection, charity workers with embryonic social work interests, and teetotallers concerned to improve the attractions of home and hearth. As one report noted:

So long as workers' homes exhibit the extreme discomfort and cheerlessness which is so frequent and marked a feature, it is to be feared that the inmates will welcome any means of escape, and at present the public-houses are the readiest and most persistent attraction.[28]

The counter-attractions of clubs, societies and church organisations were few and 'when the cold winter evenings have to be filled up in cold and inclement weather, the warmth and brightness to be found only where drink is sold proved an attraction hard to resist.'

Women, in their daily work routines, shouldered the worst of the housing conditions. The impact was noted by the Edinburgh City Engineer:

. . . the discomforts and inconveniences of the common stair, the greater risks of infection, the diminished floor space offered by the tenement system . . . (and) the diminished light upon the lower floors, the absence of any piece of garden ground attached exclusively to each house, and all this absence means to the physique and morale of family life.[29]

In the management of the household budget, it was often housewives who confronted the rent collector and bailiff, and their distaste for low grade accommodation and the omnipresent threat of eviction meant that it was they who were frequently instrumental in organising local meetings and ultimately rent strikes as part of a developing resistance to landlords and their factors. It was women, therefore, who made critical contributions to the emergent Labour party in the west of Scotland since housing and letting matters provided issues on which nascent political parties could cut their teeth.[30] Local organisations responded to local issues. Workers' discontent on housing topics, therefore, was not the product of dislocated circumstances during wartime but the result of cumulative grievances over rent levels and the terms of tenancy. Significantly, a Royal Commission commented on the injustices of the Scottish housing system before 1914 by concluding that 'bad housing may fairly be regarded as a legitimate cause of social unrest.'[31]

The causes of Scottish housing problems

Two key factors influenced the quality of Scottish housing. First, there was the pattern of weak and unpredictable incomes in Scottish burghs; second, the legal code which underpinned the framework of the building industry. Combined, these two central elements produced the construction of high density accommodation with shared amenities. Tenements, therefore, were an architectural solution to the need to divide site development and other construction costs amongst as many tenants as possible.

By British standards, nineteenth century Scottish wages were low. In the 1830s and 1840s Scottish wages were commonly 20–25 per cent below those in comparable English trades. From mid-century the gap narrowed to between 16–19 per cent in the 1860s and to 9–13 per cent in the 1890s.[32] Even in 1905, in no other area of industrial Britain were real wages lower than in Scotland. Once the cost of living was taken into account the purchasing power of urban Scots fell further behind other regions. Indeed, the Board of Trade estimated in 1905 that for a shopping basket of twenty-nine essential items of weekly consumption Scottish prices were 2 per cent above those of central London and as much as 11 per cent above prices in Midland boroughs and the industrial North of England. So though coal, oil, milk and mutton were cheaper in Scotland than elsewhere in the United Kingdom, the price of flour, butter, tea, eggs, cheese and beef in the four major Scottish cities, and Greenock, Paisley, Kilmarnock, Leith, Falkirk, Galashiels and Perth, was significantly higher than in seventy English and Welsh boroughs. As a consequence, the Board of Trade in 1912 recorded a real wage disadvantage to urban Scots of approximately 10 per cent.[33]

Demand in Scotland was weak. It was further weakened by the structure of Scottish employment. About a quarter of the male workforce and a slightly lower proportion of females in the Scottish cities encountered a period of unemployment each year.[34] Since seasonal factors and the incidence of unskilled, casual work were very pronounced in Scottish burghs, irregular earnings undermined already below-average wage rates, transforming them into yet weaker purchasing power with important implications for the quantity and quality of housing which was affordable.

Housing standards were also influenced by land tenure. In Scotland, the vendor relinquished the title to land but did retain the right to an annual payment in perpetuity—the 'feu-duty'. For several reasons, this unique Scottish combination of an outright sale of land and an annual levy tended to inflate land prices and adversely affect housing quality. Firstly, since there were no reversionary rights, as in much of English tenure, the landowner or superior either sold his land at the highest available price, or held the land off the market in expectation of yet higher land prices in the future, thereby squeezing the supply of building land and further bidding up its price. Land hoarding contributed to the inflation of land values. Secondly, once the feu-duty was set it could never be changed; accordingly, to take account of long run price trends in the land market, superiors had an interest in pitching the annual levy at a level which would not quickly be eroded by inflation. Occasionally, and according to set procedures, superiors exacted further amounts called 'casualty' payments from vassals equivalent to an additional feu-duty, with the consequence that property burdens were increased, passed on to tenants, and ultimately diminished the amount of housing space affordable. Thirdly, and most importantly, was the inflationary influence on land values of the practice of 'sub-infeudation'. Entitlement to an annual feu-duty passed successively with the transfer of land from landowner, to developer, to builder, to landlord, to occupant. In effect, a chain of feu-duty obligations compounded the amount to be paid. As each individual in the chain was personally liable for payment to his immediate superior, there was an incentive to ensure that any defaulters were covered by receipts from other vassals. This was achieved by increasing the feu-duty payable by all vassals. Finally, 'feu-farming' had a similar inflationary effect on Scottish land prices. As feu-duties were a first charge on a bankrupt's estate they were a desirable and secure basis on which to raise capital. The effect was to encourage builders to offer for sale the right to exact or 'farm' inflated feu-duties in return for lump sum capital advances which they then used to build the properties from which the duties would be obtained. Re-feuing in this way certainly added to the cost of land, so much so that land charges added 10–14 per cent to the gross rental of tenement property.[35] The Land Enquiry Committee commented that 'it is necessary for the builder to erect tenements in order to spread the high cost of land over a large number of houses,'[36] and yet, in an interconnected way, it was tenement building which itself boosted the value of land. The feuing system, with its effects on the supply of builders' capital and inflated land prices, reinforced the peculiarly Scottish pattern of high-rise tenement housing.

The building industry influenced the standard of accommodation in Scotland most conspicuously because of the extreme instability in its output. Annual variations in housebuilding between 1880 and 1914 were not uncommonly 30 or 40 per cent, sometimes higher (see Figure 2.1), a level more than double any other industrial sector. The narrow margin of error in builders' operations combined with the preponderance of small firms in over 100 Scottish burghs, where more than half the proposed building applications were for a single house and four-fifths for only one or two houses, meant that minor changes in the local economic climate could produce a spectacular crop of building bankruptcies. Subtle monitoring of demand changes, cushioning one project with cash flows from another, and accessing alternative capital supplies all proved difficult in an industry dominated by small scale production levels. The result was a level of volatility which encouraged basic designs, scamped standards and rushed completions in an effort to escape the sequestrator's bankruptcy proceedings. Unseasoned timber, shallow foundations, fewer coats of plaster, lower grade lime and lead in cement and paint, and the employment of unskilled operatives among other short cuts were techniques used to maximise short term gains to building firms at the expense of long term maintenance costs to landlords and discomfort to tenants.

To complete a property and repay or refinance a bond secured on the sale of the house was the primary objective of many builders' strategies; their liquidity depended upon it. Though a considerable number of firms built under contract with assured finance and final sale, the continuation of at least half the number of builders was dependent on skills in financing and renegotiating advances.[37] Such priorities and the absence of a regulatory agency to control those who designated themselves as 'builders' meant standards of building competence were secondary considerations. Apart from customary sources of capital—private contacts, widows' and trust funds accessed through solicitors, trade credit—builders' finance depended to a considerable extent on the sale of the right to collect feu-duties, compounded at from 25 to 30 years' purchase of the annual value, or alternatively on the raising of a bond secured on this annual income. So long as the prospects for collecting the annual feu-duties were bright, then feu-farming was attractive and the supply of building capital

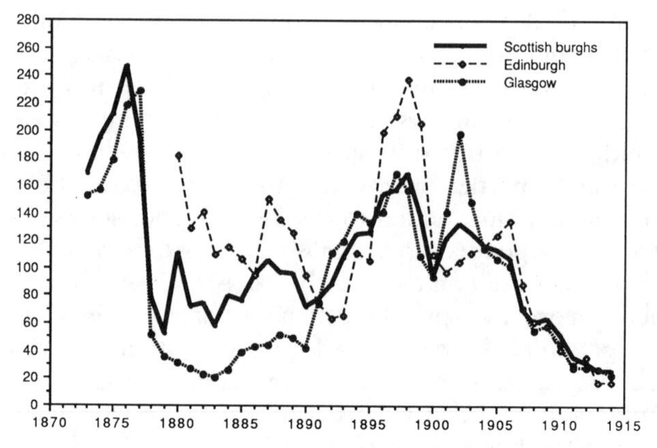

A All Scottish burghs, Edinburgh, Glasgow

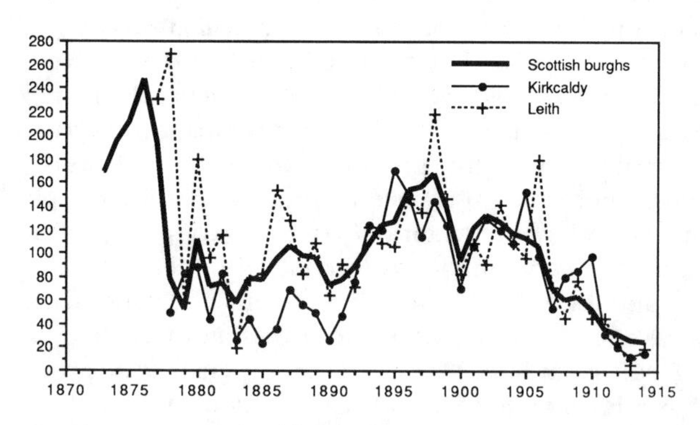

B Kilmarnock, Kirkcaldy, Leith

Figure 2.1 Fluctuations in Scottish housebuilding: selected burghs 1873–1914

forthcoming. But any rise in the numbers of unlet properties, or a downturn in the local economy caused investors to be sceptical about advances to builders. The valve of building finance was abruptly turned off. So the peculiarly Scottish system of tenure and its potential for raising capital for building purposes contributed to the exaggerated dynamic of the Scottish housebuilding industry.

Some signs of diminishing instability were evident after 1880. Larger firms, heavier representation of small firms in the bankruptcy courts, a more circumspect policy of credit advances from finance houses, and signs of a developing sense of responsibility amongst builders themselves all contributed to a more subdued amplitude of building fluctuations after 1880. However, this should not be construed as reversing the essentially small scale and unstable nature of the Scottish building industry; it represented a limited, moderating force on such characteristics.

Despite this moderation, between 1870 and 1914 the Scottish building industry in large and small burghs alike experienced two cycles of approximately twenty years' duration, with an amplitude of fluctuation highly exaggerated compared to other parts of Britain. The structure of Scottish employment suppressed working class purchasing power and compressed the effective demand for additional housing space into just a few years of the cycle. Booms flourished and faded in the space of a few years. Such demand conditions created enormous difficulties to which Scottish builders adjusted with difficulty, and their attempts to avoid bankruptcy often resulted in the completion of houses long after the boom conditions had evaporated, the resultant legacy of unsold and untenanted houses frequently taking several years to be absorbed. This stop-go cycle of working class housebuilding did little to improve the quality of accommodation.

The bases of tension and frustration 1885–1914

Builders, landlords, property managers, landowners, tenants, ratepayers, voluntary associations and town councils each experienced difficulties from the 1880s in the pursuit of what they perceived as their legitimate interests. It was not that their individual problems were entirely new; but their intensity and seeming intractability induced deepening disaffection with housing matters. For builders and landlords the combination of strengthened municipal byelaws and statutory responsibilities circumscribed managerial independence and was regarded as an affront to business autonomy. Resistance resulted. Tenants and pressure groups, including church representatives, were no longer content to remain mute when confronted by hardship and inequity. Nor was tension and frustration among housing interests simply a product of recession, though a trade cycle trough in the early- and mid-1880s may have contributed to a dismissal of housing problems by the Royal Commission as essentially temporary. Despite the underlying structural problems of the British economy in the late-nineteenth century, the Scottish economy, driven by shipbuilding, marine engineering, coal, banking and financial services, and a miscellany of other manufacturing interests, enjoyed with local exceptions a period of expansion before 1914.[38] If, then, housing matters produced deep-seated antagonisms under favourable market conditions, it was unsurprising that they should surface at other times. What forms did this antagonism take?

Housebuilders' frustration was based on complaints about rising building costs; interference by town councils in the rented sector which undermined new building opportunities; unavailability of sites cleared of slums for housebuilding; and, predictably, about the power and quality of labour. Each of these, builders claimed, undermined their profitability with adverse effects on the supply of working class housing. Their irritations were not unfounded. Building costs rose by almost 40 per cent between the 1880s and 1914—by more if expressed in real terms.[39] Such pressures on builders' profits came principally from two directions: compliance with sanitary standards and building regulations, and, from rising labour costs. To combat the worst environmental consequences of uncontrolled building and non-existent sanitary provisions,[40] the Burgh Police (Scotland) Act 1862 and successive local improvement acts enabled burghs to frame building regulations.[41] After their initial introduction in Glasgow in the 1860s, building regulations spread rapidly to other burghs—Partick, Dundee (1873), Govan (1874), Irvine (1876), Leith (1877), Port Glasgow, Kirkcaldy, Perth (1878), Edinburgh, Aberdeen, Kilmarnock (1880). From 1893 it was compulsory for all large burghs to adopt and enforce minimum building regulations; by 1900 more than 200 burghs did so.[42] Sanitary stipulations as to water supplies and WCs, drains and sewer connections were allied both to structural and safety standards relating to dampcourses, foundations, roof joists, chimney construction, guttering; the quality of lime, mortar, slates and other materials was specified, and conformity to the approved plan required. Though circumvented to some extent, builders bitterly resented the new structural specifications as these far exceeded standards applicable in English boroughs.[43] Since higher building costs promptly filtered through to the tenant in the form of increased rents, the introduction of Scottish building byelaws had substituted sound but costly tenements for cheap and insanitary ones. Tenants could afford better but less space; builders suffered a reduction in demand.

Builders' annoyance over building regulations with one external agency, the burgh corporation and its planning committee, the Dean of Guild Court, was reproduced with another group, the building trades unions. Rising wages, a working week shortened to 54 hours, restrictive practices, for example, limitations on the number of bricks to be laid per hour, and annual wage agreements were features cited as adversely affecting profit margins.[44] Wages rose by about 30 per cent in the period 1885 to 1914, but other builders' grievances, though real, were probably less justified. Undoubtedly there were instances where efficiency was impaired by slowing work and delaying completion dates, the 'ca-canny' strategy of operatives, but not all were in unions, nor was the labour market so tight that they could dictate terms. The reduction of the working week also meant lower wage bills, and since tasks might still have been accomplished in the shorter working week and annual wage agreements ensured a measure of continuity to production, employers' antagonism towards labour was to some extent misplaced. Indeed, the displacement of labour by a limited amount of machine preparation such as steam hoists, machine-dressed stonework and planing equipment, and the substitution of concrete for labour intensive stone mullions, rybats, stairs and pavements, gave considerable force to the views of labour officials that workers and wages were not responsible for the housing problem.[45] Even so, builders believed that labour held them to ransom. Bankruptcy was never far away, and Scottish builders, sensitive to any influences which might impel them in that direction, were quick to point the accusative finger in the direction of daily operational conflict, the workplace, when danger threatened.[46]

Builders also reserved some of their animosity for the town council. As one critic observed, some of our enthusiastic Councillors get carried away by the feeling that (municipal housing) is paying its way . . .'.[47] Thus, the function of the Municipal Housing Commission set up in 1902 was not to resolve the deepening housing crisis but to contain the financial implications of the Glasgow City Improvement Trust's activities.[48] Six criticisms were frequently advanced: that councils were able to obtain capital at below market interest rates; that slum clearance powers put land into councils' hands and their failure to release it for building purposes forced up urban land prices generally; that where modest council housing had begun[49] then it was artisans who were selected as tenants, not those in greatest need; that building work sub-contracted by the Corporations was usually 'scamped' (inferior); that council encroachments on and unfair competition with builders' and landlords' activities created uncertainty and deterred further commitment to it, with prejudicial effects on the supply of housing; and, that slum clearances, land hoarding and re-housing at rents below market levels each represented a charge on ratepayers.[50] At the core of these objections to local authority intervention in the housing market lay the notion that it represented a 'rate-in aid' of wages, subsidising employers who paid low wages, and distributing, albeit by another name, poor relief.

Ratepayers were occasionally able to signal their opposition to grandiose council projects in the most dramatic terms. For example, the extravagance of Glasgow City Improvement Trust caused Lord Provost John Blackie to lose his seat on Glasgow Council in 1867, and again in 1902 opposition to council housing proposals ousted Glasgow Lord Provost Samuel Chisholm and applied a brake to doctrinaire extensions of municipal socialism.[51] Mostly these flamboyant gestures were unnecessary since important committees such as the Dean of Guild Court designated their membership to be composed in part from building industry interests, ostensibly to lend technical expertise on planning matters.[52] In addition, technicalities in Scottish electoral rules confined voting to artisans and the middle class; property and rates qualifications excluded tenants in the lowest rented accommodation.[53] The urban political system, therefore, remained in the hands of property owning interest groups resolutely committed to restricting additions to municipal rates. Though Scottish civic authorities acquired a considerable reputation for their municipal interventionism, it was not an open-ended approach, since unlike English councils, the Scottish intent was to provide cheap, basic amenities and not to generate a surplus from municipal trading to offset the rates. Nonetheless, slum clearances, advantageous terms for site acquisition and capital supplies, and the progressive extension of local authority powers from the removal of individual insanitary properties to dealing with specified areas and, in 1890, to housebuilding itself, introduced a neurotic preoccupation with the defence of their interests amongst builders in the major Scottish burghs.

Landlords, both as ratepayers and more emphatically through their professional bodies, the House Factors' associations, vigorously represented rentier views of housing to town councils, their sub-committees, and to official investigations. In Edinburgh, 80 per cent of councillors in 1875 (72 per cent in 1905) were landlords, and on important committees which set the rates and approved building proposals—the Treasurer's Committee, Lord Provost's Committee and the Dean of Guild Court—landlords were even more strongly represented.[54] Such political influence meant that official documents and policies, for example, housing enquiries in Glasgow in 1891 and 1904, were strongly influenced by landlords' perspectives on housing: 'Any industry, which on an average of years is unprofitable, naturally decays. Investors seek for more profitable investments in which to place their capital.'[55] Yet despite this apparently collusive relationship over the broad framework of urban capitalism, town councils were by no means exempt from landlords' criticisms. Landlords felt threatened by municipal intervention. Direct involvement in housebuilding and house letting by civic authorities complicated landlords' cartel-like rent fixing and housing management strategies;[56] slum clearance, street widening and municipal operation of transport networks from the 1890s again disturbed the rental market; oligarchic landowners' and property developers' decisions were subject to some degree of external scrutiny, even though they often remained able to circumvent building and other controls through administrative and political channels. Rising municipal expenditure significantly added to rates, the burden of which could not easily and completely be passed to tenants, and allowances to landlords for the collection of rates were successfully averted in the drive to contain municipal spending.

Municipal responsibilities introduced by central government and those voluntarily assumed by council imposed a mounting strain on civic finance after 1870. To cope with expanded responsibilities the combined general, school, poor and police rates increased by respectively 64, 51, 30 and 27 per cent in Edinburgh, Glasgow, Aberdeen and Dundee between 1890 and 1914.[57] The core of the municipal fiscal system, property taxation, was under severe pressure. Non-payment of rates was in Glasgow ten times higher in poorer districts than for the city as a whole, and, more alarmingly to contemporaries, the cost to the civic purse of burials, vaccination, general cleansing and house inspection and the staff costs associated with the administration of these and other functions was four times heavier in the poorer wards than in the city as a whole.[58] Accordingly, better quality housing shouldered a disproportionate burden of local taxation. The spectre of subsidisation, of the rates levied on one segment of local taxpayers used to maintain another, was, even in the heartland of municipal socialism, a political terrain contested by landlords and ratepayers.

The upward trend of municipal expenditure brought two major responses from the participants. The corporation, through the considerable scope for greater administrative efficiency,[59] sought to raise more revenue from the limited tax base; and proprietors viewed the basis of assessment and escalating local taxation as a further assault on the profitability of house ownership and accordingly defended their position by opposing further rates increases and by seeking preferential treatment when housing issues came under discussion. Not without cause, property owners maintained that the incidence of local taxation fell more squarely on landlords than any other group.[60] A particular irritation, directed at landowners, was that undeveloped land was virtually exempt from rates. In 190 Scottish burghs vacant land in 1914 represented 37.3 per cent of the urban area, yet paid only 0.3 per cent of municipal rates.[61] Land hoarding and the eventual untaxed windfall gain or betterment associated with the enhanced capital value of the land annoyed landlords who paid disproportionately in annual local taxes with no equivalent benefit. Town councils, landlords and tenants urged local taxation based on site value rather than the annual income of land, and although this proposal appeared in the Royal Commission report in 1885,[62] landowners successfully resisted its introduction.

A second source of landlords' grievance was the basis of tax assessments. Scottish rates were calculated on gross rather than net rent, that is, before deductions were made for repairs, insurance and owners' taxes, a practice universally employed to determine English assessments to local taxation where a rental of £19.10s was treated as having a net rateable value of only £13.[63] In addition, owners were obliged to pay parish rates on unlet property. Thirdly, and more vehemently, landlords were aggrieved at the onerous tax collection duties which they discharged *gratis* for the town chamberlain's department. Only on properties rented at less than £4 per annum was a small rebate or 'compounding' allowance allowable to landlords for their efforts. Although 43 per cent of total Scottish rates collected in 1901 were paid directly by property owners to the city treasury (and a further significant proportion collected from occupiers and forwarded to the Treasurer's Departments), owners got almost no financial recompense for this effort, unlike English landlords whose compounding allowance applied to all properties. Only on a tiny minority of properties—2.2 per cent in Glasgow in 1906—were rebates available to landlords.[64]

The bone of contention between local authorities and landlords was how to increase the yield of the rates. In the seven fiscal years 1899/1900 to 1905/6, unpaid, and thus irrecoverable rates, on houses rented at £4.1s to £10 averaged 22 per cent.[65] More precisely, the loss of yield on Glasgow rates in 1905/6 was heavily concentrated in the £4–7 rental bracket (18.9 per cent), compared to houses rented at £7–10 (loss of 2.3 per cent), or those over £10 (0.4 per cent). Municipal authorities, therefore, reckoned that any increased rebates given to landlords for their trouble in collecting rates on a regular basis on properties rented at more than £4 would be more than offset by the net additions to civic coffers. The central problem was that to diminish tax defaults greater frequency of collection was required, and that interfered with landlords' strong preference for letting property for a year, rather than, as in English boroughs, for much shorter periods. The needs of municipal finance and the interests of property owners were in conflict.

To what extent were landlords prepared to compromise on the issue of long lets? About 80 per cent of all working class houses were let on a yearly basis, with rents paid monthly, quarterly, or half-yearly.[66] Perhaps later industrialisation in Scotland inhibited the development of a more mobile workforce,[67] but more likely, the characteristic form of tenure, feuing, contributed to inflated urban land values in Scotland, a dense and high rise building form, the tenement, and a correspondingly reduced need for labour to relocate in the event of a change of employment. For whatever reason, the proportion of short let houses was diminishing before World War I.[68] Uniquely, Scottish tenants were obliged to sign a 'missive', a written agreement to rent a flat when it became available on the expiry of the yearly let—'Whitsunday' (the actual date for legal, letting purposes being fixed in Scotland on 28 May). Tenants were, therefore, legally bound, and to their even greater annoyance, were pressurised to sign the 'missive' by Candlemas, 2 February.[69] If they did not, their existing home might be let to another tenant prepared, as early as 2 February, to make the commitment to rent for the following year. For landlords the system of yearly changes in lets had several administrative advantages and thus management cost implications. Property ownership in Scottish burghs was not as concentrated as in English cities; there was a broader participation in property ownership. For example, in Glasgow in 1900 private individuals constituted 64.4 per cent of landlords, and owned 56.1 per cent of properties; trusts accounted for a quarter of both.[70] Rather than deal with the management of tenements themselves—repairs, rent collection, payment of taxes, insurance—many landlords preferred to place these responsibilities in the hands of a specialist agent, the house factor, to whom an annual fee was payable. Long lets, dovetailed at a given point in the year, possessed an administrative simplicity appealing to landlords, since reminders to tenants, monitoring missives and tenants' replies, court proceedings for eviction could be dealt with collectively, rather than individually. Factors were disinclined to concede long lets willingly.

Tenants complained vehemently about both the letting and local taxation systems. To pay rates in a lump sum imposed considerable strains on household budgets, particularly when these were due in difficult months of irregular winter employment, and when occupiers were already accustomed to smaller, more frequent payments, as with their subscriptions to insurance, co-operative, and friendly societies. Non-payment resulted in disenfranchisement; in 1906, 9 per cent of Glaswegian householders were unable to vote for this reason. Long lets were inflexible, inconvenient, and unfair since there were financial penalties if the tenant did not complete the letting period. The rent was still due if the property was unlet, and even if sub-let, landlords charged a 5 per cent fee on part or all of the rent unpaid. Annual term dates for signing and moving in to properties caused stress and congestion. Obtaining a flat was uncertain and tenants were dependent on a factor's line, effectively a character reference; as removals were not staggered through the year considerable pressure accumulated on the availability of carts; and since repairs and maintenance were usually undertaken around the changeover in lets, frenetic small building work often went unsupervised, scamped and incomplete. Another irritant, as explained by the secretary of the Aberdeen Trades Council, was that if a worker did receive a wage increase it was unfair to him and his family to have to wait twelve or even up to sixteen months to translate it into improved living accommodation; and similarly, adjustment to a wage cut would be assisted by a prompt move to a cheaper house.[71] In a wider context, the house-letting system impaired the operation of the labour market as workers were often disinclined to take better employment opportunities because to uproot their family involved expense. Alternatively, rather than relocate the family, terminate the let and negotiate another often inferior one mid-term, the worker might prefer to go into lodgings, or to commute. Either solution imposed financial burdens on the family budget. What particularly irritated tenants was their non-existent freedom of contract when it seemed that employers and landlords could terminate agreements virtually at will.[72]

The balance of power: evictions and landlord–tenant strife

Property management could be undertaken personally, by a rent collector, by a house 'farmer' who paid a fixed rent to the owner and earned a living according to the differential between this and the rent charged to a tenant, or by a house factor with responsibilities beyond those of simple rent collection—insurance, repairs, letting. The increasingly specialist knowledge relating to public health matters, building regulations, legal procedures and valuation, not to mention tax and accounting complexities meant house farmers and factors were the preferred solution of many Scottish owners since they were confronted with more tenants than their English counterparts.[73] This accorded Scottish landlords enhanced power and influence in three respects. Firstly, the daily involvement of professional property managers generally gave them greater acquaintance with property law, and a willingness to invoke it to redress owners' grievances. Secondly, because of the numbers of factors and property agents, their professional associations were viable and actively represented their interests through newspaper columns, articles and personal networks to councillors, MPs, and official inquiries. Thirdly, this public image of solidarity encouraged unity amongst landlords when, for example, high levels of empty property might incline a wavering member towards rent reductions or some departure from the long let strategy. Cohesion amongst landlords strengthened their position in the housing market.[74]

Landlords' solidarity was buttressed by the law relating to rent arrears. The Scots Law of Hypothec, enforceable through the Sheriff Courts, meant that a tenant's furniture, furnishings and tools were liable to sequestration from the moment he occupied the house; the threat of seizure was a sanction which landlords held over tenants should they get into rent arrears. It was 'a form of privileged coercion', and offered a measure of security which was 'guarded jealously by proprietors.'[75] The process was enforced on application to the sheriff, possessions were sold, and the proceeds paid off rent due mostly in short let and thus low quality property. Sequestration for rent rose dramatically between 1900 and 1912; the increase was 50–60 per cent between 1899 and 1907; by 1909, rent recovered through the courts was in Glasgow 227 per cent above and in Scotland 204 per cent above the 1899 levels, before tailing off after 1911. Property owners and factors were evidently unprepared in times of difficult employment, as in 1904–5 and 1908–9, to allow rent to accumulate, even though the proportion of unlet houses was rising so steadily that in 1910 one in ten stood empty.[76] Recourse to the law with such frequency was one indicator of the escalation of conflict between landlord and tenant before 1914.

Another indicator of intensified landlord–tenant conflict was in landlords' actions for eviction. Rent arrears might prompt such an attempt, but vandalism and immorality were among the other reasons which led owners to seek a tenant's removal. This legal process was routed through the Burgh Court which was cheaper and more convenient for the landlord to utilise.[77] The extraordinary numerical scale of such attempts to deal mainly with evictions from short let property was reflected in the fact that warrants for eviction in

London between 1886–90 were in a ratio of 1 to every 1,818 inhabitants; in Glasgow the average annual estimate of 20,000 petitions for eviction was equivalent to a ratio of 1 to every 54 inhabitants. As if this level of antagonism was insufficient, the Housing, Letting (Scotland) Act 1911[78] accelerated the already speedy Scottish eviction process, since 7 days arrears of rent allowed the landlord to give 48 hours notice of eviction, on the expiry of which landlords could obtain a summary application for removal, giving the tenant a further 48 hours to vacate the house.

Under the threat of such sanctions it was clear that the balance of power in the rented housing market lay firmly with the property owners. Tenants might flit, run up rent arrears, remove fixtures, and cause wilful damage to the fabric of the house but landlords could speedily limit such practices. Though the overwhelming majority of court actions referred to short let and inferior properties, the spectre of such legal power was never far removed from other tenants, whose compliance with landlords' wishes it largely guaranteed. Property interests not only deployed the workings of the market to their advantage, but also activated the legal machinery to supplement it.

Housing and political alignment

The power of landed and property interests over eviction and redress for rent arrears was in some measure a reflection of urban politics in Victorian Scotland.[79] Though reformed in 1833, the extended franchise included less than one in twenty of the population in the cities. Such a narrow electoral base meant that middle class interests were most strongly represented, and if the new city electors nurtured a resentment to those landowner interests who had opposed the extension of the franchise, it was not expressed as an assault on their privileged position and even less on alliances with working class interests. An un-represented, and later under-represented, working class was more concerned to win the vote than to concentrate on specific issues such as poor housing conditions. Though Trades Councils and Working Mens' Associations gave some exposure in the city chambers to working class interests from the 1850s, only from the 1870s, once the vote had been significantly extended, did working class political action on specific issues gain momentum.

Another contributory factor to the establishment of a working class political identity in late-Victorian Scotland was the moribund nature of the Liberal Party. In urban Scotland, the Liberals had been the only party returned since the reforms of the 1830s. Though there were important factional differences, Liberal party organisation and policies had never been revised in the manner of English Liberals so as to take account of their opponents' strategies. Thus the major issues of the 1880s—disestablishment of the church in 1885 and Home Rule in 1886—irreparably split Scottish Liberals. The vacuum created an unusual opportunity for new party formations at a time when working class interests rejected alliances with radical Liberals in favour of independent Labour representation. Whereas in 1885 there were no Labour councillors in Scotland, by 1898, 14 per cent of Glasgow councillors—and by 1914, 17 per cent—were Labour and precisely to counteract their rising influence, the Citizens' Union was formed to oppose increasing levels of municipal expenditure on slum clearance and council housebuilding. It was this issue of escalating council expenditure on housing, trams and other projects, and of cross-subsidisation between them, which emerged in 1902 as a potent electoral force, causing the chairman of the City Improvement Trust, Samuel Chisholm, to lose his seat, and effectively blocking further progess on municipal housing for several years. It was a demonstration of how limited was Labour's municipal power in reality, and indicative of a switch in national political priorities towards the unemployment issue in the years 1902–7. The formation of the Glasgow Labour Party in 1911, though suspending slum clearance projects, was based on a platform of taxation of site values, equalisation of rates between landlord and tenant, a renovation programme for tenements, and a commitment to the provision of cheap council houses. The launch of Labour on Clydeside therefore owed much to its stance on housing issues.

Housing was not the sole factor in the emergence of political polarisation from the 1880s, but it was an important strand and was instrumental in bringing organised labour into local politics. Though the inconvenience of the missive—'this absurd system'[80]—was recognised by landlords, factors and occupiers, and voluntary schemes to amend the practice had failed in the four Scottish cities, property interests strongly opposed short lets. Factors' and landlords' associations from burghs throughout Scotland were 'unanimous in their opposition both to short lets and to compounding,' as were locally influential individuals.[81] Working mens' organisations—Trades Councils in Aberdeen, Leith, Dundee, Falkirk; Partick Labour Representation Committee, Glasgow Independent Labour Party, and Cooperative Societies; all building trades unions, as well as Clyde-based representatives of both the Blacksmiths' and Horsemen's Unions, and the Lanarkshire Miners' Union; and tenants' associations in Glasgow and Paisley—were 'unanimously in favour both of a shortened interval between taking a house and entry and short lets.'[82]

Such solidarity amongst tenants lent support to the claim, that 'agitation in favour of short lets' formed part of 'a general socialistic programme' politically orchestrated by English activists working in Scotland.[83] Though the conspiratorial theory was firmly rejected, more significant was the explicit official acknowledgement of the authentic grievances of Scottish tenants. Tenants' views regarding the objectionable practices of yearly lets and signed commitments to take flats were increasingly voluble and sustained between 1900 and 1914, and submissions to elected representatives and at political meetings made plain their opposition to the housing system in no uncertain terms. The missive issue was 'canvassed at meetings of landlords' factors, and tenants' associations, and at public meetings convened for the purpose,' was the subject of questions in municipal and parliamentary elections', and 'The attention of the Secretary for Scotland was called ... (to the missive) ... by deputations, and in a memorial signed by fifty-three Scotch members.'[84] Political figures such as local councillors in Greenock, Glasgow, Falkirk, Kilmarnock, Paisley, and Clydebank, the Provost of Hamilton, and C E Price and J W Cleland, the MPs for Edinburgh Central and Glasgow Bridgeton in

1907 also opposed the missive system. As to municipal views, though the corporations of Edinburgh and Dundee remained undecided, the town councils of Ayr, Clydebank, Falkirk, Glasgow, Govan, Greenock, Kilmarnock, Leith and six others were in favour of short lets and compounding; only Partick, Aberdeen, Rothesay and town councils in other resorts opposed both.

It may be that the Scottish house letting system, in that it remained unresponsive to reform, demonstrated the residual power and authority of landlords. After all, their ability to resist the combined forces of town councils, tenants' organisations, emergent Labour parties, and many prominent and influential local individuals' pleas left the missive system and long lets largely intact before 1914. An alternative interpretation is that the system of long lets was the contested terrain for much larger opposing forces, between capital and labour, and was the instrument by which much deeper forces in society—the rise of organised labour and the enfranchisement of the working class, the bureaucratisation of municipalities in the wake of their enlarged responsibilities, and the escalating scale of business and financial interests in the late-Victorian period—attempted to gain leverage over rival forces. The status quo in the housing market, therefore, does not reflect either the absolute domination of property interests or the absence of conflict, but the outcome of a rough temporal equivalence of opposing forces resulting in no significant restructuring in the housing market. It did not reflect indifference amongst the participants; it did reflect the changing balance of the social order such that no longer could a single element—landowners, landlords, builders, councils or even tenants—ride roughshod over other participants' interests. In that sense the housing conflict between 1890 and 1914 illuminates the broader stage of class relations.

Demoralisation and impotence: anxiety among housing interests

The cumulative threat to builders' interests posed by municipal housing and clearance schemes, land and building control policies of town councils, company housing programmes, and the growing muscularity of twentieth century building unions was interpreted by builders as a challenge to their managerial functions and entrepreneurial independence. Institutional interference affected the workings of the market—the pricing of wages, capital and land. The building industry operated with long-term horizons and so short-term disturbances, already considerable, were intensified in the 1890s by the uncertainty created by council policies affecting clearances, low-rented accommodation, and cheap capital supplies through the Local Government Board. Conformity with building standards added to costs, choked back an element of low income demand, and altered the framework of supply within which builders operated. Their response was to suspend building (see Figure 2.2). No English or Welsh regional building index collapsed to the same extent as that in Scotland after 1904.[85]

Landowners' and landlords' interests were no longer sacrosanct in the twentieth century. Compulsory purchase, reduced rates of compensation, and

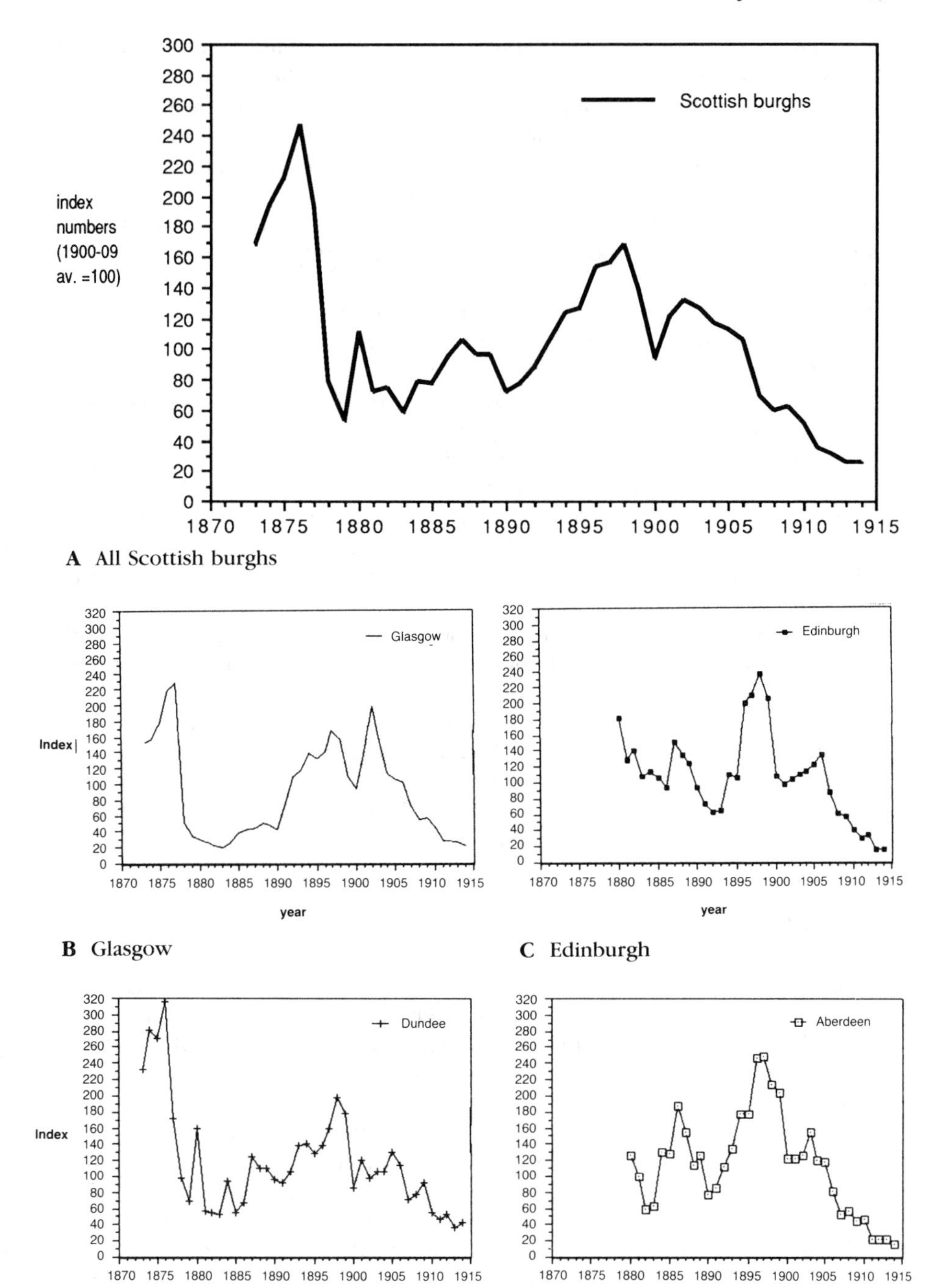

A All Scottish burghs

B Glasgow

C Edinburgh

D Dundee

E Aberdeen

Figure 2.2 Scottish urban housebuilding 1870–1914

the encroachment of suburban railways signalled the importance of external factors in the determination of property rights. If the balance of power remained with them, their omnipotence was no longer automatically assured. In particular, the crisis in municipal finance cast doubts on the accrual of land value appreciation to property owners; the threat of site value taxation to cream off the unearned increment in land values could no longer be dismissed lightly, as the submission of successive bills before parliament 1899–1905 and the inclusion of such proposals in Lloyd George's budgets of 1909 and 1914, indicated.[86]

Anxiety permeated the area of housing management too. For Scottish landlords' management problems became increasingly complex. Regulatory controls circumscribed the density of occupancy, notwithstanding the intense degree of overcrowding in many Scottish burghs. The burden of paperwork in connection both with local authority taxation and planning applications, and the possibilities of spot checks to enforce standards and fines for non-compliance left less room for manoeuvre and correspondingly narrower margins for landlords. And for house factors and bailiffs, seen as agents of the rentier class, rent collection and the enforcement of eviction orders brought vilification and increasing personal confrontation both with individual tenants and with their organisations.[87]

Perhaps most important, it was investors who increasingly adopted a sceptical view of the profitability of the property sector. Alternative investment opportunities, starting with the increased attraction of gilts at the time of the Boer War, placed property in a shadow. Rising numbers of empty houses indicated to some the saturation of the rental market. The prospect of council housing threatened the independence of the rented market and created anxiety over the capital value of, and rental income from, housing; neither possibility did much to allay the fears of investors.

Conclusion

Arguably the fears amongst housing interests were more imagined than real. Conceivably the anxiety was contagious, self-fulfilling. The concern may have been conditioned by cyclical factors which periodically afflicted the building industry, or even stage-managed to gain sympathy for builders and landlords in inquiries and their reports.

The evidence suggests otherwise. There were factors of deeper significance at work in the property sector before 1914 of which the tension and frustration expressed by builders, landlords, tenants and others were indicative of long-term structural problems superimposed upon short-term cyclical ones. The protracted downturn in housebuilding and the resilience of the percentage of empty houses to demolition rates, minimal new building and new family formation intensified the cyclical problems which, following the 1902 peak in Scottish housebuilding, might reasonably have been reversed before 1914. Patience with the autonomous recovery of the housing market was however exhausted because a crop of new and contentious social issues concerned with the distribution of capital and unearned incomes, physical welfare and standards of material well-being sensitised Scottish public opinion in the areas of housing quality. The engagement of such issues, however tentatively, itself fuelled uncertainty amongst suppliers of housing and deepened the crisis of accommodation. But it was symptomatic of a political engagement, mainly by radical liberals, with matters of wealth creation and distribution and of equity principles. That in Scotland tension and confrontation between the various property interests surfaced should be unsurprising since such issues raised fundamental questions about the structure of urban power; arguments, grievances and counter-claims were all part of the predictable manoevring for position. Tenants, builders, landlords, and property owners each had a different perspective on how that power should be redefined.

In the thirty or so years before World War I Scottish housing occupied a position of some importance on the contemporary political agenda. Occasionally this took a visible, specific and pressing form, as in the government's urgent need to house dockyard workers relocated in Scotland for whom the forbidding tenement form held little appeal; or, as when pressed by deputations of Scottish Miners' Federation leaders and MPs from mining districts, to urge action to improve living conditions for their constituents. It would be simplistic to argue that the Royal Commission of 1885 represented an emphatic turning point. Yet it was significant in several respects, not least because it represented a high-water mark in middle class power, of bourgeois hegemony. Thereafter, by design or by default, housing matters and property relations were never the same again.

Appendix 2A Overcrowding in Scotland 1861–1911

	Persons living more than 2 per room		Persons living more than 3 per room		Persons living more than 4 per room	
Year	[%]	[millions]	[%]	[millions]	[%]	[millions]
1861	58.6	1.732	33.8	1.036	18.7	0.575
1871	53.9	1.811	31.4	1.056	16.5	0.554
1881	50.8	1.896	27.7	1.034	13.2	0.493
1891	48.2	1.939	25.3	1.019	11.3	0.455
1901	45.7	2.042	22.9	1.024	9.6	0.428
1911	43.6	2.077	21.1	1.005	8.3	0.397

Source: Census of Scotland 1911, Report, *PP 1913 LXXX*, p. 568

Appendix 2B Distribution of Scottish houses by size 1861–1911

Year	[1 Room] [000s]	[%]	[2 Rooms] [000s]	[%]	[3 Rooms] [000s]	[%]	[4 Rooms] (000s)	[%]	[5 Rooms] [000s]	[%]	[6 Rooms] [000s]	[%]	[7 Rooms] [000s]	[%]
1861	227	34.0	247	37.9	76	11.1	37	5.5	20	3.0	15	2.3	37	5.6
1871	237	32.1	275	37.2	93	12.6	44	6.0	24	3.2	18	2.4	47	6.3
1881	211	26.0	316	38.9	120	14.7	55	6.8	30	3.7	22	2.7	58	7.4
1891	193	22.1	341	39.1	143	16.1	66	7.5	36	4.1	26	2.9	68	7.8
1901	170	17.6	385	39.9	178	18.5	85	8.5	44	4.5	30	3.1	77	7.9
1911	130	12.8	409	40.4	205	20.3	95	9.3	55	5.4	34	3.5	83	8.2

Source: Census of Scotland 1911, Report, *PP 1913 LXXX*, p. 568

Appendix 2C Distribution of population by house sizse 1861–1911

	[Person in Houses of]													
Year	[1 Room] [000s]	[%]	[2 Rooms] [000s]	[%]	[3 Rooms] [000s]	[%]	[4 Rooms] [000s]	[%]	[5 Rooms] [000s]	[%]	[6 Rooms] [000s]	[%]	[7 Rooms] [000s]	[%]
1861	863	26.2	1155	37.7	388	12.7	197	6.4	112	3.7	90	2.9	291	9.5
1871	797	23.7	1286	38.3	465	13.9	226	6.7	127	3.8	101	3.0	350	10.4
1881	670	18.0	1476	39.5	603	16.4	282	7.6	157	4.2	120	3.2	425	11.4
1891	573	14.3	1587	39.1	722	17.9	334	8.3	184	4.6	138	3.4	486	12.1
1901	493	11.0	1767	39.5	890	19.3	407	9.1	218	4.9	154	3.5	542	12.1
1911	400	8.4	1882	39.5	1006	21.1	456	9.6	258	5.4	175	3.7	584	12.3

Source: Census of Scotland 1911, Report, *PP 1913 LXXX*, p. 568.

Notes

1. Royal Commission on the Housing of the Working Class (subsequently RC 1884–85), Second Report, PP 1884–85 XXX, C 4409, p.4.
2. RC 1884–85, Evidence of Walker, Q18363.
3. RC 1884–85, Second Report, 7–8; Evidence of Walker Q18352–65, Collins Q19332, D Crawford Q18556–78.
4. Ibid, Evidence of Hannan, Q19291–4.
5. Deputations to the Secretary for Scotland 19 January 1909 (Edinburgh), 26 April 1911 and 20 November 1911 (London).
6. Reports of the Local Government Board for Scotland for 1910, PP 1911 XXXIII, p.lxvii, and for 1911, PP 1912–13 XXXVII, p.lix.
7. Report of the Royal Commission on the Housing of the Industrial Population of Scotland, Rural and Urban (subsequently RC 1917), PP 1917–18 XIV, and Minutes of Evidence, 4 vols, HMSO, Edinburgh, 1921.
8. E Gauldie, *Cruel Habitations: A History of Working-Class Housing 1780–1918*, 1974, p.285.
9. For example the *Pall Mall Gazette*, *National Review*, *Nineteenth Century*, and *Fortnightly Review*.
10. O Hill, *Homes of the London Poor*, and A Mearns, *The Bitter Cry of Outcast London*, reprinted as Cass Library of Victorian Times 1970 vol 6. For further details on contemporary tracts c 1880–1914 see L Lees and A Lees (eds), *The Rise of Urban Britain* (1984) for 35 titles reprinted by Garland publishing. See also D Englander *Landlord and Tenant in Urban Britain 1838–1918*, 1983, pp.326–8. See also A S Wohl, *The Eternal Slum: Housing and Social Policy in Victorian London*, 1977.
11. H D Littlejohn, Edinburgh Medical Officer of Health 1865–1908; J B Russell, Glasgow MOH 1872–98.
12. A list of publications by J B Russell is provided in O Checkland and M Lamb (eds), *Health Care as Social History: the Glasgow Case* 1982, pp.256–9.
13. Other influential lectures by J B Russell's lectures included: 'The house' (Glasgow Health Lectures 1881); 'Children of the city' (Edinburgh Health Lectures 1886); 'On the sanitary results of the Glasgow Improvement Act' (British Medical Association, Sheffield 1876); 'The house in relation to public health' (Glasgow 1887).
14. Presbytery of Glasgow, *Report of Commission on the Housing of the Poor in Relation to their Social Condition* 1891; Dundee Social Union, *Report of Investigation into Social Conditions in Dundee* 1905; City of Edinburgh Charity Organization Society, *Report on the Physical Condition of Fourteen Hundred School Children in the City together with some account of their Homes and Surroundings* 1906; Glasgow Municipal Commission on the Housing of the Poor (subsequently GMC), *Report* 1904; Scottish Land Enquiry Committee (subsequently SLEC), *Scottish Land* 1914.
15. Scotch Education Department, *Report on the Physical Condition of Children Attending the Public School of the School Board for Glasgow* 1907; Census of Scotland 1911, PP 1912–13 XIX; see also articles in *The Lancet*, *The Sanitary Journal*, *The Builder*, and local journals and magazines.
16. Applications to Dean of Guild Courts in the 1880s mushroomed as a result of innumerable plans for the addition of WCs. See for example Galashiels Dean of Guild Court Registers 1893–1914; Cullen Registers of Plans and Sections 1893–1914, Moray District Record Office ZB Cu D3; Kirkcudbright Dean of Guild Court Register of Plans and Sections 1893–1914. See also RC 1917, Evidence of Kelso, Q37911.

17. 'Urban' is defined as those resident in burghs over 2,000 inhabitants.
18. SLEC, *Report*, p.287.
19. Sir Halliday Croom to the Annual Meeting of the National Vigilance Association (Edinburgh), quoted in the *Glasgow Herald*, 21 November 1913.
20. Rooms in Scottish houses were generally larger than in English ones. The cubic capacity of Scottish rooms might be as much as 50 per cent greater than rooms in English housing, but once adjustment is made for the higher ceilings of Scottish properties, floor space might only be 20–25 per cent greater. Furthermore, sculleries were common in English houses, yet did not form part of the calculations regarding the floor area of the house.
21. RC 1917, para pp.571–2.
22. For further consideration of the impact tenement design on daily routines see R G Rodger, 'The Victorian building industry and the housing of the Scottish working class', in M Doughty (ed), *Building the Industrial City* 1986, pp.153–69.
23. SLEC, *Report*, p. 371.
24. Ibid., and see also A K Chalmers, 'The death rate in one-apartment houses: an enquiry based on the Census return of 1901', *Proc. of the Royal Phil. Soc. of Glasgow*, **34** 1902–3, pp.125–46.
25. Scotch Education Department, *Report on the Physical Condition of Children attending the Public School of the School Board for Glasgow* 1907; Dundee Social Union, *Report of Investigation into Social Conditions in Dundee* 1905; City of Edinburgh Charity Organization Society, *Report on the Physical Condition of Fourteen Hundred School Children in the City together with some account of their Homes and Surroundings* 1906.
26. Dundee Social Union, op.cit., Part 1. Medical Inspection of School Children, pp.31–7.
27. Sample sizes were respectively 787 and 755.
28. Dundee Social Union, *Report on Housing and Industrial Conditions*, p.xv.
29. RC 1917, para 479.
30. J Melling, *Rent Strikes: Peoples' Struggle for Housing in West Scotland 1890–1916* 1983, pp.27–34.
31. RC 1917, para 2223.
32. For an elaboration of this point see R G Rodger, 'The Victorian building industry and the housing of the Scottish working class', in M Doughty (ed), op.cit. (note 22), pp.169–74.
33. *Report of an Enquiry by the Board of Trade into Working Class Rents, Housing and Retail Prices*, PP 1908 CVIII, p.xl; *Report of an Enquiry into Working Class Rents, Housing and Retail Prices etc*, PP 1913 LXVI.
34. J H Treble, 'The market for unskilled male labour in Glasgow 1891–1914', in I MacDougall (ed), *Essays in Scottish Labour History; a Tribute to W H Marwick* 1979, 115–42; R G Rodger, 'Employment, wages and poverty in the Scottish cities 1841–1914', in G Gordon (ed), *Perspectives of the Scottish City* 1985, pp.25–63.
35. RC 1917, Appendix CXXI.
36. SLEC, *Report*, p. 293.
37. R G Rodger, 'Speculative builders and the structure of the Scottish building industry 1860–1914', *Business History*, **20** 1979, pp.226–46.
38. A Slaven, *The Development of the West of Scotland 1750–1970* 1975; S G E Lythe and J Butt, *An Economic History of Scotland 1100–1939* 1975; R H Campbell, *Scotland since 1707* 1985; B Lenman, *An Economic History of Modern Scotland 1660–1976* 1977.

39. R G Rodger, 'Scottish urban housebuilding 1870–1914', unpublished PhD thesis, Edinburgh 1975, Tables 8.5, 8.8.
40. Certain building control functions existed from early modern times, but had progressively fallen into disuse. See R G Rodger, 'The evolution of Scottish town planning', in G Gordon and B Dicks (eds), *Scottish Urban History* 1983, pp.71–91.
41. G Best, 'The Scottish Victorian city'. *Victorian Studies*, **11** 1968, pp.329–58; G W Barras, 'The Glasgow Building Regulations Act (1892)', *Proc. Royal Phil. Soc. Glasgow* **25** 1894, pp.155–69.
42. Report on the Judicial Statistics of Scotland for 1900, PP 1902 CXVIII.
43. GMC, Report and Recommendations, p. 22; Minutes of Evidence, Eadie, Q7184; Watson Q11161, 11080, 11199, 11204.
44. GMC, Binnie, Q6468; 1917, Auld, Q39919–26.
45. GMC, McGillivray and Fraser, Q13175; Carson and Boyd, Q12388–9.
46. R G Rodger, 'The Victorian building industry and the housing of the Scottish working class', in M Doughty, *Building the Industrial City* Leicester, 1986, pp. 151–206 expands various aspects of the structure of the Scottish building industry.
47. J Mann, 'Better houses for the poor—will they pay?', *Proc. Royal Phil. Soc. Glasgow*, **30**, 1898–9, p.93.
48. C M Allan, 'The genesis of British urban redevelopment with special reference to Glasgow', *Economic History Review*, **18** 1965, pp.598–613.
49. Approximately 3,500 families were housed in council properties in 1913, with 63 per cent of these in Glasgow, 17 per cent in Edinburgh and the remaining 20 per cent distributed amongst Aberdeen, Bo'ness, Clydebank, Greenock, Hamilton, Kilmarnock, Leith, Oban, and Perth. City of Glasgow Housing Committee, *Housing Centenary: A Review of Municipal Housing in Glasgow from 1866 to 1966* Glasgow, 1966, p.10.
50. SLEC, 420–23; GMC, Eadie, Q7184 p.336; Nisbet, Q1431, 1490–97; Gilmour, Q7401 p.346; Patterson, Q7798; Binnie, Q6587–6613, 6687, 7100, 7152; McGillivray, Q13302, 13222–4; Mann, Q8488; Carson, Q12220, 12306, 12441; Lord Provost's Sub-Committee on Housing, quoted in T Cooper, *Report on the Work of the Burgh Engineer's Department for the Year 1893–94* Edinburgh, 1894, p.44.
51. T C Smout, *A Century of the Scottish People 1830–1950* 1986, p.46.
52. R Miller, *The Edinburgh Dean of Guild Court; A Manual of History and Procedure 1887; J C Irons, Manual of the Law and Practice of the Dean of Guild Court* 1895.
53. M Atkinson *Local Government in Scotland* 1904, p.35; A Walker, *City Rating* 1911. For a useful summary see W H Fraser, 'Labour and the changing city', in G Gordon (ed), *Perspectives of the Scottish City* 1985, pp.164–5.
54. B Elliott, D McCrone and V Skelton, 'Property and politics in Edinburgh 1875–1975', in J Garrard (ed), *The Middle Class in Politics* 1978, pp.99–109.
55. Presbytery of Glasgow, *Report*, 26. (See note 14.)
56. S Damer, 'State, class and housing: Glasgow 1885–1919', in J Melling (ed), *Housing, Social Policy and the State* 1980, p.91.
57. SLEC, *Report*, p. 395.
58. J B Russell, 'Sanitation and social economics', *Proc. Royal Phil. Soc. Glasgow*, 1889, pp.1–21.
59. Royal Commission on Local Taxation, Final Report (Scotland), PP 1902 XXXIX, 7. Parish councils, county councils and town councils were responsible for levying and collecting rates. Each employed a separate staff, and each ratepayer had to pay local taxes to two, and in Police Burghs, to three collectors. The Local Government Act, 1894 empowered local authorities to consolidate their rate collecting

machinery, but by 1902 only a few had done so. The scope for improved tax collecting efficiency was considerable. Nine different types of assessment might apply:

Parochial poor rates (spent by parish council)
Parochial school rates (spent by school board)
Burgh general rate (spent by town council on police, street cleansing and sanitation)
Public health rate (spent by town council and county council on sanitation and other public health matters)
Lunatic asylums rate (spent by district lunacy board elected by town, county and parish councils)
Roads rate (spent by town council and county council road board)
County police rates (spent by county council on police)
County general (spent by county council on administration)
County general purposes rate (spent by county council on non-specific matters)

60. Departmental Committee on House-Letting in Scotland, vol 1, *Report*, PP 1907 XXXVI, 3–6 contains a useful summary of local taxation procedures in Scotland. Subsequently cited as DC 1907.
61. Burgh (Areas and Rates) Scotland, PP 1914 CXLIV, 571 quoted in *Glasgow Herald*, 18 October 1913, and SLEC, *Report*, p. 479.
62. RC 1885, Report pp.69–70.
63. R G Rodger, 'The law and urban change: some nineteenth century Scottish evidence', *Urban History Yearbook*, 1979, pp.85–6; DC 1907, *Report*, 6 and Q11159–65, 10485.
64. RC on Local Taxation, *Final Report*, Scotland, 4; DC 1907, *Report*, 5. The compounding allowance, though fixed by the Burgh Police (Scotland) Act 1892, Section 345, at 10 per cent in Scottish burghs, was substantially higher under local acts: 15 per cent or 25 per cent in Glasgow, Greenock 20 per cent or 25 per cent, Paisley 10 per cent or 25 per cent. Compounding allowances applied only to certain elements of rates.
65. DC 1907, *Report*, p.20.
66. Ibid., p.3.
67. D Englander, *Landlord and Tenant in Urban Britain 1838–1918* 1983, p.167.
68. J Butt, 'Working class housing in Glasgow 1815–1914', in S D Chapman (ed), *The History of Working Class Housing* 1971, p.71.
69. DC 1907, *Report*, 6; R G Rodger, 'The law and urban change', op.cit, (note 63) p.86; D Englander, op.cit, (note 67) pp. 162–73 provides an excellent summary of the missive system.
70. N J Morgan and M J Daunton, 'Landlords in Glasgow: a study of 1900', *Business History*, **25**, 1983, p.261, 274.
71. DC on House-Letting in Scotland, PP 1908 XLVII, evidence of, Johnston, Q10368.
72. Ibid, *Report* 3.
73. M J Daunton, *House and Home in the Victorian City: Working Class Housing 1850–1914* 1983, p.168, 173; 'What may be accepted without reservation is the fact that landlords in England had less power over their tenants than in Scotland.' p. 149.
74. S Damer, Estate, class and housing: Glasgow 1885–1911, in J Melling (ed), *Housing, Social Policy and the State*, 1980, pp. 73–112.
75. D. Englander, op.cit, (note 67), p.30.
76. Ibid, p.31.

77. Presbytery of Glasgow, *Report*, p.96.
78. 1 and 2 Geo. V. C.35.
79. What follows is based on D G Southgate 'Politics and representation in Dundee 1832–1963' in J M Jackson (ed), *The City of Dundee* 1979; M Dyer, 'Mere detail and machinery: the Great Reform Act and the effects of redistribution on Scottish representation 1832–68', *Scottish Historical Review,* **62** 1983, pp.17–34; F W S Craig, *British Parliamentary Election Results 1832–85* 1974 and *1885–1918* 1979; W H Fraser, 'Trades unions, reform and the election of 1868 in Scotland', *Scottish Historical Review,* **50** 1971, pp.138–57; J G Kellas, 'The Liberal Party in Scotland 1876–95', *Scottish Historical Review,* **44** 1965, pp. 1–15; D Savage, 'Scottish politics 1885–86', *Scottish Historical Review*, **40** 1961, pp.118–35; J McCaffrey, 'The origins of Liberal Unionism in the west of Scotland', *Scottish Historical Review*, **50** 1971, pp.47–71; W H Fraser, 'Trades Councils in the labour movement in nineteenth century Scotland', in I MacDougall (ed), *Essays in Scottish Labour History* 1975; W H Fraser, 'Labour and the changing city' and W Miller, 'Politics in the Scottish City 1832–1982', both in G Gordon (ed), *Perspectives of the Scottish City* 1985; J Melling, *Rent Strikes: Peoples' Struggle for Housing in the West of Scotland 1890–1916* 1983; S Damer, 'State, class and housing: Glasgow 1885–1914', in J Melling (ed), *Housing, Social Policy and the State* 1980.
80. DC on House-Letting, Evidence of, McBain, Q5627.
81. Ibid, *Report*, p.9.
82. Ibid, *Report*, pp.7–9.
83. Ibid, p.4.
84. Ibid, p.6.
85. J P Lewis, *Building Cycles and Britain's Growth* 1965 Appendix 4.
86. P J Waller, *Town, City and Nation: England 1850–1914* 1983, p.261; J E Pointing and M A Bulos, 'Some implications of failed issues of social reform: the case of leasehold enfranchisement', *International J Urban and Regional Research*, **8** 1984, pp.467–80; B K Murray, 'The politics of the "Peoples' Budget", *Historical Journal*, **16** 1973, pp.555–70; B B Gilbert, 'David Lloyd George, the reform of British landholding and the budget of 1914', *Historical Journal*, **21** 1978, pp.117–41.
87. S Damer, op.cit, p.91.

3 Clydeside rent struggles and the making of Labour politics in Scotland, 1900–39

Joseph Melling

In the closing decades of the twentieth century Scotland has struggled to retain its distinct economic and political identity in the face of industrial decline and urban decay. The Scottish cities have provided the setting for some of the more spectacular failures in policy-making as successive governments sought to rebuild the basic industries and renovate the great conurbations that surround them. Following their disastrous experience in the Scottish shipbuilding sector during the early 1970s, the Conservative Party reviewed the problems they faced north of the border. Policy strategists concluded that the damage inflicted on Conservatism was attributable not merely to the strength of unionised labour but also to the weakness of the Conservatives' urban political base. The sheer scale of public sector housing in cities such as Glasgow had eclipsed the role of the private landlord without laying the foundations for a property-owning democracy of house buyers.[1] In their search for a natural constituency of individual houseowners and ratepayers the Conservatives have greatly expanded the scheme of council house sales during the 1980s but their impact in Scotland remains limited.[2]

The controversy which enveloped the housing policies of different governments over recent decades only underlines the simple point that the approach to urban questions is as highly charged by political ideology and interests as the handling of industrial relations or the reform of local government. At the heart of the political debates on housing provision since the early twentieth century has been the question of rent and the legitimate claims of the private landlord on the housing market. The imposition of legislative controls on rents which began in 1915 have survived in various forms until the 1980s, though each attempt to reform the restrictions has provoked bitter conflict—in the 1920s, late 1950s and early 1970s.[3] At such moments there appeared a profound difference between those who understood the housing market as a healthy area of profitable activity once official restrictions were lifted, and those who defended the protection of the tenants as a basic duty of government which must place the needs of the occupier above the returns to the private investor.[4]

These debates have been echoed in the different interpretations offered by historians for the peculiar evolution of British housing over the twentieth century and the criticisms levelled at the private landlord. The recent study by M. J. Daunton offers a formidable challenge to accounts which assume the inevitable demise of the private rented sector and the relentless march of public housing.[5] His work suggests that the difficulties faced by the housing investor in modern Britain was not due to any crisis in the structure of the market or the limited real income of working class tenants, but to a *political* failure of the landlords to compete with the tenants in the arena of electoral influence. The failure of the housing interest to assert itself in any of the major parties during the Edwardian years left the landlords vulnerable to the introduction of legislation which seriously damaged the profitability of their investments. The arrival of rent restrictions and local authority housing after 1914 further distorted the industry and inhibited the ability of the private investor to provide a reasonable service in subsequent decades.[6]

Such an argument still leaves unanswered the question why such an enormous number of large and small investors should have found no way to influence the major parties and precisely how the mass of private tenants has compelled successive (mostly Conservative) governments to introduce and sustain rent restrictions since 1915. The rise of the Labour Party is a crucial factor in the growth of public housing and tenant protection in Britain, but it has held office for a fairly limited period even since 1945. Moreover, Labour's policies on housing and industry have not secured its position with the British electorate in the 1980s, when the privatisation of public assets (including housing) has confirmed the appeal of Conservatism. In contrast to the resilience of Labour support in Scotland and Wales, Labour's electoral appeal has been crumbling, somewhat unevenly, since the peak of 1951.[7]

The progress of rent legislation has been directly affected by struggles and political initiatives which went far beyond the electoral performance of Labour or the political ineptitude of contemporary landlords. This chapter will examine the precise relationship between the tenants' campaigns and the making of Labour politics in west Scotland. This involves some review of the general arguments about the origins and rise of Labour and its constituency, as well as the recent appraisal of the 'Red Clydeside' years in west Scotland. The contribution of the tenants' movements to the building of Labour and socialist support in the region can be evaluated and the consequences of Labour's policies assessed. It can be shown that Labour harnessed and orchestrated the tenants' movements in their early stages but were only partly successful in containing the struggles within the limits of constitutional action. Equally apparent is the importance of economic conditions in the industrial districts in moulding the housing market between the Wars, as well as influencing the tactics pursued by organised labour. Any effective explanation must take into account the particular problems of Scottish industry at this time. It was as much the basic facts of supply and demand that determined the scope for private investment in inter-war Scotland as the activities of the organised tenants, though the activists were able to establish the argument that contemporary landlords could not profitably provide the standard of accommodation needed by the tenants at acceptable rents.

Labour support and the achievements of 'Red Clydeside', 1900–18: significance and interpretation

The achievements of Scottish tenants and the significance of rent strikes in Scottish urban politics have been discussed in numerous accounts of 'Red Clydeside'. Among the most influential portraits of housing campaigns and local leaders are those provided by the autobiographies and biographies of prominent activists, such as the vivid testament of William Gallacher and the tributes to John Maclean.[8] These partisan memoirs were written during the turmoil and setbacks of the 1930s and 1940s, as their authors sought to establish the credentials of the competing Communist and socialist organisations and the heroic achievements of an earlier generation. Widespread disillusionment with the Labour Party after 1931 and the influence of brilliant trade unionists in the Communist party ensured that the earliest versions of Red Clydeside gave an overwhelming prominence to the workplace struggles of the early twentieth century and the revolutionary potential of direct action in industry.[9] Both the importance of the tenants' campaigns and the role of the early Labour Party in building a working class constituency of support was obscured in the detailed descriptions of shop steward campaigns and the impact of the Russian Revolution on 'British Bolshevism'.

This subtle distortion of popular politics has been confirmed, rather than corrected, in recent years by historical research on the region. New Left historians have offered a serious and provocative interpretation of shop floor conflict before and during World War I, documenting the important continuities of syndicalism and the shop stewards' movement. The contribution of the Clyde to revolutionary politics is reviewed mainly in terms of the industrial campaigns of the time, culminating in the post-war unrest and the formation of the British Communist Party.[10] These accounts have emphasised the miscalculations of the early Communists as well as the empty rhetoric of social democrats in the trade union movement and the Labour Party.[11] Radical historians explain the failure of the existing unions and Labour politicans to provide an effective leadership for their constituents by emphasising the prevalence of 'Labourist' ideologies and the constraints of bureaucracy in these organisations. Committed to Victorian notions of responsible market bargaining outside political controls, labour leaders were caught between craft conservationism and the upsurge of workplace militancy. The whole mentality of Labourism led the organised working class away from the possibilities of socialist politics and towards the disastrous compromises of the inter-war years.[12] The real promise of Red Clydeside was betrayed by the labour leaders long before the defeats of 1926 and 1931.

This radical view of early Labour politics has itself been criticised in the work of liberal revisionists, who offer an alternative version of working class campaigns. These writers emphasise the fragmentary and sectionalist character of industrial production and the limited workplace consciousness of the labour force. The structure and ideology of the liberal state also inhibited the spread of Marxist class politics before 1914, denying any government responsibility for the workings of a market economy.[13] In this view the character of early

Labour Party politics was determined by the incoherence of the industrial economy (and its workforce), as well as the institutional and ideological heritage of Victorian liberalism.[14] An important issue in the rise of the Labour Party, McKibbin argues, was the growing commitment of the trade unions to an independent voice in national politics. World War I only confirmed this relationship and the 1918 party constitution should be seen as an acknowledgement that Labour would pursue a 'kind of reformism' rather than revolutionary socialism.[15] Although the trade unions expressed a class identity, their class consciousness was a traditionalist and defensive outlook which inspired the labour leaders to pragmatism rather than radical innovation. The cautious progress of the Edwardian years established a powerful continuity of ideas and practices which carried the Party towards constitutional temperance.[16]

This liberal revision of working class politics has reached to Red Clydeside, with Iain McLean's study of Scottish labour conflict. His account of these years suggests that the industrial politics of Clydeside industry were overshadowed by craft conservatism rather than socialist agitation, providing no secure bases for stable class politics in west Scotland. The shop floor activists consistently misunderstood or misjudged the true character of wartime politics and only threatened the popularity of Labour by the strange blend of craft elitism and sectional militancy they showed in 1919.[17] The real sources of electoral strength lay in the highly effective housing campaigns of Wheatley and his Labour colleagues, which created a much wider constituency of support than was ever possible in the munitions industries. Wheatley and Dollan were also able to attract votes from the Irish community and cement a coalition which brought Labour to power in both local and parliamentary elections in the following years.[18] Only by breaking with the chaotic industrial unrest of the 'Red Clyde', could the party strategists create the real constituency for constitutional socialism in Scottish society.

The great advantage of such a liberal reappraisal of Labour politics is its sharp focus on the part played by housing conditions and other social questions in the growth of political consciousness. Earlier treatments of Clydeside often explained decisive shifts in class conflict wholly in terms of industrial unrest, excluding from serious attention the unorganised and the non-socialist groups in existence at this period. More recent Marxist research has acknowledged the relevance of popular culture and political traditions in the progress of Clydeside socialism, emphasising the continuities between Edwardian radicalism and the libertarian views of the Independent Labour Party.[19] There are also real weaknesses in the version of popular movements offered by the liberal revisionists. In criticising radical scholars for exaggerating the role of workplace unrest in the making of British socialism, the liberals frequently adopt a similar approach to political change, sharply distinguishing the narrow sectionalism found in industry from the wider world of electoral campaigns. Workplace interests are usually portrayed as revolving around the conservative sensibilities of the craftsman or the threat posed by innovating management. Marxists and liberals alike tend to regard the skilled trades as a flat reservoir of craft conservatism, disturbed only by the introduction of new technologies or the onset of a government dilution scheme. The direct experience of deskilling created the conditions for shop floor militancy but it was a minority of politically educated socialists who welded this unrest into an instrument of class politics.[20] Similarly, the different schools of historical writing have portrayed the trade unions as conservative institutions concerned with the particular interests of themselves and their members. These selfish and unimaginative organisations were responsible for the cautious compromises of the war years and their influence in the higher reaches of the Labour Party helped to steer the mass of the working class away from the rapids of revolution and towards the reformism of the 1920s. Basic differences remain in the interpretations of the Red Clyde era, though a number of arguments converge as to the distinct areas of industrial, social and electoral politics.

It is possible to derive an understanding of Scottish society of this period which does not endorse these arguments but which emphasises the changing character of Labour politics and the importance of the relations *between* the different areas of struggle on Clydeside in these years. The following section gives a brief outline of the economic and social forces which brought the housing issue to the forefront of political debate in west Scotland before 1914, and the immediate context for the explosion of tenant unrest that occurred in wartime Glasgow.

Housing and politics in west Scotland, 1900–14

In the second half of the nineteenth century Glasgow was transformed from a significant trading and manufacturing area into a massive industrial conurbation with a great frontage of shipyards and engine shops. The most spectacular rates of growth were recorded in the shipbuilding burghs that clustered along both banks of the Clyde. Govan rose from a small settlement of 15,000 to a boom town of 280,000 in the four decades after 1851, enclosing in its boundaries some of the most famous shipbuilding and engineering names on the river.[21] As Govan, Partick and Linthouse crowded more firms onto the waterfront, industrialists began to develop the open spaces of Scotstoun, Clydebank and Dalmuir further down the Clyde. By the turn of the century the new industrial suburb of Clydebank employed well over 20,000 workers in the two yards (one in Dalmuir) and sewing machine factory, with rapid growth down to the outbreak of war. Meanwhile, Glasgow itself was confirming its reputation as the engine shop of the Empire with massive machinery fitted to the vessels launched on the Clyde. Beyond the Clyde industrial basin the scattered coalfields, ironworks and textile factories helped to sustain the regional economy and provide employment for the growing population.

Housebuilding struggled to match the expansion of industry during most of the nineteenth century, with appalling consequences for the health of the urban working class. Until the major clearance programmes of the 1860s, Glasgow's central district was an incubator for contagious diseases and respiratory illnesses—particularly amongst the poorer migrants who crowded into the cheaper slums in search of work.[22] Such boom towns as Greenock, standing at the mouth of the Clyde, acquired such a reputation for squalor and violence that the local authorities felt compelled to inspect and police the poorest housing as the breeding ground of 'the dangerous classes'.[23] The petty capitalists who supplied provisions and spirits to the locals were frequently the owners of the tenements and cellars rented to the inhabitants. This 'shop-ocracy' included the small merchants, pawnbrokers and tontine-sellers of the immigrant communities as well as native Clydesiders, owning perhaps two-fifths of working class housing in the later decades of the century.[24] They were being seriously challenged as the dominant property investors by a rising group of trustees, lawyers and factors who were engaged in servicing the mass of Scottish housing, but who were also becoming a powerful body of owners in their own right.[25] It was this crowd of medium and small investors which provided the immediate demand for tenements suitable for renting out to working class tenants in the years before 1914. Much of the actual investment capital was raised by mortgage loans and bonds, yielding interest to the rentier class as well as enabling the house owner to secure a return on his own capital.

The houses were physically supplied by the army of small builders which assembled in the great building booms of the nineteenth century, culminating in the wave of tenement construction during the years 1893–1904.[26] Needing limited capital equipment or overheads the speculative builder contracted to complete a small number of dwellings before selling to the ready market, meeting debts and realising the profit which allowed him to undertake another tenement or cottage. These market conditions were primitive but highly competitive and provided Glasgow with tens of thousands of new dwellings in each decade, until by the 1890s the urgent shortage of accommodation in the city began to subside.[27] Although this housing was frequently of a high standard in its construction and substance, there were serious and continued problems of inadequate living space, cramped sleeping quarters and bleak sanitary facilities. In the pre-war years there were still thousands of families spending every minute of their domestic life in a single room, whilst tens of thousands of labourers expected no more than two rooms to house their wives and children at a time when Glasgow was experiencing the greatest industrial prosperity it had ever seen.[28]

It was the urban labour market and the level of real income which determined the effective demand for working class housing, with rising real incomes and growing population stimulating the upturns in the building cycle in the 1890s. After 1904 the rapid rise in prices, an increase in interest rates and investment opportunities elsewhere, and the decline in real wages seriously dampened demand in Glasgow. It has been argued that a surplus in houses was only gradually soaked up before 1914, with the housebuilding industry in virtual abeyance.[29] Offer and others have suggested that the whole structure of Edwardian investment and property markets was failing (quite literally) to meet the demands made on the urban economy.[30] New municipal politics was threatening the property owners with improved standards and burdens that they were unable or unwilling to shoulder. These views are rejected by historians such as Daunton who want to demonstrate the viability of the pre-war housing industry and the intrinsic stability of the private rented sector.[31]

In the Glasgow context the relevant question is not the degree of equilibrium between supply and demand but the clear resistance of working class tenants to paying the rent levels which would have made the continued construction of houses a viable proposition. Not only was there a strong aversion to paying a higher proportion of the household budget in rent (reinforced by a cultural preference for other kinds of consumption in urban Scotland), but the worst-housed groups depended on a range of casual occupations that did not permit an alternative to overcrowding and squalid insecurity. In contrast to the strongholds of building society activity to be found in northern England, the Clydeside working class laboured in trades notorious for their insecurity and relied on the fraternity of the public house rather than the friendly society lodge to discuss problems of income. There was neither the economic or the cultural base from which to establish the principles of regular thrift and steady individual mobility, even if significant numbers of foremen and chargehands could aspire to petty investments.[32] In the new booming burghs of the lower Clyde employers found that they could not depend on the speculative builder to supply the tenements they desperately needed to house the skilled ironworkers before 1914, such was the scepticism about the returns to be expected from housing the working class.[33]

The Glasgow landlords not only faced a stubborn resistance to higher rents in this period. There was a growing tendency for tenants to openly challenge the legal authority of the owner and his agent (the factor) to the point of court appearances against eviction.[34] The traditional resistance to the landlord would take the form of arrears in rent, frequently followed by illicit flight (or 'flit') in the quiet of night, leaving the factor to report the matter to his client. In the years before 1914 there was a noticeable tendency for tenants to stand their ground, compelling the house owner to apply to the local sheriff's court for a warrant of ejectment to remove the defaulting occupant from the premises.[35] The fact that the tenant could appear to plead against his summary eviction also complicated the factor's life. Rising Labour stars such as the barrister Rosslyn Mitchell and journalist John Wheatley seized the opportunity to represent or speak for tenants facing eviction, threatening to turn the proceedings into a melodrama of class confrontation. If the landlords could employ a large body of professionals to service the property relations of urban Glasgow, the tenants were able to recruit a growing number of self-educated intellectuals, trained lawyers and small business people to present their case in public. Sustained by the growth of services and literacy in industrial society these groups struggled to create new progressive politics in Scotland, transforming the existing institutions of the urban working class and introducing a fresh agenda of municipal reform.

Much of the argument about the character of early Labour politics turns on the historical relationship between working class institutions and British liberalism. Saville and others have stressed the importance of the 'new model' era in the aftermath of Chartism, when craft unions learned the rules of the game in both collective bargaining and bourgeois politics.[36] The leading organisations of the working class defined their interests in relation to specific material gains rather than general political ideals and sought to reach a working accommodation with the agents of bourgeois society. Even when a distinctive working class culture surfaced in the closing decades of the nineteenth century, radical artisan politics declined and the foundation of the Labour Party appears as 'a defensive solution to the employers' counter-offensive' rather than a confident assertion of political ambition.[37] The ideology of labourism which had been bred in the compromises of the 1850s was imported into the politics of the new Labour Party, stifling the efforts of revolutionary socialists and removing the political leadership from the everyday concerns of the workshop and neighbourhood. Although the Liberal party was to decline and then collapse in the decade after 1914, many of its fundamental ideas (and personnel) were incorporated in the policies of Labour.[38]

These arguments appear to offer a powerful explanation for the strength of early Labour in the regions where liberalism had been resilient and its comparative weakness in such strongholds of Tory populism as Liverpool.[39] The specific culture of nineteenth century Scotland, including its rigorous theological and religious loyalties, informed the attitudes of the free-thinking radicals and the first generations of socialists who practised their arguments at Glasgow Green.[40] Many elements of this argument carry conviction, but there are difficulties in the general orthodoxy of 'Labourism'. One of the key constituents of the national Party was the Independent Labour Party (ILP), formed in the aftermath of the bitter industrial dispute at Manningham Mills and drawing support across the trades in the West Riding. The experience of the early 1890s had demonstrated the weakness of unions based on a single occupation and the severe limitations to industrial struggle in a period of general depression. These conditions explain the unusual prominence of the local trades councils and political organisations in West Yorkshire, where the early ILP could appeal to Christian socialists and intellectuals as well as trade unionists.[41] West Scotland had a very different industrial structure and a much greater concentration of skilled journeymen, dominating a distinctly masculine labour market of ironworkers, but it was also weakly unionised until the 1880s. The late arrival of the great artisan unions in a period when 'artisan politics' was subsiding in the face of new initiatives at the workplace and in national politics, ensured that the formative years of union building in Scotland were quite different from those of industrial Lancashire or London. Moreover, the delayed and fragmentary character of Scottish trade unionism enabled the inter-union trades councils to occupy a critical place in the industrial politics of the late nineteenth century.[42] As in the West Riding, the Clydeside ILP could build on a situation where intense workplace sectionalism (between trades and grades) was countered by an unusual degree of cooperation and mutuality in the chambers of the Glasgow, Govan and Clydebank trades councils. There was an early appreciation of the importance of political campaigns and the role which organised labour could play in these matters.

The effort of the Glasgow Trades Council (GTC) to establish a separate political presence for the interests of labour came as early as the 1870s, with their decision to contest local School Board elections. Even in an area so sharply defined by religious sectarianism as education, the trades councillors were unwilling to simply accept that Glasgow Liberalism expressed all their aspirations in local government.[43] After its formation in 1888, Keir Hardie's Scottish Labour Party attracted the support of the GTC, though it was the coming of the ILP to the local parish and town council elections in the 1890s that changed the political climate in Glasgow. Building support in the most immediate organs of government, responsible for social services and medical inspection, the ILP was able to politicise every election with an evangelical style of campaigning that gradually overcame the barriers of religious sectarianism and ethnic conflict. The ILP remained the real force behind the Labour Party Representation movement in Glasgow, reaching a peak of 1,200 members in 1913 and helping to achieve the respectable parliamentary vote for Labour at Blackfriars and Govan in the election of 1905–6.[44] It must also be acknowledged that Scottish Liberalism retained its hegemonic position in parliamentary elections until the ruptures of World War I, as socialists concentrated their energies on local burgh and municipal elections in a bid to establish the crediblity of Labour administration.

It was in this context that John Wheatley discovered the political significance of the housing question in Edwardian Glasgow. The Labour party had carefully orchestrated its local campaigns on social conditions and urban amenities since the 1890s. Its progress was overshadowed by the resurgence of the Irish question before 1914 and the influence of nationalist politicians in the poorer quarters of the city, which provoked the Labour weekly paper (edited by Thomas Johnston) *Forward*, into a direct attack on the 'slum property owners, model lodging-housing keepers and provision merchants' who held sway there.[45] The Glasgow Labour Party realised that an effective organisation was essential to the success of the housing campaign and set up the party's own Housing Association, staffed by such dedicated crusaders as Andrew McBride and William Regan. Elections to the City Council were fought on the housing question and began to attract the support of voters across the city. Painstaking work in individual wards was beginning to yield political dividends even if Labour remained a minority voice in the city chambers.[46]

Although Labour activists were busy mobilising support for the Wheatley proposal of cheap cottages financed with subsidies from the Glasgow tramways' surpluses, they were not the only group engaged in the movement for better housing. The growing appeal of the campaign was due to the contributions of other bodies, many of which did not have any direct affiliation to Labour politics at all. Trade unions and trades councils had raised the housing issue as early as 1902, when the Govan and Clydebank branches of the powerful Boilermakers' Society joined with tens of thousands of other workers to demand a reversal of officials' personal liability for damages caused in pursuit of union business—the Taff Vale decision (1901).[47] They moved across to the Labour camp before the War, but the Co-operative societies retained their separate identity throughout the period. Societies were formed in areas such as Govan, Partick and Shettleston to directly challenge the hold of unscrupulous victuallers and traders, securing their own position by high retail standards and by intervening in ward and burgh politics from the 1880s onwards.[48] Broadly aligned with the progressives in such contests, the cooperatives retained their independence and female cooperators organised the Women's Co-operative Guild to attract support across the political and sectarian divisions in west Scotland.[49] Only in 1917 did the Co-operative Union join with the Wholesalers and the Scottish TUC in forming a Scottish Co-operative and Labour Council as an alliance of cooperative and Labour interests.[50]

In addition to their participation in the Co-operative Guild before 1914, Scottish women were prominent in a whole series of campaigns including that for female suffrage.[51] Outstanding trade union organisers such as Agnes Dollan worked among the telephonists and waitresses, as well as the industrial occupations to build up support for unionism and Mary Macarthur's Federation of Women Workers, before 1914. Before World War I the growth of female employment in industry and the expanded professions of teaching, commerce and medicine helped women to assert themselves against the overwhelming dominance of male control and craftism, even if numbers unionised remained limited.

Middle class women already enjoyed an established role in the philanthropic and religious agencies which attempted to relieve poverty in shipbuilding districts such as Partick and Govan.[52] As a number of radical clergymen began to support the socialist cause they met or married women who adopted an equally progressive position. One of the most brilliant campaigners and feminist orators of the period was Helen Crawfurd (wife of a Glasgow minister), who rivalled James Maxton of the ILP in the power and imagination of her political speeches. Such women were able to persuade younger colleagues to join the Labour and suffrage movements before 1914.[53] After the outbreak of War, Helen Crawfurd and Agnes Dollan were instrumental in arranging the Women's Peace Conference of 1916, which gave birth to the Women's Peace Crusade and cleared a space for anti-war speakers to address Scottish crowds throughout the War.[54]

The relationship between these feminists and the wider Labour and socialist parties were frequently tense and rarely unambiguous. Whilst the ILP adopted an early stand of conscientious opposition to the War, the party's executive sought to defer the issue of women's suffrage until the hostilities had ceased. Both Fenner Brockway and Ellen Wilkinson forced the 1915 party conference to confront the issues of female employment, suffrage and the peace initiatives under way.[55] Many male socialists remained deeply suspicious of middle class feminists and insisted that class issues should take priority over the suffrage question.[56] Just as there were rival parties to the ILP in campaigning on the question of unemployment, wages and housing before the War, so there were also groups of women who addressed the issue of housing as one of a wide range of concerns—some of which brought them into conflict with the demands of the Labour or Cooperative movements.

Similarly, local housing groups such as the Govan Women's Housing Association organised by the gifted Mary Barbour were set up on the eve of the War with strict rules of open access to all women irrespective of political loyalties. These key organisations were often affiliated to Labour Party housing

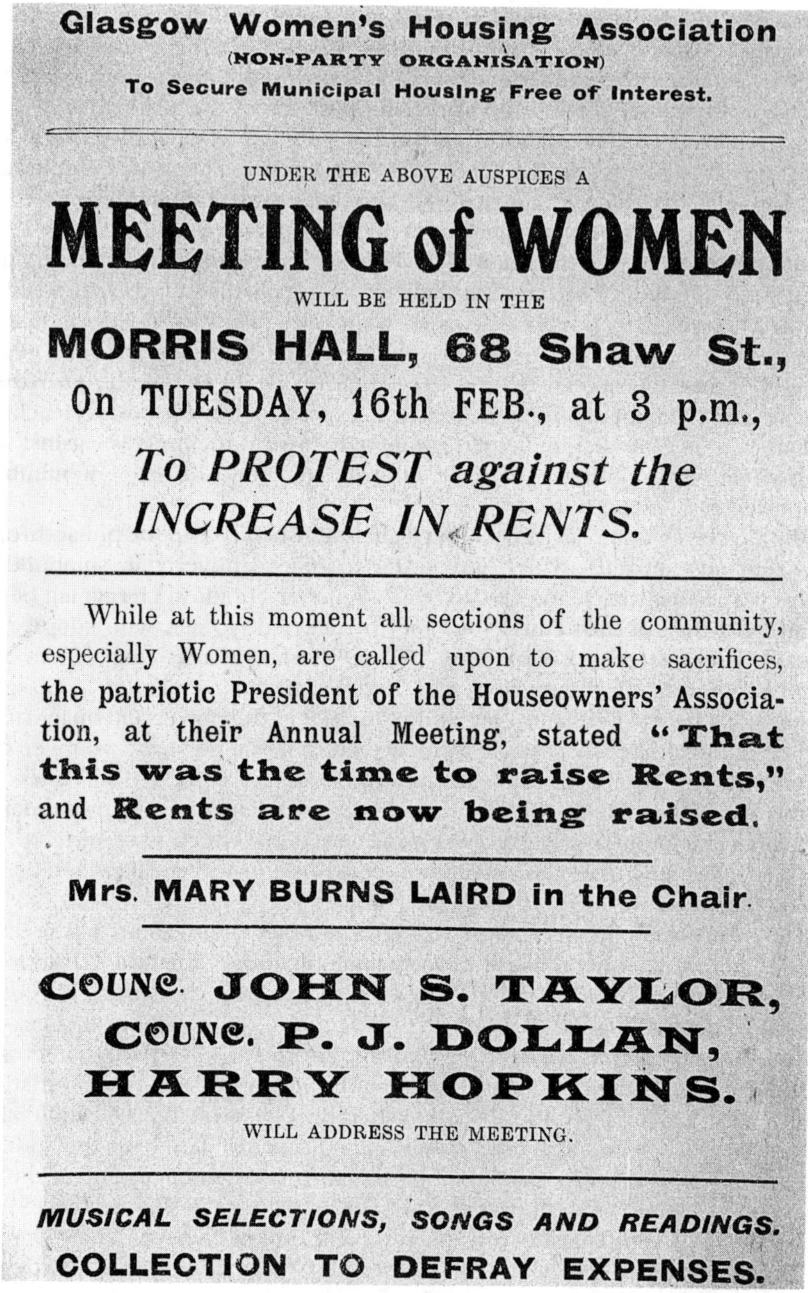

Glasgow Women's Housing Association

(NON-PARTY ORGANISATION)

To Secure Municipal Housing Free of Interest.

UNDER THE ABOVE AUSPICES A

MEETING of WOMEN

WILL BE HELD IN THE

MORRIS HALL, 68 Shaw St.,

On TUESDAY, 16th FEB., at 3 p.m.,

To PROTEST against the INCREASE IN RENTS.

While at this moment all sections of the community, especially Women, are called upon to make sacrifices, the patriotic President of the Houseowners' Association, at their Annual Meeting, stated **"That this was the time to raise Rents,"** and **Rents are now being raised.**

Mrs. MARY BURNS LAIRD in the Chair.

COUNC. JOHN S. TAYLOR,
COUNC. P. J. DOLLAN,
HARRY HOPKINS.

WILL ADDRESS THE MEETING.

MUSICAL SELECTIONS, SONGS AND READINGS.

COLLECTION TO DEFRAY EXPENSES.

Figure 3.1 Notice of a protest meeting, 1915 (courtesy of Mr L Rosenberg)

federations and shared leading personalities with the Party, but their constitution remained that of a local campaign open to working class women of the immediate area. In this way the individual burghs could maintain the support of local housewives on a non-partisan demand for improved housing without provoking open controversy.

The structure of the tenement blocks in which the great majority of working class families lived actually compelled the inhabitants to share the basic amenities and frustrations of cramped housing. Pressure on the lavatory, communal washing house and refuse area could become almost unbearable in the summer heat or the extreme cold of winter.[57] The enforced fraternity of the tenements fuelled the campaign for cottage accommodation which would give the occupants privacy and space, but the same conditions of tenement life also provided a basis for a commonplace culture which bound the tenants together against the power of the landlord. It was this everyday experience that helps to explain the growing popularity of housing campaigns in these years. The Labour Party (and more particularly the ILP) carefully orchestrated the disparate groups of tenants around the Wheatley programme of better housing though the campaigns did not originate with the Party and their appeal went far beyond the constituency of Labour activists. It was the events of 1915–18 which transformed the situation and gave a fresh direction to both the housing campaign and the socialist politics of the Clyde.

Rent strikes and Labour politics on the Clyde, 1914–18

The housing struggles of the decade after 1914 changed the course of Labour politics and had a direct influence on the housing of the British population. There had been endemic conflicts between landlords and tenants throughout the nineteenth century but there was little opportunity for concerted action and no scope for collective bargaining where the consumers were so dispersed and transitory. Political campaigns for better 'workmen's housing' had been launched in the 1880s but these national bodies directed their energies towards political reform and regulation rather than direct action at the point of consumption.[58] Tenants could retaliate against the landlord by refusal to pay, vandalism and flight from debt, but there was no legal appeal or arbitration against an increase in rent or deterioration in conditions. The law assumed an equality of choice between the two partners to the contract. Even the housing legislation passed after 1890 empowered local authorities to build houses and clear slums but did not interfere in the relationship between landlord and tenant, nor did it result in any substantial improvement in the bulk of working class housing.[59]

This situation changed fundamentally in the early years of World War I. The immediate cause of the rent strikes of 1915 lay in the mass mobilisation for total warfare. Tens of thousands of servicemen were recruited to the forces and left behind dependents on limited incomes. The demand for munitions and armaments brought thousands of migrants to the great industrial and shipbuilding centres of Britain, including the premier shipyard river, the

Clyde. Any available housing quickly disappeared as the engineering, shipbuilding and armament workers were offered almost unlimited overtime. Prices rose more quickly than basic wages and immigrants were forced to pay shortage rents for scarce accommodation near the largest yards and plants. Even if the herded conditions of tenement life had not already pushed local people into a common antagonism to the landlords, the frustrations and pressures of 1914–15 deepened the 'rebellious character of the Clydeside workers'.[60] It was the prospect of wartime scarcities forcing up weekly rents that galvanised the opposition to the 'monopoly' power of the owners in 1915, provoking a series of resistance campaigns in the summer and autumn against attempts to increase rents.

The success of the rent strikes in forcing the wartime coalition government to introduce rent restrictions in the late autumn of 1915, within weeks of statements that no interference was necesary or practicable, surprised even the strike leaders. This remarkable achievement was completely unprecedented in the field of housing and needs some explanation. To portray the struggle as a spontaneous outbreak of class warfare is to ignore the moving coalition of interests which conducted the campaigns against the landlords. Similarly, those accounts which suggest that the Labour Party leadership orchestrated the movement and exploited the rents question as another step towards an urban power base is to credit Wheatley and his contemporaries with an extraordinary degree of insight and influence in the confusion of 1915–16. The actual events of these turbulent months suggest that the key to victory in the battle against the house owners was found in the active support given by a range of distinctive organisations and groups, many of whom were radicalised by their direct experience of the conflict. Drawing on these diverse, largely apolitical, bodies for the conduct of the campaign, rent strike leaders developed a particular kind of urban politics which took both landlords and Government by surprise.

From the Government's viewpoint the Clydesiders established themselves as troublemakers before the end of 1914, when the most powerful engineering union—the Amalgamated Society of Engineers (ASE)—prepared for a substantial wage increase of 2d an hour or equivalent to an increase of about 20%. In early 1915 the London ministers were desperately anxious to avoid industrial unrest and meet the enormous demand for shells and other munitions from the armed forces. The February strike on Clydeside was ended by a hasty compromise of higher wages and followed by a national agreement on the output of shells and fuses in March.[61] The utter dependence of the industrialists on the skilled craftsmen to maintain and increase output was demonstrated throughout the spring and summer of 1915, with engineering tradesmen in Glasgow, Paisley, Johnstone and Govan able to resist any moves towards a reorganisation of production using untrained labour. It was not until the spring of 1916 that Lloyd George and the new Ministry of Munitions (formed in June–July 1915) was able to overcome the resistance in the engineering shops and introduce a massive programme of industrial dilution, using unskilled male and female labour on machining operations.

Historians have reiterated the significance of the dilution struggle and the divisions of craftism and radicalism which the campaign opened up amongst the Clydeside engineers. Probably more important for an understanding of industrial politics on the Clyde is an assessment of the quite distinct movement against the imposition of labour regulations under the Munitions Acts and Defence of the Realm Acts during the summer and autumn of 1915. This involved thousands of workers from a wide number of trades in the shipyards and the engineering shops of the region. The privileges of a particular craft were not at risk but rather the prerogatives of trade unionism in general. By insisting on 'leaving certificates' being issued by the employer (or manager and foreman) before the employee could move job or firm, the Munitions Ministry gave the boss a powerful weapon in the labour market. Not only did it prevent wage rises through firms bidding for scarce labour but it confirmed that every aspect of work and wages could be regulated in favour of the employers. The attempt of the State to enforce these measures through local munitions tribunals imposing fines and imprisonment on Scottish tradesmen led to a major crisis in the autumn of 1915. A series of protests and stoppages were organised to defeat the legislation, directed primarily by Harry Hopkins (the ASE activist) as leader of the influential Govan Trades Council. The uproar over the gaoling of shipyard workers helped to undermine the parallel policy of introducing dilution schemes in west Scotland during these months.

The impact of the wartime legislation and government controls over production was to politicise industrial relations and provoke controversy over the fundamental rights of capitalist management. There was also a growing tendency for trade unions to confront their employers and politicians with the facts of working class lifestyles. From early 1915 unions were emphasising the rapid rise in food prices and the enormous profits being made by the essential war industries. The shortage of housing and the problems of overcrowding in the shipbuilding and engineering centres was also a cause for complaint in the spring and summer months, as thousands of men left for active service and migrants flooded into the Clyde Valley to replace them at the workshops. Worst affected by the mounting pressure on housing were the strategic areas close to the shipyards and munitions centres, particularly in Govan, Parkhead and Clydebank. Empty flats were quickly filled and overcrowding worsened as many families 'doubled up' to take in lodgers or housed relatives unable to find even a 'single end' flat comprising a room and kitchen. In these districts the landlords and their factors began to demand higher rents, secure in the knowledge that virtually no fresh housebuilding could take place and shortages would grow as full employment continued.

The support of the industrial workers for the principle of rent controls gave the wartime housing campaigners a trump card in their dealings with the Government.[62] But it was the women active in each district of the city who initiated and carried the rent strikes through to a decisive conclusion in the summer and autumn of 1915. Local housing associations had been set up before the War and appealed to the working housewives of the immediate area. Even the Govan Association under the brilliant leadership of Mrs Mary Barbour called on the support of all women, irrespective of their party allegiances, throughout these years. Such bodies depended on a close network of activists for their vitality, including two or three generations of Labour women, but they claimed housing as an issue which rose above party loyalties and that only women—excluded from the parliamentary elections by the largest parties—could appreciate the fundamental need for good housing.[63] The prohibition against women's membership of the most powerful institutions of the time may have helped the local activists to organise the opposition to the factors, since they did not carry with them the burden of sectional and sectarian divisions which were to be encountered in the shipyards, pubs and football park. The formal divisions of religion and politics were not ignored but they did not shape the housing market and tenant loyalties in the way that they overshadowed the labour market and male recreations. When the housewives in Govan and Partick led the rent resistance by refusing to pay the higher rents demanded by the factors in 1915, Protestant and Orange Lodge housewives were ready to participate alongside Catholic supporters of the Labour Party.[64] Their freedom from the discipline of male associations also meant that the women's groups were able to devise highly effective tactics against the invading factor. The sharp humour of Glasgow people was expressed in the contemporary music hall sketches based on the shared experience of the tenement wash house and the everyday competition for access to this basic laundry.[65] The rent strikes and political activists recognised the great advantage of the forum created by the tenements surrounding the washhouse and midden heaps at the rear of the buildings. One ILP veteran recalls how Agnes Dollan persuaded her to address the inhabitants of the Govan Road tenements from the top of the wash house, which was in direct contrast to her earlier genteel conduct when visiting the homes of the poor with an aristocratic patron.[66] This strong element of street theatre was continued with the arrival of the factor or clerk. Expecting the traditional deference due to his person, dressed in sober suit with bowler hat and watchchain, the factor was met with ridicule and derision when he threatened the tenants with eviction. Bells were borrowed from a fishcart or market-place and rung to warn local housewives of the approach of the landlord's agent. Their weapons were the flour and pease-meal used in every kitchen and after treating the rent collector to a chorus of derision and the rough music of pots and pans he was frequently thrown into the midden before departing in disarray.[67] Behind this carnival lay a serious purpose of humiliating the man who accused them of failing to meet their responsibilities. Throughout the rent strikes of those months, which culminated in an active resistance of many hundreds or thousands of families, the women and men insisted that they were patriotic, respectable people willing to meet their obligations as long as they were fairly treated. This defence, of their respectability, was particularly important for women who frequently did not have the support of their husbands in the struggle, since it took real courage to stand up to the authority of the landlord.[68]

The women of each neighbourhood provided the shock troops of the rent strikes, frequently developing a system of street lieutenants to coordinate resistance when thè bailiffs sought to evict a particular tenant or attack one 'close' or tenement. Local housing associations covered particular burghs of the city and the riverside, but it was the Labour Party's own Housing Association that provided a voice for the whole city in 1915. When the spread of housing and industrial unrest in the autumn of that year threatened to engulf the whole shipbuilding and engineering district of Glasgow, the Government appointed a Commission to enquire into the scale of rent increases. Although the evidence suggested that significant rises were confined to such areas as Govan, Labour spokesmen led by Andrew McBride, John Wheatley and Patrick Dollan made such a powerful impression on the Commissioners that a case was made for some form of public regulation. The Labour Party had been pressing for a system of 'fair rent courts' since the pre-war years, offering the tenant a forum of appeal against the landlord and some basis for an independent review of rents. This was accompanied by the demand for rent regulation until local authorities were able to provide adequate dwellings at reasonable rents, though it was assumed that municipal corporations such as Glasgow should be able to finance their own schemes of housing and local services. The effect of the rent strikes on Clydeside and elsewhere in 1915 was to shift the focus of agitation from local rent courts to a demand for national protection of working class tenants from *any* increases during the War. The remarkable success of this demand and the restrictions on increases of rent in the bulk of rented dwellings obscured the broader programme of the Labour Party for improved housing, but in the longer term it made further state intervention an essential starting point for post-war housing. At the same time that working class rents were frozen, so also the Rent Restriction Act of 1915 committed the great body of housing capitalists to an investment which would yield low returns for the foreseeable future.

The Labour Party had greatly extended its influence and popularity as a result of the rent strikes and Andrew McBride quickly moved to consolidate the Glasgow Association and set up a Scottish Housing Association under the aegis of the Scottish party in 1916–17. William Regan of Rutherglen (Glasgow) also pressed the conference of the ILP to advance a programme which would go far beyond the support for rent restrictions after the War and demand a government which would undertake a national housing scheme, based on grants and loans as well as rates, thereby eliminating 'profit and interest from housing'.[69] The Glasgow socialists were now committed to a national housing plan based on need rather than market demand and to the principle that working class housing was not an appropriate area for profit-seeking investment. There was still considerable support for the legal defence of tenant rights in the courts, particularly as the Labour barrister Rosslyn Mitchell had distinguished himself in the famous trials of tenants during October and November 1915, but the energies of the housing campaigners was now drawn towards the reconstruction schemes for post-war housing.

The Scottish campaign was greatly assisted by the endorsement of the trade unions and the contemporary debates on the future of industrial management. A Royal Commission appointed to enquire into Scottish industrial housing before the War finally reported in 1917 and offered a detailed indictment of the housing conditions to be found in the coalmining districts and the urban centres of Scotland. Coalmining unionists such as Robert Smillie drew upon the appalling revelations of the Ballantyne Commission as the principal evidence

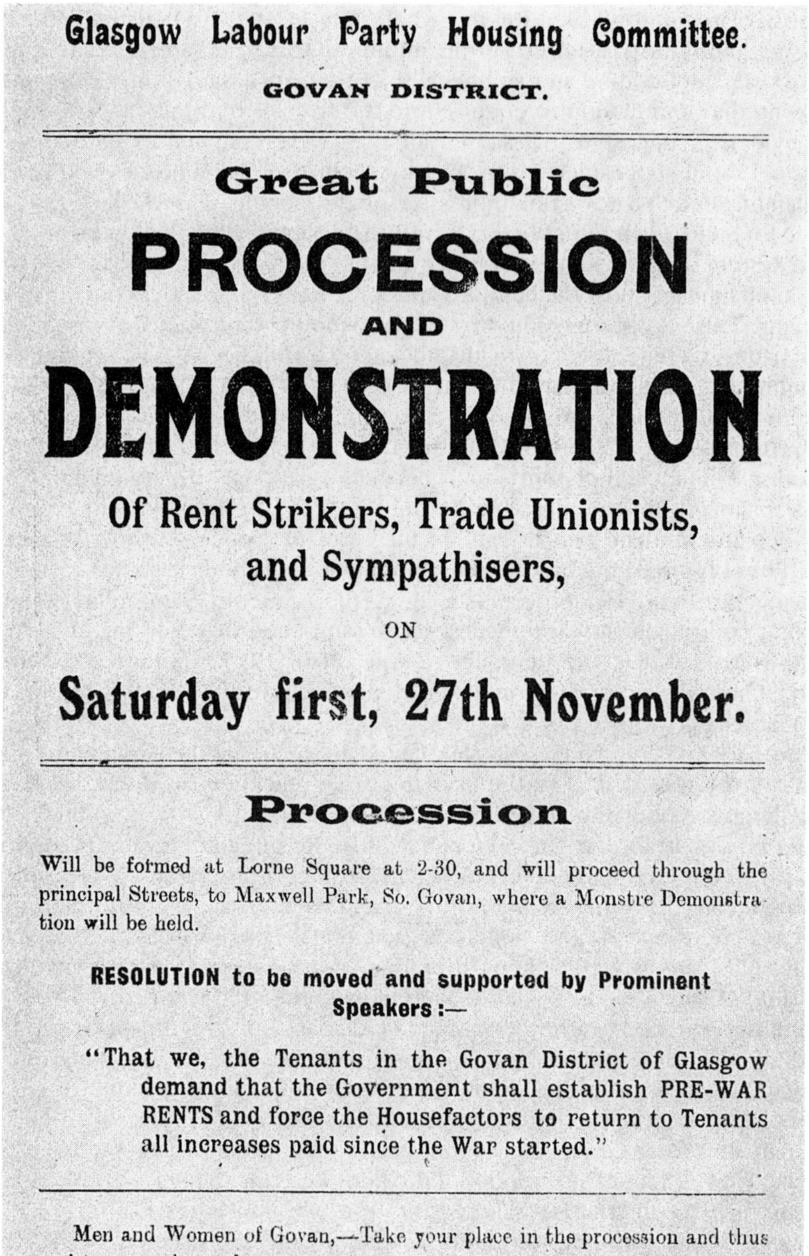

Glasgow Labour Party Housing Committee.

GOVAN DISTRICT.

Great Public

PROCESSION

AND

DEMONSTRATION

Of Rent Strikers, Trade Unionists, and Sympathisers,

ON

Saturday first, 27th November.

Procession

Will be formed at Lorne Square at 2-30, and will proceed through the principal Streets, to Maxwell Park, So. Govan, where a Monstre Demonstration will be held.

RESOLUTION to be moved and supported by Prominent Speakers :—

"That we, the Tenants in the Govan District of Glasgow demand that the Government shall establish PRE-WAR RENTS and force the Housefactors to return to Tenants all increases paid since the War started."

Men and Women of Govan,—Take your place in the procession and thus register your demand.

Figure 3.2 Notice of a protest meeting, 1915 (courtesy of the Mitchell Library, Glasgow)

against the coal owners in the subsequent debate on the nationalisation of the industry and the defects of industrial capitalism in Britain.[70] In the shipbuilding and engineering stronghold of Govan, Harry Hopkins went on from his leading role in the anti-Munitions Act and rent strike campaigns of 1915 to build an industrial base for Labour in the burgh, carrying the ASE District Committee into the great Forty Hours Strike of 1919 in Glasgow.[71] Those writers who stress the divide between shop floor militants and Labour activists based in the urban constituency overlook this continuing relationship between industrial and political campaigns during and immediately after World War I.

Another source of strength for Labour in these years was the rebuilding of the Scottish cooperative movement in the aftermath of the rent strikes. Prominent cooperators took part in some of the tenant campaigns of 1915–16 and were particularly aggrieved at the treatment of employees by local conscription officers who discriminated against the societies. In 1917 the Scottish cooperators joined the British movement for cooperative representation in Parliament, creating a Co-operative Party in 1919. A merger of the Labour and Co-operative Parties did not occur in 1919–21 as anticipated but the local organisation joined with the ILP to secure the election of MPs in Partick and Tradeston during the early 1920s.[72] World War I marked a watershed in the course of consumer politics by offering different groups the scope for organisation on the supply of food, housing and essential goods. The health and habitation of the population became, temporarily, major questions for policy-makers in the Reconstruction era.

Housing and consumption politics did not all converge on the refounding of the Labour Party in 1918, nor did divisions amongst progressives disappear. Socialist feminists such as Sylvia Pankhurst and Helen Crawfurd advanced from their pioneering role in organising rent strikes in London's East End and Glasgow to demand more rigorous class politics than that provided by the ILP.[73] The politics of Clydeside in the years 1918–20 saw the gradual divergence of Labour and Communist politics, as Henderson and the Labour leaders pressed for a disciplined constitutional party whilst the revolutionary socialists moved to form the new Communist Party.[74] The ILP still provided most of the individual members of the parent Labour Party and was badly divided by the struggles of 1920. The elections of 1920–4 paved the way for the first Labour Government and the return of the famous 'Clydesiders' to the Commons, but they also undermined the broad coalition of groups which had been formed as a result of the wartime housing and industrial campaigns.[75] Bitter conflicts emerged between the competing Labour and socialist organisations in west Scotland during the years 1922–4, particularly as a result of the refusal of Labour (and the ILP) to accept Communist candidates in local elections.[76] These frictions opened the gates to resurgent conservatism and sectarianism, though the official Labour Party was able to establish its dominance in key working class constituencies by the time of the 1923–4 elections.[77] The Labour Party which emerged from these elections and entered office in 1924 may have appeared as the embodiment of Red Clydeside when veiwed by London journalists, but the MPs were only a partial reflection of Clydeside politics in the years 1914–22.

These political developments provide the general context for the conduct of the rent struggles in west Scotland during the post-war years. The following section reviews the progress of the rent struggles and housing policies after 1918.

Rent struggles and Clydeside housing politics, 1918–39

Before 1914 the housing conditions in Glasgow had excited bitter controversy in the City Chambers as John Wheatley pressed his scheme for 10,000 municipal houses at the low rental of £8 per year.[78] There was no widespread belief that the housing market itself was in crisis, however, and the rising wages after 1910 enabled many skilled workers to move into the houses left vacant at the end of the great housebuilding boom before 1906. By 1918 the situation had changed dramatically. Population growth and immigration had quickly absorbed the spare capacity in the housing market and the post-war boom gave ready employment to munitions workers and soldiers returning from the front. Pressure on available housing continued to grow in west Scotland and most other industrial districts. The lapse of housebuilding during the War had created a situation of real scarcity, though the rent controls introduced in 1915 prevented landlords from exploiting their natural advantage.

The achievement of housing campaigners and wartime inquiries was to force the Coalition Government to acknowledge the primary importance of a national housing problem and the urgent need for a subsidised programme to deal with it. In fact, equal emphasis was placed on the absolute shortage of dwellings for working class tenants and the poor quality of many houses which were standing. A succession of inquiries and commissions between 1917 and 1921 discovered that more than 100,000 new houses were needed in Scotland to overcome some of the more immediate problems.[79] The Housing and Town Planning (Scotland) Act of 1919 was designed as part of the general Addison initiative to build 'homes fit for heroes' throughout Britain. It proved an abysmal failure as far as Scottish families were concerned. Post-war boom prices and wages meant that even subsidised housebuilding was not profitable enough to tempt local builders and by 1921 it was noted that 'speculative building as it was known thirty years ago is practically non-existent.'[80] The cost of materials and labour did not decrease significantly until 1920–1 by which time the Addison programme was already under threat from the Conservatives. Only 22,000 houses were under contract to be built in Scotland by 1921 and a miserable 2000 had actually been constructed.[81]

The War had also transformed the whole housing market in regions such as west Scotland. Private landlords had been the major customers of both speculative builders and the mortgage brokers who offered loans for the purchase of tenements. Rising interest rates, alternative investments, high maintenance costs and rent restrictions combined to make working class tenants a much less attractive area for profitable business than they had been in the 1890s. The Clydeside property owners and their factors had accepted rent controls as an inevitable evil during the War, particularly as mortgage interest was also regulated, but looked forward to increases of 50 per cent in rents within a year of the War ending. Andrew McBride and John Wheatley devised the case for the tenants when two government committees reviewed rent controls in 1918–19. Their arguments had been sharpened in the 1915 rent struggles and elaborated in the Glasgow and Scottish Housing Associations' conferences. They adopted the axiom that rents should continue to be regulated by the Government until such time as adequate housing was provided for the broad mass of the population at reasonable rents. Their second position was that the private landlord had demonstrably failed to create and sustain a supply of good quality dwellings before the War and that the State should assume full responsibility for the housing of the people. When it was suggested that rent restrictions worsened the situation by destroying the profitablity of rented dwellings, the Labour Party insisted that a free market in scarce and poor quality housing would only exacerbate a dangerous situation. The blatant failure of the owners to even maintain their property during the War only confirmed their ineligibility as the managers of working class housing. A limited increase in rents could be allowed as an incentive to improvements and repair of controlled dwellings but tenant protection must remain until the State met the widening gap between need and supply.[82] The logical conclusion to be drawn was that private landlords had a limited future in housing the Scottish working class.

These general arguments on the continuing crisis of housing provision were widely accepted by contemporary enquiries. The reconstruction of slums in the inner cities and the older industrial centres was recognised as a long-term problem which would not be eradicated by poorer working class groups moving into the housing abandoned by the artisan. The slum inhabitant would 'remain in his present environment until that environment is altered.'[83] There also remained the fear that the worst conditions of urban life would transform the labouring classes into the dangerous classes of industrial Scotland. These pressures secured the retention of rent controls under the Rent Restrictions Act of 1920, which extended protection to a higher grade of dwelling while permitting limited increases of 15–25 per cent in rents on controlled houses. These long-awaited rent rises came just at the moment that the Scottish industrial economy slipped from boom conditions to the sharp and sustained depression of the 1920s and 1930s. Shipbuilding, engineering and building wages were cut drastically in the early 1920s as unemployment reached unprecedented levels in the heavy industries. After more than a decade of high employment and powerful bargaining, organised labour faced defeat and some demoralisation in these years.

It was against this background that increases were demanded in west Scotland during 1920–1. The Glasgow Labour Party's housing organisation prepared for a fresh rent strike against the rent rises, with crowds addressed by Wheatley, Kirkwood and McBride as the housing spokesmen in the city. Many of the scenes of 1915 were re-enacted as housewives mobilised under street captains and a younger generation of women were drawn into the struggle against the factors and bailiffs.[84] Wheatley and Dollan distributed pamphlets to raise support and Labour newspapers tried to hold the line against the landlords. It soon became clear that the rent strikers were isolated and their factors were able to divide the tenements in a way that had not been possible in 1915.[85] Labour used the agitations to promote the popularity of their cause but even McBride and Dollan had to concede that some increases were unavoidable.

At this stage the centre of resistance moved down the Clyde to the new industrial burgh of Clydebank, where Shinwell and Kirkwood met the crisis by fighting legal battles in the Sheriff's courts against eviction orders.[86] Once again Labour was able to harness the support generated by a populist housing movement (steered by a local tenants' organisation under an engineering worker) which forced the rent war into the national press as the guerilla attacks on landlords continued in 1922–3.[87] The Clydebank struggle also maintained the pressure on the assorted government committees and inquiries which reviewed rent controls in the 1920s, though by 1925 it was apparent that the strikers were on the defensive and could achieve little beyond a cancellation of arrears and a staged introduction of new increases.[88]

The rent struggles of the post-war years offered an ideal platform for the veterans of the wartime Labour movement to consolidate their reputations in the Clydeside story. Leading lights in the Labour Party and ILP used the housing issue in the elections of 1922–4 to strengthen their following in the poorer districts of Glasgow as well as the artisan neighbourhoods.[89] Wheatley, Kirkwood, Maxton and Shinwell were given a rousing send-off from St Enoch's Station on their way to Westminster in 1924, while Patrick Dollan remained behind to build up an efficient electoral machine in the municipal constituencies. Labour was rewarded with the capture of the city in the early 1930s, inaugurating a long and almost unbroken era of political control down to the present day, enabling the Party to build a massive public sector and virtually eliminate the private landlord from large areas of Clydeside.[90]

Over the period 1918–39 the politics of the tenants' movements reflected the wider changes in the Labour movement. It has been suggested that the vital factor in the electoral success of the Labour Party was the appeal of the housing issue in the slum districts and the winning of Irish support in the building of a political machine under Dollan.[91] The evidence from the early 1920s points to a more complex political alignment, involving Labour's relationship with other socialist parties as well as a shift of the Irish vote. The new Labour constitution of 1918 and the subsequent debates on the reconstruction of industry had confirmed the role of both trade unions and the ILP in the Party.[92] Former members of the Socialist Labour Party, including William Paul and some of the best known shop-floor activists of the war years, were still uncertain of their political future. John Maclean was also striving to build an independent Marxist party for Scottish socialists and introduce a Bolshevik republic to Britain.[93] After 1920 the sectarian divisions among the various groups hardened as local elections in Motherwell, Paisley and Kelvingrove revealed a growing hostility between the Labour and Communist Parties.[94] While Labour supporters moved away from direct action towards electoral success and constitutional power, the Communists defended the relevance of the Bolshevik model to Britain and debated Moscow's directives.[95] Even in the excitement of the Clydebank conflict, Labour councillors were ready to resort to legal and judicial methods of defending the tenants rather than relying on street battles to resolve the dispute. The impact made by mass unemployment and the industrial defeats of 1919–23 persuaded Wheatley and his colleagues that parliamentary power would be a more secure road to socialism than a syndicalist challenge to the State. Communists such as Gallacher and Bell, on the other hand, looked to the industrial confrontations of the War as the greatest moment of class struggle, besieging the bourgeoisie and its capitalist government. By the time rent strikes were organised in Clydebank, Communists were assuming a prominent role in the street politics of Clydeside and advocating a united campaign on the issues of unemployment, rents and legal rights.[96]

In the aftermath of the rent strikes and the General Strike of 1926, the Communist Party focused its activities on the organisation of the unemployed and gaining local power in the 'Little Moscows' of the period. Formidable personalities such as Gallacher, Finlay Hart and Harry McShane contributed to the Unemployed Workers' Movement as well as attracting a sizeable following in areas such as Clydebank. During the 1930s the impetus of tenant organisation and rent strikes moved to London and the Midlands, with Communists like Phil Piratin leading the attack on private landlords and demanding protection for municipal tenants.[97] The Labour Party argued that a war of position and attrition was needed to make progress in local conditions, rather than the heroic direct action of earlier years. After acceding to parliamentary government in 1924 the Labour Party was firmly set on legislative measures to improve housing, rather than grounding its politics in the industrial and social strategies developed during the original rent strike era. In doing so, it arguably lost the capacity to replace the politics of constitutional liberalism with the socialist government demanded by the activists of 1914–19 but Labour could claim a considerable achievement in terms of housing reform.

The Addison programme of 1919 envisaged the construction of at least 300,000 houses in the immediate post-war years, completed to the high standards recommended by the Tudor Walters Committee. By the end of 1920 a mere 29,000 had been built in England and Wales with less than 2,000 undertaken in Scotland.[98] In 1921 this ambitious scheme of high quality dwellings was abandoned by the Lloyd George coalition and Addison virtually dismissed as Minister of Health. Labour activists including Mary Laird and Mrs George Kerr of the Women's Labour League in Glasgow argued that overcrowding in Scottish housing demanded special consideration.[99] They were also able to emphasise the vital part played by rent controls in protecting people suffering from these conditions. The 1917 Report of the Royal Commission on Scottish Housing estimated that about a quarter of a million houses were needed, whereas Labour saw an urgent demand for one million homes throughout Britain in the immediate post-war era.[100] Until these were provided and the disorders of the housing market resolved, Labour argued that rent restrictions were an essential part of any housing policy.

The Conservative prescription for housing, embodied in the Chamberlain Act of 1923, enjoyed very modest success in Scotland and the depressed industrial districts of England and Wales. There the obvious need was for basic accommodation at reasonable rents rather than private building for owner occupation, and it fell to the local authorities to fulfil this demand. Chamberlain's measure led to a total of 75,000 dwellings for local authority rental whereas the ambitious Wheatley Act of 1924 could claim to have provided more than half a million homes in the inter-war years—virtually all of them for public sector tenants. As the powerful Minister of Health in the first Labour Government, Wheatley devised a formula for subsidising local authorities which began to meet the mass demand for standardised dwellings at affordable rents.[101]

The Labour Governments of 1924 and 1929 were committed to the maintenance of rent controls and the improvement of working class housing, but the Wheatley Act itself did little to alleviate the slum problem. Rent restrictions in fact created a safe ghetto of older, poorly maintained and frequently overcrowded dwellings which could be rented for well under ten shillings a week. Their occupants were reluctant—especially in the climate of the 1920s and early 1930s—to abandon these controlled houses and venture into the free market. Good quality local authority dwellings were rented out to better-paid manual workers and those lower middle class groups who enjoyed a secure income in the depression years. Even the Glasgow Corporation was anxious that the new housing stock should not be damaged by irresponsible tenants and defaulting families.[102] The Labour Government of 1929–31 introduced the Greenwood Act to deal with slum clearance and offered subsidies based on the numbers rehoused, but the Labour vision of a 'reconstructed' housing stock was unfulfilled in 1939.

The limits of the inter-war housing programmes illustrates the critical importance of rent controls to the great bulk of working class tenants in west Scotland and elsewhere. At the outbreak of War there were still four million dwellings under rent protection and a quarter of these were let out for five shillings a week or less.[103] As soon as war broke out in 1939, general controls were imposed over rented dwellings and these continued intact until the Conservatives' Rent Act of 1957. The obvious failure of this latter measure to regenerate private investment in the rented house market and landlord abuses provoked the controversies of the 1960s over 'fair rents'.[104] Once again, Scotland was able to retain a much greater degree of control over rents and its massive public housing stock was expanded until the 1980s.

Clyde rent strikes and Scottish Labour politics: a longer perspective

By the 1930s the impact of the General Strike and the fall of Labour from office created widespread disillusionment with the parliamentary road to socialism. Writing in the years of European fascism and the defeat of the Spanish republic, many veterans of the Scottish labour movement looked back to the wartime struggles as the heroic era of working class struggle against a capitalist state. Leading Labour figures such as David Kirkwood presented his life as the culmination of a long struggle for the working class but both the Communist and ILP supporters emphasised the revolutionary potential of popular movements in wartime Scotland, claiming that John Maclean and the early Marxists were the authentic representatives of the socialist cause. It was in these years that the competing mythologies of Red Clydeside were established and the rent strikes were placed in a sequence of events that usually led to the foundation of the Communist Party. Marxist historians have subsequently qualified the portrayal of revolt on the Clyde given by Gallagher and others but have usually confirmed the importance of industrial struggle and the compromises imposed on the militant working class by trade union and Labour leaders. The pervasive ideology of 'Labourism' and the moderate acceptance of the liberal state led to the betrayal of socialist revolution by the recognised leadership of the workers—during the War and throughout the inter-war years.

Liberal historians have criticised this interpretation of Labour politics at many points but they also share and confirm some of the more important assumptions in the analysis. Marxist accounts are attacked for exaggerating workplace militancy and misrepresenting the intentions of contemporary politicians and civil servants but liberal historians also represent the evolving Labour Party as a conservative institution committed to steady reformism before and after the 1918 constitution was drafted.[105] The liberal revision of Red Clydeside by McLean reaffirms the radical view that industrial militants struggled against a mass of craft conservatism in the wartime conflicts and the argument that leading shop stewards had little to do with the campaigns on rents and housing which were conducted outside the workplace.[106] The only realistic road to power for the working class, it is argued, lay in the pursuit of housing reform and the building of an urban political machine which could attract the Irish constituency. This was possible only after the crushing of wartime militancy in industry and the adoption of responsible electoral tactics by the official Labour Party. Thereafter the skilful party bosses could secure their own base and literally construct a wider constituency by removing the private landlord and making the mass of working class tenants dependent on the municipal housing sector.

Serious research on the Scottish rent strikes of these years indicates that the new liberal revisionism actually endorses many of the assumptions of the Marxist interpretation while in other respects it merely replaces the older mythologies with a new legend of moderate Labourism. The significance of the housing question is that it created a sustained coalition of different movements and organisations which had previously ignored or been excluded from the world of urban politics. The Glasgow Trades Council and its constituent unions began to press for improved housing at the turn of the century and thereafter supported the cause of housing reform in Glasgow, Govan, Clydebank and elsewhere. During the War the local trades councils were not only instrumental in mobilising resistance to State coercion of labour in west

Scotland and mounting a challenge to the authority of employers and government, but they also played a vital part in organising support for the rent strikers. The coalmining districts of west Scotland as well as the metal industries were able to make housing conditions part of a general case against the continuation of private investment and an argument for the nationalisation of production as well as state control of the housing sector.[107] By the end of the War the unions had a social as well as an industrial agenda and were recruiting members at an unprecedented rate in their claims for greater workers' control and a new deal for labour in post-war society.

The struggle for improved housing and fair rents also had the effect of transforming consumer politics during the War. The sluggish cooperative movement was galvanised into greater campaigning by the controversies over rents, food prices, rationing and conscription until by 1918 the Co-operative Party was ready to join the Labour campaign for a major reconstruction of society. Radicals and temperance reformers who had started the attack on the Glasgow victuallers and spirit dealers during the 1880s were naturally carried towards the Labour cause for better food and improved housing in such areas as Govan and Partick. Similarly, a whole generation of small professionals, clergymen, self-made businessmen (such as Wheatley), journalists and educationalists were, from the 1890s, joining Labour in a movement which provided the Glasgow working class with an urban leadership to counter that of the propertied interests and the professionals who serviced housing capital. The principal agency in this creation of an alternative political and moral economy for the Scottish workers was undoubtedly the Independent Labour Party, with its network of leading personalities drawn from the engineering and shipbuilding trades as well as the small independent class. It was Maxton and the ILP who provided a form of socialist evangelism which brought women and men from the good causes of Victorian Glasgow to the platforms of Edwardian politics.[108]

The ILP and the Labour Party clearly orchestrated the housing campaign before 1914 and the rent strikes of the years 1915–25, which became one of its most successful electoral appeals. It is equally apparent that there was an upsurge in activity and organisations in different areas of west Scotland which formed an autonomous movement of tenants demanding better housing and rent protection. An important reason for the success of these local bodies was their appeal across party boundaries and their insistence that adequate housing was a basic social right. These groups overcame the resistance of the ratepayers to local reform and engaged in a particular kind of political discourse which was effective in converting large numbers of Clydesiders to the novel idea that tenants had rights which did not depend solely on their contract with a particular landlord. By the later years of the war these organisations had not only forced the State to intervene in an unprecedented move to suspend market relations in an indsutry, but they had also persuaded official inquiries to accept the principle that rents should be controlled until the private landlord or the government could resolve the housing crisis. These doctrines owed much to the arguments of the Labour rent strike spokesmen but they also derived from the commonsense beliefs concerning fairness, respectability and patriotism that were translated by working class women into the direct action of the rent strikes themselves. The Labour Party encouraged these claims and appropriated some of the political benefits of the rent strike successes but it did not initiate the struggles nor did it fully encompass the wider popular movement behind the housing and rents demands.

Probably the most effective contribution to the rent struggles throughout these years was made by the working class and middle class women of west Scotland. A number of powerful personalities, such as Helen Crawfurd, Agnes Dollan and Mary Laird had already distinguished themselves as feminists and socialists in pre-war Glasgow. They went on to pioneering work in the pacifist and anti-military campaigns of World War I and helped to place Clydeside on the map as one of the great political cities of Europe in the years after the Russian Revolution.[109] Other women such as Mrs Mary Barbour and Mrs Ferguson were drawn into organised politics as a direct consequence of the rent strikes and went on to distinguished careers in municipal government. For the generation of women who fought the rent campaigns of 1915–25 the experience was a moment of political education which equalled that of the industrial shop steward. As one of Mary Barbour's daughters (herself a veteran of the 1920 strike) explained:[110]

> Well, we were *young* you see, and it was great fun! ... And it gets hold of you, when you've been used to it. When you've been a member of a thing like that, it just never leaves you.

Women who had enjoyed contacts through the Co-operative Guild and the Women's Labour League before the War were quickly mobilised behind the housing cause and readily assumed key roles in the local housing associations. A greater number had no previous experience of organisation but responded to the crisis by drawing on the resources of the neighbourhood to defend the area against the factor. After a lifetime of deference and grinding responsibility, ordinary women suddenly rebelled against the authority of their landlords. Loyal supporters of the Orange Lodge, the Tory Party and the war effort found a common cause with Catholic socialists, pacifists and feminists.

The explanation for this 'remarkable and spontaneous coming together of active spirits' is to be found not only in the leadership provided by Mary Barbour and her contemporaries.[111] The structure of the working class family economy meant that the housewife had to bear the responsiblity for meeting the various demands made on the housekeeping budget allowed by the male wage earner. As one participant of the period noted, 'it was the women that had to do if there wasn't any money to pay the rent. A man doesnae bother about rent!'[112] Although the women would attack the factor and court officers with ferocity and bitter ridicule, they always presented themselves as utterly respectable and responsible housewives and were almost invariably referred to as 'Mrs' Barbour, Laird or Ferguson. The street processions to the City Chambers were remarkable for the high standard of marching order and the care with which the women dressed themselves and their children for the public spectacle. Their placards proclaimed the patriotism and fairness of their cause, denouncing landlords as 'profit huns' betraying their husbands and sons fighting in the trenches. These women were deeply convinced that their campaign was one for common justice and the rule of law, as one Sheriff discovered when he heard the cases of numerous rent strikers who denied that their factors had any legal right to raise rents or evict the families of men so vital to the whole war effort.[113] Many of the women involved clearly believed that they were restoring the sound basis of landlord–tenant relations rather than challenging the authority of property or the state.

This does not prove that the strikers were basically moderates seeking a return to the status quo. Many of the leading shop stewards who determined on a disciplined campaign of resistance against Lloyd George and his allies would gather in their best suits and bowler hats to debate strategy or hear John Maclean deliver a lecture on Marxist economics. Wartime campaigners were striving to demonstrate that they could present a coherent case for the opposition, whether in the court room or the public meeting and were well equipped to ground their arguments on points of principle and of experience. The women who gathered around 'close committees' to defend the entrance to a tenement block were also able to see beyond the horizon of the washhouse or street corner. In 1915 the analogy between the industrial stoppages of the shipyard or workshop and the refusal to pay rent rises was often drawn by local speakers, hence the prominence of 'munitions' workers in the court dramas. By 1920 the economic climate had changed and again the housewives were faced with the dilemma of meeting increased rents at a time of growing unemployment and hardship. The rent struggle acquired a significance that implied a much deeper political challenge to contemporary society. As a prominent rent striker emphasised:[114]

> They werenae just labourers' wives that were on strike against the factors. No matter who you were, what you were or what you did. That was it. You were on strike against the factors. In fact, you were on strike against the whole blooming thing because the men were getting the bag, and they hadnae the money, some of the people. So they just objected absolutely to it. So they just took the bull by the horns.

This dawning realisation that a confrontation with the landlords also involved a struggle against the wider power of the whole system of production and distribution was shared by a limited number of women and men in 1920, but the moral authority of these local leaders was established in a way that secured the future of Labour in Clydeside politics.

The campaigns for better housing and fair rents did not remove the shadow of religious sectarianism from Glasgow society but they expressed political aspirations in which religious loyalties played little part. The tensions between competition and collective interest remained a feature of industrial bargaining, with its craft sectionalism, as well as urban culture. The structures of production and consumption forced distinct groups to define their particular interests in relation to their standing in the labour market or the neighbourhood. It had also become apparent through the campaigns of the 1890s to 1920s that these specific groups could achieve little without the support of other organisations and a political understanding of contemporary society. Some of these bridging

Figure 3.3 Rent strikers, Glasgow, 1915 (courtesy of the Mitchell Library, Glasgow)

agencies, such as the trades councils, already existed in urban Scotland but many other bodies had to be constructed in these years by dedicated activists.

The late arrival of massive industrialisation on Clydeside and the birth of many campaigns at this period of socialist debate helps to explain the peculiarities of the Scottish scene. Defeat and disunity in the 1920s did not appear to affect the west Scotland constituencies where both the Labour Party and the socialist parties consolidated their position. They were helped by the rise of a strong wave of nativism and political self-confidence at this time, expressed in republicanism and support for national independence. Labour organisations retained their national identity and the Labour Party's housing campaigners used the opportunity to emphasise the distinctive problems of Scottish tenants throughout the inter-war years.

Standing on the socialist left of the Labour Party the Clydesiders were able to escape from the crisis of 1931 with some dignity, though it was not until World War II that the departure of the ILP and the demoralisation in the ranks was overcome. In the post-war era the dominance of Labour in central Scotland has enabled the urban politicians such as Patrick Dollan to build up a massive public housing sector and effectively exclude the private landlord from the mass market for rented accommodation. During the 1970s the nativist alliance of unions, urban organisations and local government re-emerged to oppose the Conservative policies on industry and housing. Their effectiveness helped to undermine the Conservatives in 1971–4 but it also provoked a radical right-wing appraisal of future policies amongst Scottish Tories and laid some of the intellectual foundations of Thatcherism.

Conservative housing policies in the 1980s were designed to uproot public sector socialism in urban Scotland, reforming rents and rates in favour of propertied groups and extending the practice of home ownership among the working and lower middle classes. Financial inducements and government support for property investors and the suppression of local authority building in a period of rapid house price rises has served to resuscitate the private landlord in many urban centres. High rents and ready profits are being realised in many English and some Scottish cities as increasing numbers of people are denied access to house ownership and public housing. Unfortunately for the Conservative visionaries, economic decline has placed a major obstacle on the road to increased home ownership in urban Scotland. Only by offering the most attractive council dwellings for sale to tenants on extremely favourable conditions (usually below any realistic valuation) can the Conservatives hope to, paradoxically, advance the philosophy of market freedom in working class housing.

The political consequences of these radical housing measures are still being assessed, though it seems unlikely that the party loyalties of urban Scotland has been fundamentally changed in the Thatcher years. The continued damage to the industrial heartland of central Scotland has undoubtedly weakened trade union confidence. Home ownership appeals to a wide range of tenants who demand greater control over their own lives and recognise the opportunity for gain. Yet the base of support which was created by the combined industrial and housing movements of the early twentieth century remains largely intact and suggests that the political demand for decent housing at fair rents will remain part of the code of popular values in urban Scotland for the remaining years of the twentieth century.

Notes

1. Bob Patten, *et al*, *Eclipse of the Private Landlord: a study of the consequences*, London, Conservative Political Centre 1974, pp.4, 10–11. This is discussed in John Foster and Charles Woolfson, *The Politics of the UCS Work-In*, Lawrence and Wishart, 1986, pp.380–81 and *passim*. The Conservative pamphlet in fact accepted the demise of the private landlord as inevitable, op.cit., pp.13–14.
2. M Foulis, 'The effect of sales on the public sector in Scotland', in D Clapham and J English (eds), *Public Housing* Croom Helm, 1987, pp.93–8. About 63 per cent of Glasgow's housing was public rented stock in 1981.
3. J B Cullingworth, *Essays on Housing Policy* London, Allen & Unwin 1979, pp.62–4, 70–3; S Merrett, *Owner-Occupation in Britain* London, Routledge & Kegan Paul, 1982, pp.134–9.
4. P N Balchin, *Housing Policy and Housing Needs* London, Macmillan 1981, pp.114–19, 127–9, *passim*; D Maclennan, 'The pricing of public housing in Britain: an overview of issues and experience' in *Rent Schemes in British Public Housing* CURR Papers, 18 University of Glasgow, 1984, pp.5–13.
5. M J Daunton, *House and Home in the Victorian City: Working-Class Housing 1850–1914*, Arnold, 1983.
6. Ibid, pp.287–95, 302–4, *passim*.
7. E Hobsbawm, *The Forward March of Labour Halted?* London, Verso 1981, pp.1–19, 173 and *passim*.
8. W Gallacher, *Revolt on the Clyde* Lawrence & Wishart, 1936, 1977, and *Last Memoirs* Lawrence & Wishart, 1966; J Broom, *John Maclean* Loanhead, 1973, p.56 and *passim*; T Bell, *John Maclean: A Fighter for Freedom* Glasgow, Scottish Committee of Communist Party 1944.
9. Gallacher, op.cit. (note 8); T Bell, *Pioneering Days* London, Lawrence & Wishart, 1941; also D Kirkwood, *My Life of Revolt*, London, Harrap, 1935.
10. J Hinton, *The First Shop Stewards' Movement* London, Allen & Unwin, 1973; J Hinton and R Hyman, *Trade Unions and Revolution: the Industrial Politics of the Early Communist Party* London, Pluto 1975; R Challinor, *The Origins of British Bolshevism* London, Croom Helm, 1977.
11. Ibid; cf H Pollitt, *Serving My Time: an Apprenticeship to Politics* London, Lawrence & Wishart, 1940.
12. J Saville, 'The ideology of Labourism' in R Benewick, *et.al.* (eds), *Knowledge and Belief in Politics* London, Allen & Unwin, 1973, pp.214–15; see also D Coates, 'Labourism and the Transition to Socialism', *New Left Review* (NLR) **129** (1981), pp.19–22; T Ali and Q Hoare, 'Socialists and the crisis of Labourism' *NLR* **132** (1982, pp.68–74, 80; G Stedman Jones, 'March into history?' *New Socialist* **3** (1982), pp.12–15.
13. R McKibbin, 'Why was there no Marxism in Great Britain?' *English Historical Review* **XCIX** (1984), pp.305–22, *passim*.
14. Ibid, pp.326–7.
15. R McKibbin, *The Evolution of the Labour Party, 1910–1924* Oxford University Press, 1974, pp.236–41.

16. Ibid, pp.235–44.
17. I McLean, *The Legend of Red Clydeside* Edinburgh, Donald, 1983, pp.107–9, 157, *passim.*
18. Ibid, pp.91, 186–7.
19. Joan Smith, 'Labour tradition in Glasgow and Liverpool', *History Workshop Journal* **17** (1984), pp.32–56; Jim Smyth, 'The political impact of Labour: Glasgow, 1880–1914' [unpublished paper] Edinburgh, 1987.
20. Hinton, op.cit. (note 10), McLean, op.cit. (note 17), pp.97–109.
21. R A Cage (ed), *The Working Class in Glasgow, 1750–1914* London, Croom Helm, 1987, pp.8–17.
22. Ibid, pp.57–62; J A Handley, *The Irish in Scotland* University of Cork Press, 1947, p.279.
23. Ibid, pp.279–80.
24. J Butt, 'Housing' in Cage, op.cit. (note 21), pp.37–9.
25. Ibid, pp.39, 44–5; J Melling, 'Scottish industrialists and the changing character of class relationships in the Clyde region, 1880–1918' in T Dickson (ed), *Capital and Class in Scotland* Edinburgh, Donald, 1982.
26. J Butt, loc.cit. (note 24); J Melling, 'Clydeside housing and the evolution of State rent controls, 1900–1939' in J Melling, *Housing, Social Policy and the State* Croom Helm, 1980, pp.138–67, for general background.
27. J Butt, loc.cit. (note 24), p.45.
28. J Butt, 'Working class housing in Glasgow, 1900–1939' in I Macdougall (ed), *Essays in Scottish Labour History* Edinburgh, Donald, 1978.
29. Ibid.
30. A Offer, *Property and Politics 1870–1914* Cambridge University Press, 1981, pp.384–406 and *passim*; cf Daunton, op.cit., (note 5) pp.289–92.
31. Ibid, ch 5–7.
32. J Melling, 'Employers, industrial housing . . . in west Scotland, 1870–1920' *International Review of Social History* **XXVI** 1981, pp.255–301.
33. Ibid.
34. D Englander, *Landlord and Tenant in Urban Britain 1838–1918* Oxford University Press, 1983, pp.162–89.
35. Ibid, Englander also provides a valuable survey of pre-1914 rent struggles in Yorkshire and the Midlands.
36. J Saville, loc. cit. and also 'Trade Unions and Free Labour: the background to the Taff Vale decision' in A Briggs and J Saville (eds), *Essays in Labour History* London, Macmillan, 1960, particularly pp.331–2.
37. G Stedman Jones, 'Working Class Culture and Working-Class Politics in London, 1870–1900: Notes on the remaking of a Working Class' *Social History* **VII** (1974), pp.485–9, 499.
38. G Stedman Jones, 'March into History' loc.cit.
39. Joan Smith, loc. cit. (note 19); P J Waller, *Democracy and Sectarianism . . . Liverpool 1868–1939* Liverpool University Press, 1981, ch 16–17; T Lane, *Liverpool: Gateway of Empire* London, Lawrence & Wishart, 1987, pp.123–39 and *passim.* It is arguable that both Smith and Waller exaggerate the importance of religion in inhibiting the rise of Labour and also the actual time lag between Labour acquiring power in major urban centres—Labour's electoral successes date from the period 1930s–40s in most cities.
40. H McShane and J Smith, *Harry McShane—No Mean Fighter* London, Pluto, 1978; E Shinwell, *Conflict Without Malice* London, Odhams, 1955, p.63 and *passim* for generation which included Harry Hopkins of Govan.
41. The Independent Labour Party, *Report of the Second Annual Conference of the*

I.L.P (1893); *Report of the Annual Conference* (1895), pp.7–8, 16. Copies of ILP conference reports and other pages in Broady Collection, Glasgow University Library, ref A202-04, etc.

42. W H Fraser, 'Municipal Socialism and Social Policy' SSRC Conference Paper University of Glasgow [unpublished] (1979); W H Fraser, 'Scottish trades councils . . .' in MacDougall (ed), op.cit. (note 28).
43. I G C Hutchinson, 'Glasgow Working-Class Politics' in Cage (ed), op.cit. (note 21), pp.111–12.
44. Ibid, pp.119–20.
45. Quoted in ibid, p.134.
46. J Melling, *Rent Strikes: Peoples' Struggle for Housing in West Scotland 1890–1916*, Edinburgh Polygon (1983), ch 3–4.
47. J E Mortimer, *History of the Boilermakers' Society, 1834–1906* Allen & Unwin (1973) London, p.147.
48. P J Dollan, *Jubilee History of the Kinning Park Cooperative Society Ltd* Glasgow, Society, 1923 pp.4–5, 37. Dollan was part of the network of Cooperators, Labour spokesmen and housing activists in such strategic areas as Kinning Park and Govan. For the parallel temperance movement in Govan see J F Leishman, *Matthew Leishman of Govan* Paisley, Garner 1921, pp.182–3 for the Scottish Temperance Society and the 'wee Frees'.
49. Mary Cordiner, oral transcript (August 1978), p.10: 'There was an awful lot of Tories in [the Women's Co-operative Guild]'.
50. R McKibbin, op.cit. (note 15), pp.179–82.
51. J Melling, op.cit. (note 46), 1983, ch. 3.
52. Interview with Mary Cordiner and Harry McShane, oral transcript (23 August 1978), p.11 for account of visit to the poorer Govan tenements in Autumn 1914.
53. Ibid, pp.11–12, for impact of Agnes Dollan and Helen Crawfurd.
54. H Corr, 'Helen Crawfurd (1877–1954): Suffragette, Independent Labour Party Activist, and Communist Party Organiser' in W Knox *Scottish Labour Biography* Edinburgh, 1984.
55. Independent Labour Party, *Report of the Annual Conference of the I.L.P.* 1915, Broady Collection A219, pp.15, 56.
56. T Bell, *Pioneering Days* 1941, pp.86, 96.
57. Ibid, p.18: 'We did not live exactly in a slum but in something next door to it. Imagine a block of buildings less than fifty yards square; with a courtyard; twenty-five families . . . one water-tap outside to each group of families; two open wet closets; a central midden joining them, and one wash-house for the lot . . .'.
58. D Englander, op.cit. (note 34), Chapter 6 for tenants' defence organisations and national housing campaigns.
59. Ibid, M J Daunton, op.cit. (note 5), pp.30–31, *passim*, Melling, op.cit. (note 26), 1980, 'Introduction'.
60. T Bell, op.cit., pp.18–19. The structure of Glasgow's tenements and their impact on the enforced fraternity of working class tenants is discussed in Melling, op.cit. (note 46), 1983.
61. J Hinton, op.cit. (note 10); McLean, op.cit. (note 17), pp.83–5 and *passim*; cf W Kendall, *The Revolutionary Movement in Britain, 1900–1921* London, Weidenfeld & Nicolson, 1969, p.354 note 59 for the significance of the Fairfield shipwrights and the Munitions Act controversy in the rebirth of the Clyde Vigilance Committee itself—rather than the dilution struggle. This would confirm the significance of the generalised anti-State conflict rather than the specific production issues facing the craft engineers.
62. Letter to J Kennedy of the Govan Branch of the Shipwrights' Association to the

Scottish Secretary, McKinnon Wood, 9 October 1915, outlining the three resolutions against rent increases, Munitions legislation, and Munitions Tribunals and fines. Scottish Record Office HH 31/22, copy loaned to author by Dr A J Reid. This would also illustrate the central role of Hopkins and the Govan Trades Council in co-ordinating the resistance on rents and industrial grievances at this time.

63. Jessie Barbour (senior), Jessie Barbour (junior), Mary Barbour (junior), and William McShane, oral interview transcript (16 August 1978), pp.4–5, 7, 14. Mrs Jessie Barbour senior was the daughter-in-law of the original Mary Barbour who led the rent strikes in Govan in 1915 and was herself an active participant in the struggles of 1920.
64. James McFarlane, oral interview transcript (17 August 1978), pp.3–7. Mr McFarlane was the son of an active rent striker and Orange Lodge supporter in Partick, where sectarian riots had occurred in the 1860s–70s. Elizabeth McNab, oral interview transcript (14 August 1978), p.4, for another Orange Lodge family in Govan.
65. James McFarlane, op.cit., pp.6–7; 'The idea was to get each tenant one day a week, but there were probably more tenants and you couldnae fit them in. . . . Its really a bit of a joke, but there were supposed to be lots of fights over this washing house key. . . . It was real Glasgow you see, so everybody enjoyed it.'
66. Mary Cordiner, op.cit. (note 49), pp.5, 11.
67. Jessie Barbour senior, op.cit. (note 63), pp.5, 11.
68. Elizabeth McNab, op.cit. (note 64), p.6; Mary McNab at ibid, p.4.
69. Independent Labour Party, *Report of the Annual Conference of the ILP*, 1916 in Broady A220, p.92 for William Regan.
70. J Melling, loc.cit. 'Scottish industrialists and . . . class relations' op.cit. (1982), for some background.
71. H McShane (ed), *Glasgow 1919: The Story of the 40 Hours Strike* Glasgow, Molindar Press, 1970 gives some details.
72. R McKibbin, op.cit. (note 15), pp.150, 181–2; Dollan, op.cit. (note 48).
73. R Challinor. *The Origins of British Bolshevism*, p.168; Corr, op.cit. (note 54), S Macintyre, *A Proletarian Science: Marxism in Britain 1917–1933* Cambridge University Press, 1980, pp.23–24 for context.
74. McKibbin, op.cit. (note 15); L Macassey, *Labour Policy – False and True* Thornton London, Butterworth, 1922 p.23, for Henderson; A J P Taylor, *English History 1914–1945* Oxford University Press, 1965, pp.127–29.
75. Challinor, op.cit. (note 10), p.244, 252–53; R K Middlemass, *The Clydesiders* London, Hutchinson, 1965, pp.79–83 and *passim*; C Cook, 'Labour's electoral base' in C Cook and I Taylor (eds) *The Labour Party* Longman, 1980, pp.85–9.
76. McKibbin, op.cit. (note 10), pp.186–8, 196–8.
77. Ibid, pp.193–95; Cook, loc. cit., p.86; Middlemass, op.cit. (note 75).
78. W H Fraser, 'Municipal socialism and social policy' 1979, pp.18–19; I S Wood, 'John Wheatley, the Irish and the Labour Movement in Scotland' *The Innes Review* **XXXI** 1980, 75–6 and *passim*.
79. *Report of Committee of Inquiry into the High Cost of Building Working Class Dwellings in Scotland* [Currie Committee], Scottish Board of Health, Cmd 1411, 1921, p.7.
80. Ibid, p.24.
81. Ibid, pp.24–25; M Swenarton, *Homes Fit for Heroes* London, Heinemann 1981; L F Orbach, *Homes for Heroes: a Study of the Evolution of British Public Housing, 1915–1921* New York, Seeley, Service, 1977, pp.96–9.
82. *Report of the Committee on the Rent Restriction Acts* [Constable Committee]

Cmd 2423 1925, pp.6–8 provides an outline of legislation and the increases permitted and enforced as well as the *Kerr v Bryde* case. Patrick Dollan's 'minority' report and recommendations included the argument that the 'popular demand of the tenants is for a return to pre-war rents for pre-war houses. That demand arises from economic necessity.' Ibid, p.41.

83. Currie Committee, Cmd 1411, op.cit. (note 79), pp.25–6.
84. Elizabeth McNab, op.cit. (note 64), pp.4–6.
85. Jessie Barbour senior, op.cit. (note 63), pp.2–4; McLean, op.cit., (note 17) pp.170–2.
86. Constable Committee, Cmd 2423, op.cit. (note 82), pp.15–28 for Constable's detailed discussion of the Clydebank situation; Shinwell, op.cit. (note 40), for an heroic interpretation of his own role in the rent struggles.
87. S Damer, *State, Local State and Local Struggle: The Clydeside Rent Strike of the 1920s* CURR Paper No 22, University of Glasgow, 1985, pp.12–27, for an illuminating discussion of the Clydebank conflict.
88. Ibid, pp.31–32.
89. McLean, op.cit. (note 17), pp.187–90.
90. C Harvie, *No Gods and Precious Few Heroes: Scotland 1914–1980* London, Arnold, 1981, pp.70–2, 154–5 for a critical view of Labour's housing achievement.
91. McLean, op.cit. (note 17), pp.201–18 and *passim.*
92. I McLean, 'Party organisation' in Cook and Taylor (eds), op.cit., (note 75) pp.15–16.
93. Challinor, op.cit. (note 10), pp.244, 253; see W Paul, *The State: its Origin and Function* Glasgow, Socialist Labour Press, c. 1912, pp.169–92 for the earlier SLP politics of Paul.
94. McKibbin, op.cit. (note 15), pp.186–98.
95. Hinton and Hyman, op.cit. (note 10), pp.53–61; Macintyre, op.cit., pp.226–34.
96. Damer, op.cit. (note 87), pp.27–28.
97. P Piratin, *Our Flag Stays Red* [Foreword by William Gallagher] London, Lawrence & Wishart [1948], 1978 ed, pp.37–45.
98. Orbach, op.cit. (note 81), pp.51–2, 62–3, 119.
99. Ibid, pp.56–9; Melling, op.cit. (note 46), 1983, for Mary Laird and other leading personalities.
100. Orbach, op.cit. (note 81), pp.72–3.
101. J Burnett, *A Social History of Housing 1815–1985* London, Methuen, 1986, p.233.
102. Ibid, pp.239–40; J Melling 'Introduction' to *Housing Social Policy and the State* (1980), for the Glasgow tenant policies and concern to let to reliable 'artisan' workers and lower middle class rentpayers.
103. Cullingworth, op.cit. p.62.
104. Ibid, pp.63–6.
105. McKibbin, op.cit. (note 15).
106. McLean, op.cit. (note 17), p.157 and *passim*; Hinton, op.cit., p.127.
107. Orbach, op.cit. (note 81), pp.66–7 for Lanarkshire Miners; Melling, loc.cit. (note 46) 1983, gives some details on coalmining and nationalisation.
108. Mary Cordiner, op.cit. (note 49), pp.1–2 is an example; (note 41) p.3 for Ben Tillett's salvationist view of the Labour cause.
109. Harry McShane, oral transcript (23 August 1978), p.5 recalls some of the major figures.
110. Jessie Barbour senior, op.cit., pp.9–10.

111. Baillie Jack Davies, 'The End of an Epoch' *Govan Press*, April 1958 for an obituary of Mary Barbour including this vivid phrase. In a contemporary review, W C Anderson (Parliamentary champion of the rent strikers) had described the rents struggle as the achievement of 'hundreds of thousands of discriminating and undiscriminating minds'. *Forward* 13 November 1915.
112. Jessie Barbour senior, op.cit., pp.2–4.
113. Sheriff Lee quoted in the *Glasgow Herald* 18 November 1915. The local judiciary of urban Scotland played a prominent and usually constructive role in resolving industrial and housing conflicts and frequently defended the rights of the tenants in the period 1914–25.
114. Jessie Barbour senior, op.cit., p.5.

4 National policies and local tensions

PART 1 STATE HOUSING AND THE GREAT WAR[1]

David Whitham

In *Cities in Evolution*, published in 1915, Patrick Geddes, Scotland's visionary advocate of planning and housing reform, attacked the tenement tradition, denouncing even the New Town of Edinburgh as a 'super slum'.

In the first decade of this century tenements, each of which could contain up to sixteen two-roomed 'houses' reached by a common stair, were still being built in Scotland, and Geddes illustrated, with particular outrage, a new tenement village at Duddingston housing workers for a new group of breweries outside Edinburgh, an ideal place it would seem, for an exemplary garden suburb. He despaired sarcastically of a people 'whose high and abstract cultivation thus lifts them above common ground wherever they may go' and said:

> We must fall back on importing missionaries! Happily, these sometimes desirable aliens have lately been forthcoming. Like honey from the carcase of the lion, a peaceful advance of industry and well-being may be gained from the very heart of war. Thus the transference of some hundreds of torpedo workmen from Woolwich to the Clyde lately brought with it the needful discontent with tenement conditions ... and a garden village for those soundest, wisest, and most successful of strike-leaders—let us hope some day strike exemplars—is therefore already in progress.[2]

The reference to the torpedo workmen provides the starting point for this chapter on the approach to state housing in Scotland in the years immediately before and during World War I. It begins by examining the response to local housing crises at Greenock and Rosyth. Each crisis was due to the Admiralty's need for skilled civilian workers, but the causes were not otherwise connected.

Woolwich, as a former naval dockyard and a centre of arms manufacture remained a suitable place to make torpedoes, but the Thames estuary for obvious reasons was not a suitable place for testing them. The Clyde, on the other hand, besides its established engineering tradition, had access to quiet stretches of water undisturbed by sea-going traffic and the decision was taken to move the torpedo factory to Greenock with a nearby testing range in Loch

Long. The establishment of a dockyard at Rosyth, and the more northerly base at Invergordon was in response to increasing German naval power threatening the North Sea and Baltic approaches.

This first section of the chapter then discusses the production of munitions housing during the war and seeks to demonstrate a continuous development of commitment and policy on the part of one government department, the Local Government Board for Scotland (LGBS), from 1910, towards state intervention in housing.

Greenock

The decision to move the torpedo factory to Fort Matilda at Greenock had been made in 1907[3] but must have become generally known some time in 1909. At the beginning of 1910 the housing question raised its head. The Woolwich workers knew what they were in for even before they saw the Clyde, for a member of an advance deputation, Mr W Coton, wrote before visiting Greenock to John Burns, the responsible minister for housing in England and Wales asking him to use his influence with the authorities at Greenock to 'stimulate them into some action' to meet the housing needs of the four or five hundred men and their families who expected to be transferred that year. They had been informed that in May there would be about 700 vacant houses but 'about two-thirds of these are entirely unsuitable for our people being mainly one-room "houses" in slums.'[4]

The letter was passed to Lord Pentland, the Scottish Secretary, and on its receipt Pentland's private secretary minuted proposals for a conference, saying that the Secretary was already aware of the problem—he must have heard directly from Burns.

In March 1910 the Greenock Industrial Building Society wrote to the Scottish Secretary proposing a 'garden suburb', including houses for sale and to let and requesting loans at low rates of interest to facilitate it. The LGBS replied referring to provisions of the 1890 (s.67) and 1909 (s.4) Acts permitting public works loans to be made to public utility societies for up to two-thirds of costs, but internal minutes showed distinct lack of enthusiasm for the proposal, suggesting it was too late.[5] This sounds odd, in view of the length of time that the Greenock problem was to persist, but the LGBS might have accepted reassurances from the Admiralty, whose real troubles were yet to come. The complacency of that department was shown in replies to parliamentary questions. In April 1910 the First Lord, Mr McKenna, agreed that Woolwich workers were raising objections to the housing in Greenock but hoped that suitable houses would be provided by private enterprise: the Admiralty had never contemplated buying land for housing. On 19 July in the Navy Estimates debate, Mr Lambert, the Civil Lord, said that the Admiralty had made an arrangement guaranteeing rents for 100 houses 'which are to be provided by a private company'.

Such arrangements could not allay the immediate discontent and the 'strike' to which Patrick Geddes referred consisted of a downright refusal by some of the transferred employees to move to Greenock, as a result of which some men apparently were dismissed. Asked about this at Estimates on 17 March 1911, Dr Macnamara, First Secretary to the Admiralty, said that the delay 'was due to various causes of which housing the men is one . . . in particular they did not take kindly to the tenement system'.

In Greenock, attitudes to the housing problem were far from complacent and the concern was of long standing. A popular housing movement founded in 1865 had built model tenements and some cottages on land feued at low rates but had to abandon the development due to high building costs. Generally, in Scotland, when land was feued for a specific purpose, the feudal superior (himself a vassal in succession, eventually to the Crown) lost the use of it forever, receiving in exchange an income, the feu duty, which was fixed once and for all. The system meant that landowners drove hard bargains for building land and the resulting high and recurring charges were the most important single reason for the small houses and high densities which characterised tenement development. In 1877 Greenock was among the first authorities to operate the Artisans' and Labourers' Dwellings Act of 1875 with a clearance area extending over eight acres in the lower part of the town, redeveloping half the site itself and feuing the remainder at preferential rates for private building.

Despite further building of 200 dwellings under the 1890 Act, those early initiatives had little effect on conditions in 1910. In his 1911 report the burgh sanitary inspector warned the council that the scarcity of houses for workmen earning up to one pound a week was 'a menace to public health' and cited cases of extreme overcrowding of one and two-roomed dwellings by as many as four families. The only way that low-income families could find housing at all was by sub-letting.[6]

Another witness of housing conditions in Greenock was T W Hamilton, architect and surveyor to the Greenock estate of Sir Hugh Shaw Stewart.[7] Hamilton had a longstanding interest in housing, had visited Bourneville, Port Sunlight and Letchworth and was an advocate of the garden city and tenants' co-partnership movements. The Greenock estate itself had a creditable planning record; the development of the largely middle-class western area of the town had been controlled by an early nineteenth century development plan, and land for the working men's housing trust of 1865 had been allocated at preferential rates by Sir Michael Robert Shaw Stewart, the seventh baronet.

There were special problems in the way of 'garden suburb' development in Scotland where the feudal system of land tenure formed a formidable obstacle to providing low density housing at any reasonable cost, but by 1911 the Admiralty had entered into an agreement with a garden suburb company at weekly rents of up to eight shillings and sixpence excluding rates. Sixteen houses were to be ready by Whitsuntide and the company would try to complete fifty. This was the Scottish Garden Suburb Company, which started building that spring on a site outside Greenock, about half a mile west of the factory, but progress was not to be as rapid as the Admiralty had hoped.

When a second scheme was reported the point about land costs was well made. Greenock Garden suburb (founded by Glasgow Garden Suburb

Tenants Ltd) secured thirty acres at Cartdyke, where

> The landlord, Sir Hugh Shaw Stewart, has treated us most liberally, feuing the ground at £16 per acre, whereas in the near neighbourhood they get £70 per acre for building tenements.[8]

Glasgow Garden Suburb Tenants Ltd were an established society having already acquired 210 acres of land at Canniesburn at £13 per acre annually.[9]

By the beginning of 1913 the town council and citizens of Greenock were even more worried about the housing situation and in February the secretary of the Greenock Housing Council wrote to the Admiralty, with a copy to the Scottish Secretary, urging that their lordships should ensure that suitable accommodation was available before any more workers were transferred to the district. The earlier transfer, he maintained, was an important element in the acute shortage of 'accommodation of the artisan type', resulting in a general rise in rents and serious overcrowding, and concluded, referring to the recent appointment of a royal commission on housing in Scotland, by suggesting that the government should be especially careful not to contribute itself to the housing problem.

The LGBS, thus provoked, themselves wrote to the Admiralty, receiving an even more than usually complacent reply, explaining that the Admiralty had already assisted in promoting the building of cottages, but that the Scottish Garden Suburb Company had 'by no means taken full advantage' of their assistance, and repeating that, 'in a populous place like Greenock', needs should be met by local enterprise.

But by August 1913 further expansion of the factory was proposed, amounting to about 300 workers, 200 of them newcomers to the district, and a delegation representing the LGBS, Greenock and Gourock town councils, Scottish Garden Suburb Tenants Ltd and the factor of Major Darroch's Gourock estate met at Fort Matilda to appraise the situation.

An inventory of new housing development showed:

1. Scottish Garden Suburb Tenants Ltd had built forty-eight houses on their site at Gourock with twelve more to be completed by November. All but four of the forty-eight were let or sold to torpedo workers (forty let, four sold). The company regarded their agreement with the Admiralty as fulfilled. Eight shillings and sixpence was too low a rent and any further houses would be sold at £300;
2. Gourock and Greenock Tenants Ltd, a society formed by torpedo factory employees, building on land feued by Major Darroch had built four houses, with four being built and four more sanctioned;
3. Greenock Garden Suburb Tenants Ltd, on their thirty acres, had six cottages under construction;
4. The only current corporation housing scheme, at Serpentine Row, was for slum clearance;
5. Private development in Gourock would provide a number of small villas and flats.

The LGBS's reporter found no lack of housing in the area (presumably numerically) but no room for new transfers. Purely speculative housing was 'almost dead' in the district. Moreover the torpedo factory employees preferred renting to purchase. Many had previously owned at Woolwich but had difficulty in selling their houses there. Perhaps a 'syndicate', as proposed at Rosyth should be formed.[10]

Private enterprise, garden suburbs and altruistic landowners had failed to meet the new housing need. And it appeared there might be limits to altruism. A Nurse Campbell wrote from Greenock 26 April 1914:

> Sir,
> Can the Corporation of Greenock not obtain Government powers to acquire land for house-building . . .?
> Greenock has a slum area which is a disgrace to civilisation, the whole district is congested, yet it is there that the torpedo factory workmen are driven into. While there are *three miles* of ideal land for feuing, between Greenock and the Cloch the property of Hugh Shaw Stewart, who will neither feu, let, nor sell, as he objects to have the common people within miles of his policies . . .

The LGBS replied on 28 April 1914 saying that the local authority had powers under the Housing Acts to acquire land for housing purposes either by agreement or compulsorily and that a public inquiry was about to be held into housing conditions at Greenock.[11]

The inquiry was held on four days in April and May 1914 and its recommendations included that the authority should immediately proceed to build 250 houses to be followed by a further 250. LGBS inspectors would advise on the best use of the available land at Roxburgh Street.[12] But not until June 1915 could the LGBS write to the Treasury and to the Admiralty reporting that Greenock had resolved to build 144 houses at Roxburgh Street, all to be completed in nine months, and the first houses to be ready in five months. They would be available to Admiralty employees for two years or more, at rents to cover costs. Though 'not a model scheme . . . it is one that would provide very acceptable housing accommodation for the Admiralty employees and later would materially assist the local authority in their scheme for slum clearance'.

Earlier in June the Admiralty had at last awakened to the seriousness of the housing question at Greenock and had written to the LGBS seeking help. The 'dearth of housing' at Greenock was serious and production of torpedoes was affected. At a meeting a week later the Admiralty produced desperate ideas for Greenock; commandeering existing housing (what about the locals?), trains from Glasgow and Paisley (themselves overcrowded), boats from Dunoon (some workers were being turned out at *Greenock*, to make room for summer visitors), huts, and renting the SS *Uranium*, an ex-prison ship, for £2,300 per month. It was in that context that the Local Government Board produced Roxburgh Street: only 144 dwellings, but twice as many as their Lordships had obtained from 'local enterprise' in more than five years.

In 1916–17 200 more houses and flats were built in Greenock and Gourock under the instigation of the LGBS, half of them directly provided by the Office of Works. Greenock was a test case. With the neighbouring towns of Gourock and Port Glasgow it provided a thriving market. Mr Godfrey Collins, MP for Greenock, reckoned that the total population increase due to the torpedo factory was about 7,000, a 10 per cent increase.[13]

Those households must have been classic 'good tenants', skilled men in regular employment, willing to rent good homes, and private enterprise had failed them utterly.

Rosyth

In contrast to Greenock, at Rosyth there was nothing. Dunfermline, about two miles away, was a small town with a limited industrial tradition.

Land for a new dockyard at Rosyth, on the north side of the Forth estuary about two miles west of the railway bridge, was purchased by the Admiralty in 1903 and construction work had started in 1909.[14] The size of the workforce had already affected housing conditions in the area although at first the demand was mainly for lodgings for single men. The longer term question of permanent housing was already being discussed in 1910 and a progressive solution proposed. At the first annual meeting of the Scottish branch of the Garden Cities and Town Planning Association in May, Professor Lodge referred to:

> ... the exciting problem of Rosyth. Here (we have) on land owned, or partly owned by the State the prospect of building up a very considerable dockyard town ... it was no secret that the Admiralty was disposed to consider favourably any scheme on what might be known as garden city lines. Secondly it was no secret that the Scottish Local Government Board was eager and willing to use all the powers which the Town Planning Act gave it to encourage development on these lines.

William Robertson, of the Carnegie Trust, talked about the high cost of developing 600 acres at low density due to servicing and feus. It would only be possible if the Admiralty would 'hand over the 600 acres to a society such as this' considering the land 'as a sort of by-product of the Naval Base'.[15]

In the following year concern about conditions in the district increased. A LGBS inspection reported that about 2,000 workers were employed at the base, about one-third of them married, and 'it was hard for them to find good homes'. In 1911 also, Dunfermline Burgh floated a private bill to extend its boundaries to include the whole of the Admiralty's land and this was enacted on 18 August. The LGBS annual report for 1911 stated officially the objective, to create 'a town on garden city lines' at Rosyth. Towards this end the local authority at least was wasting no time. By 9 October the first plans had been prepared and the burgh's intention to prepare a town planning scheme under the 1909 Act was advertised on 11 December 1911. The authority had also, on the strength of negotiation with the Admiralty and LGBS, commenced an extensive drainage scheme for the 600 acres of land which had been designated for housing. This land lay on either side of a new road, running east–west behind the naval base, and it had been taken for granted that the part to the south, nearer the works and better building land, would be developed first. But it appeared in 1911 that the Admiralty had changed their mind. They were prepared, they said, to fall in with any town planning scheme for the area *north* of the new road, but refused to consider preparing any scheme of their own.

The advantages of an Admiralty promoted town planning scheme for the land they had acquired had been pressed on their lordships by the LGBS since the beginning of 1910. Negotiations with adjoining owners would have been no great problem and there would have been no need to wait for the Dunfermline extension Act. But the Admiralty remained adamant that it was none of their concern, and that no part of the cost of preparing or implementing any plan should fall upon naval funds. After an unproductive meeting on 19 January 1912 the LGBS wrote formally to the Secretary for Scotland to expose the impasse at political level.

The LGBS's letter explained that 2,500 dockyard employees were likely to be drafted to Rosyth by 1916. Dunfermline's planning proposals were unlikely to be approved before 1914 but the council had no responsibility for providing housing for incoming workers: their duty ended with the production of a scheme for town planning the area. It was the duty of the Admiralty at the very least to provide land for housing and they should state as early as possible the terms on which they were prepared to feu the ground to the north of the new road, the numbers and types of houses that would be required and the rents that could be paid. There was no room for delay, and in the opinion of the Board, unless the Admiralty took immediate action they might experience 'in an intensified degree' the difficulties they had met at Greenock.[16]

Despite these hard words the Admiralty, at a subsequent meeting, repeated that they would not propose a town planning scheme but would fall in with any scheme proposed by the LGBS. The fact that the Dunfermline scheme might not be ready in time did not affect the Admiralty's decision. Could not the LGBS prepare a scheme: the Admiralty would provide a brief? This last suggestion was considered, but how could the Board act? Its power under the 1909 Act presumed default by the local authority; and the local authority was doing its level best. Dunfermline had made formal application under the Act on 14 March. They were authorised on 22 May 1912 to prepare a town planning scheme to cover 4,970 acres and in July appointed J E Wilkes, from the Birmingham city surveyor's department, and two assistants as town planning staff.

There was evidently no way forward but by diplomacy, and perceptible progress with the Admiralty took another year. The result was a public advertisement—such was the Admiralty's trust in private enterprise—and the text was agreed in April 1913, on the basis of a LGBS draft (so much for the Admiralty's offer to provide a brief) except for the crucial issue of feu-duty. The LGBS suggested £10 per acre, but the Admiralty wanted tenders stating *interalia*,

the feu duty which the applicant is prepared to pay, the classes of house which it is proposed to erect, number of houses to the acre, number and classes of houses to be completed by certain dates and guaranteed rents.

The advertisement went on to summarise a rate of occupation somewhat lower than previous estimates; 500 men by 1916, 2,500 men by 1918, and 5,000 men by 1920, and their wage levels.[17]

Several offers were received but the LGBS, clearly unhappy about a form of tender that effectively allowed the contractor to write his own brief, continued to press the Admiralty to appoint a consultant. J S Nettlefold was suggested, but on 3 July, after a further meeting, the Civil Lord informed the Vice-President of LGBS that the Admiralty had appointed 'a Mr Unwin' to advise them. In December 1913 the Admiralty wrote to Dunfermline Corporation, accepting their planning proposals in full and undertaking to instruct Raymond Unwin to lay out 300 acres, thus effectively adopting the course recommended by the LGBS in 1910.[18]

In the spring and early summer of 1914, between the LGBS, Dunfermline Burgh and the now more conciliatory Admiralty, a solution was hammered out. As to the urgent need for houses there was no dispute, but none of the offers to develop the 300 acres had been entirely satisfactory and there was no prospect of a speedy approval of Dunfermline's town planning scheme. The chosen instrument was to be that old favourite of housing legislation, a public utility society, later to be unveiled as the Scottish National Housing Company Ltd.

Paul Wilding's account of the parliamentary housing movement up to 1914 ends with the second reading on 24 July, of Walter Runciman's bill to give the Board of Agriculture power to build houses in agricultural districts,[19] but the long title of that bill continued, '... and to make provision with respect to the housing of persons employed by or on behalf of the Government where sufficient dwelling accommodation is not available'.

This referred to an apparently secondary purpose, embodied in clause 2, which would give the Local Government Board (LGB), or the LGBS in Scotland, powers to make arrangements with an authorised society for the provision of dwellings, gardens or other works or buildings for persons employed by or on behalf of government departments where sufficient accommodation was not available, or for the Commissioners of Works, with Treasury consent and after consultation with LGB or LGBS to provide housing—or to contribute towards its provision—by their own hand.

Runciman actually mentioned Rosyth in connection with the later clauses of the bill, but that was hardly noticed by the Commons in their heady pursuit of another rural housing bill. Every Tory member, by birth and heritage, was an expert on rural housing, as much as every liberal representing a county constituency was convinced of its inadequacy, and the anecdotal verbiage of this debate occupies pages of Hansard with scarce mention of Rosyth.

But war was less than three weeks away, and at the committee stage on 31 July Runciman did a surprising thing, moving the postponement of clause 1, and deletion of each mention of his own department from the bill, 'in pursuance of an agreement made yesterday in order that we may make some progress with the latter part of the bill which is known as the Rosyth clauses'.[20]

Walter Runciman's rural housing measures were to be embodied in the Housing (No 2) Act, 1914, but the 'Rosyth clauses' received Royal assent on 10

August as the Housing Act 1914.[21] Really a Scottish local government board bill, passed within a fortnight, it was to be the instrument for providing Britain's first state housing.

Public sector housing was not new: local councils had built housing schemes in London, Liverpool, Glasgow and a number of other places including Greenock. Since 1890 they had been able to provide housing to meet general needs in their areas as distinct from slum clearance and in some cases had been urged to do so by the local government boards. Rosyth was something new; not only was a housing scheme directed by a central government department, but the government was prepared to subsidise it.

The LGBS annual report for 1914, published in the first year of the war, was quietly jubilant. It reported the two housing acts, but devoted most space to the proposed Dunfermline town planning scheme, particularly in relation to Rosyth:

> As the base approaches completion, the question of accommodation for the Admiralty employees becomes more urgent ... As the Admiralty cannot see its way to undertake the work, both Departments have agreed that it should be entrusted to a Housing Company operating under our supervision. To this end we propose to avail ourselves of our powers under the Housing Act 1914 ... (and) we are arranging for conveyance to us of that portion of the Admiralty lands available for feuing. We have also under consideration an agreement with an 'authorised society' to be charged with the erection of the requisite houses and other buildings.[22]

The Scottish National Housing Company had already commissioned a housing scheme from Barry Parker and Raymond Unwin, which must have been just about their last joint commission before Unwin joined the Local Government Board in London in August 1914.

In 1915 came an unexpected and ridiculous setback. The Private Bill commission in Edinburgh had accepted proposals by a tramway company to change the route of its line, contrary to the proposals of the Dunfermline town planning scheme. Whether the scheme was retained as lodged with LGBS, or whether it was amended, one party or another, operating with government assurances, would stand to lose. The Housing (Rosyth Dockyard) Bill, consisting of one clause providing, in effect, that Government operating in arrangement with a public utility society comprised a town planning scheme all on its own, saved the situation and went from first reading to royal assent in three days.[23]

Building commenced at Rosyth in September 1915. By the end of the year contracts had been placed for 292 houses and it was expected that 150 would be ready for occupation in the spring of 1916.

The 1914 Act did not restrict the proportion of exchequer assistance to societies operating under its terms and the Scottish National Housing Company Ltd was almost entirely publicly financed. Its commitment was to erect 3,000 houses at an estimated total cost of one million pounds: towards this the government would advance up to £900,000 at three and a half per cent. The principal shareholder was Dunfermline Burgh, holding 50,000 shares bought with a public works loan at 4 per cent: other shares taken up by December

1916 totalled only 21,000 and the company could pay shareholders up to 5 per cent. A LGBS memo of 26 December explored the implications of these arrangements.

Earlier in 1916 it had become apparent that increasing building costs would not permit the company to pay a dividend of anything like 5 per cent, so a supplementary agreement had to be arranged between the LGBS, Admiralty and the Treasury providing:

(a) that the company was not bound to erect 3000 houses, but should build a first instalment of 600 on terms enabling them to pay 5% (but before the end of the year the Admiralty demanded another 1000 houses), and
(b) Mr Walker Smith (LGBS's Engineer) should join the executive committee of the company to represent government interests.

But at this, Dunfermline Burgh, who were becoming increasingly fed up at the way their town planning scheme had been taken over by the government, announced that they would take control of the company and oppose any LGBS appointment.[24]

The LGBS contemplated buying £100,000 of shares to give them control but such extreme expenditure was apparently not necessary. Dunfermline withdrew their objections and in January 1917 ten shares each were transferred to six members and staff of the LGBS (including Walker Smith) to give them directors' qualifications. But whether they were in control of the company or not, the implications to the Government were now clearly seen. The Treasury was committed to an open-ended subsidy, not only to housing but to shareholders, including Dunfermline Burgh, who had bought their shares with a low-interest treasury loan. There were probably better ways of subsidising housing.

In the absence of plans or illustrations of Rosyth, a brief description is necessary. The site runs east–west along a shallow valley and the principal access road contours round it. The form of the estate is therefore an elongated 'U' with its top to the west, but in the garden city manner the building line is elaborated by *culs de sac* and lateral crescents. Down the valley, seen best from the back windows of houses on the inner bend of the 'U' is a splendid view of south Dunfermline town dominated by the abbey.

The houses however, are less successful, and show their wartime origins. They are in the most cottagey of styles with dormers, hips and valleys and grey harled walls. Internally the rooms are small and often of awkward shapes. Their tenants have always been critical of these features and in February 1918 their association wrote to the Admiralty criticising the design of the houses and the high rents. Houses were 'cold and draughty owing to badly fitting doors and windows, sloping roofs in bedrooms and the large number of corners'. Some houses had only one room downstairs. 'In EE type the lavatory is upstairs and inconvenient for the garden.' Terrace houses had no rear access. The letter concluded with heavy sarcasm:

Eminent hygenists tell us that corners harbour dirt, and bring disease. This being the case, the houses here must have been designed by a German, with the idea of spreading disease. There are more corners in one of these houses than in any polygon which you gentlemen can conceive.

Early in 1918 also, the Treasury questioned the value of the Scottish National Housing Company—should it be continued or dissolved? The Scottish Office was inclined towards dissolution:

... it seems clear that the company can no longer form an effective buffer between the Government and its employees who live in houses nominally provided by the company ... but we ought to consult LGBS.

The LGBS disagreed strongly, urging that the company should not be dissolved for the following reasons:

(a) It would be a mistake to interrupt present contracts;
(b) Future work would fall not to LGBS but to the Office of Works (under the 1914 Act), involving a waste of past experience; and
(c) 'we may need such bodies as the company in the event of local authorities failing to undertake housing schemes and indeed it is likely that this particular company's work will be extended after the war.'

The Secretary for Scotland agreed, and told the Treasury so.[25]

By that time the LGBS, like its London counterpart, was preparing a state-aided housing drive after the War, but without clear details of how it would be organised. Their realisation that Scotland's special problems and special needs might call for a means by which government could build houses quickly and by its own hand was farsighted indeed, though it was only in 1937 that such an organisation was created in the Scottish Special Housing Association (SSHA). A Second Scottish National Housing Company was formed in 1925, to foster and build Weir and Atholl steel houses, early examples of system building, and the first and second companies were eventually taken over by the SSHA which has modernised, and still manages, the houses at Rosyth.[26]

The Ministry of Munitions

The housing problems at Greenock and Rosyth were the consequences of long-term developments by the Admiralty, begun in peace time. The third case study in this section examines the relationship between the LGBS and the Ministry of Munitions in the war years from 1915.

Failure to supply guns and ammunition to the front in 1915 was an important reason for the fall of the Liberal government and the formation of Asquith's coalition administration on 25 May 1915. But on 8 April Asquith had set up a cabinet committee, the Munitions of War Committee, with Lloyd George, then Chancellor of the Exchequer, as chairman, an appointment celebrated in the famous *Punch* cartoon, 'Delivering the Goods' of 21 April 1915.

The Ministry of Munitions was formed on 9 June 1915 'to stimulate and control government war supplies'. It employed more people than any previous government department. Iron and steel, chemical and engineering industries were brought under its control. The Royal Ordnance factories expanded and multiplied under its management. It controlled imports of arms and strategic materials from abroad. It controlled rates of pay, conditions of work, welfare and housing. In its heyday it occupied both sides of London's Northumberland Avenue. It created a model of the modern corporate state. Its senior members represented a remarkable range of talents selected from the industrial and academic as well as the political field and included E S Montagu, Christopher Addison, Winston Churchill, Seebohm Rowntree, Eric Geddes, Professor A M Bowley and G M Booth. The formation of this super-ministry involved secondments and transfers from other departments, and housing staff was seconded from the Local Government Board, Raymond Unwin becoming housing architect in the explosives division.

The Scottish Local Government Board, however, was at pains to maintain its integrity, referring in its annual reports for 1915 and 1916 to assistance to the Admiralty and the Ministry of Munitions in providing housing for war workers, which, it confidently expected, 'will be readily absorbed after the war'.[27]

Thus the LGBS preferred to provide a consultancy and enabling service to the Ministry of Munitions which as the War progressed was seen as invaluable experience in mounting a state-propelled housing programme for Scotland. In 1917 the LGBS claimed that the number of houses provided was 4,276 but that seems to have included acquisitions and requisitions.[28]

Scottish Office and LGBS staff were at the same time supporting the Royal Commission on housing in Scotland (RCHS), appointed in 1912 under the chairmanship of Sir Henry Ballantyne.[29] The Commission began hearings of evidence in March 1913 and continued until October 1915 by which date drafting of some sections had begun. Although the report was not published until 1917, after suspension of work on it for nearly a year on Treasury instructions, LGBS officers would be well aware of its direction of thought, that private enterprise had failed and that state subsidised housing would be the necessary remedy, probably by the agency of enlarged and strengthened local authorities.

Wartime housing in Scotland can now be divided into three categories. First there was housing for government employees at new and expanding establishments such as Rosyth, Greenock and later, Invergordon. Such housing was not new in principle; housing had for long been provided for coastguards and for naval and military personnel in remote places. What was new was its provision by civil agencies; a housing association at Rosyth and the local authority at Greenock.

The second category was housing for employees of private industry, albeit for establishments engaged entirely on munitions work. These schemes were mostly in the west of Scotland, associated with the expanding steel industry in areas where housing conditions were notoriously bad, as in landward districts of Lanark and Ayrshire, and with shipbuilding at Clydebank, but other schemes supported industries quite new to Scotland such as aircraft manufacture at Inchinnan in Renfrew and at Alexandria. In all about 2,200 dwellings appear to have been built for private industry in Scotland by or on behalf of the Ministry of Munitions.

The third category was the most mysterious and in some ways the most adventurous of the wartime housing processes, the settlements built by the ministry's explosive division with minimal involvement of any other agency. Such a project was Gretna, ignored by LGBS's annual reports and hardly mentioned in Scottish Office records. Gretna is discussed by John Minett in the second section of this chapter.

In 1918[30] the LGBS published details of the war housing in which they had been involved, amounting to more than 3,000 dwellings, though their summary did not include another 1,100 dwellings for private industry in Scotland mentioned in other sources.[31] These are tabulated in Appendix 4A, which is arranged so as to permit comparison with Appendix 1 of the *Official History of the Ministry of Munitions*, vol V.

Did the investment of time and energy by the LGBS in the unaccustomed task of building new houses result in direct benefits for Scotland in terms of post-war housing policy and production? Members and officers certainly believed at the time that it should.

At the end of July 1916 Vaughan Nash, on behalf of the Reconstruction Committee, wrote to the Secretary for Scotland asking five questions about housing:

(a) What will be the probable housing shortage in Scotland at the end of the War?
(b) What will be the probable distribution of any shortage?
(c) What causes produced shortage before the War?
(d) Whether those causes are likely to operate after? If so how to remove them and encourage the resumption of private enterprise, and
(e) What action should be taken by the State?

A formal acknowledgement from the Scottish Office said that the Secretary was consulting the LGBS but there is no record of an official reply; instead Nash was supplied with a copy of a long memorandum dated 22 August 1916 from Dr W Leslie Mackenzie, medical member of the LGBS and a member of the Royal Commission, suggesting that the information asked for was in large measure contained in evidence to the RCHS, but within the last year 'very important developments had taken place in Lanarkshire, Renfrewshire and Dumbartonshire', the pressures of war having 'altered the whole problem of housing, particularly in Glasgow'. Dr Mackenzie went on to urge that the housing commission should be revived (this was in the period of suspension decreed by the Treasury) to receive additional evidence on the methods employed in providing wartime housing and the town planning schemes which had been submitted to the Board as indicators of the direction in which housing policy after the War should go.[32]

The strength of the Scottish evidence was accepted: a printed memorandum, 'The housing question' by Nash to the Reconstruction Committee dated 30 November 1916 agreed that housing need must be met by public authority building on a large scale and estimated the amount of subsidy that would be required. For England and Wales, grant to meet a total deficiency of 200,000 houses at the end of 1917 would be £12 million; for Scotland 120,000 houses would require grant of £7.2 million—to be almost doubled if current standards of habitability were to be raised. Scottish housing needs were thus recognised as disproportionately greater than the respective national populations would suggest.[33]

The extended remit requested by Dr Mackenzie was not granted to the Scottish commissioners—though evidence on Greenock and Rosyth had already been assimilated—but completion of the report was recommenced in February 1917 for signature in September. The force of the Scottish Royal Commission's report, which can be regarded as the last in the great nineteenth century series of parliamentary inquiries on urban and housing problems is acknowledged in accounts of the development of public sector housing in Britain.

It is clear also that the LGBS's positive approach to housing influenced national housing policy after 1918. James Walker Smith, the board's engineer and housing and town planning inspector was a member of the two crucial committees appointed in 1917 to advise on post-war building and housing problems, under Sir James Carmichael on the building industry and Sir John Tudor Walters on housing provision—apart from Smith only Tudor Walters sat on both—and Walters' remit was extended to Scotland in April 1918.[34] The broad and radical approach taken by the Tudor Walters committee, which Hayes Fisher, President of the LGB, had expected to recommend a cautious economy in housing provision, is well known, and the quality of housing built under Addison's 1919 housing act is its memorial.[35] Unfortunately the Carmichael recommendations on the need for strict control and licensing of post-war building were not heeded. Most significantly, senior posts in the powerful central housing department in the Ministry of Health, formed in 1919, were filled not by LGB staff, but from the Ministry of Munitions and Tudor Walters groups, with Carmichael as Director General, Walker Smith as deputy and Raymond Unwin as chief housing architect.[36]

Despite the Scottish Board's efforts to win Scotland a head start in post-war housing the immediate results were disappointing. Against Nash's estimates of 200,000 dwellings needed in England and Wales and 120,000 (the RCHS report said 250,000) in Scotland the total numbers of houses built under the 1919 housing acts were 170,100 and 25,100 respectively.[37] The relatively poor performance of Scottish local authorities which themselves had done much to politicise the housing question suggests problems for further study.

Conclusion

This section has sought to show that the Local Government Board for Scotland adopted a positive and progressive role in implementing state housing from 1910 to 1917 and by 1919 had set up a most creditable track record, having built or otherwise commissioned over 3,000 houses in Scotland, nearly all of them 'cottages' (as distinct from tenements) and all at 'garden city' densities, revolutionary concepts for working-class housing in Scotland. The LGBS had experimented with a range of processes for building public sector housing during this time. It had made mistakes, particularly in finance, but was in a position to assess and evaluate the devices it had employed.

The board was if anything modest in its claims; there appears to be a discrepancy of nearly 1,100 houses between the summary of wartime achievement in the LGBS annual report for 1918 and the Ministry of Munitions' account of mainstream building, quite apart from Gretna and Eastriggs, explosives division projects in which the local authorities were not involved.

The strong conclusions and recommendations of the 1917 Royal Commission report, and the practical and administrative experience gained by the Scottish Local Government Board were influential in the formation of post-war housing policy not only for Scotland but for Britain as a whole.

PART 2 GOVERNMENT SPONSORSHIP OF NEW TOWNS: GRETNA 1915–17 AND ITS IMPLICATIONS[38]

John Minett

The rise and fall of Gretna provides a useful case study of development processes. It shows how problems can be solved or set aside when urgency drives, but also how vested and selfish interests can exploit situations for their own ends. Built by the Ministry of Munitions between 1915 and 1918 to house workers at a new cordite factory, Gretna was used as a proving ground for a number of social experiments. Also it was a product of its time; the work of two men determined to set the style of future planning, David Lloyd George and Raymond Unwin.

In the first year of the War the slow production of cordite caused great problems for munitions supply. The principal propellant, Cordite MD, required acetone, much of which had to be imported from America; furthermore the main British manufacturing base, the Royal Ordnance Factory at Waltham Abbey was old and unsuitable for expansion. However, by 1915 a new form of cordite, Cordite RDB, had been developed using ether and alcohol, both of which could be produced in Britain.

In May 1915 Asquith's Munitions of War Committee, which preceded the Ministry of Munitions, recommended that an entirely new factory should be built for the manufacture of Cordite RDB; such a factory would require a large site in an isolated area with 'an enormous supply of water'.[39] By the end of June an area of nearly 8,000 acres straddling the English–Scottish border near Gretna Green had been chosen, and the new Minister of Munitions had given formal approval for erecting the factory. By August 1915 work had started on site. The first Cordite RDB from Gretna reached France a year later. Planned to produce 40,000 tons of cordite a year, in the last year of the War the Gretna factory produced nearly 57,000 tons.

A brief description gives some idea of the huge undertaking. The factory covered a strip of land nine miles long by one mile wide and was divided into several sections (see Figure 4.1). At Dornock, near Annan, was a glycerine distillery and acid, nitrocellulose and nitroglycerine sections. From Dornock paste was sent eastwards to a central area at Mossband where, in eight widely dispersed units, it was made into cordite. The finished cordite was then sent further east across the border to be stored in magazines at Longtown. Near

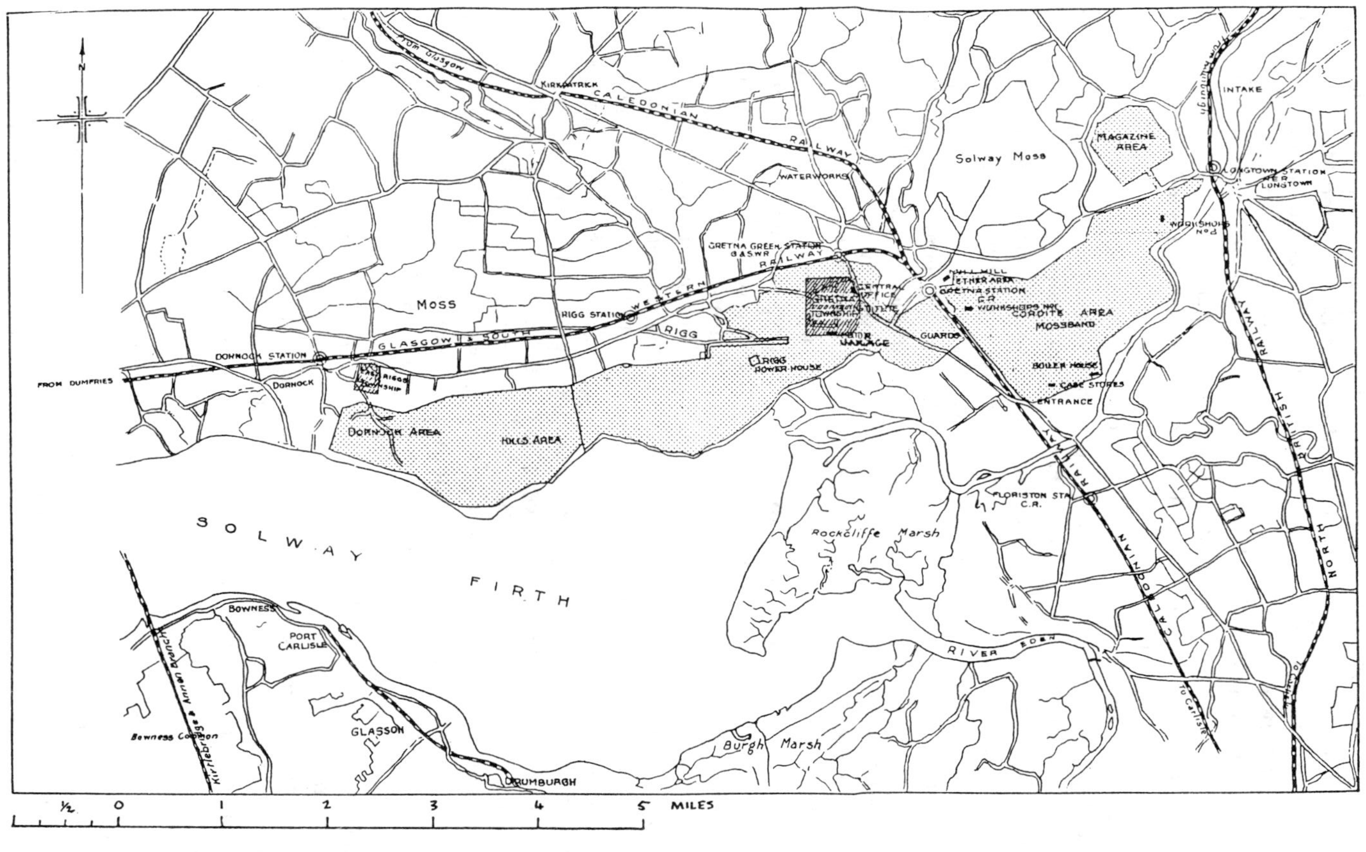

Figure 4.1 Plan of the munitions factory at Gretna

Mossband was built a separate ether section which supplied the ether–alcohol solvent. In addition to the manufacturing areas, ten acres were provided for a central electric power station at Rigg, between Dornock and Mossband; five acres were taken for the water intake and pumping station on the River Esk above Longtown and fourteen acres were used for reservoirs and filter beds. The sections were connected by a network of railway lines and the whole area was surrounded by a double line of barbed wire, patrolled by military guards. Outside the wire lay the 'townships', new villages constructed at Gretna and Eastriggs to house employees of the factory.

Such a massive operation required careful physical and social planning. In June 1915 it was estimated that the factory would employ up to 15,000 workers, and before it could start there would be large numbers of construction workers. All had to be accommodated in a sparsely populated district with no amenities. There was no electricity or water supply and virtually no shops. Its saving grace was that it was well served by railways. Into Gretna poured thousands of people from all over the British Isles. By Janury 1916 there were nearly 9,000 construction workers on site, and in the last year of the war there were 30,000. By the Armistice 11,000 people, of whom 70 per cent were women, were employed at the factory.[40] Throughout its history, one question dominated the planning of Gretna: should it be temporary or permanent? The pragmatists, represented primarily by the Treasury, wanted it to be temporary; the idealists, represented by the staff of the explosives division, saw it as permanent. This issue surfaced a number of times: especially regarding land purchase, construction of the factory and housing, and town planning.

The site was chosen because it was strategically well placed. It could not be shelled from the sea, and submarines could be stopped by netting the Solway railway viaduct (since demolished). Although remote it was easily accessible, being served by three railway companies and six stations, which was important as upwards of six hundred railway trucks would be turned round each day. The site, mainly arable farmland, was acquired compulsorily in July 1915 but settlement with the principal owner, Lord Mansfield, was not reached for over a year. Not only was there argument over its value, but there was a difference of opinion within the Government about the terms of acquisition. The Treasury suggested taking the land temporarily, for the duration of the War; the Ministry of Munitions thought that the freehold should be bought quickly before the value increased as a result of the infrastructure which would be built. Christopher Addison, Secretary of State at Munitions, was loath to see too much paid for one of the 'vacant spaces of the earth', and the Government was considering adopting powers to purchase land exclusive of the increased value due to improvements. Eventually Sir Howard Frank, a private surveyor, was called in as arbitrator. After smoothing ruffled feelings amongst government valuers, agreement was reached at about half of Lord Mansfield's initial price of £63 per acre.[41]

Security, which was obviously important, was an initial headache. Because of its location, and political differences between army and police, Gretna was for a time the responsiblity of six different authorities. For military protection there were two battalions of infantry under Western Command and seven anti-aircraft guns and crews under Northern Command. A factory police force was created which was solely concerned with security within the fence, commanded by an inappropriately named Colonel Rideout, while outside the fence jurisdiction came under two county police forces: Cumberland and Dumfriesshire. Finally a force of the Women's Police Service worked inside the factory with Colonel Rideout and in the townships with the county police. Sorting out the tangle of political and military feelings took some time, being finally resolved in 1916 by the appointment of a retired chief constable to take charge of all security.[42]

Amid the arguments over security and land values, construction went ahead but by no means smoothly. Initially it was assumed that the project could be managed from London and contracts were let to a number of contractors for different aspects of the work. But problems quickly arose, first over wage rates: not only were there different wage rates between urban and rural areas but also between England and Scotland. A further problem which soon emerged concerned the unions. Although many of the contractors were from England, it was the Scottish unions who quickly gripped the site.

In August 1915 the Glasgow District Building Trades Standing Committee wrote to the Ministry of Munitions asking for a joint meeting with the contractors and the Ministry. The Ministry replied that relations between contractors and unions were not their concern, but could not maintain that position for long. As workmen poured onto the site complaints were widely raised about the high wages being paid by some contractors. Strikes broke out. To resolve the problem the Ministry of Munitions persuaded the Treasury to appoint a general contractor, S Pearson & Co, to manage the whole site. After some difficulties, Pearsons managed to establish order and got on with the job of building the factory.

Notes by a member of the munitions directorate, after a visit to Gretna in January 1916, give a vivid impression of conditions in the early days of construction.[43] There was great praise for the Pearson staff, the way they handled labour relations and the way they had organized the site. If it was not for them the writer would 'despair of its coming to anything within a reasonable time ... The first thing that Pearson did was to use temporary railway lines everywhere. This meant tackling a big job in a big way. The earlier men had been content with road transport.'

Nevertheless conditions for the construction gangs were deplorable:

> The labourers ... are a very poor lot, ill fed, out-at-elbows, and badly booted ... along the roads, among the gangs of pipelayers there was hardly any semblance of activity as we passed ... The weather was bad and has been worse. Heavy Scotch mist alternated with a drifting sea wrack. The weather conditions are habitually uncomfortable and take the heart out of the men. Their clothes are wet early in the day, they have no change of their own, they take them off wet when they go to bed and they are still damp when they put them back on the following morning.

The men worked a ten-hour day and a six-day week, starting at 7.30 in the morning. There were canteens which provided a hot plate, but men brought their own food and cooked it during the half an hour allowed for dinner. On Saturdays there was a cinema show which was very popular.

About 3,000 men slept on the site in temporary huts in what were to become the 'townships'. The remainder travelled daily, mainly by train from Carlisle with as many as twenty people in a compartment. The Gretna township was:

> ... a conglomeration of one storey huts made of weather boards nailed to struts and lined with some sort of patent material. The place is a sea of mud. A railway track runs down the centre and alongside it a good road is being constructed. ... The actual planning seems satisfactory, but too often the siting is bad, and in all cases there seemed to be a great risk of fire because of heating apparatus built near to the wooden walls. ... The appearance of the township is, at present, forbidding. There is no provision for tree planting or for the humblest flower beds to improve its appearance.

A theme which emerges from this and other departmental correspondence is the need to improve the quality of the environment in order 'to secure respectable men and women coming to the area'. To help achieve this, Raymond Unwin, 'the chief town planning expert' of the Local Government Board was borrowed to plan the townships.

Unwin had gone to the LGB in 1914 at the invitation of Herbert Samuel. After Rosyth he had run down his practice with Barry Parker, concentrating on lecturing and advising other planners. He had helped found the Town Planning Institute in 1913 and become its first president.[44]

Unwin must have been excited by the opportunity offered by Lloyd George, for the aims and organisation of the Ministry of Munitions followed the lines of efficient industrial management which he also revered. It promised a chance to work out in practice many of the theoretical ideas he had advocated in his lectures on town organisation, low density workers' housing and communal welfare facilities.[45] But, unlike his earlier town planning work with Parker at Earswick, Hampstead and Letchworth, this time he had the power of the State behind him.

Unwin set to work quickly and by the end of October 1915 a cinema and club were in contract, and design was well advanced for shops and other necessary buildings.[46] Meanwhile the Treasury, hoping to keep costs down, pressed that as many workers as possible should be housed in the nearby towns of Carlisle, Dumfries and Annan, with housing at Gretna provided in wooden huts. Rumours spread that the permanent building works had been cancelled; only the realisation that there was accommodation available for only 4,500 people within twenty-five miles of Gretna confirmed the need for the new townships.

The issue of whether housing, in particular, should be temporary or permanent affected Unwin's role and influence. In June 1915 he had been appointed 'technical consultant' to the explosives supply division. The aim then was to provide housing quickly and prefabricated timber huts were built; four-room family houses for married men, small hostels for nine men and a housekeeper, and large hostels accommodating seventy to eighty workers. The official history reported that scarcity of timber forced the ministry to build more permanent brick buildings[47] but it was also acknowledged that the wooden buildings were monotonous in appearance whereas permanent houses introduced greater quality and variety in house types. Eventually almost all the public and community buildings, and about half of the houses were built of permanent materials, mainly brick with slate roofs. By 1917 when building was nearly complete, Unwin was director of the division's housing branch employing five architects, one quantity surveyor, six draughtsmen and a shorthand typist.[48]

The greater importance attached to housing enabled Unwin and his team to experiment with the kind of social housing which the Tudor Walters report later advocated for state housing after the War. Most of the permanent houses were built in what today would be regarded as conventional groupings; semi-detached or terraces of four, but one experiment was particularly noteworthy. Two storey brick hostels were designed which could be converted to cottages later. Writing at the end of the War, Unwin suggested that this arrangement would not only help to meet post-war housing need but would 'assist in tiding over the period of unemployment for ... men in the building trades'.[49]

The layout of the permanent parts of the townships followed many of the principles advocated by the garden city movement and incorporated Unwin's concern for spatial organisation which combined function and visual effect while preserving views and privacy.[50] The centre of Gretna was formally planned. Central Avenue was not only lined with shops, banks, a school, community halls and two of the churches, but it was also a twin carriageway with trees in the central reservation, as at Letchworth. The reservation fulfilled an industrial requirement: a railway ran along it during the War. Eastriggs, though much smaller, had proportionately more permanent houses which with the shops and public buildings, were grouped around an open space like a village green. Recreation and sports grounds adjoined the townships and surplus land was used for allotments and agriculture.

Advances were made in servicing. Electric lighting was provided in the streets and to all houses and public buildings. A more economic system of drainage was introduced whereby a number of houses shared a common drain and disconnecting trap instead of being connected separately to the sewer. This was later to become common practice in local authority housing.

Management and services

The administration of the townships, was more akin to efficient industrial organisation than to normal local government. Relations with the local authorities were minimal; as the local *Annandale Observer* commented, Gretna was regarded as a secret area, and no mention was ever made of it until after the War.

The Ministry of Munitions appointed a town manager who controlled most of the services provided for the highly organised community. He was responsible for allocating houses, collecting rents (usually deducted from wages), providing furniture if required, and maintaining the property. A catering department provided canteen services and supervised the central food stores.

Private traders were admitted but to prevent overcharging the catering department opened a shop which fixed prices in the neighbourhood. The ministry provided and operated the public services including refuse collection, and staffed the hospital and schools. The schools were managed by a local committee, presided over by the town manager.

Welfare and discipline presented great problems. Life in the early days must have been akin to the Klondyke. There was little recreational provision for the thousands of navvies and workmen and the incidence of drunkenness was high. To keep men on the site the railway companies were made to restrict the number of trains to neighbouring towns so that even on Saturday the last train from Carlisle was at 9.30pm. In August 1915, under the Defence of the Realm Act, the ministry took over all public houses near Gretna, and by early 1916 had taken over all liquor sales and breweries in the Carlisle district. A social and athletic club was formed in 1916 and by Christmas a community centre, the Border Hall, had been built with a dance floor, stage, an organ, and seating for 1,100 people. There followed, at both Gretna and Eastriggs, institutes, cinemas, meeting halls, missions and eventually four churches and chapels. As the community developed, clubs and societies for a host of activities flourished. The official history reported that dances were popular, commenting emphatically that 'for reasons of policy the Recreation Committee encouraged this form of amusement'. There were football, hockey and bowling. 'Cricket clubs existed, but as was to be expected in Scotland, the game was not very extensively played'.[51]

A particular concern of the welfare department was the large number of women working at the factory. With nearly 6,000 girls from diverse backgrounds, great care was needed. A lady welfare superintendent was appointed, with a staff of over 200 to supervise the hostels, providing both a homely atmosphere, and strict discipline. The Girl Guide movement was introduced 'with an appreciable effect on discipline both in factory and Townships'.[52] The lady superintendent acted as district commissioner and her staff were company officers.

Gretna was seen as a great success. So far as secrecy would allow, it was shown off as an example of state enterprise at its best and a model for the future, King George V and Queen Mary visiting it in 1917. Mr Burnham, the superintendent of the factory, wrote in a descriptive booklet 'No longer could it be said that a Government undertaking must be more extravagant than a private concern. Gretna provided a standing example of a contrary case, and took the lead of all other factories public or private'.[53]

After the War

The war to end wars ended. The chance to create a new civilisation appeared. Writers all over the world thought that a new society would emerge, with a new environment, the kind of environment created at Gretna. But with no more wars, what should happen to the largest munitions factory in Britain? For advocates of garden cities like Ebenezer Howard and Frederic Osborn there were no doubts: Gretna should be used as a spearhead in the drive to build new towns.[54] Reports of the reconstruction committees had stated that there would be a need for a house building programme of between half a million and a million new homes; why should this not be converted into a town building programme for a hundred new towns?[55] Osborn, in particular worked hard on members of Neville Chamberlain's committee investigating slum housing whose interim report recommended that the Government give support for decentralising population from slum areas into garden cities.[56]

In the first heady days of peace opportunities to plan the future seemed enormous. No longer would the State take a back seat and allow development to be dictated by the market. The corporatist approach developed in the War could be applied to reconstruction. Committees were set up and bills drafted to develop the new State. A housing and town planning bill was presented which required that all large and medium sized towns should plan their future expansion. The same bill would give local authorities the duty, and by providing subsidies the means to build houses. Further powers would make it simpler and cheaper for local authorites to buy land, and there would be money for land settlement by returning servicemen. The Ministry of Ways and Communications would be retained to coordinate the planning of roads and railways. Clearly Gretna should have a role in the new Britain. The question was, what?

In January 1919 the Cabinet laid down the ground rules for state involvement in industry.[57] They decided that the Ministry of Munitions should proceed without delay to sell eighty-five factories taken over during the War for arms production, preferably to trades unions, cooperative societies, local authorities or public utility societies. While the State should not compete with private enterprise in the manufacture of articles of general trade, national factories would be retained for areas where the government was the sole buyer. In these proposals Gretna was not mentioned.

A Cabinet meeting in February was concerned that too many armament factories proposed for retention were in the danger zone near London and the east coast.[58] In the same month the Ministry of Munitions set up a committee of inquiry to consider the future of the factories at Gretna and Waltham Abbey. Meanwhile the *Annandale Observer* had reported a glittering New Year Ball at Gretna 'prior to the closing of the factory'.[59]

The committee of inquiry

The committee of inquiry was chaired by Sir Edward Pearson, who had been appointed general contractor for building Gretna less than four years before. Two members of the committee were from the Ministry of Munitions, one from the Board of Trade, one from the Lands Directorate, and a member of parliament, Sir William Pearce. All but Pearce agreed that Gretna should replace Waltham Abbey as the main source of cordite in case of any future war. Gretna was modern and up to date, while Waltham was old and its capacity was too limited. It was also cheaper to produce cordite at Gretna than at

Waltham. They recognised that the factory was only useful for producing cordite, but thought 'it would be criminal to scrap it' as it was in an excellent state of maintenance and had cost a large sum to erect.[60]

Regarding the specialist plants, the committee advised that the ether plant should be retained on a commercial footing as a source of ether alcohol which, as the basis for solvents, would be required in many industries. With slight modification the plant could also be used for the production of ethyl alcohol which was a necessary component for the dye industry. They suggested that it would be advantageous to keep the production of a duty-free alcohol centralised and under government control.

The committee recommended that land near the factory should be turned into smallholdings as part of the scheme for resettling returning servicemen. The existing social and recreational facilities in Gretna and Eastriggs would provide an excellent base for a land scheme; many schemes had suffered because of their remoteness from facilities. Gretna and Eastriggs, then run as part of the factory, should be transferred to the local authorities so as no longer to be a cost on production. They concluded by suggesting that 'every encouragement should be given to induce new industries to start up at Gretna' with the government providing cheap power and use of infrastructure to help factory overheads; a foreshadow of the trading estates which were to be built in the 1930s.

Pearce disagreed. In a minority report he urged that the factory should be closed. It had cost an enormous amount, it was no longer needed and therefore the best action would be to cut losses once and for all rather than 'continue a huge factory in a locality with inherent disadvantages, which factory only a world war called into existence, and only the probability of a future world war could justify its existence'. If the War Office required a cordite factory they should keep Waltham Abbey.

Minutes of the committee suggest that there was not as wholehearted support for the majority viewpoint as their conclusions suggest.[61] While the land settlement lobby saw Gretna as an ideal place for such a scheme, industrialists were more dubious of the value of the plant. Furthermore, despite eulogies in the local press about the quality of the housing at Gretna, the local authority was not keen to take over the townships.

Gretna appeared to present excellent opportunities for land settlement: the government already owned nearly 9,000 acres and 'the social amenities of Eastriggs and Gretna are in such close proximity that there is no danger of the lives of settlers becoming dull and monotonous . . . Gretna might indeed offer a contribution to the solution of one of the problems of reconstruction as interesting and important as the output of the factory during the war'.

In contrast, an industrialist from Nobel, the explosives manufacturers, was much less hopeful of Gretna's industrial future. He saw little scope for the factory manufacturing munitions, asserting that 'the Trade' (private industry) could provide cordite cheaper. He considered the dye industry unlikely to be interested because they would rather start from scratch, and new trades would take so long to build up that the running charges would make them impracticable.

As for local authority interest, Dumfriesshire County Council, whose only involvement with Gretna during the War was policing, seemed mainly concerned about arrears of rates. The only mention of housing was a suggestion from the Local Government Board that the temporary houses might be sent to Lincolnshire for steelworkers in Scunthorpe.

The Pearson Committee officially presented their report in June 1919. Unofficially it must have been leaked, because the *Annandale Observer* commented favourably on its findings in an editorial on 23 May. It also reported protest meetings at Waltham Abbey. The editor saw no comparison from a military and strategic viewpoint: Waltham was near to the heart of the Empire; it was further for an enemy to fly to Gretna; 'It is time people in the provinces made an effective appeal against the vicious and unhealthy pull of London.

A week later the paper reported meetings at Waltham and Gretna. Waltham had 'engineered', a protest meeting in Trafalgar Square where pacifists had attacked the idea of having a munitions factory at all. At Gretna 2,000 people had called for 'a square deal'. If a factory was required then it should be judged on its technical merits. Much more harm would be done to Gretna, where unemployment would have a more serious effect and 'a beautiful social experiment run by all classes would be destroyed'.[62]

On 24 July, in response to a question in the Commons, the Minister of Munitions stated that the Cabinet had not yet considered the report. On 7 August the costs of Gretna were given at question time: the explosives factory had cost approximately £9.18 million, the cost of working the factory had been nearly £12.8 million and the value of the cordite produced was £15 million. If that had been bought from the USA it would have cost £23 million. The cost of the residential buildings, hutments and amenities at Gretna was £1.24 million which was included in the cost of the factory. On 27 October the minister stated that he could not yet answer about the future as 'the whole question of Gretna and certain other factories to form a nucleus of munitions manufacturing capacity is being considered afresh in the light of recent developments'.[63] What he meant was that the Cabinet was trying to persuade the army and navy to get their cordite from the same factory, the one at Gretna.

Meanwhile more answers in the Commons indicated the rundown taking place at Gretna. At the time of the armistice 11,477 were employed at the factory. In April 1919 the number was 3,000; by October the number had dropped to 1,319; by November it was 1,262. Nearly all the permanent houses remained occupied. By March 1920 production of cordite had ceased and the main employment was the repair of railway waggons. By June there were 909 industrial workers and 168 administrative staff; the whole place costing £20,000 a month to maintain. Empty hostels had been offered to neighbouring housing authorities. Carlisle was reported to have considered the idea but abandoned it because of difficulties of transporting people ten miles.[64] At Annan, only three miles away, the council preferred to pursue their own housing scheme, and the county saw no need.

Plans for land settlement disappeared behind a cloud of foggy answers about the price to be paid for the land by the Department of Agriculture for Scotland. Judging from the press and parliamentary answers, Gretna must have been awash with rumours of industrialists making offers for the factory, and sugar-beet growers/processors making offers for the land. In March 1921 the Department of Agriculture promised to make a statement soon, but nothing more was heard that year.

In November 1919 a special committee was appointed under Lord Moulton (who had been director-general of the explosives supply division) to decide the most economical arrangements, consistent with efficiency, for providing cordite for the army and the navy.[65] This committee concluded that Gretna should be retained and Waltham scrapped, but by the time it reported the factory had been transferred to the War Office who announced that they once again were reviewing Gretna's future.[66]

Winston Churchill, Secretary of State for War, had set up his own committee to consider the future of the national factories and was inclined towards keeping some of the factories and appointing a director-general to run them.[67] In the case of munitions the question was should it be Gretna, which produced far more cordite than was required, or Waltham, a 300-year-old Royal Ordnance factory, not really equipped for producing cordite? A counter argument was also canvassed: that the trade could satisfy much of the country's needs on its own.

Analysis was carried out of alternative ways of getting cordite and the likely amounts required. The Cabinet had decided to assume that no great war was likely for ten years, so that there was no need for productive capacity from private industry and two national factories. The General Staff, assuming a twenty-division war, agreed that Waltham could not cope but that Gretna would still have over-capacity. If new propellants were required, Waltham was unsuitable, but its discontinuance 'would raise political issues and the cost of maintaining Gretna would be very heavy and the prospect of alternative work there would not be great'.[68] The War Office was in a dilemma.

On 1 December 1920 the War Office committee reached its final, though contradictory, compromise conclusion,

> that the Government should be advised to retain Waltham Abbey for experimental and peace production and enter into an arrangement with the Trade for maintaining Gretna. So far as purely military considerations were considered it would suffice to retain Gretna for experimental work and peace production and close down and dispose of Waltham Abbey.

The decision in fact lay with the navy: would they agree to get cordite from Gretna rather than their own establishment at Holton Heath?

The issue returned to the Cabinet. The finance committee stated that Waltham Abbey was 'bad and old fashioned'.[69] The heavy capital investment in Gretna was needed in war. The War Office and the navy should sort out their differences. A War Office memorandum dated spring 1921 recorded that after discussions with the Admiralty, it was agreed that the army and navy must keep their cordite manufacture separate.[70] On 3 June 1921 the Cabinet agreed to retain Waltham Abbey, dispose of Gretna and subsidise the trade.

The decision was given to the House of Commons in reply to a question on 21 June 1921. On 29 June, again in answer to a question, the Secretary of State for War announced that Gretna had been put in the hands of the Disposal and Liquidation Commission to be sold in units or as one lot.

Disposal

The story was by no means over. It was three years before the grand auction was held. Meanwhile Gretna and other war assets were in the hands of a rather shadowy organisation, the Disposal and Liquidation Commission, set up by the Treasury to sell off war surplus stock all over the world. Its chairman was Sir Howard Frank, who had valued the Gretna lands in 1916.[71]

The three years to 1924 must have been a particularly awkward time for the remaining inhabitants while local representatives of the Disposal and Liquidation Commission ran down the townships and the plant. Parliamentary answers given indicate the hopelessness that must have been felt locally. In March 1922 it was reported that no work was being carried out at Gretna beyond the destruction of dangerous buildings and the preparation of assets for sale.[72] While every effort was being made to employ local people on dismantling and removing purchases, the government could not insist that firms buying plant at Gretna would do so.[73] Efforts were being made to find purchasers for the whole place, but despite rumours nothing materialised: it would have to be sold off piecemeal.[74] There was talk of machinery being advertised in the back streets of London and accusations of corruption. The Chancellor of the Exchequer asked for evidence, but nothing further was recorded. The only large purchases were by the Department of Agriculture for Scotland, of 4,000 acres and 24 bungalows for a land settlement scheme but that had involved dispossessing existing tenant farmers.[75]

In May 1923, there was a short debate about Gretna. Dr Chapple, elected as member for Dumfries in 1922, asked the War Office why successive governments had given no reasons for ignoring the report of the Pearson committee. 'It was intended by the government of the day, and the architects who designed it, to be a permanent centre for the manufacture of munitions. If not, it was the most criminal blunder of which this country could be guilty'. Instead of 454 empty houses in Gretna, the housing situation in Waltham could have been eased. Rather than answer, the Financial Secretary to the War Office chose to ridicule promises in Chapple's election address, to keep a factory which he knew was 'in ruins'. When pressed by others about exploring alternative uses for the factory, the Minister retorted, 'how can the War Office deal with an industrial factory'.[76] The rundown continued; the policy was to dispose of the property and stores as rapidly as possible. Auctioneers were appointed in Carlisle and the sale, in more than 600 lots, arranged for July 1924.

There appeared one last chance to salvage Gretna when the first Labour Government took office in 1924. Questioners pressed that the sale should be reconsidered; that it was against socialist principles to sell national assets; that it was wrong to sell land belonging to the nation when socialists stood for nationalisation and reconstruction of industry. But Major Attlee, Under Secretary at the War Office, argued that the government had no alternative but to go ahead. The decision to sell had been made in 1921. In any case the factory would make a loss and it would be a violation of socialist principles to run at a loss.[77]

Locally there were hopes that the sale might produce a 'fairy godmother'. Gretna's virtues as a holiday resort had been mooted in a locally printed pamphlet by an unknown author who described:

> ...houses built in a variety of designs according to the latest models; wooden bungalows of a very convenient nature; good shops; liquor trade in the hands of the Liquor Board ... The laying out of a golf course is a matter that has simply been delayed owing to the changeover of the land in the neighbourhood from the War Office to the Board of Agriculture ... The great Cordite Factory, with its offices and Townships, should form an object of interest and marvel.[78]

The auctioneers' particulars[79] of the residential areas were equally glowing but the hopes were stillborn. On 26 July the *Dumfries and Galloway Standard and Advertiser* reported the sale as 'a dismal failure'. After four days it had produced £82,456. Only bungalows, small plant and farms were sold at the auction. Mass meetings at Gretna protested against the policy of a Labour administration in allowing 'that fiasco called a sale' to go on. Why, it was asked, was land being sold to some of the original owners for less than half that the government had paid?

In fact the Government had been shamed into action before the sale. On 2 July the Home Secretary informed the Cabinet that there was some feeling in the Labour Party that the Government was in too much of a hurry to dispose of national factories and it was agreed that 'the Minister of Health and the Secretary of State for Scotland should make enquiries into the suitability of Gretna for the purposes of industry, afforestation combined with smallholdings, public health or any other purpose'.[80] On 22 July a Cabinet committee was set up of ministers for the Treasury, War, Scotland, and Works 'to consider reports ... regarding the results of the auction and proposals for utilizing Gretna'.[81] On 30 July the Cabinet agreed to stop further sales.[82]

The Minister of Health, and the Secretary of State for Scotland had moved quickly after the Cabinet meeting on 2 July and had asked for reports from all departments concerned. Replies were received from the Air Council, the Scottish Board of Health, the Board of Agriculture for Scotland, the Forestry Commission, the Ministry of Health, the General Board of Control (Scotland), the War Office, the Ministry of Agriculture and Fisheries, the Air Ministry and the Treasury. Many had sent staff to visit Gretna; most apparently went on 15 July! The reports of some, including the Scottish Board of Health, implied that it was their first visit and that they were surprised at what they found. Together the reports are illuminating because they provide a picture of a place still quite lively, despite the negative attitude of the disposals commission.[83]

Regarding specific ideas: the Scottish Board of Control considered that

Gretna 'did not offer any inducements' as a place for the feeble-minded, and in any case the neighbouring counties and burghs had just provided themselves with a sanitorium. The Forestry Commission considered the land too valuable for forestry; the Board of Agriculture had taken all the land it could for smallholdings; the War Office considered that Gretna might be useful as a vocational training centre in place of that at Catterick, but they would need to repurchase 300 acres of land at Eastriggs.

The Ministry of Health produced the longest statement and in view of their responsibilities for housing and town planning (in England and Wales!), perhaps the most illuminating. They regretted the way departmental divisions had affected Gretna, saying 'the more we examined it the firmer became our impression that it would be regrettable if the possiblities of making a more or less model township were permitted to lapse'. They noted a feeling of doubt, uncertainty, and incipient depression hanging over the district:

> The impression is conveyed that the dominating wish is to convert anything and everything into cash and to get out quickly and at all costs. The local authority, taking their cue from the atmosphere of 'unload and get out at any price', proceed to undertake the very minimum of their statutory duties and that they appear to do a little begrudgingly ... (The local authority in Annan) never had much voice or interest in Gretna. They observe the rapid decline and are not the least enthused to save at any cost of effort or money what may well appear to them to be a sinking ship ... The local authority should be persuaded to undertake their duties fully and enthusiastically.[84]

The valuation rolls of Dumfriesshire County Council show that the government continued to get rid of their holdings as quickly as they could. In 1925–6 the liquidation commission was still responsible for the power station and mains at Eastriggs, about seventy houses and workshops, and the shops in Central Avenue, Gretna. All the wooden bungalows and hostels and their adjoining land had been sold to estate agents in Blackburn, Blackpool and Carlisle. By the end of 1926 the Treasury Surplus Stores Department had divested itself of almost everything except a rather fine social club, and this they auctioned in May 1927. The factory disappears from the rolls in 1925–6, presumably because it was pulled down. Today there is no sign of it.

Dumfriesshire County Council, as the principal local authority appears to have taken little interest in the sale. It bought nine properties, including the police barracks, the school and four houses for their roadmen. The county's main interest was still to recover the seven years' unpaid rates on government property at Gretna and the dispute hinged on a private agreement by the ministry to get water from Lower Annandale.

Eventually, in a settlement of April 1923, when the government agreed to pay a sum corresponding to the rates demand without admitting liability, the county adopted the sewers, and certain of the roads, but insisted that it would construct new footpaths and fences and surface the roads, at the government's expense, and that the remaining temporary huts should cease to be used as dwellings.[85] Nevertheless the temporary houses continued to be valued, and presumably occupied, long after they had been sold to the estate agents.

Conclusion

Poor Gretna; the story is in effect Cinderella in reverse with the local authority cast in the role of stepmother. It has no happy ending except that Gretna now exists as an ordinary part of Scotland. But, in many respects it remained for years an extraordinary place—a halfway-house between garden suburb and the Essex plotlands. At the north end, lining Victoria Avenue, Empire Way, Annan Road and Central Avenue, lay the neat brick semi-detached houses and converted brick hostels, almost all in private ownership; at the south end the lines of temporary wooden huts rented from the English estate agents. In 1946 the county council at last moved into Gretna to solve its housing problems by buying land from the estate agents. There the county replaced some of the World War I 'prefabs' with new prefabs which remain to this day, refurbished and popular. In the last few years Annandale and Eskdale District Council, the present housing authority, has also built new estates. Many residents commute the ten miles to Carlisle, which the city council had found difficult to conceive in 1921.

So what was learnt from Gretna? Perhaps first and foremost the importance of power to achieve ideas. As in other emergencies, when the need required it, money was found and ideas reached fruition. Rational planning makes good sense and is relatively easy to achieve when societal objectives are unified and simple, and powers are available. The building of Gretna is a good example. Rational planning is much more difficult to achieve in a pluralist society when power is diverse and a wide variety of attitudes are allowed to flourish. Then pragmatism (to deal with issues as they arise) and inertia (to leave things alone whenever possible) become the dominant forces. Again the decline of Gretna provides a good example. After all the arguments in favour of rationalising explosives supply, the army still uses Waltham Abbey and the navy uses Holton Heath!

Between the wars four million houses were built in Britain. Idealists like Frederic Osborn and Trystan Edwards urged that these should be built in new towns to spread people more evenly all over the country and provide better environments. Proposals for garden cities and garden villages appeared in many of the regional plans of the 1920s. Lloyd George, in 1929, promised to use the regional plans as part of his programme to conquer unemployment. But only Welwyn Garden City and a handful of 'satellite towns' were started. Instead the government concentrated on providing as many houses as possible wherever builders and local authorities would build them. That policy was accepted by Raymond Unwin who as housing and planning inspector in the Ministry of Health during the 1920s was involved in the great housing drive. Defending it in a letter to Osborn, Unwin wrote

> probably most are built in the wrong place; but if not built there the right place would not have been found I fear. Folk can't be allowed to pass a certain degree of overcrowding while the world learns planning.[86]

There is nothing left of Lloyd George's social experiment at Gretna, except the effect it had on subsequent industrial relations. In contrast Unwin did leave a memorial. Sir Lawrence Weaver wrote in 1926:

The need for housing vast munition populations in new areas led in some cases to the planning of towns and suburbs in which the experience laboriously gained at Letchworth, Hampstead Garden Suburb, Ruislip and elsewhere was used with admirable effect ... The war village of Gretna, the home of a great industrial army engaged in making explosives gave great opportunity which was well grasped by Dr Raymond Unwin and those who worked with him ... It involved the solution in an incredibly short time not only of great housing and engineering problems but also of perplexing social questions known generally as 'welfare'.[87]

Furthermore, Weaver emphasised the transformation that Unwin and his team brought about in housing design, by including a lengthy quotation from a wartime description of Gretna by Sir Robert Lorimer:

The sane and extremely simple type of permanent house that was erected shows what a far road has been travelled since the days of the first cheap cottage exhibition at Letchworth, where the plain man went about tearing his hair in the hopeless endeavour to find here and there a cottage the designer of which showed the most rudimentary elements of common sense. Here all was plain and straightforward, of pleasant and reasonable proportion and mercifully devoid of ornament or prettiness ... The admirer of the Kate Greenaway type of garden city house doubtless found the Gretna variety too reminiscent of what Morris called the 'brick box with the slate lid', but these houses had to be rattled up at a tremendous pace, and a plain roof in which there are neither dormers nor gables is obviously cheaper and more rapidly constructed and slated than one that is cut up by features.[88]

Gretna provided the model for millions more houses built since.

Appendix 4A War housing in Scotland 1914–18

Place	*Number of houses*	*Date*	*Agent*	*Type of agreement*	*Firm or factory*
1 Housing for Government employees					
Rosyth	292	1915	National Housing Company Ltd	deficit subsidy	Admiralty dockyard
Rosyth	310	1916			
Rosyth	1,000	1917			
Invergordon	126	1916	direct		Admiralty
Greenock Craigieknowes	102	1916	local authority	Admiralty grant	Admiralty torpedo factory
Gourock	48	1916	direct		Admiralty torpedo factory
	50	1917	direct		
2 Housing for private industry					
Mid Lanark: Mossend					
North Road	100	1915	local authority	Min of Munitions grants	Beardmores
Coronation Road	50	1915	local authority*		Beardmores
Calder Road	50	1915	local authority*		Beardmores
Dalmuir	530	1915	?	War Office loan	Beardmores

Inchinnan	60	1915	Beardmores to plans by LGBS	War Office loan	Beardmores
Mid Lanark No 2					
Carmyle	50	1916	direct	post-war agreement	Colvilles
Calder Road	50	1916	direct		Beardmores
Coronation Road	24	1916	direct		Beardmores
Thankerton	76	1916	direct		Beardmores
Cambuslang	150	1916	direct		Stewart & Lloyds
Clydebank	160	1916	?	excess profits	John Brown & Co
Alexandria	150	1916	direct		Armstrong Whitworth
Glengarnock	250	1917	direct	post-war agreement	Colvilles
Port Glasgow	400	1917	?	excess profits	Russell & Co
Clydebank	100	1918	direct with Office of Works	post-war agreement	Singers
3 Housing for Ministry of Munitions Explosives Division					
Gretna	941 + 388†	1915	Ministry direct		National factory

Notes * 1915 schemes at Coronation Road and Calder Road were completed direct in 1916.
† 388 houses realised from 97 convertible hostels.

Sources: LGBS, *Annual Report for 1918* [Cmd. 230]
Official history of the Ministry of Munitions, vol. V

Notes

Part 1

1. This section is based on D Whitham, 'Like honey from the carcase of the lion', a paper to a Planning History Group seminar, Liverpool, March 1979.
2. P Geddes, *Cities in evolution* 1915.
3. Royal Commission on Housing of the Working Classes in Scotland, Rural and Urban (RCHS), *Minutes of evidence* 1922, para. 5828.
4. Scottish Record Office (SRO), DD6/426.
5. SRO, DD6/426.
6. Quoted in Scottish Land Enquiry Committee, *Report* 1914, p.381.
7. T W Hamilton, evidence to RCHS 6 May 1914, para. 29, p.495 *et seq*; *How Greenock grew* 1947.
8. Hamilton, lamenting the failure of co-partnership in Greenock, explained that the site offered to the torpedo workers in 1912 was that of the venture of 1866, and at the same feu-duty of £16 per acre. 'Thus the same ground was offered twice and taken back twice.' (1947).
9. Local Government Board for Scotland (LGBS), *Annual Report for 1912* [1913 Cd 6728].
10. SRO, DD6/429
11. SRO, DD6/432.
12. LGBS, *Annual report for 1914* [1916 Cd 8041].
13. Hansard, *Commons* 27 July 1914.
14. RCHS, *Evidence.*
15. *The Scotsman* 24 May 1910.
16. SRO, DD6/428.
17. Ibid.
18. SRO, DD6/431, 19 March 1914.
19. P Wilding, 'Towards exchequer subsidies for housing, 1906–1914', in *Social and Economic Administration* vol. vi 1, pp.3–15.
20. Hansard, *Commons*, 31 July 1914.
21. Housing Act 1914, 4–5 George V, C.31.
22. LGBS, *Annual report for 1914* [1916 Cd 8041].
23. Housing (Rosyth Dockyard) Act 1915, 5–6 George V, [1916 Cd 8041]. C.49.
24. SRO, DD6/444.
25. SRO, DD6/542.
26. For subsequent histories of the housing companies and of the SSHA see Tom Begg, *Fifty Special Years: a Study in Scottish Housing* 1987.
27. LGBS, *Annual Report for 1915* [Cd.8273] and *Annual Report for 1916* [1917–18 Cd 8517].
28. LGBS, *Annual Report for 1917* [1918 Cd 9020].
29. RCHS, *Report* [Cd. 8731], 1917–18: p.xiv.
30. LGBS, *Annual Report for 1918* [1919 Cmd 230].
31. Public Record Office (PRO), and *Official History of the Ministry of Munitions* (Official History), vol.V.
32. PRO, RECO1/463.
33. At 1911 Census, population of England and Wales was 36.070 million, population of Scotland 4.761 million, ie 11.7 per cent of that of Great Britain, compared with an estimated housing deficiency of 37.5 per cent of Great Britain's in 1916.
34. J Carmichael *Building industry after the war* [Cd.9197], 1918: p.vii. Carmichael

was appointed chairman of the Ministry of Munitions works board by Addison in 1917. J Tudor Walters *Building construction in connection with the provision of dwellings for the working classes* [Cd 9191], 1918, p.vii.

35. See M Swenarton, *Homes Fit for Heroes*, 1981, ch. 5.
36. Ibid, p.110.
37. See D Whitham, 'The first sixty years of council housing' Tables 1.1 and 1.2 in J English (ed) *The Future of Council Housing* 1982.

Part 2

38. This section is based on J Minett, 'Gretna – Britain's first government sponsored new town', a paper to a Planning History Group conference, Edinburgh, March 1978.
39. PRO, MUN5/365/1122/21.
40. PRO, MUN7/254.
41. PRO, MUN7/260.
42. PRO, MUN7/255.
43. PRO, MUN5/158/1122.7/1; note by G Duckworth.
44. G Cherry, *The Evolution of British Town Planning* 1974.
45. W Creese, *The Legacy of Raymond Unwin*, 1967; R Unwin in P Waterhouse and R Unwin, *Old Towns and New Needs* 1912.
46. PRO, MUN7/255.
47. Official History, vol.V, p.76.
48. PRO, MUN5/263/27.12.
49. PRO, MUN7/257, (23.11.18).
50. R Unwin, *Town Planning in Practice* 1909.
51. Official History, vol.V, ch.8, p.76.
52. Ibid, p.78.
53. Burnham in Ministry of Munitions, *HM Factory at Gretna: Description of Plant and Process* 1919.
54. F Osborn, *New Towns after the War* 1942.
55. 'New Townsman' (F Osborn), *New Towns after the War* 1917.
56. Ministry of Health, *Principles to be Followed in Dealing with Unhealthy Areas* 1920.
57. PRO, CAB23/9/514.
58. PRO, CAB23/9/533.
59. *Annandale Observer* 17 January 1919.
60. PRO, MUN5/151/1122.1/9.
61. PRO, MUN5/159/1122.7/24.
62. *Annandale Observer*, 30 May 1919.
63. Hansard, *Commons* **120**, col. 254.
64. Hansard, *Commons* **132**, col. 682.
65. PRO, CAB27/71, FC.16.
66. Hansard, *Commons* **129**, col. 2050.
67. PRO, WO32/4900.
68. Ibid., 2 November 1920.
69. PRO, CAB27/71, FC32.
70. PRO, WO32/4901.
71. The author found it difficult to locate records of the Disposal and Liquidation

Commission except for some annual reports and accounts, but no accounts were found for 1925 or later when most of Gretna was sold. The principal references in Hansard are defensive statements refuting press accusations of fraud. To this day there is talk in Gretna of members of the commission lining their pockets from the sale of surplus stock.

72. Hansard, *Commons* **151**, col. 2212.
73. Hansard, *Commons* **152**, col. 1076.
74. Hansard, *Commons* **155**, col. 1053.
75. Ibid.
76. Hansard, *Commons* **163**, col. 2253 *et seq.*
77. Hansard, *Commons* **175**, col. 582.
78. Anon. *Guide to Gretna* Gretna, nd.
79. Tiffen & Gibbings, *Sale Particular for Gretna* Carlisle, 1924.
80. PRO, CAB23/48,C39.(24)22.
81. PRO, CAB27.243/NF(24).
82. PRO, CAB23/48,C45(24)5.
83. PRO, CAB27.243/NF.
84. Ibid.
85. Dumfries-shire CC Minute Book, 1923.
86. R Unwin, undated letter to Osborn, early 1930s.
87. L Weaver, *Cottages: their Planning, Design and Materials* 1926, p.322.
88. Ibid., pp.324–8.

5 '£8 cottages for Glasgow citizens' Innovations in municipal house-building in Glasgow in the inter-war years[1]

Nicholas J Morgan

The first part of this story at least is well known. In 1919, in response to the requirement of the Housing Town Planning etc (Scotland) Act for local authorities to specify their future housing needs and plans, Glasgow Corporation submitted to the Scottish Office a detailed breakdown of the City's housing scheme. To 'adequately supply the needs of their district' the city required 57,000 new houses—of which 21,000 were to relieve overcrowding, 3,000 to replace houses 'which should be closed and demolished', 7,000 to house those displaced by improvement schemes planned under the 1890 Housing of the Working Classes Act, 15,000 to meet the estimated natural increase in the city's population between 1919 and 1922, 5,000 to meet the needs of new industries, and 6,000 to house demobilised members of the forces. All of the 57,000 houses were to be provided by the local authority. The estimated acreage required to build these houses at a density of twelve cottage dwellings per acre (or 24 for tenement houses) was put at 4,735 acres—at the time the proposal was drawn up the City possessed only 400 acres of approved building land, including the sites of Kennyhill and Riddrie (105 acres), and Mosspark (174 acres). Seven thousand of these houses (including 500 temporary wooden huts) were to be built (on around 600 acres) in three years from 19 August 1919.[2] The Act, and the Corporation's scheme, seemed to offer the realisation of earlier demands made for widespread municipal involvement in general needs housebuilding. Articulated in a Labour Party campaign in 1913 led by John Wheatley for 'Eight-pound cottages for Glasgow citizens', the scheme was to be financed out of the surplus of the City's tramway operations.[3] These demands were revived during McKinnon-Woods' enquiry into the Glasgow rent-strikes; by 1915, however, the onus had shifted to central government—it was 'from the State' that James Stewart believed that the 'million' required to solve Glasgow's housing problem should come.[4]

The realisation of these demands, and the Corporation's ambitious scheme, was never achieved—by 1922 the local authority had built only 2,242 houses, by the end of 1929 this figure stood at 21,939, by 1939 50,277, less than 7,000 short of the estimated requirement of twenty years earlier.[5] This failure to achieve the quantitative objectives of 1919, largely reflected in the experiences of other Scottish local authorities, has led historians to set housebuilding in the inter-war years in a framework governed by pessimism. This has been reinforced by a heavily critical, but largely superficial, appraisal of the actual structures that were erected by local-authorities.[6] In addition the pessimism has seemed all the more justified when data collected shortly before the outbreak of World War II showed that despite new building, nearly 24 per cent of all Scottish homes remained overcrowded—in Glasgow the total was around 30 per cent of all houses. The findings of the 1935 overcrowding survey led the Corporation to estimate that 100,000 houses were needed immediately to overcome the problem, far more than the 20,000 houses required to relieve overcrowding in 1919.[7] So persuasive has this pessimism been that few scholars have been concerned to investigate the detailed events of housing in the inter-war years in Glasgow, as if the bare figures told the whole affair.

This chapter seeks to examine some of the reasons for the so called 'failures' of the inter-war period. It will not cover all of them, but will rather present a summary of the main areas in which obstructions to the effectiveness of

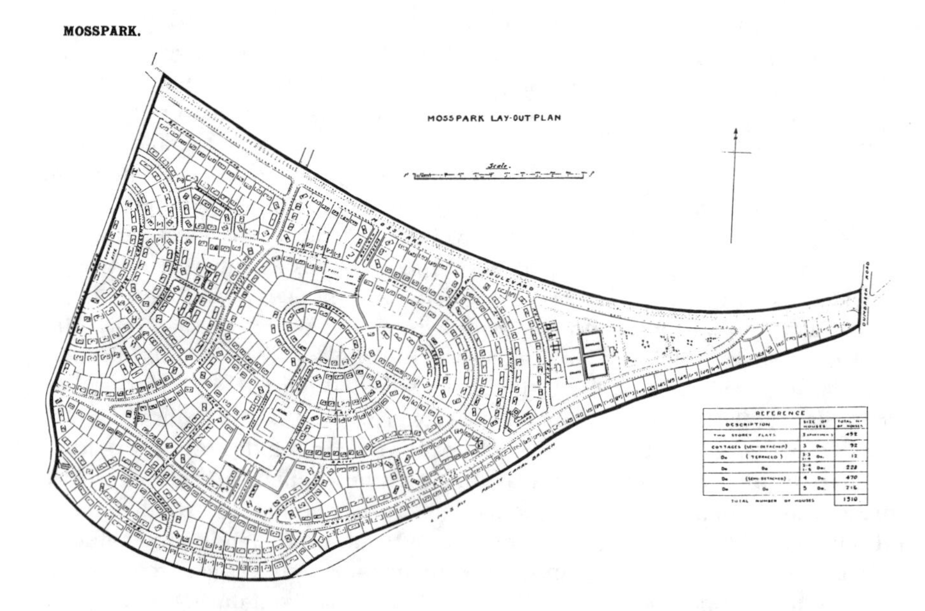

Figure 5.1 Mosspark: Glasgow's garden city housing scheme developed on a beautifully contoured site

housing policy in the City were to be found. In particular, having summarised these problems, it will concentrate on the question of building materials, and innovations in building techniques. The final part of the chapter will examine briefly the sources of innovations in local authority building during the inter-war years, and suggest some of the consequences for post-war building which stemmed from these innovations. The chapter has been written using a variety of sources: chiefly the minutes of Glasgow Corporation, and particularly of the Special Committee on Housing (later the Housing Committee), associated committee papers, Housing Department compendiums, Dean of Guild Court records, business records of firms involved in local authority contracts, and some parliamentary papers and also newspapers (mainly the

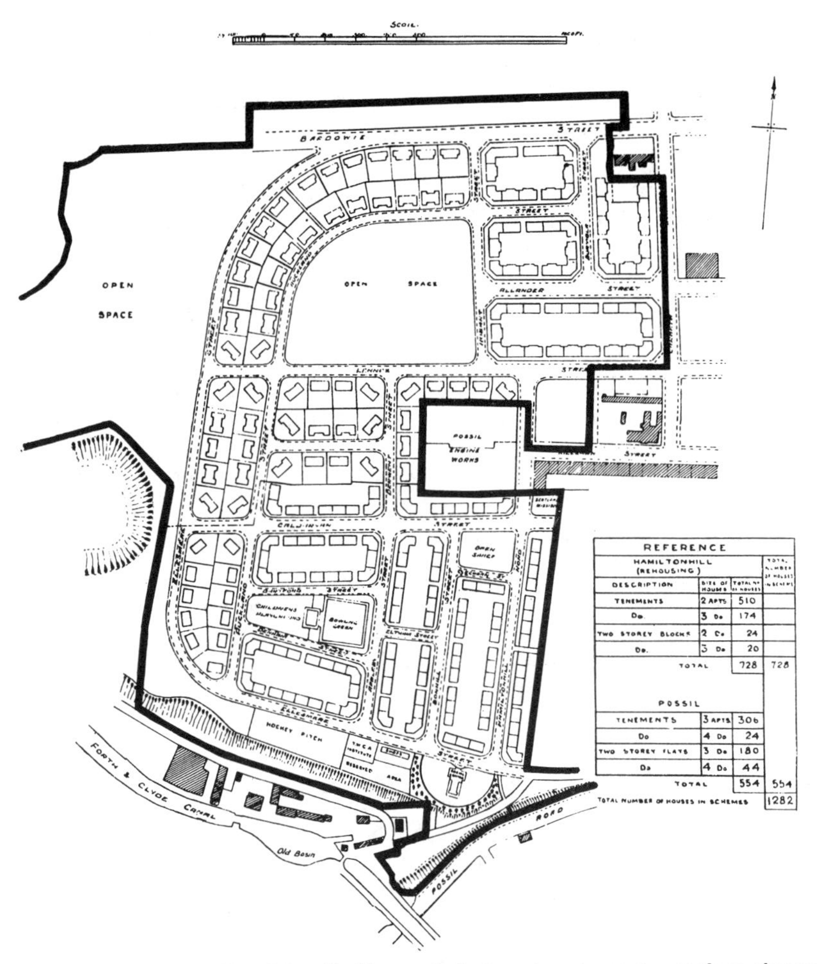

HAMILTONHILL (REHOUSING)			TOTAL NUMBER OF HOUSES IN SCHEMES
DESCRIPTION	SIZE OF HOUSES	TOTAL No. OF HOUSES	
TENEMENTS	2 APTS	510	
Do.	3 Do	174	
TWO STOREY BLOCKS	2 Do	24	
Do.	3 Do	20	
TOTAL		728	728
POSSIL			
TENEMENTS	3 APTS	306	
Do	4 Do	24	
TWO STOREY FLATS	3 Do	180	
Do	4 Do	44	
TOTAL		554	554
TOTAL NUMBER OF HOUSES IN SCHEMES			1282

Figure 5.2 Hamiltonhill and Possil: Glasgow's first venture in post-war slum clearance, with possil engine works as a centre-piece

Glasgow Herald).[8] It should not be considered an exhaustive treatment, nor is it the product of completed research. It does, however, shed a new light on house-building in the inter-war years, redressing some of the pessimism that has informed previous interpretations, and hopefully offering new avenues for research which others might wish to pursue.

A municipal mission

When Thomas Nisbet, the city engineer, reported to the Council in May 1919 on the proposed housing bill he pointed to a major drawback in its provisions—that it 'gives the Local Government Board absolutely autocratic powers'—there should, wrote Nisbet, 'be some measure of freedom of action given to a Local Authority—so far as housing is concerned. This Bill gives none'.[9] Nisbet was concerned with clauses that enjoined local authorities to refer all site and type plans, specifications and tenders, to the Scottish Office before building could commence. He was also clearly concerned at the implications this had for the independence of local government action. For all that a debate had raged in Glasgow before the War on the extent and nature of Corporation intervention in the private housing market none of the parties involved had been in any doubt that intervention would come from the municipality rather than from central Government. Indeed, it was central Government that prevented the municipality from fulfilling its historic task. Daniel Macaulay Stevenson, Lord Provost of the City, expressed this view in 1914, in the preface to *Municipal Glasgow its Evolution and Enterprises*:

> We are still in the morning of the times. There are many other ideals requiring the consideration of municipalists. Not least of these is the getting of Parliament to devolve upon the municipalities such powers as would render for ever unnecessary the waste of time, energy and money required every few years to obtain authority for carrying out the most obviously necessary municipal undertakings.[10]

The 1919 Act did the reverse of this. Nisbet's reactions prefaced a thinly disguised battle between Glasgow and central Government, which was to delay building projects by up to two years and in the process dissipate both effort and energy. The battle lines were drawn before Nisbet's report was considered as draft schemes had already been prepared in advance of the passage of the Act. The Special Committee on Housing complained in a report to the Corporation in April that:

> Glasgow local authority might safely be presumed to have suficient knowledge of the requirements of the city to be able to judge of what is satisfactory, and they feel that if they had been allowed to proceed without supervision of lay-out and type-plans they would now have been well advanced instead of nothing whatever having been done.[11]

Later in May 1919 John Wheatley, whose scheme for eight-pound cottages for Glasgow citizens had been based firmly on the premise that the Corporation would act as the provider of housing, urged the council to build regardless of Scottish Office delays.[12] As a key officer in the Corporation Nisbet was in the van of the conflict. He complained to the Town Clerk in September 1919 of the bureaucracy involved:

I wonder what the next step to be taken by the Government will be to add to the labour in the connection with Housing questions. I suggest that you call a meeting of the Committee to consider this, and whether it will be necessary for the Committee to engage a number of complete government departments to give effect to the new proposals.[13]

Disputes over the acquisition of land, permitted heights of ceilings, the size of oriel windows, the width of footpaths, internal fittings and the use of types of materials all served to delay the crucial moment at which work began on site. This was not just a Glasgow problem—'the 1919 Act was wrecked through every little authority having to send their plans to the Board of Health to sit on for a year or 18 months' complained an official from Hamilton in 1924.[14] And of course the 1919 Act had provided the greatest opportunity to tackle the problem quickly. In the case of Glasgow however, where ambitions and expectations were greater, the acrimony ran deeper and lasted longer. When Robert Bruce began his drawn-out 'overspill' conflict with central Government after World War II he was merely continuing a fight that had been begun by Nisbet nearly thirty years earlier.[15] Nor were Glasgow's relations with neighbouring local authorities much better, as the abortive attempt to instigate a joint town planning scheme between Glasgow, Dumbarton, Lanarkshire and Renfrewshire revealed. Glasgow's attempts to impinge on the land of neighbouring counties were strenuously resisted. Dumbarton County Council, for example, objected

strenuously to the Glasgow proposal for invasion of our territory at three points. In particular my committee feel that workmen's houses should not be erected in the area of 122.42 acres in proximity to Bearsden. The latter as you are no doubt aware is a residential district with many fine houses . . .[16]

The effectiveness of central control, and local administration, was determined by the available level of experience upon which newly created departments and sections could draw. At both central and local level this expertise was negligible. Perhaps the most effective figure in Edinburgh, Sir Joshua Walker Smith, was poached first to London and then to the private sector.[17] Glasgow was more fortunate in being able to appoint the talented Peter Fyfe its first director of housing in 1919.[18] However Fyfe lacked a department; following his appointment he submitted a detailed memorandum outlining the staffing requirements needed to 'accomplish the great work which lies before the Housing Department in a satisfactory manner as expeditiously as possible'. He proposed five branches, dealing with engineering, architecture, surveying, reconstruction and clerical duties; these were to be staffed partly by transfers of experienced staff from the City Engineer's Department (notably the chief engineer and Fyfe's assistant director John Bryce, and chief architect Robert Horn) and also by 'a considerable addition' of new staff.[19] However although staffing was gradually built up in the 1920s appointments tended to be made on the basis of what might now be called 'crisis management'.[20] Similarly the development of procedures to effect policy was of necessity piecemeal—this applied through the range of functions—planning, building, allocations and housing management (although these last two were undertaken by officers of the City Improvement Department).[21] That anyone could conceive of undertaking such a massive building programme as that put forward by Glasgow in 1919 (prior to which the Corporation had only built slightly over 2,000 houses) with no adequate existing administrative infrastructure seems astonishing. It reflects both the muddle-headedness of central Government expectations of local authority competence, and the confidence that Glasgow Corporation officials possessed in their own ability. It was a major part of the argument of the minority report of the Royal Commission on Housing in 1917 that the burden that would be placed on local authorities by the type of schemes that the Commission had been established to justify would be far beyond the competence of local officials.[22]

Within the Housing Department a division devoted to direct labour gradually evolved, but only in the face of severe hostility both from central government and from a large proportion of council members.[23] For the most part the local authority relied on private builders to undertake public housing contracts. The role of builders and the structure of the building industry during these years is crucial to this discussion, and has largely been misunderstood. 'Private enterprise', wrote John Butt, had 'atrophied' during this period.[24] Such a comment may be one interpretation of the available data for the completion of houses for the private sector (with or without subsidy) in Scotland between 1919 and 1939.[25] However it hardly reflects the fact that the private building industry, far from wasting away, was pivotal in the construction of the majority of local authority housing schemes during this period. Pivotal because it provided the labour and contracting expertise to both start and finish the job. Pivotal also, because in entering into contracts with local authorities that could and did take between eighteen months and two years to settle after completion, the private builders were placing in the hands of the local authorities credit without which they could not have built. As we shall see, private builders were also responsible for prompting the local authorities to explore and exploit new building methods. To suggest atrophy of the building industry in Scotland, and particularly in Glasgow, is also to misunderstand the events of the five years or so before the war. Far from atrophying, the building industry had been assassinated by the budget of 1909–10, and in particular by the introduction of Increment Duty on undeveloped building sites and also on ground annuals.[26] 'I may say', wrote the builder Archibald Stewart to Sir John Lindsay:

> that my late firm built in their day several thousand houses and greater improvements were effected from the commencement to the stoppage of these building operations by the 1910 Finance Act that never took place in any similar period in Glasgow.[27]

Stewart, like other builders, reacted to the Act by ceasing building operations and turning to the full time management of the properties he had retained as investments.[28] As a result of misguided central government intervention the building industry in Glasgow was decimated and the housing market was grossly distorted, leading to the conflicts over rents of 1915, and further intervention in the market through the Rent and Mortgage Restriction Act.[29] Almost a generation of builders withdrew from business and it is a surprise that there were any builders in the city left to take up the challenge of municipal undertakings in 1919.

Among those builders who had remained there was a small group of innovative entrepreneurs who sought to overcome some of the structural difficulties of the industry (these were largely the result of widespread multi-contracting through a variety of specialist trades) by taking on the role of single contractors.[30] This method of organisation, essential if contracts were to be managed efficiently and quickly, had been the preferred choice of John Wilson, Architectural Inspector to the Local Government Board, who in 1915 compiled a special report on house design and construction for the Royal Commission on Housing.[31] It was also the preferred choice of Glasgow's housing administrators for larger contracts, but faced opposition from vested interests within the Corporation, from small craft-employers and from the craft unions themselves.[32] Opposition to single contractors led to the adoption by these reactionary elements of policies of non-cooperation both with the corporation and the contractors.[33] This was aided and abetted by continuing trade disputes throughout the period (such as the joiners' strike of May 1920) and a reluctance by the craft unions to allow overtime on Corporation schemes.[34] This dispute within the industry was compounded by a chronic lack of skilled labour, which persisted throughout the period despite efforts at local and national level to increase the pool of trained labour.[35]

A quest for innovation

Further preventing the rapid accomplishment of the objectives of the 1919 and subsequent Acts was the problem of chronic shortages and the expense of traditional building materials, particularly bricks.[36] As we have seen, by the end of 1924 around 5,000 houses had been completed, while costs (for a cottage divided into three apartments) had fluctuated from £721 in October 1919 to a peak of £895 in September 1920 down to £425 in June 1924.[37] During this period the Corporation had purchased brickworks in Dalry in Ayrshire and contracted to take the total output of several others.[38] Production of houses, however, remained unsatisfactory. It was in this context, to be found in all the major urban centres in the UK, that a national search was launched for new building types and materials led by the government's Standardisation and New Methods of Construction Committee. By 1924 the Government enjoined local authorities to exploit any new material which would reduce the cost of construction and expedite production without prejudice to durability or appearance.[39] The penalty for neglecting innovations in building materials was a possible withdrawal of the subsidy offered under the Act. In the sphere of innovation, however, specialist authors on building have been harsh in their treatment of Scottish local authorities. In her book, *The British Building Industry*, published in 1966, Marion Bowley offered the following assessment: 'examples of extreme unwillingness to use even the most efficient of the non-traditional methods are provided by the behaviour of local housing authorities in Scotland', which were, she suggested, innately conservative.[40] This damming indictment, in a work which has become the standard for historians of the construction industry, has only served to support the pessimistic view of Scottish local authority building propounded by the majority of urban historians.

However in Glasgow the Corporation had begun experimentation before the materials and labour crisis had become apparent. By the end of 1918 it had decided to sponsor the erection of a series of experimental blocks at Gilshochill. The four blocks of unusual cottage flats were built with brick walls, stone walls, patent concrete walls, and concrete block walls. In June 1919 the tender price for the brick block was the lowest by over £200.[41] In addition members of the Special Committee on Housing began a series of visits to other sites which were exploiting new methods, both within the United Kingdom (for example the Unit Construction Company's estate at Braintree) and also on the continent (Corolite concrete housing in Holland).[42] Under the energetic leadership of Peter Fyfe the housing department began to make a variety of experiments in producing its own substitutes for brickwork—equipment was purchased for the manufacture of up to nine million clinker bricks per year.[43] The need to introduce practical innovations on schemes was clearly apparent as the supply of materials became increasingly unreliable.[44] Between January and the end of 1922 the Corporation planned (with the approval of the Board of Health) six housing schemes which were to contain at least 600 houses (about half of the total in the schemes) built from concrete or similar materials. This included the first direct labour scheme at Drumoyne and the Cathcart Road scheme built by the National Building Guild with terrazzo blocks.[45] For the Hawthorn Street scheme the Corporation petitioned the Board of Health to approve a variation in the plans to allow concrete block houses to be built 'to vary the monotony of an all brick scheme'.[46] On the majority of these schemes concrete blocks were built on site with plant owned either by the Corporation or the Board of Health. Contractors on existing schemes also recognised the potential cost saving offered by new materials. John Mactaggart, whose £1.8 million contract for the building of 1,500 houses at Mosspark was the largest single project undertaken by the Corporation in the inter-war years, had attempted to exploit a number of new methods including the use of a steam-powered brick-laying machine and plaster and cement guns.[47] As we have seen his demands for materials for the massive scheme far outweighed supply: in April 1921 Mactaggart approached the council to alter his tender to allow the construction of 100 concrete block houses for C1, C2 and G2 type designs, at a saving of between £12 and £17 per house. A year later he received permission to build an additional 150 concrete block houses at a saving of £17 each.[48] Other contractors followed this lead.

It should be stressed that concrete was not a new material as such. The use of concrete as a building material had increased rapidly in the second half of the nineteenth century. One of the pioneers of its use in Scotland was Robert (later Sir Robert) McAlpine, who was building tenements with granolithic

Type E4

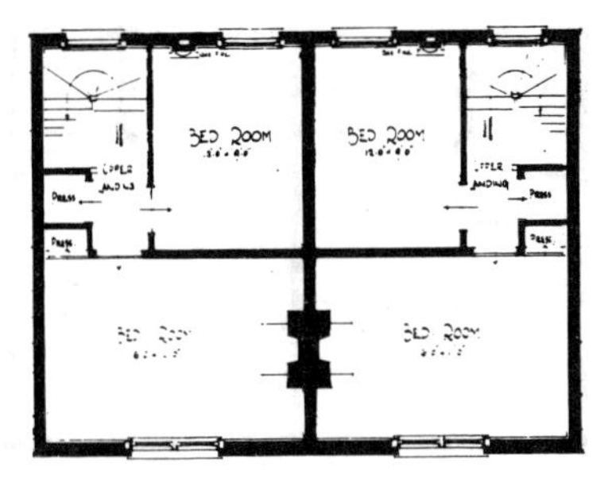

Upper Floor Plan

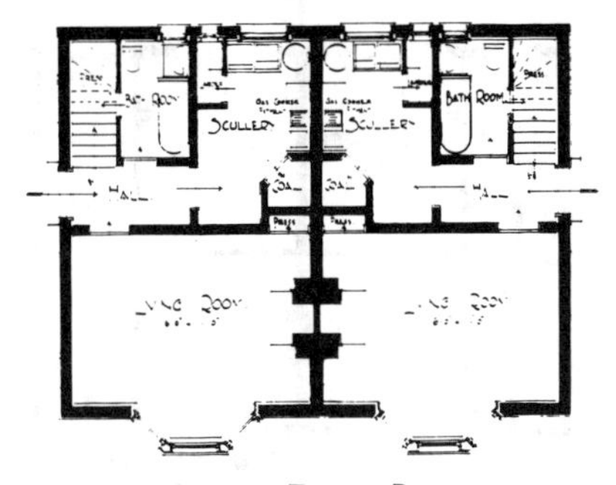

Ground Floor Plan

Figure 5.3 An economical E4 semi-detached house built with brick and rough cast. Rent about £33 pa

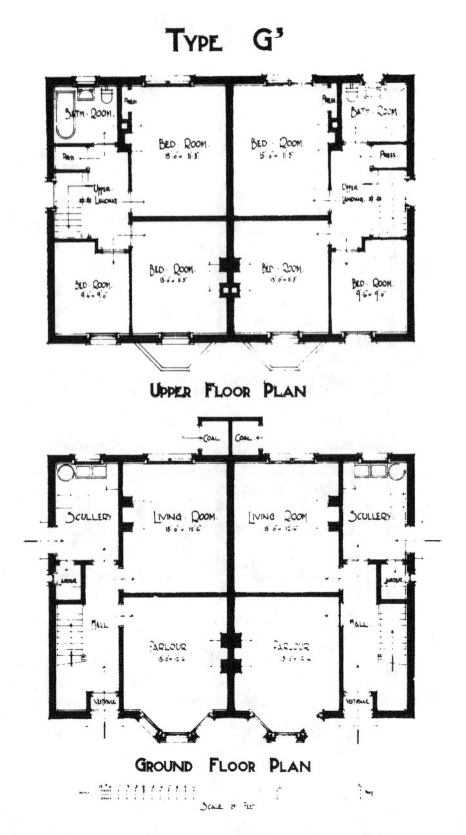

Figure 5.4 The G3—a three bedroomed house with parlour, built using concrete blocks. Rent about £40 pa

concrete (a mixture of sandstone, granite and portland cement) in Hamilton and Motherwell as early as 1873. McAlpine was following the example of other local builders who had copied a not entirely successful method of building using filled concrete shell blocks patented by J C Sellars of Birkenhead. When this method was investigated by Hamilton Dean of Guild Court in 1878 a number of builders came forward to support the general principle of concrete construction, among them Richard Waugh from Melrose, who in the early 1870s had built the Melrose Hydropathic 'largely from concrete', and from Glasgow John MacDonald, who claimed to have been building in concrete for 'about seven years'.[49] Cheaper than both stone and brickwork, concrete offered a viable alternative which McAlpine was able to exploit not only in housebuilding (he was still using it for this in 1891 when he built fourteen villas in Clydebank) but also in the many public-works contracts he undertook throughout Scotland.[50] Contractors on such schemes frequently used concrete in bridge and viaduct work, and for tunnel linings. In rural Scotland concrete was taken up by estate proprietors both for farm cottages and occasionally mansions—Glencripesdale House, a baronial style mansion at Morven was built about 1874 for the Newton family using reinforced concrete, while many of the new cottages on the Ardtornish estate at Morven were also built from concrete.[51] John Wilson, the Architectural Inspector to the Local Government Board in Scotland, reported in 1915 that concrete was widely used where neither stone nor brick was available, citing particularly the example of the Shetlands.[52]

For the enthusiasts, concrete, particularly when used in monolithic building, offered a solution to the universal problem of providing cheap houses for the working class. At the most extreme was the proposal, made in 1909, to construct cast-iron moulds for complete houses into which semi-liquid cement concrete would be poured. The resulting house, at £240 for two storeys, basement and attic, could provide two comfortable houses at modest cost. At £8,000 the moulds were however almost prohibitive, as was the cost of plant required to transport them around a site.[53] Glaswegians in particular had been attracted to less ambitious but equally innovative applications. In 1893 John Dougan, a consulting engineer in the city, presented a paper to the Philosophical Society on the Paristagan system of building, a scheme to build cheap dwelling houses using thin concrete plates or hollow blocks with an iron or wood frame.[54] A concrete house, specifically designed for the housing of the 'residuum' in the city, was proposed to the Municipal Commission on the Housing of the Poor in 1904 by the City Engineer—his scheme was warmly endorsed by witnesses such as John Mann and William Menzies who were urging the responsibility of the housing of the poorest classes in the city on the municipal authorities.[55] Non-traditional and cheaper materials, it was argued, offered a possible solution to the city's intractable housing problem—supervised concrete barracks would also provide the necessary environment to achieve the socialisation of a portion of the population who could not normally be reached in their backlands and rookeries by the agencies of law, church and education.[56] However the material was not widely exploited in house building in the city and few surviving examples of early concrete housing can be found. One example of the partial use of concrete in domestic building was the development built on the Scotstoun estate by John Mactaggart in 1914—red-brick cottage houses, themselves unusual in Glasgow, were built with flat concrete roofs with an asphalt covering (normally only used in public buildings) at a cost of £220, which Mactaggart estimated was little more than the cost of tenement construction.[57]

The immediate need to introduce new materials as a substitute for brick and roughcast receded in 1923 as the price of materials fell, bringing the cost of a three-apartment cottage flat down to £392.[58] In addition the Corporation began to find itself burdened with an excessive supply of bricks from its own works and the sources it had commissioned in 1921.[59] As a consequence concrete took a low priority in the planning of new cottage building schemes. From 1923 onwards the problem in house production became less one of supply of materials than of the output of labour. When Wheatley's Act of 1924, 'a partnership with private enterprise' was passed, great emphasis was placed on the need to bring new workers into the building industry through special apprenticeship schemes.[60] The obligation placed on local authorities to examine new methods of construction was designed specifically to speed up the building of houses. The Corporation of Glasgow, which had many discussions (both formally and probably informally) with Wheatley prior to the passing of the Act again jumped the gun by introducing a small scheme at Langlands in the summer of 1924 as a test site for experimental houses which might be put into mass production.[61]

The Langlands site was developed by a two-way process of the Corporation seeking out new house types to be tested and builders offering to erect their own new developments.[62] In all fifty-six houses were built on the site, comprising thirteen different house types, ranging from a concrete block bungalow, twenty of which were erected by the Housing Department, a Cowieson's steel house, one cast iron house, a variety of poured and concrete block houses, and a Mansard house developed by Mactaggart & Mickel. The scheme showed that the Corporation entered fully into the search for new materials and designs—in its assessment of the carefully costed experiment, which rejected the more exotic proposals in favour of the now almost traditional brick and rough cast or concrete block cavity walls, the Corporation was being no more or less conservative than authorities (and government) throughout the UK.[63] As we shall see in its continued application of new methods throughout the 1920s and 1930s Glasgow was in practice far more adventurous than most.

What dogged the Langlands experiment was the fiasco surrounding the Weir steel house. This was surely the incident which persuaded Marion Bowley to make what by now should clearly be seen as her groundless allegation about the conservative attitudes of local authorities in Scotland to new methods. Weir's scheme, to accelerate housebuilding by launching a massive auxiliary housing programme exploiting non-skilled labour to erect standardised steel houses, had been planned since an informal approach to him by Bonar Law in 1923. When he announced the possibility of such a scheme during the debate in the House of Lords on Wheatley's housing bill in July 1924 he had typically chosen an inflammatory moment to present the nation with what in many respects was a *fait accompli*. He also effectively upstaged Wheatley's proposal, as the astonishing enthusiasm for the Weir house in the national press illustrates.[64] Weir proposed a variety of house types, all of which were based on the model of a timber-framed house with walls of steel sheets.[65] The controversy which surrounded his proposal lay less in its novelty, than in the possibility of the mass production of these houses and their erection by non-unionised labour employed by non-building firms.

The labour question has dominated interpretation of the issue. Old sores from the War were undoubtedly opened by this attempt to introduce de-skilling and Taylorism on the building site.[66] But the Corporation of Glasgow, despite the presence of a number of Labour members who had been involved with the struggles against Weir in 1915, had responded warmly to his initiative. It was only when the labour question came to the fore that problems arose. It was ultimately the threat of the total withdrawal of building labour from Corporation housing schemes by the NFBTO which dissuaded Glasgow Corporation from erecting ten steel houses at Langlands.[67] Thus their refusal was a pragmatic decision designed to secure the future of existing housing schemes.

But to a large degree the building craft unions allowed themselves to be exploited in this issue by both the employers and building professionals (namely architects) whose objections to the proposal were far more bitter and fundamental. This is clear from the unpublished minutes of both the Moir Committee into New Methods of House Construction of October 1924, and the Industrial Court of Inquiry into the erection of steel houses held in March 1925 after Glasgow and other local authorities had capitulated to the threat of industrial action.[68] Witnesses before Moir, such as Sir Frank Baines, who had designed the wartime housing scheme at Well Hall, Woolwich (described by contemporaries as 'a community which ... is, from the architectural standpoint, without equal in the world') were far more critical of the house than labour representatives. Baines saw nothing useful in Weir's 'temporary house' beyond the fact that it offered a logical (but unacceptable) solution to a problem. He criticised every aspect of the construction of the house on architectural, technical and even social grounds—'with regard to internal timber', he said, 'I think it is too light, too light in the sense that I cannot imagine a Scottish worker coming home full of whisky and falling against one of these partitions, because I am afraid he will go through'.[69] Other witnesses criticised the use of non-traditional materials and methods, arguing that it was socially divisive to produce homes for the working classes that were so physically distinctive.[70] Building employers were less hostile to the house, which they rightly pointed out offered nothing more or less than was available from numerous other manufacturers in Glasgow and elsewhere, than its form of erection, which seemed to them to threaten not only the essential skill base of the industry, but also the established employers' leading place within it.[71]

The failure of the Weir proposal to win the support of local authorities led eventually to the intervention of the Government, largely as a result of the promptings of Walter Elliot. The government acted through the agency of the

A Foundations laid in Grosvenor Square 9/3/25

B Steel plates in place on timber frame 10/3/25

C Roof-trusses set and covered 11/3/25

D Interior shell, roof trusses and hearth 12/3/25

E Roof tiled, steel windows fitted 14/3/25

F Internal wall framing 14/3/25

G Completed house: the living room 19/3/25

H Completed house: scullery and living room 19/3/25

Figure 5.5 Ten days in the life of a Weir steel house

Scottish Housing Trust Company, a hybrid of the firm which had been established to build the housing scheme at Rosyth. In December 1925 the Company announced a scheme, sponsored by the Scottish Board of Health, to build over 2,000 steel houses in selected areas throughout Scotland. Local authorities refused to cooperate with the company unless the Weir house in the scheme, which made up half the original total, were built under normal conditions.[72] They clearly also held deeper suspicions that the company was an attempt by central government to impinge on local efforts and initiative. It was not until the middle of 1926 that an agreement was reached between the warring factions and building commenced. The scheme, as with the original announcement, was greeted with massive public enthusiasm. In Glasgow eighty-six houses were built by Weir at Garngad, with others erected at Shettleston. Additional steel houses of the Weir, Atholl and Cowieson variety were erected by the Scottish Housing Trust at Hamilton, Lochend in Edinburgh, Cragiebank in Dundee, and on three sites in Greenock.[73]

As we have seen the Weir controversy had little or nothing to do with the receptiveness of local authorities to new building materials and techniques. At the same time as being in dispute with Weir and the Scottish National Housing Trust, Glasgow Corporation were continuing to press forward with the exploitation of new methods and materials on housing schemes built under the 1924 subsidy. In 1927 at Carntyne and Knightswood the Corporation contracted for the erection of 500 cavity walled concrete flat roofed houses designed by the builder John MacDonald.[74] Also under the Wheatley Act the Corporation contracted for 1,004 concrete houses built by the Balshagray Building Company which had been tested at Langlands; for 300 Dennis Wild steel houses; for 188 Kane Brickwood houses, and for houses built to the Winget Pier and Panel method of construction.[75] Combined, new methods of building (principally exploiting concrete construction), accounted for in excess of 20 per cent of the 16,000 general needs houses built under the Acts of 1919, 1923 and 1924.

Clearance and concrete

It was however in the building of 'cheaper dwellings' in slum clearance schemes that concrete in particular was to make its greatest contribution to inter-war housing in Glasgow. It has been suggested that Scottish local authorities, with little regard to either house design and layout, accepted the higher rates of subsidy and housed the better-off during the early 1920s, and then ditched both principle and populace following the shift in legislation in 1930 and 1933. The result of this desertion of 'general needs' provision in favour of 'slum clearance' was the creation of a distinctive and second-class brand of housing scheme, devoid of even basic facilities, in which the socially undesirable were housed. Andy Gibb, John Butt and Sydney Checkland all illustrate this same point in the Glasgow context with the building of the Blackhill rehousing scheme between 1930 and 1936.[76] Such a treatment may be supported once more by aggregates and a too-literal interpretation of statutes. In reality the policy to build a 'second class' house had been developed much earlier: it had been implicit in the report of the Royal Commission on Housing that tenement-type houses would be built and reserved for occupation by lower paid workers.[77] The debate over housing reform in the late nineteenth and early twentieth century had also defined the need for basic accommodation for the 'residuum'—this view, and the anxiety over the lack of legislation to deal with slum conditions, was articulated by the Corporation as early as 1919. A sub-committee of the Housing and Town Improvement Committee urged that 'the Corporation get in touch with the Members of Parliament for the City, and the Scottish Office, to impress on them the necessity for drastic legislation with regard to slums'.[78] Even pioneers in the fight for higher standards such as John Wheatley pressed the Corporation to build as many two-roomed houses as possible to rehouse those from the slums who were unable to pay the rents imposed on general needs schemes by the Scottish Office, with the support of moderate or Conservative councillors.[79] In Glasgow 13,756 tenement houses were built in rehousing schemes in the inter-war years. Of these 5,990, or 43.5 per cent, were built before 1930 under the terms of specific government grants for clearance or the 1923 Chamberlain Act which offered a 50 per cent subsidy on the loss incurred on any clearance scheme.[80] It was these tenement houses of the 1920s, the result of a conscious policy to grapple with a growing problem, which established the distinctive pattern for Blackhill. The pattern was set not least in the extent to which Glasgow Corporation sought to cheapen the cost of these buildings by the use of new or experimental materials.

In March 1922 the Special Committee on Housing noted that 'the time has arrived when action should be taken to deal with the slums', agreeing that an initial scheme should be built at Craigbank comprising two and three-roomed houses.[81] The Socialists on the Committee, led by Wheatley, initially opposed the move to introduce two-roomed houses with bathrooms.[82] However six months later, following a report from the city's Medical Officer of Health which estimated that 58,000 people in the city were living in uninhabitable houses, Wheatley himself proposed a motion calling for plans to be laid for the construction of 13,000 two-roomed houses (with bathrooms and a scullery) on land owned by the Corporation.[83] The Socialists had already lost one battle in 1920 when the rents for the first completed schemes had been set at a minimum of £28 per year, a price far beyond the eight-pound cottages which they had promised Glasgow citizens at the turn of the century, and a price far beyond the pockets of all but the most highly paid skilled workers, white collar workers and even professionals.[84] In conceding to a return to two-roomed houses Wheatley and his colleagues were bowing to the inevitable pressure of an apparently insoluble problem, which meant that, in the absence of generous subsidy (when it came, the 1923 Act only paid half of any loss incurred on rehousing schemes) cheapness of site and economy of space and construction lay at the heart of any successful rehousing scheme.

The Director of Housing had a model at hand on which to base the design and management of rehousing schemes in the tenements built at Kennyhill by the Improvement Trust in 1906.[85] However these houses were built in

Figure 5.6 Early slum clearance tenements at Hamiltonhill, built using concrete blocks. Rent about £19 pa

traditional fashion using stone and brickwork—with the exception of a small number of rehousing schemes such as those at Scotstoun or Yorkhill all the tenements built under rehousing schemes between the wars (probably around 10,000 of the total of 13,700) were constructed using uncoloured concrete block hollow walls.[86] Where rehousing schemes included flatted cottages, such as Newbank or the second phase of Hamiltonhill, these were built for the most part of brick and roughcast. These high density schemes (often due to reduced subsidy) were built on less costly and less attractive sites than those chosen for general needs housing—a report on the Possilpark site, for example, commented that 'the ground might be described as "cold" in its appearance, but we see no reason why it should not be converted into an attractive area for workmen's dwellings'.[87] Built to a high internal standard, carefully supervised by caretakers and nurses, often provided with social or community centres, the schemes nonetheless lacked the aesthetic appeal of the general needs schemes, not least because of the uncompromising harshness of the materials of which they were built.[88] Efforts were made to overcome these problems—at the Springfield Road site 'with a view to relieving monotony and improving amenity' a mixture of Dorset pea pebble and ordinary concrete blocks was used on the frontages of blocks facing main and internal roads. At Ballindalloch Drive a similar contrast of concrete materials was employed, with the additional device of varied building heights.[89]

Concrete provided the answer to the need to build quickly and cheaply, but it did nothing to meet other criteria, mapped out by John Highton in 1935 following his tour of working class housing on the continent:

The strongest impression left with me as a result of my tour is that of the colourful charm and brightness of the Continental schemes ... The two elements of light and colour react favourably upon one another. Absence of colour minimises the value of light, and absence of light minimises the value of colour. Light and colour are the two elements in which our Scottish schemes are most lacking.[90]

Highton's report was largely intended to illustrate the potential offered by tenement building in an attempt to increase popularity for the Housing Act of 1935 which was designed to relieve overcrowding through wholesale clearance and tenement construction.[91] However concrete certainly provided the houses which Glasgow Corporation needed to solve, or at least abate, a problem which normal building could not address. Its use shows the extent to which councillors in the city were prepared to exploit new techniques to overcome the housing problem. They embarked on a steady programme of development—by 1938 the Corporation had produced the first block of houses built by its own 'foam slag' process which was to provide 1,600 houses after the War.[92] This was described by *Concrete Quarterly* as 'a new method of building with large precast foamed slag concrete blocks, which is entirely different from any other experiment in the United Kingdom'.[93] The social disadvantages of these means of construction, evident if not to the newly rehoused tenants then certainly to architectural critics after only a few years, could only be overcome by the provision of funding which neither ratepayers nor central government was prepared to provide.

Although there was an environment of enquiry and innovation in housebuilding techniques throughout the United Kingdom in the inter-war years it is clear that in Glasgow much of the initiative for the use of new materials and methods came from within the Corporation itself, both from officials and elected representatives. Of particular importance was the influence of Peter Fyfe. Fyfe had served a seven-year apprenticeship with a Glasgow engineering firm before joining the Corporation Sanitary Department in 1879.[94] It is thus not surprising that he adopted a view of the housing problem that saw building technique as the main issue to be resolved. In a lecture given in 1899 (by which time he was Chief Sanitary Inspector for the City) he made this viewpoint clear:

Government and municipal standards are in the main good and desirable, but infinitely more important and useful for the poor labourer are good accommodation and low rents; and, in my opinion where the former makes impossible the latter elasticity must be found in construction, as there is none in the poor man's ability to pay.

It was, said Fyfe, the 'architectural craftsman', who has the 'special knowledge and skill' to resolve the dilemma.[95] These were views which he carried into the Housing Department on its formation in 1919, leading the drive for the manufacture of composite bricks, of concrete blocks, and the adoption of standardised methods of construction.[96] He was also a man imbued with a missionary spirit; we have seen how he referred to 'the *great work* which lies before the Housing Department'.[97] In this he was ably assisted by George Morton, chairman of the City's Housing Committee. A member of one of Glasgow's first firms of concrete merchants, Morton was well able to see the practical utility of Fyfe's plans. In addition, like Fyfe, he had a great appetite for his work—'his enthusiasm in the work was infectious, and he imparted to his committee the spirit of hustle'.[98]

When Fyfe resigned from the Corporation in 1923 he did so to pursue an initiative in the private sector to produce cheap, non-traditional materials. He formed his own company, Fyfe-Stone Ltd, to exploit patents for the manufacture of artificial stone which he had acquired in 1916. The prospectus for the company began with a resumé of the poor output of the public sector since 1919, laying the blame firmly on the high cost of materials. 'Fyfe stone will rectify this and permit rapid and economical building' it declared. The stone was described as 'a superior building material for standard dwelling houses, bungalows, cottages etc, on the unit construction principle which had reached a high stage of development in the United States of America'. Fyfe and his fellow directors sought to raise capital of £30,000 to purchase specialist plant from America and to provide working capital for the manufacture of the blocks.[99] Despite his high reputation the flotation was a failure, echoing the difficulties in raising liquid capital faced by English firms involved in similar methods of concrete construction.[100]

Among the largest backers of Fyfe's abortive venture were the firm of J A Mactaggart & Co and its three directors, J A Mactaggart, Jack Mactaggart and Andrew Mickel. In his position as possibly the largest contractor to the Corporation in this period Mactaggart was clearly of influence in determining the extent to which new materials would be used. His was a pragmatic approach—he had already experimented with flat concrete roofs in the construction of workmen's cottages at Scotstoun before World War I (many of his tenements were built with flat roofs also)—and as we have seen, when the supply of bricks failed to meet the needs of the Mosspark scheme he quickly turned to the use of concrete blocks. He extended this pragmatism equally to the private sector—using a variety of materials in the construction of houses for both Mactaggart and Mickel and also for the Western Heritable Property Company of which he was a director.[101]

Less of a pragmatist and more of an idealist was the builder John McDonald of the Sunlit Building Company. Knighted in 1937 in recognition of his successful experimentation in building materials and house types, McDonald was the designer and builder of the 500 flat roofed concrete houses erected at Carntyne.[102] Next to John Mactaggart he was the second most successful builder in the city; he had acquired a large number of Corporation contracts and had, since 1924, been encouraging the local authority to adopt his flat roofed design. Cost cutting they may have been, but flat roofs also served distinct social purposes—in their view of this McDonald and his son J R H McDonald were largely informed by the functionalist European Modern Movement. They argued in favour of:

> the much lesser obstruction of sunlight by the flat roofs than by pitched roofs, and the infinite possibilities of the use of flat roofs for healthy recreation and exercise.[103]

They also praised the virtue of the (now standard) cavity wall for reducing condensation. Like Mactaggart, MacDonald took his methods into both public and private sector with the construction of his famous Carse View estate at Bearsden.[104]

Conclusion and continuities

Glasgow grappled with its inter-war housing problems with energy, imagination and innovation, adopting up to 1933 a novel partnership between private and public sectors. It should not be thought unique in terms of its innovations in materials, with similar progress being made by local authorities in Clydebank, Dundee, Edinburgh and Aberdeen, and also by the Scottish Special Housing Association.[105] However its energy and imagination in this field far surpassed any of its rivals. Raw statistics on the number of houses built by 1939, or the level of overcrowding in the city by World War II, do nothing to explain what actually happened during this period. This brief examination of attitudes towards building in new materials has shown that what happened was in many ways far more constructive, and given the constraints far more successful, than some historians have allowed. Closer examination of other areas may well give the same results.

The matter of building in new materials cannot be put to rest in 1939. During the inter-war years Glasgow built up a confidence in the application of new methods to house building which was to be tested and justified in the years after World War II. By 1944 the City's Housing Department had based its post-war programme firmly around the exploitation of non-traditional methods of building. In the ten years 1945–55, 249,345 houses were built by local authorities in Scotland—46 per cent of these were built by non-traditional methods.[106] These included nearly 18,000 Weir houses, 12,995 Cruden houses and 9,000 Orlit houses. Glasgow in particular was the site for the erection of a large number of these, built generally in low density developments such as Balornock. This second phase of experimental building was crucial to post-war recovery in Scotland. Such was the faith of the local authority in such methods that Glasgow became one of the first cities to experiment with high rise, and later system building techniques.[107] Glasgow did not need to be pressed into such options by changes in government subsidy schemes, nor was it the victim of some conspiracy by building or design professionals, rather it welcomed the continued promise of technological progress in building. Nor did this decision come about, as had been suggested, as the result of a one-off visit to France by Corporation officials in 1947 to visit the Marseilles Block, built after the style of Le Corbusier.[108] By that time Glasgow had earned itself a place at the forefront of housing innovation which it had become anxious to maintain—it was also anxious to build at high density in order to house its population within the city's available supply of land, thus avoiding the loss of population through overspill. As early as 1946 the Corporation developed the plans to build multi-storey flats up to ten storeys at Moss Heights, 'a major innovation so far as housing in Scotland is concerned'.[109] The adoption of these techniques wholesale in the late 1950s was a rational decision based on a continuity of successful innovation in building, begun by Fyfe in the 1920s. As such the Corporation should not be judged as harshly as it has been by some for the technical and social problems which were to arise from this epic but perhaps misguided building programme.

Notes

1. Earlier versions of this paper were presented at the University of St Andrews' social history seminar, 'Urban development and city planning', in March 1987, and the University of Strathclyde's History of Glasgow project one-day conference, 'Governing Glasgow: public authorities, planning and urban problems', in December 1987.
2. Corporation of Glasgow Minutes, Special Committee on Housing and General Town Improvement, 15 October 1919, draft housing scheme.
3. John Wheatley, *Eight Pound Cottages for Glasgow Citizens* no place, 1913.
4. *Departmental committee on increases in rental of small dwelling houses in industrial districts in Scotland*, Minutes of evidence, para 727, evidence of James Stewart PP, cd 8154. Stewart, whose evidence to this Committee is notable for its total failure to grasp the realities of funding and managing a public house-building programme, later became Under-Secretary of Health for Scotland in 1924, with specific responsibility for overseeing housebuilding: for a biography see William Knox (ed) *Scottish Labour Leaders* Edinburgh, 1984, pp.255–7.
5. A G Jury, *Housing Centenary* Glasgow, 1966, p.46.
6. This pessimism is probably most clearly stated in two essays by John Butt, 'Working class housing in Glasgow, 1900–39', in Ian MacDougall (ed) *Essays in Scottish Labour History* Edinburgh, 1978, pp.143–169, and 'Working class housing in Scottish cities, 1900–1950', in George Gordon and Brian Dicks (eds) *Scottish Urban History* (Aberdeen, 1983) pp.233–67. Sydney Checkland's *The Upas Tree* Glasgow, 1976, pp.35–40 offers a more objective, but ultimately gloomy view of the period. The sense of failure also haunts Andy Gibb, *Glasgow, The Making of a City* London, 1983, pp.154–9, and for Scotland generally Ian Adams, *The Making of Urban Scotland* London, 1978, pp.172–6. But see also T C Smout, *A Century of the Scottish People 1830–1950* London, 1986, pp.52–7.
7. Ian Adams, op.cit., (note 6), Table 3, p.176; Corporation of Glasgow Housing Department, *Review of Operations 1919–1947* Glasgow, 1947, pp.29–32.
8. I wish to acknowledge the assistance of Dr Derek Dow, who made available to me the set of Corporation Minutes belonging to the Greater Glasgow Health Board Archive, and Dr Irene O'Brien and her colleagues, who have been of invaluable assistance to me in my work in Strathclyde Regional Archives.
9. Corporation of Glasgow Minutes, Committee on Parliamentary Bills, 5 May 1919, report by the City Engineer on Housing, Town Planning, etc (Scotland) Bill. This minute also contains reports by the Town Clerk and by the Medical Officer of Health. The danger of conflict arising from over-centralisation was anticipated in the minority report of the 1917 Royal Commission on Housing; *Report of the Royal Commission on the Housing of the Industrial Population of Scotland Rural and Urban*, pp.1917–18 XIV, Minority Report, para 4.
10. *Municipal Glasgow, its Evolution and Enterprises* Glasgow, 1914, p.7.
11. Strathclyde Regional Archives, D–TC 8/18 (1919–20), folder 1 (1919), Corporation of Glasgow Housing Schemes, 16 April 1919.

12. Corporation of Glasgow Minutes, minute of the Special Committee on Housing and General Town Improvement, 26 May 1919.
13. Strathclyde Regional Archives, D–TC 8/18 (1919–20), folder 1 (1919), Thomas Nisbet to Town Clerk, 1 September 1919.
14. *Glasgow Herald*, 5 September 1924, report on the Jubilee Congress of the Incorporated Sanitary Association of Scotland; for an example of the relationship between a local authority and central Government in England see Robert Ryder, 'Council house building in County Durham, 1900–39' in M J Daunton (ed) *Councillors and Tenants: Local Authority Housing in English Cities, 1919–1939* Leicester, 1984, pp.50–53.
15. Urlan Wannop, 'Glasgow/Clydeside: a century of metropolitan evolution', in George Gordon (ed) *Regional Cities in the U.K. 1890–1980* London, 1986, p.88.
16. Strathclyde Regional Archives, D-TC 8/18 (1919–20), folder 1 (1919), copy letter J F Robertson, District Clerk, Dumbarton County Council, to Secretary, Housing Department, Scottish Board of Health, 8 January 1920.
17. Walker had been responsible for the 'Memorandum by the Local Government Board for Scotland with suggestions in regard to the provision and planning of houses for the working classes' (Edinburgh, 1918); for his career see also Nicholas J Morgan, *A History of the NHBC and Private Home Building* Carnforth, 1987, p.28.
18. The career and contribution of Peter Fyfe is discussed, below pp.143–4.
19. Strathclyde Regional Archives, D–TC 8/18 (1919–20), folder 1 (1919), memorandum by the Director of Housing upon the staffing of the Housing Department, 16 September 1919.
20. See, for example, Corporation of Glasgow Minutes, minute of the Special Committee on Housing and General Town Improvement, 28 March 1923: 'The Director of Housing reported, in view of the increased work required by the proposals for further housing schemes in view of the new government subsidy, it would be necessary for him to obtain additional temporary assistance, and the committee agreed to authorise the Director of Housing to engage, temporarily, two qualified engineering assistants and two engineering students from the University, and also an assistant surveyor'.
21. Corporation of Glasgow Housing Department, *Review of Operations 1919–1947* Glasgow, 1947, p.13. In order to rationalise the administration of housing matters the functions of the Special Committee on Housing and General Town Improvement, the Executive Committee on Housing, the Town Planning Committee and the City Improvement Committee were merged into a single Housing Committee in November 1923: Corporation of Glasgow minutes 1 November 1923.
22. 'As Local Authorities are at present constituted, and in view of their other duties, they do not seem to us qualified to carry out the truly gigantic task of providing dwellings for the greater part of the working-class population of Scotland; while there would be grave dangers—not least in the delay in the provision of houses—if bodies which have hitherto provided less than 1 per cent of the necessary dwellings were at once made responsible for providing perhaps 80 or 90 per cent of the new working-class houses required', *Report of the Royal Commission on the Housing of the Industrial Population of Scotland Rural and Urban*, Minority Report, para. 2. It is a remarkable reflection of the partiality with which historians have approached this report that few if any have paid due notice to the views expressed in the minority report, most of which were vindicated within a decade of its publication.
23. Corporation of Glasgow Housing Department, *Review of Operations 1919–1947*

Glasgow, 1947, pp.20–5 gives a summary of direct labour building in Glasgow. The first experiment in this direction came with the contract for the Drumoyne Housing Scheme, which was awarded to the Glasgow and West of Scotland Building Guild in December 1920; on completion of the scheme it was estimated that some £37,000 had been saved on the cost that would have been incurred by a contractor: Corporation of Glasgow Minutes, Special Committee on Housing and General Town Improvement, minute of the Sub-Committee on Direct Labour, 16 December 1920; 5 October 1923, statement showing estimated profit to Corporation by work carried out by direct labour.

24. John Butt, 'Working class housing in Scottish cities, 1900–1950', in George Gordon and Brian Dicks (eds) *Scottish Urban History* Aberdeen, 1983, p.247.
25. Private builders constructed 10,419 houses between 1919 and 1939 with the support of local authority grants under the various housing Acts—around 10,000 were built without assistance, and in addition large numbers of houses for Glasgow citizens were built privately outside the city boundaries. For data on houses built see Corporation of Glasgow Housing Department, *Review of Operations 1919–1947* (Glasgow, 1947), p.76; J Cunnison and J B S Gilfillan, *Third Statistical Account of Scotland, Glasgow* Glasgow, 1958, p.876.
26. For the background to this see Bruce K Murray *The People's Budget 1909/10: Lloyd George and Liberal Politics* Oxford 1980, pp.131–6.
27. Strathclyde Regional Archives, D–TC 8/18 (1919–20), folder 1 (1919), Archibald Stewart to Sir John Lindsay, 6 November 1919.
28. See, for example, Glasgow University Archives, UGD 208/1/1, J C McKellar Ltd, Minute Book vol. 1, 6 September 1909. The impact of increment duty on the Scottish building industry was discussed at length in the *Glasgow Herald*, 11 May 1910, p.9. Opposition from the industry within Great Britain as a whole was expressed to the Tudor Walters Committee: PP Cd 9191, *Report of the Committee appointed by the President of the Local Government Board and the Secretary of State for Scotland to consider questions of building construction* 1918, para 24. The building industry in Scotland had been 'killed', according to one contributor to the debate in the House of Commons on the 1919 Act, 'by the Land Tax of 1909. I know districts in which a great many houses were built from year to year, and as soon as that legislation came into force, the building of new houses stopped entirely from that very moment': Hansard, vol 115, 1919 col. 675–6.
29. Which is described admirably in J Melling, *Rent strikes: People's Struggle for Housing in West Scotland 1890–1916* Edinburgh, 1983, *passim*.
30. The structure of the Scottish building industry is discussed in Richard Rodger, 'Victorian building industry and the housing of the Scottish working classes' in Martin Doughty (ed) *Building and the Industrial City* Leicester, 1986, pp.174–82.
31. PP Cd 8760, *Special Report on the Design, Construction, and Materials of Various Types of Small Dwelling-houses in Scotland*, para 127.
32. Corporation of Glasgow Minutes, minute of the Special Committee on Housing and General Town Improvement, 11 April 1919. The Building Employers Federation lobbied the Corporation in December 1919, proposing 'that housing schemes should be handed over to the Federation, to be allocated among their members', and summarised some of their objections to large single-firm contracts in two letters to the Corporation in 1925, noting that 'reputable contracting firms' had not embarked on 'these speculative ventures', Corporation of Glasgow Minutes, minute of the Special Committee on Housing and General Town Improvement, 5 December 1919; Corporation of Glasgow Minutes, minute of the Committee on Housing, 9 March 1925.

33. Strathclyde Regional Archives, D–TC 8/18 (1919–20), folder 1 (1919), Peter Fyfe to Town Clerk, 20 February 1919, with enclosed circular of Glasgow and West of Scotland Master Plumber's Association, complaining about the use of sole contractors, and urging members not to tender for sub-contracts on such schemes.
34. For the joiners' strike see Corporation of Glasgow Minutes, minute of the Special Committee on Housing and General Town Improvement, 10 May 1920, 1 June 1920. The industry-wide strike in the summer of 1924 also had 'a very serious effect on output, as not only were two of the best months in the year lost, but its effect was such that it was some months before many of the contractors had their squads brought up to the previous level'. Corporation of Glasgow Minutes, minute of the Committee on Housing, 9 March 1925. The Associated Society of Carpenters, Cabinetmakers and Joiners banned overtime on Corporation schemes in September 1920: Strathclyde Regional Archives, D–TC 8/18 (1919–20), folder 2 (1919), letter from Thomas Barron to Peter Fyfe 10 September 1920.
35. The labour position was outlined in a minute of February 1920, and highlighted as a major contributory factor in delaying progress in 1925: Corporation of Glasgow Minutes, minute of the Special Committee on Housing and General Town Improvement, 20 February 1920; Corporation of Glasgow Minutes, minute of the Committee on Housing, 9 March 1925.
36. Around 45 per cent of the output of Scottish brickyards was available for housing schemes; according to an official in the Building Materials Supply Department 'it would appear that Glasgow alone could absorb the whole available output of Scottish brickyards at this time', Strathclyde Regional Archives, D–TC 8/18 (1919–20), folder 2 (1920), draft letter Peter Fyfe to Town Clerk, 4 August 1920, with letter from Building Materials Supply Department to Peter Fyfe, 4 August 1920.
37. Corporation of Glasgow Housing Department, *Review of Operations 1919–1927* Glasgow, 1927, p.11.
38. Corporation of Glasgow Minutes, minute of the Special Committee on Housing and General Town Improvement, Sub-Committee on Building Materials, 29 December 1920, 17 January 1921. The Corporation argued that bricks could be obtained on the open market at a cheaper price than from the Building Materials Supply Department: Corporation of Glasgow Minutes, minute of the Special Committee on Housing and General Town Improvement, 12 January 1921.
39. For a detailed account of developments during this period see R B White, *Prefabrication, a History of its Development in Great Britain* London, 1965, pp.49–92.
40. Marion Bowley, *The British Building Industry* Cambridge, 1966, pp.197–98.
41. Corporation of Glasgow Minutes, minute of the Special Committee on Housing and General Town Improvement, 16 June 1919.
42. Corporation of Glasgow Minutes, minute of the Special Committee on Housing and General Town Improvement, 13 October 1919, 17 November 1919, 21 May 1920, 1 September 1920, 27 April 1921; Minute of the Committee on Housing, 17 February 1924.
43. Corporation of Glasgow Minutes, minute of the Special Committee on Housing and General Town Improvement, 1 September 1920, 23 February 1921; Strathclyde Regional Archives, D–TC 8/18 (1919–20), folder 2 (1920), Report on a visit to Leigh and Wakefield to inspect lime-concrete brickmaking machinery.
44. Strathclyde Regional Archives, D–TC 8/18 (1919–20), folder 2 (1920), draft letter, Peter Fyfe to Town Clerk 4 August 1920.
45. Corporation of Glasgow Minutes, minute of the Special Committee on Housing

and General Town Improvement, 23 November 1921, 12 April 1922, 11 October 1922.

46. Corporation of Glasgow Minutes, minute of the Special Committee on Housing and General Town Improvement, 6 December 1922.
47. For the Mosspark contract see Corporation of Glasgow Minutes, minute of the Special Committee on Housing and General Town Improvement, Sub-Committee on Grounds and Properties, 10 September 1920; for the experimental cement gun see Corporation of Glasgow Minutes, minute of the Special Committee on Housing and General Town Improvement, 1 June 1921; *Glasgow Illustrated* February, 1964, 'Histories of Glasgow companies no 18, Mactaggart & Mickel Ltd'.
48. Corporation of Glasgow Minutes, minute of the Special Committee on Housing and General Town Improvement, 6 April 1921, 24 May 1922.
49. Iain Russell and George Dixon, 'Some notes on "Concrete Bob" McAlpine', *Scottish Industrial History*, **9** 1986, pp.3–10; for McAlpine generally see Iain Russell, *Sir Robert McAlpine & Sons, the Early Years* Carnforth, 1988.
50. For McAlpine's concrete houses in Clydebank see John F Hood (ed) *The History of Clydebank* Carnforth, 1988, p.37.
51. Michael C Davies, *The Lost Mansions of Argyll* (Ardrishaig, 1984) p.13; PP, c 3980, *Report by Her Majesty's Commissioners of Inquiry into the Conditions of Crofters and Cottars in the Highlands and Islands of Scotland*, Appendix A, LXXIV, statement by Walter Elliot Esq.
52. PP, Cd. 8760, *Special Report on the Design, Construction, and Materials of Various Types of Small Dwelling-Houses in Scotland*, para 51.
53. For some general observations on concrete housebuilding see G Lister Sutcliffe, *The Principles and Practice of Modern House-construction* (London, 1898) vol 1, pp.102–5. The poured concrete cottage is described in Lawrence Weaver, *The 'Country Life' Book of Cottages* London, 1919, pp.52–4.
54. John Dougan, 'On the "Paristagan" system of building with concrete', *Proc. Philosophical Soc. of Glasgow* **25** 1894, pp.90–7.
55. *Glasgow Municipal Commission on the Housing of the Poor, Minutes of Evidence*, Glasgow, 1904, para 3095, evidence of William Menzies; John Mann Junior, 'Better houses for the poor—will they pay?' *Proc. Philosophical Soc. of Glasgow* (30) 1899, p.119. See also Corporation of Glasgow City Improvement Department, *Report of the Proceedings at a Conference as to Cheap Dwellings* Glasgow, 1901, *passim*.
56. William Smart's proposed non-traditional house employed new materials as a device for disciplining tenants. It was to comprise 'four bare walls, say, of concrete, with an indestructible bedframe. So far as possible no wood to hack or burn; no plaster to pull down; no paper to tear away; no fittings to carry away by the light of the moon. . .'. *The Housing Problem and the Municipality* Glasgow, 1902. The prominent Glasgow builder Thomas Binnie had built a property at Spoutmouth, Glasgow, in 1864 with all concrete fittings for 'a very rough class': *Glasgow Municipal Commission on the Housing the Poor, Minutes of Evidence*, Glasgow, 1904, para 7114.
57. *Royal Commission on the Housing of the Industrial Population of Scotland, Rural and Urban, Minutes of Evidence* (Edinburgh, 1921) vol II, para 22, 847/28, 22,943; Mactaggart was unenthusiastic about building in concrete, either reinforced or concrete blocks: 'Good concrete blocks might make a very nice house and bad concrete blocks might make a very inferior house, but there are good bricks in Scotland, and I think brick is in every way superior to concrete as a constructive material for housing', *ibid.* para. 23,001.

58. Corporation of Glasgow Housing Department, *Review of Operations 1919–1927* Glasgow, 1927, p.11.
59. 'The Town-Clerk reported that at Dalry Brick-works the number of bricks stacked occupies the whole space at the disposal of the department, and it will be necessary, unless some outlet is obtained for the production, to obtain further ground for stacking purposes', Corporation of Glasgow, Minute of the Committee on Housing, Sub-Committee on Direct Labour and Building Materials, 19 February 1924.
60. 14 & 15 Geo. 5, cap 35. 'By promoting a larger market for houses I am creating a field for private enterprise that it could not have in anything but these proposals': *Hansard* 175 (1924) col 101, speech of John Wheatley.
61. 'The Convenor reported that he has had a conversation with the new Minister of Health with reference to housing matters, and that the Minister had stated he would welcome a deputation from the Housing Committee to confer with him as to the Government housing policy...' Corporation of Glasgow, minutes of the Committee on Housing, 30 January 1924.
62. Corporation of Glasgow, minutes of the Committee on Housing, Sub-Committee on Sites and Buildings, 15 January 1924.
63. The scheme is described in full in the report of the Director of Housing to the Committee on Housing in May 1925: Corporation of Glasgow, minutes of the Committee on Housing, 9 March 1925.
64. Nicholas J Morgan, 'Stone, style and steel: sources for the study of three Scottish house builders, 1850–1930', *Proc. Annual Conference 1986 of the Business Archives Council* London, 1987, pp.33–4.
65. Glasgow University Archives DC96/11/2, *Some Notes on the Weir House* Glasgow, 1926.
66. The background to Weir's turbulent relationship with Glasgow's trade unions is admirably described in Iain McLean, *The Legend of Red Clydeside* Edinburgh, 1983, pp.5–110.
67. Glasgow University Archives DC96/11/9, correspondence relating to early proposals for steel houses; Corporation of Glasgow Minutes, 14 January 1925, 22 January 1925; Corporation of Glasgow, minutes of the Committee on Housing, 17 December 1924, 14 January 1925, 25 February 1925.
68. Glasgow University Archives, DC96/11/2, minutes of a Court of Enquiry into the erection of steel houses; DC96/11/2, minute of an inquiry by the Committee on new methods of house construction held at Glasgow 4 October 1924. See *Interim Report of the Committee on new methods of house construction* (London, 1925); *Report of a Court of Inquiry concerning Steel Houses*, 1925 Cmd 2392.
69. Glasgow University Archives, DC96/11/2, Report of a Court of Inquiry concerning Steel Houses held at Glasgow, 4 October 1924, p.524.36, evidence of Sir Frank Baines.
70. 'It is going to set workers as a class apart ... it is going to confirm the workers in their class antagonism', Glasgow University Archives, DC96/11/2, Report of a Court of Inquiry concerning Steel Houses 1925, Cmd 2392; DC96/11/2, p.14, evidence of R Coppock.
71. Glasgow University Archives, DC96/11/2, minutes of a Court of Enquiry into the erection of steel houses; DC96/11/2, pp.53–66, evidence of William H Nicholls.
72. Tom Begg, *50 Special Years—a Study in Scottish Housing* London, 1987, pp.51–5.
73. *Glasgow Herald*, 1 September 1926, 19 October 1926.
74. These houses are described and illustrated in John R H McDonald, *Modern Housing* Glasgow, 1931.

75. These figures are taken from site plans included in Corporation of Glasgow Housing Department, *Review of Operations 1919–1927* Glasgow, 1927. The Winget Pier and Panel house and the Dennis-Wild house are described in the Scottish Office Building Directorate's recently published and generally useful (although not exhaustive) *Guide to Non-Traditional Housing in Scotland* Edinburgh, 1987; see also 'House construction third report' *Post War Building Studies No. 25* Edinburgh, 1948. Plans of all these house-types (including MacDonald's flat-roofed house) can be found in the collection of plans submitted to the Glasgow Dean of Guild Court, held in the Strathclyde Regional Archives.
76. Andrew Gibb, *The Development of Public Sector Housing in Glasgow* Glasgow, Centre for Urban and Regional Research discussion paper no. 6, 1982, pp 12–13; Andrew Gibb, *Glasgow the Making of a City* London, 1983, pp.155–9; John Butt, 'Working class housing in Glasgow, 1900–39', in Ian MacDougall (ed) *Essays in Scottish Labour History* (Edinburgh, 1978) pp.164, and 'Working class housing in Scottish cities, 1900–1950', in George Gordon and Brian Dicks (eds) *Scottish Urban History* (Aberdeen, 1983) p.259; Sydney Checkland, *The Upas Tree* Glasgow, 1976, pp.39–40.
77. PP, Cd 8731, *Report of the Royal Commission on the Housing of the Industrial Population of Scotland Rural and Urban*, para 536–7.
78. Corporation of Glasgow, minutes of the Special Committee on Housing and General Town Improvement, 28 February 1919; 'There was submitted as letter from the Medical Officer of Health, reporting on the number of slum properties in the city which required demolition. The report was submitted to the Sub-Committee on Ground and Properties, along with Councillor M'Connell, to have a plan prepared showing the positions in the city of these tenements, with a view to reconstruction schemes', Corporation of Glasgow, minutes of the Special Committee on Housing and General Town Improvement 4 September 1919.
79. In September 1922 Wheatley moved that 'in view of the report by the Medical Officer of Health that 58,000 persons occupy 13,195 houses in the city which are not reasonably fit for human occupation, the Director of Housing be instructed to submit plans for lay-outs and the erection of two-room and kitchen houses, with bathrooms, on the building sites presently held by the Corporation, and to report on such other sites, giving the probable cost, as may be suitable in or near the city, with a view to the erection, with all possible speed, of 13,000 such houses': Corporation of Glasgow, minutes of the Special Committee on Housing and General Town Improvement, 20 September 1922.
80. Corporation of Glasgow Housing Department, *Review of Operations 1919–1947* Glasgow, 1947, pp.68–74.
81. Corporation of Glasgow, minutes of the Special Committee on Housing and General Town Improvement, Joint Sub-Committee on Slum areas, 21 March 1922 (memorandum by the Director of Housing upon slum clearances and the housing of the dispossessed therefrom), 24 March 1922.
82. Corporation of Glasgow Minutes, 30 March 1922.
83. See above, note 81.
84. Corporation of Glasgow, minutes of the Special Committee on Housing and General Town Improvement, 30 January 1920; Corporation of Glasgow Minutes, 18 March 1920, 25 March 1920—the first discussion of rents in a meeting of the full Corporation was terminated due to 'disorder' in the Council Chamber—the second, which agreed the proposed rent levels witnessed the suspension of Emanuel Shinwell, for 'obstructive conduct'.
85. *Municipal Glasgow its Evolution and Enterprises* Glasgow, 1914, 65–7.

86. This estimate probably understates the use of concrete in these houses—Corporation of Glasgow Housing Department, *Review of Operations from 1919–1927* Glasgow, 1927, p.19, gives figures for early rehousing schemes—for materials employed in later developments, see, for example, Corporation of Glasgow Housing Department, *Completion of the 40,000th House and Opening of the Scheme at Springfield Road* (Glasgow, 1935), pp.9–10; *Housing Inspection and Ceremony of Cutting of the First Sod at Pollok Housing Scheme* Glasgow, 1937, pp.6–17.
87. Strathclyde Regional Archives, D–TC 8/18 (1919–20), folder 1 (1919), various reports on possible building sites, 2 October 1919.
88. Corporation of Glasgow Housing Department, *Review of Operations from 1919–1927*, Glasgow, 1927, pp.9–10; Corporation of Glasgow Housing Department, *Completion of the 40,000th House and Opening of the Scheme at Springfield Road* Glasgow, 1935, 7–8.
89. '... in the past, through anxiety for speed and for financial reasons, a certain slumping or grouping of the same type of houses has been employed in particular areas, but an endeavour is being made in recent schemes to relieve monotony...'. ibid. pp.7–10; For the scheme at Ballindalloch Drive see *Housing Inspection and Ceremony of Cutting of the First Sod at Pollok Housing Scheme* Glasgow, 1937, p.10.
90. Department of Health for Scotland *Working Class Housing on the Continent. Report by Mr. John E. Highton* ... Edinburgh, 1935, pp.19–21.
91. 25 & 26 Geo. 5., cap 41. The Act is explained in R D Crammond, *Housing Policy in Scotland 1919–1964* Glasgow, 1966, pp.21–2.
92. For the foamed-slag house see Glasgow Corporation Housing Department, *Review of Operations 1919–1947* Glasgow, 1947, pp.56–60; Scottish Office Building Directorate, *Guide to Non-Traditional Housing in Scotland* (Edinburgh, 1987) pp.156–8. See also 'House construction second report' *Post War Building Studies No. 23* Edinburgh, 1946, pp.13–19.
93. *Concrete Quarterly* 3 March 1948 p.20.
94. *Glasgow Herald* 15 May 1923; for Fyfe see also *The British Builder* November 1921, p.79.
95. Peter Fyfe, *Housing of the Labouring Classes* Glasgow, 1899, p.19.
96. Fyfe's enthusiasm for new building methods can be seen in the numerous papers and reports on the subject in the Housing Department files contained in Strathclyde Regional Archives D–TC 8/18.
97. Strathclyde Regional Archives, D–TC 8/18 (1919–20), folder 1 (1919), memorandum by the Director of Housing upon the staffing of the Housing Department, 16 September 1919.
98. *Glasgow Herald* 6 May 1937; see also Nicholas J Morgan, *'Pavement' Glasgow: Scott Rae Stevenson 1838–1988* Glasgow, 1988.
99. Scottish Record Office, BT2/12983 Fyfe-Stone Ltd.
100. Sheila Marriner, 'Cash and concrete. Liquidity problems in the mass-production of "Homes for Heroes"', *Business History* **18** 1976.
101. For Mactaggart see A Slaven and S G Checkland (eds), *Dictionary of Scottish Business Biography*, vol. II, (forthcoming, 1989).
102. *Glasgow Herald* 3 February 1964; for McDonald see also R L Nelson 'To what extent was J R H McDonald's designs at Carse View a practical application of theories put forward in his book of 1931, *Modern Housing*' (unpublished typescript, nd).
103. J R H McDonald, *Modern Housing* Glasgow, 1931, p.93—they also argued that

flat-roofs could be used for putting greens—'if we all had this chance of putting practice we could find a Britisher to bring one or other of the British Golf championships back from America', ibid. p.96.

104. These houses are described in Charles McKean *The Scottish thirties: an Architectural Introduction* Edinburgh, 1987, pp.171–3.
105. For Clydebank see Nicholas Morgan, 'Housing 1914–1845' in John H Hood (ed) *The History of Clydebank* Carnforth, 1988, pp. 87–92; for Aberdeen see, for example, Scottish Office Building Directorate, *Guide to Non-Traditional Housing in Scotland*, Edinburgh, 1987 pp.35–7; for Edinburgh see ibid. pp.40–4; for Dundee see ibid. pp.38–9. Clearly all of these cities are subjects for further intensive research.
106. PP Cmd 9366, *Housing Return for Scotland* (December 1954) p.13.
107. Corporation of Glasgow Housing Department, *Review of Operations 1919–1947* Glasgow, 1947, pp.47–50. For a review of the construction of the reinforced-concrete framed flats at Crathie Drive, Partick see *Concrete Quarterly*, 2 February 1948 p.9.
108. For which see Strathclyde Regional Archives 'Report of a deputation to inspect the "Marseilles Block"' (1954); I H Adams, *The Making of Urban Scotland* London, 1978, p.180.
109. Corporation of Glasgow Housing Department, *Review of Operations 1919–1947* Glasgow, 1947, pp.50.

6 Policy and politics in Scottish housing since1945

Andrew Gibb

At first glance the title to this chapter might appear tautological, since politics is the science and art of government, embodying its political principles, and policy is the course or general plan of action adopted by government. However, other definitions of policy include prudent conduct or sagacity, a definition open to more subjective interpretation of values, modes of implementation, and effectiveness. On a more obscure level there is also the meaning of a document containing a contract of insurance for the future, arguably one of the most cogent interpretations of the term with its connotations of sound economic investment, and sustained social welfare and well-being. Even the solid rock of 'politics' crumbles in the face of warring ideologies, operating not only sequentially, to amend or undo the work of previous administrations, but also concurrently, at national, regional and local levels of interest. These aspects of complexity underlie the Scottish housing experience of the post-war period, and provide some explanation of its unique characteristics.

Problems and early responses

The distinctive tenurial and structural characteristics developed in Scottish housing during the period of rapid industrialisation have been discussed earlier in this volume and widely elsewhere.[1] Fundamental problems of dwelling infrastructure and public health were echoed in concentrated nodes of economic development throughout Scotland, in the small and medium-sized towns of Fife, Lothian and Ayrshire, the larger urban units of Stirling, Aberdeen, Dundee and Edinburgh, and above all in the dynamic, dense conurbation stretching from the docks of Greenock through the sprawl of Glasgow's industries to the coalfield towns of Lanarkshire. That these problems confronted the planners of the post-war period on such an enormous scale is a function of limited response; none whatsoever from the private sector, and painfully slow growth of action from a public sector implementing new and tentative policies while developing its own operational infrastructure and constructional and managerial experience.

Problem perception and problem response varied between local and national levels, providing a fore-taste of tensions to come. The small-scale surgical operations of City Improvements Acts throughout Scotland were overshadowed by the effects of the 1912 Royal Commission into Industrial Housing in Scotland. With its report in 1917 to the effect that private enterprise had failed to meet the housing needs of the working classes, although it overwhelmingly dominated the market, and that only the State, acting through local authorities, could and should take responsibility to meet such requirements, the first operational links between levels of government were forged. The Addison Act of 1919 forced Scottish local authorities to submit proposals on working class housing schemes to the Scottish Board of Health, and in offering generous subsidies not only encouraged them to act quickly, but transferred most of the financial burden of house provision from local rates to national taxes. The national purse remained open for over sixty years, under varying strictures, encouraging attitudes towards public sector house provision which had to be traumatically revised when the drawstrings tightened and closed in the 1970s and 1980s.

Early Scottish problems exerted an important influence on national policy. The Mortgage and Rent Restrictions Act of 1915, the source of national rent control legislation, found some of its roots in the Glasgow and West of Scotland rent strikes,[2] while the Scottish Royal Commission report influenced the decision by national Government to involve itself in the provision of public housing on a large scale throughout Britain. These two elements, of state supply and rents fixed below market levels, were and are important tenets of Socialism, manifested strongly in Scottish urban areas, where the bulk of the working class voting population lay. While central government was able to exert certain controls, on scale and type of public developments, local authorities followed their political instincts. The 1917 Royal Commission had identified a need for a quarter of a million new houses in Scotland. Between 1919 and 1939, 337,000 houses were built, two-thirds within the public sector in strong contrast to the 25 per cent in England and Wales. As political interest and power became more and more strongly consolidated around housing tenure interests, so tenure divergence became more progressive, and by 1945 Scottish housing was clearly distinguished from that of the rest of the UK by a high level of dependence on state housing commanding only low and often nominal rents. Over the next thirty years this pattern intensified, opening up huge gaps between realisable income and expenditure on construction and maintenance, and ultimately between diminishing supply and increasing demand.

Wartime planning for post-war needs

Although house construction virtually ceased during World War II, advanced planning for post-war requirements continued. A 1942 survey of housing needs showed a desperate desire among the working population to escape from overcrowded and insanitary tenements after ten or twenty years on the housing list.[3] The Minister of Health responded directly to this need by announcing in 1944 that in order to secure the largest possible numbers of dwelling units in the two years after the war, work was to proceed simultaneously on the construction of both temporary and permanent houses. Two reports by the Scottish Housing Advisory Committee introduced a revised scale of overcrowding and proposed evaluation of housing need on a national basis, phasing and locating housing development along with industrial development.[4]

The two Housing Acts of 1944 at first ignored the latter recommendation, but the 1946 Act included a response to more general housing needs, widening both the responsibility and the powers of local authorities. As a final crucial step in this strengthening process, the 1949 Act, by deleting all references to 'working classes', entrusted local authorities with providing for the housing needs of all members of the community. The total of over one million houses constructed in Scotland by 1984, over 76 per cent by public sector agencies, provides physical evidence of the pre-eminence of local authorities in the housing field. However, the bare figures disguise the struggle between levels of government, with central Government devising policy instruments of compulsion and financial inducement to aid the implementation of changing regional economic policies, while local government either seized eagerly upon the chance to expand their housing stock in favoured economic circumstances and locations, or fought desperately to deal with overwhelming housing need and the dispersal of their industrial and population bases, in areas of economic decline.

In terms of national need, post-war Scotland revealed a housing deficit on an enormous scale. Over 120,000 unfit houses required immediate replacement, while a further 200,000 were classified as being overcrowded. War damage and special needs added a further 64,000 and 134,000 newly formed households required accommodation. To this daunting total of more than half a million houses required as a matter of immediate necessity, a second wave of need consisting of approximately 405,000 houses technically 'fit for habitation' but lacking sanitary conveniences or internal water supply had to be added.[5] In geographical terms, while rural Scotland exhibited all the characteristics of housing decay and housing need typical of the country as a whole, it was in the urban areas and their satellite zones that the clotted masses of tenements crowded together the greatest proportion of households in need of accommodation.

The concentration of population reflected itself in political power. The Glasgow conurbation contained around 35 per cent of the total Scottish population in contrast to London's 18 per cent of the English population. The central Lowlands as a whole contained 75 per cent of Scotland's people, and the historic drift of the nation's population to this urbanised core was still intensifying in the post-war decades. In 1951 the urban component of the Scottish population amounted to 82.9 per cent, and by 1961 this had risen to 85 per cent.[6] Suburbanisation of more affluent middle-class voters intensified the political characteristics of the cities, and local politicians as well as national sought to maintain their electoral support by the provision of mass public

Table 6.1 Houses by size and region: Scotland 1951 (percentage of total)

No. of rooms*	Scotland	Northern	East Central	West Central	Southern	Crofting Counties
1	5.2	2.3	3.5	7.9	1.7	1.4
2	26.3	16.5	26.2	31.3	17.5	12.5
3	31.2	29.7	34.1	30.2	30.3	25.8
4	21.5	25.2	21.8	19.3	24.9	30.6
5	7.7	11.6	6.9	6.2	10.0	13.5
6	3.4	6.2	3.0	2.2	5.8	7.3
7+	4.7	8.5	4.5	2.9	9.8	8.9

Note: In reckoning the number of rooms in a house, kitchens are counted as rooms, but not kitchenettes, sculleries, closets, bathrooms, landings or rooms occupied as offices, shops, or for other business purposes.
Source: Census of Scotland 1951 Vol. III.

housing. The powerfully evocative image of housing as shelter, and the right of the individual to partake in such a basic commodity, took root in the minds of supplier and consumer alike, engendering a relationship of devouring dependency.

Perception of housing need was made complex by changing standards of evaluation of housing fitness, involving the function of rooms within the house and the status of children under ten. The 1951 census was the first occasion when questions were asked on a uniform basis about the availability of conveniences such as piped water, fixed baths and water closets, and together with information on house and household size they provided evidence of a clear hierarchy of need. Table 6.1 indicates the preponderance of small houses in central Scotland as a whole, but especially in the west-central area, while in contrast, the southern and crofting counties were better endowed with larger dwellings. Table 6.2 shows the overwhelming concentration of small houses in urban areas, and especially in Glasgow. Over 78 per cent of single apartment and almost 66 per cent of two-apartment houses were located in urban areas, and Glasgow alone contained virtually half of the Scottish population who lived in one-roomed houses.[7] With over 130,000 houses overcrowded, and

Table 6.2 Urban concentration: percentage of small houses and population within them: Scotland 1951

	1 room		2 rooms		3 rooms	
	houses	people	houses	people	houses	people
Glasgow	45.2	49	29.5	32.2	19.3	20
Other 3 cities	16.1	13	18.3	17.3	17.9	17.3
Large burghs	16.9	15.9	18.1	17.8	17	17.4
Counties	21.8	20.7	34.1	32.7	45	45.3

Source: Census of Scotland 1951 Vol. III.

thousands of others rendered sub-standard on a sanitary or piped water basis, Glasgow occupied an unenviable position at the top of the hierarchy.[8] Edinburgh, Aberdeen and Dundee occupied the next lower tier, with very large proportions of dwellings classified as unfit. The smallest numbers of houses were required in landward areas of counties, many of which had drawn on inter-war subsidies to greatly reduce their housing needs, already proportionately smaller than those of urban areas.

Policy response: an era of consensus

Policy response to the urgent demands of the post-war housing situation was swift, decisive, and substantial in scale. At both national and local levels, Conservative and Labour administrations saw the need for efficient programmes of land acquisition and public housing construction, and for twenty-five years this consensus of thought dominated Scottish housing policy and provision, though not without the appearance of differences of opinion, some extremely substantial and damaging. Massive investment in public housing was perceived as the solution to Scotland's housing problems, and that investment was to be sustained by a programme of economic growth, recovery, and relocation in industry. The degree to which economic growth failed to sustain itself, proceeding instead in a series of fits and starts as enormous structural changes took place in Scottish industry and vital markets were lost to overseas competitors, obviously had serious effects on the level of commitment to public housing investment.

The period between 1945 and 1970 may be divided into two sub-phases, from 1945 to 1957, and from 1957 to 1969. In the earlier of these sub-phases a vigorous programme of housing developments was undertaken on large-scale suburban greenfield sites. Construction consisted largely of tenemental family houses of three and four apartments, built under general needs subsidies to provide necessary reception areas for overcrowded urban slum-dwellers. The second sub-phase was characterised by the introduction of approved houses (Figure 6.1). The high rate of construction continued, but under more specific direction from central government on type, location, function and size of house, including overspill houses or others designed to integrate housing and industrial incentives along the lines proposed by the Scottish Housing Advisory Committee. At the same time, as peripheral housing schemes, New Towns, and overspill agreements absorbed thousands of families, removal of unfit housing could begin under comprehensive development area policies.

Strategies for house construction and location were not always decided upon and did not always operate as smoothly as the preceding paragraphs and the outline in Figure 6.1 might suggest. Inevitably there were conflicting notions of how rehousing populations could be achieved, and inevitably, where neither side was willing to give ground, these led to damaging delays and fragmented effort. The most serious divergence of opinion between national and local administrations took place in the west of Scotland, where the recommendations of the government-sponsored Clyde Valley Regional

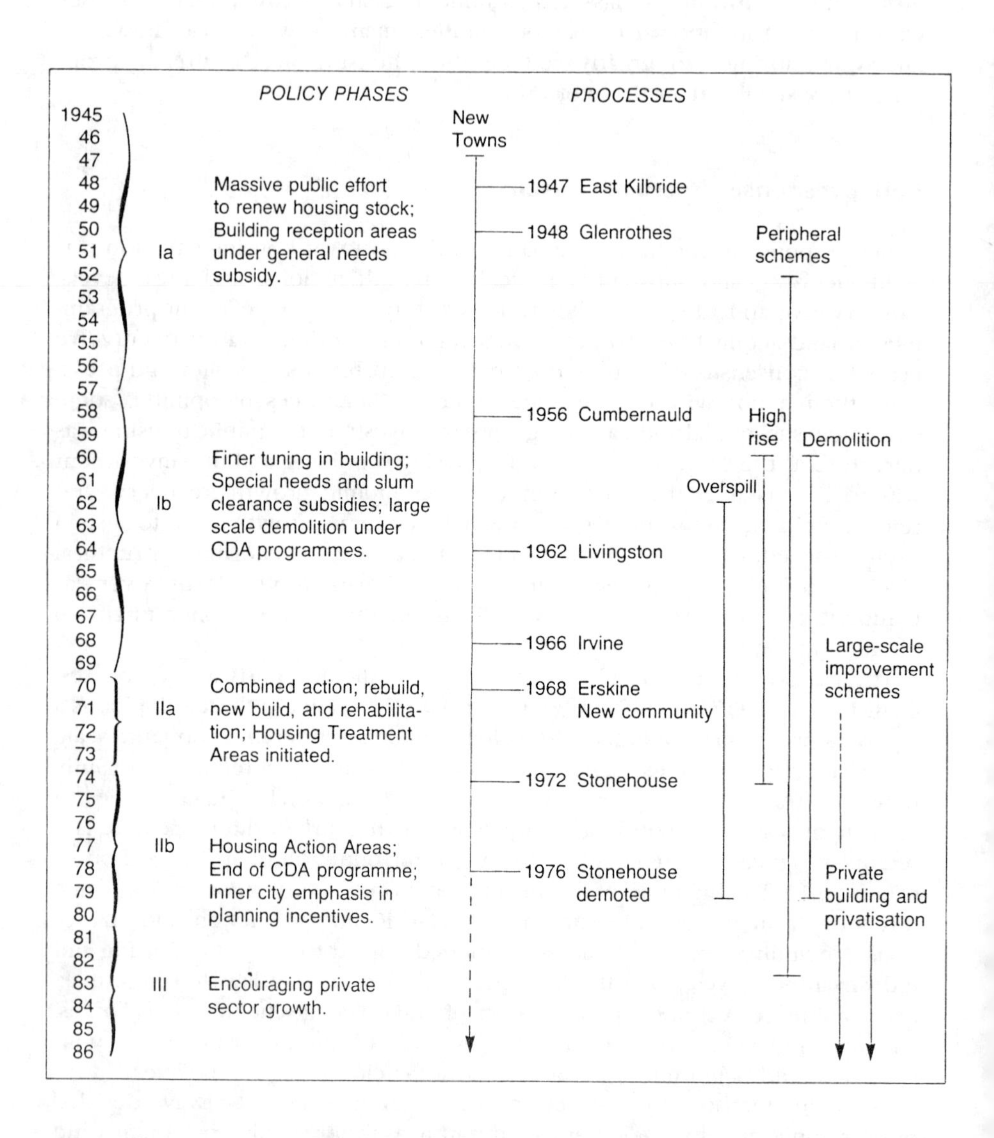

Figure 6.1 Housing strategies in Scotland 1945–86

Plan of 1946 clashed head-on with the Bruce Plan of the same year, produced by Glasgow's City Engineer. In the case of Glasgow, the Clyde Valley Regional Plan proposed a limit on further peripheral growth of its built-up area, with around 250,000 people to be settled between existing city limits and the inner edge of the proposed green belt. This in itself posed no serious obstacles, but strong opposition was mounted to its next proposal. In line with national government's strategy of creating new economic and population growth poles by dispersing congested industries and their workers, 250–300,000 people from the Glasgow conurbation were to be relocated as overspill population in expanded existing towns and in specially-created New Towns.[9]

Local authority opposition was personified by Robert Bruce, the Glasgow Master of Works and City Engineer, who believed that the 316,000 new houses which Glasgow would require by 1986 could be sited, at a range of appropriate densities and with a suitable proportion of gardens or public open space, within the city boundaries. Glasgow Corporation therefore strongly opposed the designation of East Kilbride as a New Town, stubbornly insisting that they would maintain their million plus population, and for a time they were effective in delaying the overspill programme. By the early 1950s however, they were forced to accept East Kilbride's reality, as it had been under way since 1947, and they agreed also to the designation in 1956 of Cumbernauld New Town as a further reception centre for Glasgow families. Spurred by reappraisals of the necessary scale of population loss, which predicted high levels of natural increase and diminishing rates of undirected migration, the original figure of around 250–300,000 was revised to a shedding of 400–500,000.[10] A further series of overspill agreements was made with fifty-seven existing towns, from Irvine in the west to Haddington in the east, and from Stranraer in the south to Wick in the north.

The effects of this struggle with and eventual concession to national Government were far-reaching. The inception of huge peripheral housing programmes was delayed, so that more and more thousands of Victorian slum tenements slid further into decay and dissolution as overcrowding increased. The resultant urgency in housebuilding dictated a 'houses only' policy. Politicians and people alike demanded a visible and swift tally of new housing units to relieve inner city misery. Services and amenities could wait, in the prospect of a successful national economy generating sufficient surplus for the provision of town centres, clubs, cinemas, churches and health centres on the pattern of the growing New Towns, once the all-important houses had been built. The eventual result was economic downturn, subsidy and rating base restriction, and in terms of provision of the most basic elements of social support, far too little, far too late. The other side of the coin was the rapid absorption of slum dwellers once the schemes were under way, and in the 1957–69 phase of development, the opportunity for large-scale demolition of inner city tenements. Opportunity rapidly became perceived as necessity, and for more than a decade the engine of destruction ran at full throttle, resulting in population displacement, social disruption, and the isolation of residual, aged and unskilled groups. The whole process of urgency deciding scale, scale providing speed, and speed and scale together spawning huge problems for the future, was one which local and national politicians alike, with few exceptions were unable to grasp.

Whatever the drawbacks and hidden costs of peripheral schemes, the houses were of solid, traditional construction, relatively expensive to erect, and therefore funded largely by generous subsidies. In 1957 and 1962 central Government began to exert stronger control over housebuilding, using the subsidy mechanism. The 1957 Housing Act reduced the basic subsidy to £24, a severe reduction from even the lowest rate of the 1952 Act. The special needs of rural areas were recognised by a £36 agricultural worker subsidy, increased by a further £12 for remote areas, following the Commission of Inquiry into Crofting Conditions and the establishment of the Crofters' Commission in 1954.[11] New Towns, centres accepting overspill families, and expanding industrial areas were also favoured by both the 1957 and 1962 Acts. Perhaps the provision of greatest consequence related to houses in blocks of flats of more than six storeys, where the basic needs figure of £24 was supplemented by an allowance of two-thirds of any surplus over the average cost of approved houses. The 1962 Act increased the multi-storey basic figure to £40 in an effort to raise the totals of housing unit completions and to encourage higher and mixed-density usage of available sites. With no real possibility of cutting back on urgent housing programmes, local authorities, especially those of the larger urban areas, committed themselves to the large-scale adoption of high-rise building, a decision encouraged by a 1965 circular in which the Minister of Housing proposed 'to launch a concentrated drive to increase and improve the use of industrialised methods in housebuilding for the public sector'.[12] Scottish local authorities were instructed by the Scottish Office to combine where feasible or necessary and choose among types of industrialised building schemes for the public sector. System building had been given the stamp of national approval.

Subsidies and Agencies

There is no doubt that the sytem of subsidy operated by central Government stimulated house construction on a massive level. Examination of the numbers and percentages provided by various agencies shows an interesting pattern, dominated by two major peaks (see Figure 6.2). In the first two years after the War totals were small, a reflection of post-war shortages and controls. Completions then rose to over 20,000 per annum until 1952, when a total of 30,000 presaged a productive decade during which totals never fell below 25,000 per annum, and sustained levels of over 30,000 for most of the period. The second peak represents a surge between 1964 and 1972, with totals always over 35,000 and for five years over 40,000 per annum. The first major phase produced around half a million new housing units, while the second added a further 400,000. Responsibility for these totals lay mainly with three sets of agencies, namely local authorities, the Scottish Special Housing Association, and New Town development corporations, all acting within the public sector. Among these three, the outstanding contribution undoubtedly came from the

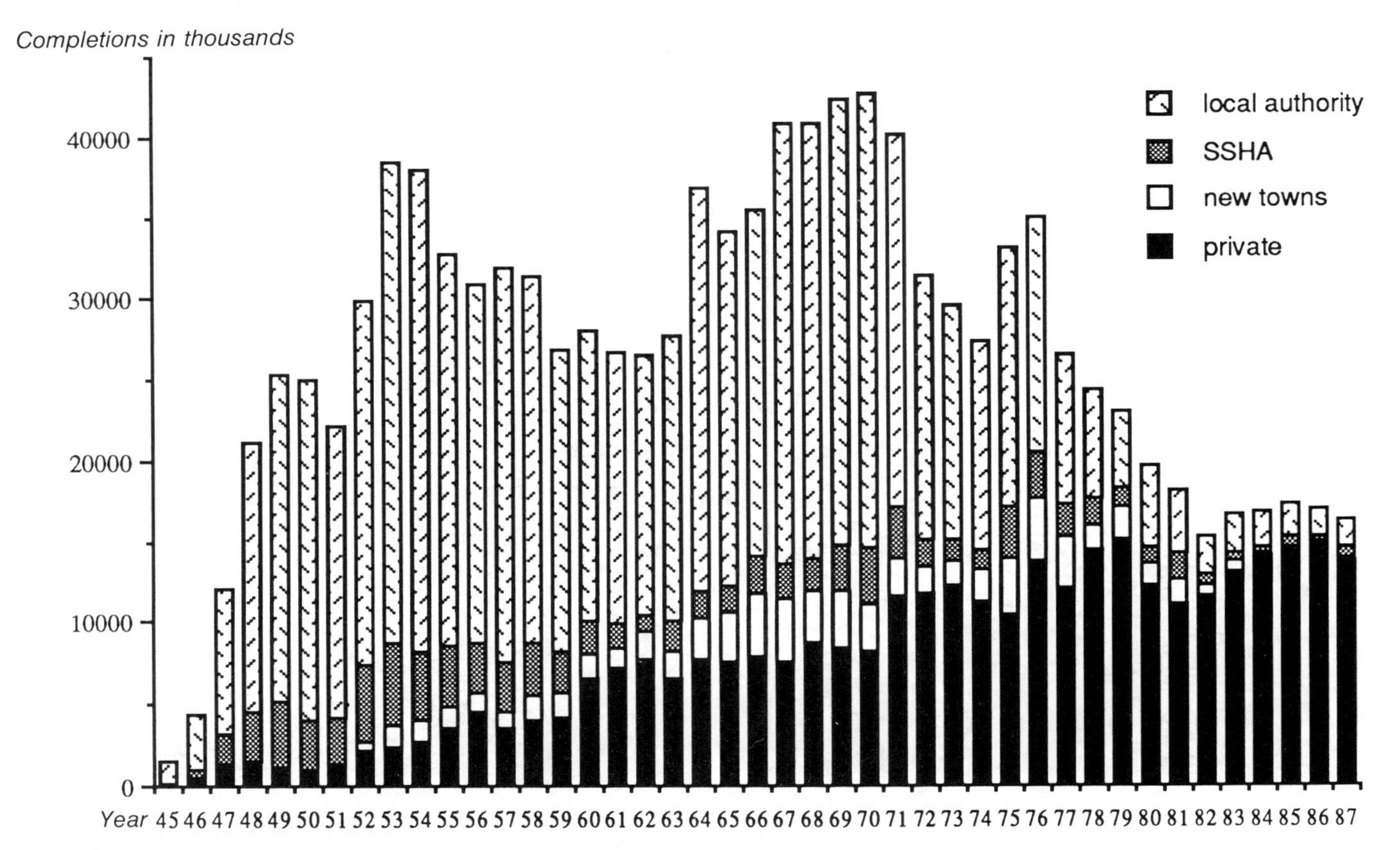

Figure 6.2 House completions by agency: percentage of total, Scotland 1945–82

local authorities, who between 1946 and 1970 completed more than half a million dwellings, more than 70 per cent of the total. This was due to the pattern of subsidy in post-war Housing Acts, which in many ways replicated those of the inter-war period. From 1945 to 1953, the peak year of the first surge, with over 40,000 completions, the local authority share of building never dropped below 80 per cent and often hovered around 85 per cent. As other agencies, especially the private sector, shouldered an increasing proportion of the burden, this share gradually dropped to below 70 per cent in 1959, and stayed in the middle sixties with minor fluctuations, until 1971. It is fashionable, particularly among right-wing politicians, to use the emergence of management and social problems to call into question the long-term efficiency of massive public housing investment in a mixed economy. It is impossible to dismiss the enormous constructive achievements of thirty-eight years of energetic striving and their effects on relieving the overall Scottish housing shortage.

Of the other agencies involved, the Scottish Special Housing Association, discussed elsewhere in this volume, had perhaps the most varied role. Provided with extra funding to experiment with building methods suited to unskilled workers, it was established in 1937 to provide houses and employment within the Special Areas designated for economic assistance. The 1944 Housing Act allowed it to extend its operations throughout Scotland, and it concentrated upon areas of greatest need in large cities and in providing overspill housing. From 1946 to 1953 it contributed between 12.5 and 17.5 per cent of annual completions, dropping to between 9.5 and 10.5 per cent until 1959, and thereafter contributing a percentage which fluctuated around 6 per cent with annual peaks of 9 per cent and troughs of 3 per cent. By 1970 it was the second largest public sector landlord in Scotland, responsible for around 80,000 houses. Between 1947 and 1970, the Scottish New Towns constructed 50,000 public sector units, taking advantage of central government strategy of concentrating investment on new industrial growth poles. Whatever the justice of contemporary claims that the older urban centres were being starved of funds in order to benefit New Towns, the new locations for housing investment attracted private funds on the strength of the spillover effects of their industrial and service infrastructure. At the same time they contributed to the relief of pressure on older inner cities, permitting slum demolition, particularly in Glasgow and Edinburgh.

Private sector activity of course did not benefit from direct large-scale subsidy, and its housing output until the 1970s was dwarfed by that of the public sector. However it grew steadily in absolute and proportional significance both by means of new construction and by the transference of rent-controlled dwellings from private renting to owner occupation. Private investment capital was obviously drawn to the urban areas where the greatest potential market lay, but the relatively small numbers of builders in the immediate post-war period found access to desirable sites restricted by local authorities, anxious to secure land for their own building programmes. The 1946 Building Materials and Housing Act expressed the consensus of opinon on the need for public housing programmes by ensuring that priority in scarce building materials and labour went to those in greatest need, namely local authorities. In many cases, even when the acute shortages were easing, those same local authorities demonstrated a political commitment to exclude or at least make life extremely difficult for private builders, a course of action which when fossilised as political dogma ensured future friction with right-wing governments, even those not notedly of a radical non-interventionist persuasion. Severe restrictions included the necessity to obtain building licences, only granted by local authorities where exceptional need could be demonstrated, and only under strict controls on house size and selling price. Building controls were not abolished until 1954, and from this time the private sector began a steady rise, as completions climbed from the 3–6 per cent of the previous six years to levels of 12–16 per cent between 1956 and 1959, then in the building boom of the 1960s a virtually uninterrupted level of around 20 per cent lasting until 1971. The general affluence of a rising middle class was reflected in the proliferation of suburban owner-occupied housing estates, flourishing in areas beyond the immediate periphery of Labour-controlled cities and their green belts. Conservative-dominated rural or small town councils were swift to seize upon the twin opportunities of expanding their rating base and consolidating their political support by providing a conducive environment for private builders.

The effects of this large scale expansion were far-reaching spatially, structurally, and socially. Around the larger urban centres concentric sprawls of suburban private estates developed rapidly, consolidating and expanding existing middle class residential settlements such as Bearsden and Milngavie, or giving a new lease of life to decayed industrial villages like Hardgate and Duntocher. This undirected overspill affected settlements all through the urban hierarchy as private house buyers sought to balance their aspirations between proximity to the larger centres of employment and the more distant tranquility of rural life. Another kind of expansion took place also, beyond the solidity of inter-war bungalows and semi-detached houses, to include a wider range of private dwellings including terraces and flats. The 'semi' and its derivatives remained the firm favourite however, although its internal characteristics underwent considerable change. In the 1960s and 1970s there was an increasing convergence of working class and middle class housing in terms of size, but a divergence in terms of internal fittings and finish. As the general cubic footage of all houses shrank, so the private house became distinguished by its central heating, fitted kitchen, and integral garage.

The transportation needs of these new communities were met from two directions. Extensive programmes of suburban electrification cut journey times for the new commuters, while a massive increase in car ownership was reflected in new road construction, with motorways and their feeders, such as the Lomond motorway and the Clarkston expressway, cutting swathes of destruction through older urban centres. The presence of tributary populations and the possibility of easy access along new roads, prompted a revolution in retailing, with large scale supermarkets, do-it-yourself and furnishing stores locating at nodal points between the urban periphery and the new satellite settlements. As well as creating pressure on smaller urban and rural authorities to invest heavily in physical and social service provision, these new communities affected the older urban centres in two fundamental ways. The migration of retail outlets, while providing for the needs of a largely car-borne public, reduced the facilities available for the remaining populations of the inner cities. At the same time, the successful growth of new private housing areas in the 1960s and 1970s greatly enhanced social polarisation, reinforcing and extending a concentric pattern of inner city residual population, ageing, socially immobile and low in employment skills, surrounded by young, skilled and upwardly mobile families. Central area regeneration in the 1980s has begun a new cycle, as relatively affluent groups begin to return to the old urban cores.[13]

The political consensus on public housing development helped forge a crucial identification of the provision of public housing as a prime component of Labour Party policy in Scotland. The processes of house building described above, the physical types of the houses and their geographical locations had created clearly identifiable and often strongly polarised political constituencies. Public housing in the peripheral estates and the rebuilt Comprehensive Development Areas (CDAs) contained high proportions of skilled and unskilled working class voters. Private housing in residual urban enclaves and suburban commuter settlements contained high proportions of managers and professionals. In 1973, this spatial perpetuation of class divisions was reflected in the fact that Labour won every urban ward with less than 10 per cent managers and professionals in its electorate, while the Conservatives won the rest.[14] The long tradition of Labour domination of Scottish politics at all levels was reinforced by the huge public sector housing programme, and the equally long tradition of Labour involvement with housing issues as a part of their socialist programmes developed into a powerful political weapon. Using the Scottish Office as a kind of federalising filter, and the necessarily heavy involvement of local authorities in housing supply and management as a lever, Labour politicians created and politically exploited a relationship of dependency between themselves and the mass of the population inhabiting the public sector. Dependency developed along two basic lines, that of spatial segregation of populations, and within those discrete areas, complete control of housing and its environment. In spatial terms the housebuilding programmes of the 1950s, 1960s and 1970s were heavily concentrated on greenfield sites within which housing was overwhelmingly dominated by the local authority. In Glasgow's four main peripheral public sector housing schemes of Drumchapel, Castlemilk, Easterhouse and Pollok for instance, local authority housing accounted for between 98 per cent and 98.8 per cent of all stock. At the same time, the local authority controlled a broad range of functions, including transport, schools, environmental improvement, waste disposal, and retail provision, even to the issuing of licences for mobile traders, invaluable in the serviceless deserts of the peripheral schemes. In housing, as in virtually every aspect of the way of life of these segregated populations, with religious worship the outstanding exception, the local authority controlled every step from initial delivery through to the management and maintenance, and the local authority was motivated by the political will of its councillors. Existence in the next world had its own channels of communication, but in the living world only the Council could provide.

This dependency enabled Labour councillors to frustrate and delay housing initiatives, on funding, tenure, and rehabilitation, which the national Government was able to introduce in England and Wales. The end result by the 1970s was a Scottish housing system overwhelmingly publicised, monolithic and monotonous in structure, inadequately managed and maintained, and providing precious little reward for decades of consumer loyalty.

The built environment

In 1972 the Scottish Housing Advisory Committee produced a report based on information provided by Scottish local authorities to the Scottish Development Department.[15] It admitted that while the acute housing shortage of the immediate post-war period had been substantially met in many areas, there were still long waiting lists for houses, and much substandard and unsuitable stock in existence. It advocated a radical departure from the sheer provision of quantity, the goal of so many fund-raising politicians, and a comprehensive approach to the total needs of the community, to the quality of housing needed. Housing as both an outcome and a generator of social policy, meeting the requirements of special needs groups, and evolving supply, maintenance, management and mobility systems within existing stock, provided the main thrust of the document. While this pointed the way to the future, it said little about the legacy of the past, already beginning to reveal its ghastly contours after only twenty-five to thirty years of construction, and by the time its recommendations were being acted upon, in the late 1970s and early 1980s, a full crop of disasters had come to fruition.

The problem was basically one of compartmentalisation of interests. At one end of the spectrum lay the politicians who sustained themselves on high completion figures. Next in the chain came the commissioned architects, supplying structure and estate layouts to direct labour organisations or commissioned builders. At the receiving end, with no canvassed opinion or input other than rental payments, sat the consumer. As long as the chain of production relied upon traditional methods of construction the end product was reliable, whatever the environmental inadequacies of 1950s and 1960s peripheral estates. However, from the middle 1960s, the adoption of system-building techniques introduced into Scottish housebuilding a whole series of vested interests, tied to quantity and speed of production, and providing the potential for a wide series of problems. The use of factory-made components, to be assembled by industrial methods, introduced a level of technological dominance over skill, one in which quality was essential, but operating within an incentive system which rewarded careless completion and penalised painstaking care.

Building designs totally unsuited to the Scottish climate and to the mass incarceration of humanity were symptomatic of the lack of architectural conception and commitment, producing built environments of stultifying insensitivity and monotony. Flat roofs failed to shed heavy rainfall and acted as reservoirs for rainwater which percolated through inadequately sealed joints to the dwellings below. Cladding slabs were secure by ferrous pins which rusted rapidly in the moist climate and in the worst cases gave way entirely, hurling their half-ton burdens hundreds of feet to shatter on the paving slabs below, or occasionally left them perched, the object of costly and dangerous removal attempts. Steel-framed windows which no amount of painting could protect from corrosion, and which acted as reservoirs for condensation, thin interior divisions which transmitted the slightest noise, and uninsulated exterior walls which permitted expensive heat to drain away were but a few of the basic structural drawbacks. In addition to these, underfloor electric heating which produced differential expansion cracks (in the cases where householders could afford to use it), uninsulated water tanks and pipes which were liable to burst in frost, and ineffective ventilation systems which encouraged severe levels of condensation were among the catalogue of architectural absurdities which perhaps reached their nadir in systems provision for high-rise buildings. Windows lacking safety catches, common landings with no access to fire doors except through houses, steel fire doors on the main walls of bedrooms, elevators never designed to cope with twenty-four hour usage, metal rubbish chutes and doors seemingly designed to provide the maximum noise above ground level and a noisome eyesore on the ground, ludicrously inadequate drying and storage facilities and noisy plumbing systems which provided perfect fire transmission ducts where preventive collars had been omitted to save a few pounds of costs, were built in as additional features of frustration.

The initial architectural and systems provision conception may have been shallow enough, but these inadequacies were compounded by a culpable lack of quality control at the component fabrication and assembly stages. Mass production of components, often by a range of fly-by-night manufacturers or giant combines setting up instant production lines to cash in on the subsidy bonanza, shoddy workmanship by hastily recruited staff operating under inadequate quality control ensured a sufficient supply of substandard items to provide a scattering of malfunctioning systems and crumbling, cracking or corroding structural members throughout a diversity of housing types. Penalties for failure to meet contractual deadlines ensured a blind eye on the part of management and supervisors during both manufacturing and construction, where piece-work payment encouraged slipshod assembly of prefabricated components. At all stages, from design through production and construction to mute consumer acceptance, quality was sacrificed for false economy in an orgy of profit and prestige generation which brought fortunes and reputations to an influential few, and misery to gullible millions. These products of technocracy rendered ludicrous claims of cost-effectiveness, many of them destined for demolition before the interest on their construction loan was paid, and the remainder constituting an architectural time-bomb, ticking towards an estimated cost (in 1983 terms) of £3,000 million nationally for rehabilitation to a habitable standard. If misspent capital was not enough, the huge social problems which rapidly surfaced in these dwellings gave impetus to the desire for a change of direction in housing the Scottish people.[16]

Change was necessary in almost every aspect of housing supply, maintenance and management. The awful legacy of nineteenth century industrialisation had shaped a perception of need which focused solely on house size and sanitary provision. In terms of encouraging investment and producing results this was also an easy and safe political package to deliver. The promise of infrastructure and amenities to come held potential voters in religious thrall, with no recourse but to housing management. The highly centralised bureaucratic structure of management organisations threw the needs of the consumers back in their faces. The job of management was to control access to the system, often by the crudest measures of need, to gather the due rent and rates payments, and to ensure the good behaviour of tenants by threat of expulsion. Sensitivity to tenant needs or desires in terms of changing household profiles, satisfaction with service delivery, from fabric maintenance to environmental enhancement, was absent. The very nature of the housing stock itself, designed for the average family, excluded large groups of the population who could no longer be dismissed as residual casualties of urban renewal. The decade of the 1970s was the stage upon which a panorama of changes was to take place.

Plural policies and crumbling consensus

It has been agreed that the post-war consensus of approach to housing between Labour and Conservative governments was broken only by the 1979 Conservative administration and its successor, but consensus was by no means clearly defined either between party, or between level of government. The strategies adopted towards Scottish housing from the early 1970s lagged behind the multiple approaches of the rest of the UK, but echoed strands of difference of opinion, of political and ideological attitudes, which had been apparent for decades. The 1979 and subsequent administrations merely continued and enhanced these differences.[17] Change in approach was the keynote at every level, from the grand strategy of national design in investment, through decisions on tenure and sector preference, to finer threads in house design and purpose, estate layout, management style, and most significantly, fabric retention and enhancement in preference to removal (see Figure 6.1).

At this strategic level, the most significant change of approach was the diversion of attention from New Towns to older urban centres, in particular their inner areas. From the first, New Towns had been conceived as an aspect of urban redevelopment policy, though their potential role in regional economic policy underscored this aim. By the later 1960s, they had shown how successfully they could attract industry, and their size, infrastructural linkages, and investment patterns were being carefully reconsidered more from the regional economic policy aspect than from the point of view of urban renewal and housing provision. At the same time, the socially disruptive and physically destructive effects of clearance and demolition programmes in inner urban areas were beginning to become evident. Within the cities themselves, socially polarised and spatially segregated communities had developed. The massive building of 'family' houses in public sector estates had brought about serious distortion of the demographic profiles of inner areas, where residual elements of elderly, single homeless, unskilled, handicapped and other special needs groups existed in blighted landscapes constrasting strongly with the solidity and affluence of middle-class residential enclaves. Distortion was further enhanced by the twin processes of officially-encouraged decentralisation or overspill schemes, and the voluntary migration of the socially mobile, away from the deteriorating older urban economies towards the opportunities for employment presented by newer, more successful centres.[18] Thus as the population as a whole lost vital younger age groups, so the urban labour force lost its more highly skilled and qualified elements, many of them in a step form of migration, to peripheral schemes at first, then out of the cities altogether, on the heels of disappearing industries.

By the end of the 1960s it was recognised that much of the poorest quality tenemental stock had been removed from Scottish towns and cities, and that alternative approaches were possible in the case of surviving stock. A 1967 report on Scotland's older houses pointed out that strategies for modernisation had been outlined as early as 1947, and included the subdivision of large houses and flats, modernisation of self-contained houses and flats, and the combination of small houses and flats.[19] It pointed out that there was also a need for the rapid replacement of over 250,000 houses in a continuing programme, far greater in scope than the current one, and involving both rehabilitation and newbuild. It also very strongly condemned central Government for failing to provide the necessary leadership, and the resources to encourage, assist and compel local authorities to act.[20] Viewed as a plea for strong intervention, this critique had interesting implications for future policy decisions, but perhaps its most immediate effect was an acknowledgement, in the 1969 Housing (Scotland) Act, that rehabilitation of existing tenemental housing stock was a feasible and attractive proposition. In fact, the Act began to open the doors to a range of initiatives in Scottish housing which made the 1970s a decade of radical departure from its predecessors.

The framework for change was provided not only by developments in housing legislation, but by major revisions of Scottish local government and the Scottish planning system. The 1972 Local Government Reform Act set up a two-tier system of authorities at Region and District levels, to replace the old county and town councils. A two-level planning system, designed originally in the 1960s for unitary local authorities, divided responsibility into strategic issues which were to be the responsibility of Regions, and would be expressed in Structure Plans, and more localised issues, which would be dealt with by Districts in their Local Plans.[21] Local authority administrative functions were also divided, and housing, perceived as a local issue, was given to Districts. However, since functions such as roads and sewers, fundamental components of any housing development, and social work, important to the identification and satisfaction of special housing needs, were put in Regional hands, the potential for conflict of interest was built into the system. At the same time the avowed intention of central government to play a more strongly directive role, and their strictures to planning authorities to undertake increased consultation with the public added opportunities for future friction.

In a strategic sense, the aspect of change in planning ethos with the greatest implications for housing was the end of the guiding principle of decentralisation, born in the immediate post-war years and given added impetus by the growth pole strategy in economic planning of the 1960s. The new policy to be applied to all of Scotland's run-down industrial areas was one of consolidation and improvement of existing elements in the fabric, including housing wherever possible. The euphoria of New Town designation, with Livingston in 1962 and Irvine in 1966, reached its peak with the addition of Stonehouse to the remit of East Kilbride Development Corporation. Within a few years, the situation had changed completely, spurred on by developments in the area of greatest population concentration, the West of Scotland. A study jointly commissioned by the local authorities of the Clyde Valley and the Scottish Office, an example of consensus in perception of need if not policy outcome, was published in 1974.[22] The West Central Scotland Plan recommended improvement in existing settlements and an end to decentralisation. The visible fruits of this recommendation came in the form of the announcement of the Glasgow Eastern Area Renewal (GEAR) Programme, in May 1976. This was to be an integrated, multi-purpose, large-scale, inner city planning initiative, involving a group of participating bodies under the overall coordination of the Scottish Development Agency.[23] Significantly, of the seven participating bodies, the Housing Corporation and the Scottish Special Housing Association were to contribute virtually one-third of the total first quinquennial budget, while of Glasgow District Council's one-third contribution, a very large proportion was earmarked for housing.[24] In 1976, Stonehouse was demoted, and in 1977 action was taken to terminate Glasgow's overspill agreements. The inner city policy was well under way.

Within the broad framework of these strategic moves, a series of finer threads in housing policy were implemented, leaving behind forever the old simplistic approach of public housing as the only solution to Scotland's housing problems. Figure 6.1 shows the chronology of the introduction of new methods, emphasis on alternative tenure, and cessation of damaging policies, a combination which characterised the 1970s. 1970 itself was the peak year for house completions, with over 43,000 built, 81 per cent by the public sector (65 per cent by local authorities). From then until the 1980s, house completions exhibited a gradual diminution, with the exception of a surge in 1975 and 1976, partly explained by a response to the need for houses in the oil development areas of Scotland, met by both public and private sectors.[25] More interesting perhaps than actual numbers is the changing sectoral composition, with the private sector gradually rising to the position of dominance which it was to enjoy in the 1980s.

A drastic reduction in its share of completions, from 81 per cent in 1970 to 39.5 per cent in 1980, marks the changing role of the public sector (Figure 6.1). New Town growth had been throttled back, and first generation New

Towns especially were finding it necessary to pay attention to special needs groups such as the elderly, within a reduced housing provision. The role of the Scottish Special Housing Association remained steady in terms of output, but it began to extend its activities in other directions, notably towards rehabilitation of older local authority stock. The principal changes took place within local authorities themselves, as their orientation towards stock increase began to diminish, and more attention was paid to new approaches to management. As decentralisation on the grand scale was being abandoned as a strategy for urban renewal, so it was increasingly being adopted by housing management, employing better-trained management staff to respond to the participative needs of tenants. At the same time, criteria of eligibility for entry to public systems were being revised, particularly after the passing of the 1978 Homeless Persons Act.

Ever since 1919, central government subsidy provision had been crucial to local authority behaviour towards housing provision, and the 1970s proved no exception. Until 1976 the old type of fixed-term subsidies, defined under the various housing Acts, displayed a minefield of complexity in their provisions. Belated Labour Party attempts to reduce public spending, not just in Scotland, brought about more direct Scottish Office funding of management and maintenance costs, and in 1978 the Housing Support Grant system was introduced in Scotland, providing for a firm direction by central Government of the spending powers and patterns of local government. In contrast to this introduction of inflexible control, the Labour Party's 1977 Green Paper on Housing Policy for Scotland,[26] embodied a broad, multi-faceted approach to housing policy, reflecting the distinctive needs of Scottish housing. In terms of major party consensus, there was little difference between statements in this paper, and the approaches to housing adopted by the successor Conservative government. The whole thrust of the document was towards widening people's choice of tenure, and breaking down the barriers between tenures. This was to be done partly by introducing intermediate forms of tenure and encouraging local admixtures of tenure types in order to break the rigidity of social and spatial segregation still prevalent. Co-ownership schemes, equity sharing, co-operatives and housing association experiments would be encouraged by legislative arrangements to make subsidies more flexible and allow local authorities to acquire private builders' houses, or to build for sale themselves, and to shed portions of their stock under safeguarded selling procedures.

Criticism of the outlined agenda centred on certain crucial issues. Firstly, the central Government assessment of the peculiar needs of Scottish housing was, to say the least, optimistic, since not only did 160,000 houses not meet the minimum tolerable standard, but another 250,000 houses, equal to 14 per cent of the total stock, were the shelters for households living in 'unsatisfactory conditions', on central Government's own definition.[27] Therefore the notion that the quantitative problem had been solved, in terms of sheer numerical provision ignored both the poor quality of the most recent and most numerous crops of completions, and the gathering storm of problems resulting from inadequate cyclical maintenance of 1950s and 1960s stock. Diversion of attention towards a broader tenure mix and greater inter-tenure mobility merely masked the manifest inability of public sector authorities, particularly large local authorities, to adequately, reasonably, economically or at the very least sympathetically manage the stock which they already had in hand. To the hard left the document was anathema, if only because of its commitment to tenures other than public rental, but especially because of its heretical notion of selling public assets. To the hard right, it was permissive in its continued consideration of welfare policies and the proposed vast drainage of the national purse into housing support. To the middle ground of all political colours it was insufficient in all of its recommendations. Between national and local government there was greater diversity than a simple scan of the political spectrum might reveal. Urban authorities viewed with horror the implications of ownership change, tenure shift, and the effects of a regeneration of urban social mobility on their secure voting base. The response was entrenchment, perhaps a perceptive preparation for the next few years, since while the 1978 Housing (Financial Provisions) (Scotland) Act came into operation, in many ways providing local authorities with greater flexibility over types of expenditure while maintaining a firm hand on its upper limits, the change of national government in 1979 effectively slowed full implementation of measures which the Conservative central authorities were to enforce with enthusiasm in their ensuing administrations.

Positive change: retention and rehabilitation

If the hostile attitudes of Scottish local authorities towards any breaching of their public management monopolies had negative effects in delaying implementation of change, then change when it came was not only peculiarly Scottish in character, but in many aspects had beneficial effects absent from similar changes elsewhere in the United Kingdom.[28] The 1969 Housing (Scotland) Act was a relatively ineffective instrument in inducing a transfer of local authority efforts from removal to renovation. While it encouraged the definition of Housing Treatment Areas (Figure 6.1) within which grant-aided work might be undertaken on substandard houses, it was neither sufficiently compulsive nor flexible. A major step forward was embodied in the 1974 Housing (Scotland) Act, whereby local authorities could respond to the needs of private owners and housing associations, apart from their own requirements, by declaring Housing Action Areas, within which the range of available approaches gave scope for imaginative combinations of treatment. There were three main methods of implementing rehabilitation schemes. Firstly, private property owners could be funded to undertake the necessary work, but the fragmented nature of tenement ownership, even where large factorages administered blocks of dwellings, slowed and often precluded the necessary processes of application and implementation. In the remaining rump of tenemental stock lying within the private rental market, surviving the depredations of comprehensive redevelopment, there was no real incentive for landlords to undertake, let alone share, the costs of extensive rehabilitation, at any level of subsidy. Secondly, local authorities could undertake improvement within Housing Action Areas, but lack of proper decanting accommodation and reliance on improperly costed direct works organisations slowed their efforts to such a degree as to render them impractical in many cases. By 1979, forty-nine out of sixty-one authorities were involved in basically small-scale rehabilitation projects, but four-fifths of expenditure was concentrated in seven districts, with Glasgow alone accounting for 59 per cent of total expenditure.[29] This reflection of the discretionary powers of local authorities in the definition and declaration of Below Tolerable Standard (BTS) housing, and the choice of strategies with which to treat it, resulted also in an extremely uneven spatial pattern of expenditure.

The third and most significant component of the rehabilitation movement involved area-based housing associations, acting as agents for the local authority, but acting without local authority restraints, funded by the Housing Corporation. Established by Parliament in 1964 to promote voluntary, non-profit making housing associations, it now funds and supervises 2,600 housing associations in Great Britain, eighty-five of them in Scotland, each run by a committee of volunteers to provide homes for people in need. In sharp contrast to the swingeing reductions in other sectors of public housing expenditure the Corporation has retained its level of funding, currently accounting for approximately one quarter of public housing investment, principally on rehabilitation, but also on newbuild programmes.

Groups of houses in clearly identifiable geographical areas were passed to the control of resident groups who forged a development policy involving responsibility for rehabilitation, maintenance and management, throughout the forseeable life of the renovated properties.[30] However, while central government provided policy instruments which were favourable to rehabilitation by housing associations, local authority discretion was one important element in shaping the scale, type, and location of housing associations up to 1980. From a pre-1974 total of fifteen, the number of associations had increased to fifty-three by 1980, but these operated only in nine Scottish local authority areas, with an extremely uneven level of input of expenditure among them. 75 per cent of the national total went to Strathclyde Region, and within that, 65 per cent of the national total went to Glasgow. As Maclennan and Brailey point out,

> This highly concentrated pattern of expenditure, with real programme totals of around £70 million per annum by 1980, did not emerge from an explicit, rational capital allocation process by central government or the Housing Corporation over different areas. Instead it reflected essentially where housing associations existed and where they could organise feasible rehabilitation contracts.[31]

By 1980, Glasgow had thirty locally-based housing associations, Edinburgh had sixteen, Dundee had three and Aberdeen had two. While to a limited extent these numbers may seem to reflect different sizes of population and therefore different needs and potential, this is only a crude approximation of the truth. Local authority attitude was of fundamental importance in ensuring success as a multiplier in housing association foundation. There were strong contrasts between the aggressive promotional policy of the Housing Corporation in Glasgow and the '*laissez-faire*' attitude in Edinburgh, in both cases encouraged by the district councils. In Glasgow the council encouraged targeting of medium-scale priority areas in which concentrated inputs produced successful rehabilitation, rapidly emulated by newly-forming housing associations. In Edinburgh, success was more limited, because of the stressful contacts between organisational systems designed to cover several large geographical territories, and the approval of piecemeal improvements within those territories, sometimes of single houses, rendering cost-effective repair and management impractical. It is significant that the formation of new associations beyond the two cities has shown a clear bias for the Glasgow model, and these local authorities have shown the same willingness as Glasgow to cope with the complexities of dealing with multiple organisations, rather than following the supposedly managerially more simple Edinburgh model.[32]

Whatever the spatial and concomitant financial inequalities of the Scottish rehabilitation programme, there can be no doubts concerning its effectiveness at all scales of examination. By 1980 almost 20,000 dwellings had been rehabilitated by the combined efforts of local authorities, the Scottish Special Housing Association, and area-based housing associations funded by the Housing Corporation, and the considerable momentum of the programme was to carry it buoyantly into the next decade. At the scale of the individual dwelling the provision of adequate living space and acceptable internal facilities, including bathroom and kitchen space, necessarily involved amalgamation of existing flats and a reduction in the number of dwelling houses in most, though not all, tenement closes. However, the end product, in terms of commodious and well-appointed flats in buildings of traditional and proven structure, administered with a sympathetic and intimate knowledge of inhabitant and neighbourhood needs, was a large number of highly desirable residences which in their local groups provided attractive housing possibilities for a range of household profiles.

At the area scale there was obviously a reduction in local population density, but this was more than compensated for in the overall retention of local inhabitants, often remnants of communities with deep historical roots. The identification of community with area was enhanced by the preservation of street layout and building fabric, the physical and social antithesis of the grinding programmes of comprehensive redevelopment of the late 1950s and 1960s. In tandem with the gift of prolonged life to familiar and endearing structures went the sigh of relief for the breathing space which promised a future for beleaguered communities, and an end to the dispiriting downward spiral of fabric decay and social degeneration. Beyond the immediately recognisable physical and social transformations, further effects began to materialise. Stability, confidence and the potential spending power of present and future inhabitants of these rejuvenated and regenerated areas began to attract the attention of private capital. Spillover effects ranged from the measurable, in the tangible terms of service provision involving both enhancement of existing premises and introduction of completely new services, to the intangible locational decisions of private builders at all scales, perceiving the possibilities of following pump-priming capital from the national purse. Thus to successful area rejuvenation was added social admixture, and the resultant urban renewal involved not only enhancement of the built environment but more importantly the development of social groupings with built-in potential for growth, continuity and stability.

The broadest scale was that of the individual city, for while policy instruments provided national opportunity, in practice it was those urban areas which seized the proferred chances, and enthusiastically channelled Housing Corporation finance into their development strategies, who reaped the greatest benefits. In Glasgow the improvement programme was providing jobs for around 2,500 people by 1980, mainly construction workers, but also professional and clerical workers. In the job-hungry northern cities, this kind of programme showed the potential to become an important counterbalance to spiralling industrial redundancies. Apart from the catalytic effect on small local construction companies, which admittedly provided only a limited input to the larger urban economy, the broader environmental impacts and effects of the programme set in train long-term developments of external perception of the urban environment and the possibilities of attracting manufacturing and service industry back to cities previously shunned because of their image. The whole rehabilitation programme, with all of its instruments and agencies, may be seen as a successful component of a broader philosophy regarding approaches to urban regeneration. From the middle 1970s the spotlight had switched from New Towns to the decayed older urban centres, and housing was one element of an approach involving employment, environment and public health, aimed at inner city regeneration.

The 1980s: piecemeal policy and public sector crisis

In the mid 1980s some observers were predicting the imminent arrival of a new national housing crisis, and forecasting this crisis would be the result not of an end to political consensus on housing policy, and a radical post-1979 change of direction by Conservative governments, but simply the accentuation and in places exacerbation of trends in housing policy which were already clearly defined.[33] Others argued that there had been a fundamental policy shift since 1979, consisting almost entirely of public sector cuts, unaccompanied by any form of extensive policy restructuring.[34] The truth lies along the spectrum between these two poles of thought, and the fact that it lies closer to the latter than the former point of view stems from the more prominent role played by the public sector in Scottish housing. The wide range and tenure-sector orientation of policy instruments employed by the Scottish Office on behalf of central Government, necessarily implies an imbalance both sectorally and spatially, as encouragement of the private sector is more than matched by disinvestment in the public sector.

The end of the public dream?

From the end of World War II until the 1970s, the dominant attitude towards public sector housing was that sustained investment, maintained on the basis of economic growth, would solve Scotland's housing problems. The economic realities of the later 1960s and the 1970s put an end to these ideas, incidentally undermining the existing complexity of subsidies. By the 1980s, the need to restrict public spending of all kinds forced central Government pressure on local authorities, and housing expenditure bore the brunt of cutbacks. Consumers, both of structures and services, found themselves on a battlefield of ideals, with on the one hand, largely socialist local authorities ideologically committed to public housing and on the other a Conservative central Government determined to curb their general profligacy and prepared to act firmly to achieve its ends.

In housing terms, some idea of the spatial imbalance of such policies within Scotland may be gleaned from Table 6.3. The long tradition in Scotland of commitment to the provision of public housing on a large scale meant that by 1981, 54.6 per cent of Scotland's houses lay within the public sector, compared with only 26 per cent of houses in England and Wales. However, while 54.6 per cent represented the national average, nineteen of the fifty-six Scottish district authorities represented either completely or dominantly urbanised areas, with large concentrations of people, and therefore large numbers of houses. In the cases of Glasgow and Dundee, for instance, in the 60–69 per cent group, their public sectors equalled approximately 166,000 and approximately 39,000 houses respectively. In contrast to this, authorities with less than 50 per cent of their houses within the public sector represented largely rural areas, with the exceptions of Bearsden and Milngavie, and Eastwood, at the lowest end of the scale, and representing the outward mobility of contiguous Glasgow's middle classes. Public sector cuts thus concentrated their effects spatially within the central lowlands, especially the western central lowlands, among traditionally socialist-voting populations now also experiencing the worst effects of rapidly rising unemployment levels.

Between 1980 and 1984 a sustained pattern of reduction in housing programme expenditure meant an overall loss of 30 per cent for Scotland. This looks favourable against a 50 per cent loss for England and Wales in the same period, but the pattern for cuts affected Scotland, with its dominant public sector, much more strongly. While subsidies to the private sector actually increased in real terms, Housing Support Grant (HSG) fell heavily, from around 39 per cent of Housing Revenue Account (HRA) income in 1979 to around 7 per cent in 1985, and in fact around half of Scotland's District Councils were by this time receiving no HSG at all. Limited by central Government controls on the amount of Rate Fund Contributions (RFC) upon which they could draw without attracting upon themselves 'rate-capping' penalties, even diehard socialist councils were forced to jeopardise their voting support by raising council house rents. However satisfying this might have seemed to a central Government bent on forcing rent rises to meet a greater proportion of HRA outgoings, the general effect on reducing public expenditure was negated by the growing number of households qualifying for Housing Benefit.

Hapless district councils, forced since 1977 to lay out their strategy in housing plans, and squeezed in the vice of diminishing or disappearing HSG income, found themselves having to give ground on the most sacred of

Table 6.3 Public sector housing: percentage of housing stock in district council areas: Scotland 1981

80–89	70–79	60–69	50–59	40–49	30–39	20–29	10–19
Clydebank	Cumnock & Doon	Dundee	Aberdeen	Caithness	Shetland	Orkney	Bearsden & Milngavie
Monklands	West Lothian	Clackmannan	East Lothian	Ross & Cromarty	Sutherland	Western Isles	Eastwood
Motherwell	Cumbernauld & Kilsyth	Dunfermline	Roxburgh	Inverness	Moray	Skye & Lochalsh	
		Kirkcaldy	Lanark	Banff & Buchan	Badenoch & Strathspey	Gordon	
		Falkirk	Lochaber	Berwickshire	Perth & Kinross	Kincardine & Deeside	
		Midlothian		Ettrick & Lauderdale	Argyll & Bute		
		Cunningham		Annandale & Eskdale	Nairn		
		Kilmarnock & Loudon		Nithsdale	Stewartry		
		East Kilbride		Wigtown	Edinburgh		
				Kyle & Carrick	Tweeddale		
		Renfrew		Stirling	NE Fife		
		Inverclyde		Dumbarton			
		Hamilton		Strathkelvin			
		Glasgow		Angus			

Note: Scottish average is 54.6%
Source: Census of Scotland, 1981.

ideological issues, the sale of council houses after the 'right to buy' legislation introduced in 1980. Given the rapid closing of the HSG pipeline of public funds, councils might have begun to welcome additional revenue from sales had not central Government, through the Secretary of State for Scotland, imposed severe restrictions on how and when such revenue might be used. Forward planning is therefore done in an atmosphere of considerable uncertainty as to projected income and spending permission, while the requirement to use the revenue in the year in which it is provided adds an unwelcome note of urgency to the proceedings.

Figure 6.2 shows some of the physical effects of policy in terms of house completions. The graph lines for completion in the public and private sectors crossed in 1977, at which time 55.5 per cent of all completions were in the public sector. By 1982 that proportion had dropped to 28.8 per cent and thereafter continued on its downward spiral. As significant as the severe reduction in overall completions was the need to concentrate almost entirely on construction for special needs, such as the elderly and disabled. Rapid rises in rates of household formation in the 1980s therefore exerted greater pressure on stocks of 'family'-size public sector houses, which stocks were themselves being gradually reduced by sales. At the same time, spending on maintenance and modernisation of existing stocks has not grown rapidly enough to meet the requirements of hundreds of thousands of both traditional and system-built houses sliding ever more rapidly into conditions of gross disrepair. The Glasgow Energy Enquiry of 1986 estimated that £600 million was required to tackle dampness alone in 520,000 Scottish houses, while Glasgow District Council estimated that £1.3 billion would be required to bring the city's below tolerable standard houses, more than half of which belong to the Council, to a state of reasonable repair.[35]

One undoubted effect of central Government's restrictive housing policy has been increased competition for houses remaining. While the public sector has steadily become more and more residualised in terms of catering for less mobile social groups such as single-parent families, large families, and homeless persons, the level of homelessness has still risen sharply. A Shelter report esimated that in 1986, one Scottish family in every hundred was homeless. In 1985, more than 23,000 families had applied for help under the Homeless Persons Act, and the large municipal authorities were facing staggering increases. Between 1983 and 1985, Glasgow and Edinburgh recorded rises of 36 and 38 per cent respectively, Aberdeen and Dundee an appalling 248 per cent.[36] Over large areas of public sector housing, particularly in peripheral estates, a deadly combination of insufficient maintenance, high levels of environmental pressure, and concentrations of multiply-deprived households generating no rental stream, accelerated the growth of the new slums of the 1980s.

The private sector and its alternatives

The other side of the coin of central Government's negative attitude towards public sector housing in the 1980s has been its positive and active promotion of private sector activity, together with a range of peripheral or alternative forms of tenure. While it is possible to argue that the private rental sector has been ignored in policy terms, the promotion of housing association activity, though including newbuild, has been strongly concentrated on rehabilitation for rent. Although the Housing Corporation is basically using public funds, its provision of low-rent, inner city accommodation may be seen as an attractive alternative to the private rented sector, and helps explain the lack of central Government interest in the sector, demonstrated by their reductions in improvement grant availability.

Important though this activity is, and in capital terms that amounts to £80–90 million pounds per annum by 1983, the major thrust of housing policy was directed towards increasing levels of owner-occupation. In 1981, 34.7 per cent of Scottish households owned the houses which they occupied, compared with 58 per cent for England and Wales. The strong Government commitment to home ownership therefore faced a much greater uphill struggle in Scotland, and represented a more extreme reversal of policy. Continuation of positive tax benefits for home owners, including the raising of the tax relief threshold to £30,000 in 1983, and private sector improvement grant provision, represented further use of existing policies, but new measures to induce accelerated sector shift involved the sale of public sector houses to sitting tenants at extremely favourable discounts. By 1984, four years after the introduction of legislation, and despite the intransigence of local authorities and local government unions, around 60,000 public sector houses had been sold. The predicted concentration of such sales in the most desirable groups of housing type not only restricted mobility generally within the public sector, but created spatial disparities between rural areas where high levels of desirable stock were sold, and urban areas, where the levels were much lower. Together with efforts by urban local authorities, particularly Glasgow District Council, to release land on favourable terms to private builders in order to provide cheap starter homes, encouragement of owner-occupation brought the Scottish average to 38 per cent by 1984, in comparison to 63 per cent for England and Wales.

Moving beyond straightforward reliance on increasing home ownership, by the mid-1980s central Government was exerting pressure on local authorities to take active steps towards greater diversification of tenure. In many cases they were preaching to the converted, since the Convention of Scottish Local Authorities (COSLA) had set up a Special Housing Group as early as 1963, in order to encourage better housing by improving the provision, management and maintenance of the Scottish housing stock. However, it was really during the 1980s that a wide range of effective schemes of tenure diversification got under way. Provision of new housing for sale or rent, involving cooperation between private and public capital and expertise, self-build housing schemes, community ownership housing, improving housing for sale, homesteading, par-value and tenant cooperatives, partnership schemes of all kinds, were under way from Edinburgh to Argyll, with Glasgow the acknowledged leader in the field.[37] Ministers responsible for both housing and Scottish local government have stated clearly that sales of council houses alone will not transform Scottish council housing, and that large estates must be broken up into a number of smaller communities characterised by their variety of tenure. Firm warning was given that local authorities must move away from concern merely with houses which they own control, and establish themselves more as enabling agents, helping other agencies to provide housing within the areas which they administer.

Conclusion: the 1980s and beyond

It is possible, and reasonable, to debate the applicability of the term 'consensus' to the politics of Scottish housing in the post-war period, and to the policies developed and implemented during that time. However, there was at least a general level of agreement, across the political spectrum, and through the political hierarchy, of the need for swift production of large numbers of new houses as a response to Scotland's severe housing problems. Even in the 1970s, when the perception began growing that the purely numerical problem had been solved, and considerations of type, quality and location should assume dominance, there was still a planned, pluralistic approach to Scottish housing. The introduction of Housing Plans and Housing Support Grant may be viewed in this light, at least in their earliest manifestations, as genuine attempts to devolve policy formulation to local authorities on the ground. Prior to the advent of the 1979 Conservative government, the strongest pressures on local authorities were imposed principally by Labour governments striving for equality and uniformity, and the measures of the 1970s began to relieve such pressure.[38]

The 1980s saw a complete turnaround in relationships. Central Government steadily increased its influence over local authorities, paralysing their power to act autonomously and crushing their independence in order to reduce public expenditure. Annual cash limits on spending were and are enforced through the medium of fiscal penalties, with inevitably harsh effects on the provision of public services such as housing.[39] All scope for investment or spending discretion has been lost to local authorities, with concomitant effects on imaginative initiatives. Each act of defiance or intransigence, or even exploitation of existing loopholes by a local authority has brought down the wrath of the Scottish Secretary in the form of new restrictive legislation. Purposive, planned housing policy has been sacrificed to the primal urge of public spending reduction.

It is possible to discover positive aspects of this piecemeal and largely accidental policy framework of the 1980s. Forced marriages between public sector agencies and the deployers of private capital have produced many concrete developments, lasting benefits, and initiatives for the future. Release of inner city land to private builders has acted in conjunction with massive Housing Corporation investment to revitalise run-down inner areas and rejuvenate the housing cycle. However, the present policies of public sector curtailment, in aggravating the effects of decades of inadequate cyclical maintenance, are sowing the seeds of potentially massive problems for the next decade. The deprived deserts of outer urban areas, creations of decades of energetic striving in the post-war period, must swiftly become the focus of policy concern, if all of that valiant effort is not to be undone.

Notes

1. R G Rodger, Crisis and confrontation in Scottish housing 1880–1914; above pp.25–53 and, for example A Gibb *Glasgow, the Making of a City* ch 5–7 London, 1983; I H Adams *The Making of Urban Scotland*. London, 1978, ch 5–9.
2. J Melling, *Rent Strikes: Peoples' Struggle for Housing in West Scotland, 1890–1916* Edinburgh, 1983.
3. D Chapman, *Wartime Social Survey; the Location of Dwellings in Scottish Towns* Edinburgh, 1943.
4. Scottish Housing Advisory Committee, 1944: (a) 'The design, planning and furnishing of new houses in Scotland'; (b) 'Distribution of new houses in Scotland'.
5. Scottish Housing Advisory Committee, 1944 (a), op.cit. pp.10, 11.
6. Census of Scotland, enumeration abstracts, 1951, 1961.
7. A Gibb, 'The development of public sector housing in Glasgow', University of Glasgow, Centre for Urban and Regional Research, Discussion Paper No 6, 1982.
8. J Cunnison and J Gilfillan (eds) *The Third Statistical Account of Scotland; Glasgow* Glasgow and London 1958 Table LXXIV p.469.
9. P Abercrombie and R H Matthew *The Clyde Valley Regional Plan* 1946 pp.176–85.
10. E Farmer and R Smith 'Overspill theory: a metropolitan case study' *Urban Studies* 1975, pp.153–5; Corporation of Glasgow, *First Quinquennial Review of the Development Plan* 1960, p.8.
11. Department of Agriculture for Scotland, *A Programme for Highland Development* 1954, report of the Commission of Enquiry into Crofting Conditions, [Cmnd 9091].
12. Ministry of Housing and Local Government, 'Industrialised building', Circular 76/65, 1965.
13. N J Burnett, *A Social History of Housing 1815–1985* (2nd ed) 1978, 319.
14. W Miller, 'Politics in the Scottish city 1832–1982' in G Gordon (ed) *Perspectives of the Scottish City* Aberdeen 1985, p.203.
15. Scottish Housing Advisory Committee, *Planning for housing needs: pointers towards a comprehensive approach* Edinburgh, 1972.
16. A Gibb and D MacLennan 'Policy and process in Scottish housing, 1950–1980' in R Saville (ed) *The Economic Development of Modern Scotland 1950–1980* Edinburgh 1985, pp.282–3.
17. F Brown and D Green 'Housing in the cities: the end of consensus?' in P Lawless and C Raban (eds) *The Contemporary British City* London, 1986.
18. A Gibb, 1983, op.cit. pp.155, 156.
19. Scottish Housing Advisory Committee *Scotland's Older Houses* Edinburgh, 1967, p.15.
20. Scottish Housing Advisory Committee, 1967, op.cit. p.24.
21. J Forbes, 'A view of planning in Scotland 1974 to 1984' *Scottish Geographical Magazine* 100(2) 1984, p.105.
22. *West Central Scotland Plan*, 1974 Synopsis, Glasgow.
23. Scottish Development Agency, 1978. *The future for G.E.A.R.: Key issues and possible courses of action* 1978, p.4.

24. A Gibb, 1983. op.cit. p.175.
25. C Jones and D MacLennan *North Sea Oil and the Aberdeen Housing Market* Final Report to the Social Science Research Council North Sea Oil Panel, 1983.
26. Green Paper on Housing Policy for Scotland. 1977 [Cmnd 6852] Edinburgh.
27. A Macleary and N J Williams 'A Critical Overview of the Government's Green Paper on Scottish Housing' in D MacLennan and G Wood (eds) *Housing Policy and Research in Scotland: A Response to the Green Paper on Housing*. Department of Political Economy, University of Aberdeen, 1978, pp.2–13.
28. D MacLennan and M J Brailey *Housing Associations and Rehabilitation in Scotland* University of Glasgow, Centre for Urban and Regional Research, Discussion Paper 13, 1984.
29. D MacLennan, M Brailey and N Lawrie *The Rehabilitation Activities and Effectiveness of Housing Associations in Scotland* Scottish Development Department, Central Research Unit Report, 1983.
30. D Robertson, *Revitalising Glasgow: Glasgow's Improvement Programme 1964–1984* University of Glasgow, Centre for Housing Research, Discussion Paper 3, 1985.
31. D MacLennan and M J Brailey, 1984, op.cit. (note 28) p.7.
32. D MacLennan and M J Brailey, 1983, op.cit. (note 29) pp.9–14.
33. F Brown and D Green in P Lawless and C Raban, 1986, op.cit. (note 17) p.63.
34. D MacLennan and A O'Sullivan 'Scottish housing policy and spending since 1979' in *The Thatcher Revolution*, Modern Studies Association, 1986.
35. *Glasgow Herald* 15 November 86, 27 February 87.
36. *Glasgow Herald* 10 July 86.
37. Scottish Local Authorities Special Housing Group *Alternative forms of housing finance and tenure*, Housing management paper No 9, 1982; Glasgow District Council, Housing Department *Community Ownership in Glasgow*, 1985.
38. W Miller, 1985, op.cit. (note 14). p.209.
39. J Forbes, 1984, op.cit. (note 21) p.106.

7 The Scottish Special Housing Association and the implementation of housing policy, 1937–87[1]

Richard Rodger and Hunain Al-Qaddo

Acute housing problems have been endemic in Scotland for at least a century. Overcrowded block dwellings, deficient in amenities and with adverse vital statistics—child, infant and maternal mortality, and life expectancy—and other social indicators such as under-developed physiology, violent crime and delinquency, have characterised high-rise Scottish tenement dwelling and social relationships in stark contrast to the English pattern of terraced living.[2] Though acute, the Scottish housing problem was not unique; pockets of English and Welsh housing deprivation, notably on Tyneside, in South Wales, and East London were conspicuous[3] but nowhere was the phenomenon as universal as in the Scottish burghs. Urban Scots were five times more over-crowded than their English counterparts in 1911, an adverse comparison which induced government statisticians to amend the Scottish criterion so that it should appear less unfavourable.

Complex historical forces explain the peculiarly Scottish urban form and the adverse living conditions associated with it. On the supply side, strict building regulations and severe instability among builders and suppliers were important considerations. The legal framework as it specifically related to tenure, a unique form of which, feuing, existed in Scotland, had crucial implications for land release and building finance, and the operation of the Scottish rating system adversely affected the provision of housing for letting. But the composition of demand was vital. Scottish industry and commerce, faced with penetration from their English counterparts competed principally through lower wage costs.[4] Average wages and incomes have historically been substantially adrift of those in identical grades in England, and though narrowing over time the differential was, even in 1939, at least 5 per cent.[5] Consequently, relatively weak effective demand for consumer goods and conspicuously for housing accommodation resulted. In addition, the narrower economic base, substantially dependent on textiles, iron and steel, and heavy engineering, induced problems of a structural and cyclical kind during the inter-war period, and which even today remain difficult to reverse.

Deficient Scottish housing conditions were explicitly recognised in two ways by the British Government in the quarter century before 1939. Firstly, central Government granted subsidies to Scottish local authorities for council housing under preferential terms compared to those in English boroughs; and, secondly, except for London, private sector rents were more vigorously controlled in Scotland than elsewhere in recognition of the fundamental housing disequilibrium.[6] Notwithstanding the very real achievements of Scottish local authorities during the inter-war period, the disparity between English and Scottish housing standards remained evident (see Table 7.1), and along with wider Health Department issues, frequently drew the Scottish Office into conflict with Whitehall as the former sought to sustain special terms to deal with social conditions north of the border.

The scale of the building programme, and the composition as between State and private sector schemes, is shown in Table 7.1, the Scottish performance contrasting markedly with that of England and Wales. Table 7.1 demonstrates, among other things, the emphatic wedge driven between private and municipal housing, the basis for the eventual elimination in Scotland of the private landlord, and the implications for a structural shift in landlord–tenant relations. The local authority to private housebuilding ratio was inversely related on either side of the Scottish–English divide: the ratio was 70/30 in Scotland and 28/72 in England and Wales and formed the basis of a subsequent concern,

Table 7.1 Housing and housebuilding 1919–41

	Scotland		England & Wales	
		%		%
Population	4,842,980		39,952,377	
No. of houses	1,146,852		9,399,535	
Unfit houses	66,538	5.8	472,000	5.0
Overcrowded houses	258,987	22.6	341,554	3.8
Houses of 1 & 2 rooms	504,615	44.0	432,328	4.6
Houses built 1919–41	344,209		4,233,712	
by local authorities	241,018	70.0	1,178,021	27.8
by private enterprise	103,191	30.0	3,055,691	72.2
by private enterprise				
(a) with subsidy	40,873	39.6	433,980	14.2
(b) without subsidy	62,318	60.4	2,621,711	85.6
Housebuilding:				
Average annual output	17,200		211,700	
Peak annual output (1938)	26,070		346,053	

Source: Scottish Housing Advisory Committee, *Report on the Distribution of New Houses in Scotland*, Cmnd 6552, 1943–44, para 23.

namely, the council as a 'monopoly landlord'.[7] It was this decisive dependence upon Scottish council housing in the inter-war years which accentuated the tradition of architectural monotony in the Scottish urban setting at an early stage, reinforced in a suburban context by a private enterprise preoccupation with bungaloid development, itself more homogeneous than English semi-detached housing forms. Table 7.1 pinpoints the chronic overcrowding problem in dwellings of two or fewer rooms in Scotland, ten times more numerous than in England and Wales and the basis in Victorian times of objections based on decency and morality. Even though Scottish overcrowding was halved between 1911 and 1935, it was still six times above levels prevailing south of the border.

Policy reorientation and the foundation of the SSHA

To some extent, the Royal Commission on Scottish Housing which reported in 1917 recognised and perpetuated the special pleading to deal with intense housing problems in Scotland. The more generous financial provisions for Scotland in 1919 and 1924 were explicit acknowledgements of such needs—and a brief departure from the pro rata formula (based on a simple proportion of Scots in the UK population) to allocate funds to Scotland devised by Goschen in 1888. Yet Conservative policy thinking was opposed to such preferential arrangements and favoured standard subsidy payments to all parts of the UK. The Scottish Office view, tenaciously represented by Walter Elliott (MP for Lanarkshire 1919–23, Kelvingrove 1924–45) and Parliamentary Under-Secretary for Health at the Scottish Office, was geared to obtaining special terms for Scottish housing programmes, which if they prevailed occasionally, were generally at odds with those of Whitehall from a early stage.[8]

Contemporary analysis of the economic misfortunes of Britain in the 1920s focused on cyclical or short run dislocation allied with post-war conditions, international monetary instability and exchange rate uncertainties.[9] Gradually a diagnosis emerged which implicitly recognised more fundamental, structural causes of the economic malaise of the late 1920s and 1930s. De-rating and industrial transference schemes to alleviate local revenue shortfalls and labour oversupply problems in the late 1920s heralded a different approach to economic problems, and with the suspension of the gold standard late in 1931, and tariff protection and imperial preference from 1932, the external dimension in economic policy receded. As a consequence, domestic issues involving a more interventionist stance towards economic management were somewhat reluctantly embraced. In a sense, the Clyde Valley Regional Planning Committee (1927) anticipated this deliberate move to regional policy, a move more expansively reflected in the Special Areas Act (1934), and which with other locally based economic initiatives gathered pace and was more fully recognised in a more ambitious Act in 1937. The SSHA, therefore, was a particular instance of this wider assault on regional unemployment problems, though deep-seated concern regarding the defective character of Scottish housing, as frequently expressed in the House of Commons,[10] remained an ever-present concern.

The depth of recession in the Scottish heavy industries and its pervasive impact on other parts of the Scottish economy produced unemployment rates double those of the UK as a whole, and so any reliance on a demand driven expansion in private sector housebuilding to rectify the legacy of a defective housing stock was unlikely to prove successful. Scottish local authorities had demonstrated considerable energy and imagination, as Morgan has shown,[11] in developing new materials—clinker and composite blocks—as well as utilizing steel framed, flat-roofed, and other designs in efforts to produce non-traditional solutions to the housing problem, and in the 1920s the Scottish National Housing Company's programmes encouraged alternative designs, steel materials and new financial apparatus. But despite these initiatives, the legacy of nineteenth century Scottish housing problems was compounded in the inter-war period by at least five problems—first, and most serious, was the continued weak purchasing power of Scots; second, there were major logistical difficulties in the organisation of supplies from a building industry unaccustomed to large scale production; third, the political imperatives of containing tenants' rent increases strangled landlords' incentives to build more houses for rental; fourth, trade unionists' opposition to the dilution of building skills as a result of new materials and pre-fabricated processes curtailed housing output; and fifth, changing housing subsidy arrangements created financial uncertainty among local authorities and tension between them and the executive arm of central Government. Under these conditions it was not surprising that inroads into the quantitative needs for Scottish housing were not met during the inter-war years, and that towards the end of the period some further recognition of special initiatives was required.

No less important in the birth of special housing arrangements for Scotland was the appointment of Walter Elliott as Secretary of State for Scotland during 1936–38, and his convincing demonstration that Scottish housing deficiencies were not being eliminated, that shipbuilding and rearmament would increasingly deflect non-traditional materials from housing supply, and that in the Scottish National Housing Company the administrative precedent already existed for targeting housing black spots and redirecting resources in their direction. The birth of the Scottish Special Housing Association, therefore, was closely identified with a policy of regional industrial regeneration.

The SSHA and Scottish housing politics 1937–47[12]

The interconnected assault upon housing standards and industrial recovery was signalled by the immediate appointment of the Commissioner for Special Areas in 1937 as chairman of the SSHA. The initial problems of the SSHA were daunting; there was no managerial or organisational structure, no technical analysis of non-traditional housing designs and their relative merits, ill-defined housing production targets, no powers of compulsory purchase, and cautious not to say hostile reactions from councils towards SSHA functions, and from

Labour MPs in the House of Commons highly critical of the SSHA's rate of housing progress in 1938–9. In addition, SSHA responsibilities were to be discharged bearing in mind the need to generate employment within the Special Area, and with regard to a 'fair wages' clause. Against such odds the subsequent success and longevity of the SSHA owed much to the masterly management of the media by Walter Elliott and his opportunism in using the royal visit to Lanarkshire in May 1938 to quell ILP opposition to the SSHA.[13] Favourable press coverage of SSHA housing assured that Labour party critics were thereafter on the defensive, and although by 1939 only two houses had been completed, 1,364 houses were under construction and 2,026 under contract, and a further 2,141 had been approved. In less than two years more than 5,500 dwellings were authorised on approximately twenty-five sites, and some momentum had been gathered.

By 1939 the SSHA was authorised to build 30 per cent of its houses outside the confines of the Special Areas, and came more directly under the control of the Scottish Office than the Special Areas commissioner. Whether, as has recently been argued, this progressive acceleration in the SSHA building programme between 1937–9 heralded a new era in Scottish housing, and spurred on by Walter Elliott, whether the SSHA would have offered a remedy to the endemic Scottish housing problem must remain conjectural, but certainly 'Hitler's war' caused an interruption to housebuilding which for Scotland it has been claimed was 'a national disaster' in that it absolutely curtailed experimentation in new designs, and delayed revisions regarding the form and function of Scottish housing.[14]

Wartime conditions predictably impinged on SSHA activities. Building was suspended where foundations were not already down, site acquisition ceased, and labour and materials supplies were in grave shortage due to government requisitioning, the combined impact of building quotas and permits, and to the non-availability of manufactured fittings. Equally serious were labour shortages, and the inadequate substitution of unskilled, aged and infirm labour with low productivity levels for the able bodied. Contractors were most acutely affected since their liquidity was jeopardised by an inability to complete and sell houses commissioned by the SSHA.

Despite these wartime constraints on the original intention to supplement Scottish housing stocks through selective SSHA initiatives, the war presented new opportunities for the SSHA. Wide powers, new responsibilities, political leverage with different authorities, and most critical, the assumption of a central position in any subsequent Scottish housing strategy were conspicuous gains to the SSHA. From the outset, the SSHA proved responsive to the urgent constructional needs of war related activities. Aircraft and naval workers' housing at Hillington, Rosyth, Edinburgh and Kirkwall, and industrial and munitions workers' hostels in Clydebank and Greenock typified the rapid provision of specialist housing where no obvious or willing authority existed. Such SSHA involvement was not without difficulty: Glasgow City Corporation were initially obstructionist over the 1,500 houses planned for Rolls Royce workers at Hillington, and eventually abruptly insisted on taking over the entire project, keeping external agencies such as the SSHA at arm's length and signposting future friction between central and local government. Wartime responsibilities, which besides new building for military personnel included the management of evacuation camps in Perthshire and Midlothian and hostels and other hutted encampments in the Strathclyde region, meant that the SSHA emerged in 1945 with more than the rudimentary administrative machinery and consultant architect with which it had commenced operations; it had become a fully fledged government agency with full time and experienced technical and housing management officers, and a geographically widespread presence.

Accordingly the SSHA was well placed to participate in wider responsibilities and general housing requirements outside the strict geographical confines of the former distressed or special areas designation and was empowered to move into the field of general housing provision by the Housing (Scotland) Acts of 1944 and 1950.[15] To some extent the SSHA had already secured a prominent, even permanent, position in housing provision by involving itself in 1943–44 with post-war reconstruction plans. The SSHA cemented more than just houses when it undertook to provide 600 houses for the Department of Health and to manage about 700 houses for the Ministry of Fuel and Power; it had significantly enhanced its scale and scope of operations, and moved decisively into long-term housing management. The functions of landlord and builder became firmly fused with these additional SSHA contributions to post-war reconstruction, and, perhaps most importantly, the Association became an instrument by which a separate housing policy for Scotland was implemented, simultaneously strengthening the grip of the Scottish Office while weakening that of Whitehall.

By willing compliance with requests from government departments the SSHA ensured its continuity and guaranteed goodwill from powerful allies. This was further buttressed in the 1940s, as indeed later, by housebuilding for agencies—hospital, lighthouse, fire, hydroelectric and forestry interests each sought and obtained SSHA housing, thereby overcoming their own financial and constitutional restrictions.[16] And equally important in the process of securing its future was the direct access which the SSHA had to the Scottish Office, as for example in 1942 when the SSHA chairman was also Parliamentary Under-Secretary of State for Scotland. The presentation of technical information to the Department of Health had secured the influential support of the chairman of the Scottish Housing Advisory Committee, and in 1943 the powerful Scottish Secretary of State, Tom Johnston, added to the stature of the SSHA, stating:

> We already have a national housebuilding agency in Scotland, the Scottish Special Housing Association. This Association can provide housing in any part of Scotland and I am at present planning for a large scale programme of building after the war.[17]

To capitalise on post-war opportunities the SSHA urgently needed to resolve materials and labour supply problems. Brick and bricklayer shortages, as in 1937, necessitated a non-traditional approach to construction methods.[18] Through prior experience the SSHA was well placed to address the problem; indeed, it became something of an SSHA hallmark. Obliged to employ unskilled labour, it was imperative that the SSHA sponsor and adopt alternatives to craft building techniques. Swedish government sponsored timber houses figured in these experiments to develop alternative building technology in Scotland, as did examples from Canada and the USA, and various types of concrete and steel construction were considered in a group of innovative designs and constructional methods developed at Sighthill in Edinburgh from 1944. The SSHA showed experimental flair in searching for models and materials which might alleviate post-war housing problems intensified by the neglect of repair and maintenance work during six wartime years, (see Figure 7.1).

It was Dutch experience with concrete which proved technically preferable. The 'no-fines concrete' construction method enabled concrete to be made with larger particles of aggregate cemented together, without the use of sand or 'fine' aggregate, the resultant concrete being poured into prepared shapes formed from metal pans with wooden posts.[19] Two or three skilled tradesmen working with a gang of forty-eight shutters and concreters could construct a three-room house in four days. The SSHA also supported the site development and layout for a number of other innovative housebuilders, especially for steel framed houses (British Iron and Steel Federation, Atholl Steel, Weir), timber construction (Swedish schemes), and pre-cast concrete construction (Orlit, Hilcon and Whitson-Fairhurst). To respond rapidly to the pressing general post-war housing needs the SSHA also modified its own original techniques along Wimpey lines for poured cellular concrete housing and refined them so that new 'no fines' housing commenced in Fintry (Dundee) in 1950 with a 'no fines' squad of twenty-five people capable of producing 8–12 houses per week.[20]

Post-war labour availability and construction costs endorsed the SSHA's view that new techniques were critical in achieving their production targets. By the later 1950s non-traditional houses and no-fines techniques together represented the majority of SSHA houses, though of the first 30,000 built, at least 50 per cent were of more conventional brick and mortar construction.[21] Despite the SSHA's position as a technological leader in the use of building materials and methods, its expressed wish to provide housing 'with due regard to the social needs of the people'[22] in contrast to austere local authority housing, made limited progress. Architecturally innovative excursions proved largely stillborn: a Modern Movement inspired design at Grangemouth proved so troublesome that the SSHA reverted to layout designs using perimeter access roads which became known as 'bastard garden city'.

With technical solutions on the horizon, emphatic cross-party political support for its wartime role, administrative powers extended by the 1944 Housing Act, and instructions to build 10,000 more houses, the SSHA had effectively secured a central position in Scottish housing policy after 1945.

Yet it was precisely because of the success and influence of the SSHA that political obstacles were quickly positioned. To address the most acute post-war housing problems the SSHA planned to concentrate 78 per cent of its new housebuilding programme in the cities and major burghs of central Scotland. This policy was perceived as a multiple threat to local councils: it potentially undermined their revenue base and political autonomy. Because of its

A Canadian timber houses 1939

B Myton, Tarran Clyde, 1947

Figure 7.1 SSHA experimental designs and materials

C Traditional design, Carskeogh, Patna, 1951
Figure 7.1 cont'd

D Weir quality steel flat roof (Four room semi-detached and terraced houses. Concrete foundations, prefabricated gauged steel sheet cladding, jointed and bolted. 1st floor steel joists on steel beams. Cast iron chimney, steel casement windows.)

E Orlit Bellrock 1949. (Loadbearing, pre-cast reinforced concrete structural frame, concrete outer wall, inner wall of pre-cast gypsum, hydrated calcium and sulphate, concrete.)

Figure 7.1 cont'd

F Miller O'Sullivan Construction 1952. (Three rooms, cavity brick walls, roughcast, on a concrete strip base. O'Sullivan system used patent 'on-site' aluminium alloy moulds to construct dense concrete walls.

Figure 7.1 cont'd

interaction with the local economy, housing supply affected local economic prospects, and the presence of a housing stock owned and managed by an agency outside the burgh constituted a drain on council rental income, and reduced the volume of council controlled labour directly employed by municipal housing departments.

In the struggle for political dominance, the SSHA had become sandwiched between the massed forces of local government and the Scottish Office; between labour councils, mostly in west central Scotland, and the executive arm of St Andrew's House; and between ideological perspectives which favoured integrated planning and those clinging to their historic civic identity. By flexing their political muscle local authorities had endorsed their independence, yet paradoxically had undermined their strength, since in view of the severity of post-war problems, economic planning could no longer be conducted except by reference to regional issues and by agencies with terms of reference broader than purely municipal. Housing policy, therefore, as presented by the SSHA endorsed integrated regional economic planning; as presented by local councils, housing policy remained an instrument of narrow local political control. In redirecting SSHA policy away from the urban areas to rural ones, the new Labour Under-Secretary of State George Buchanan, ex-

Glasgow city councillor and former member of the ILP group critical of the SSHA, acceded to the interests of city councils. The dismemberment of the top tier of SSHA management was, therefore, sought and in 1946 obtained by the new Scottish Under-Secretary in his loyalty to Labour councils whose ideological drive towards greater local authority ownership of the housing stock necessitated the disablement of an effective SSHA managerial team. Though SSHA activities were, therefore, sidetracked to more marginal rural housing it was a temporary diversion; by the late 1950s the SSHA had recaptured the initiative and its participation in broader economic policy was assured.

Post-war activities of the SSHA

Perceived by Labour councillors as an agent of central Government and thus as a political threat to both the local control of council jobs and the political support of the Scottish working class, the SSHA was for some years after 1945 diverted from those areas of chronic housing need. Nonetheless the SSHA addressed its redefined responsiblities with characteristic energy, and in so doing refused to be permanently sidelined. The political climate also changed. By 1947, Buchanan had been replaced as the minister responsible for Scottish housing by a former SSHA Council member, J J Robertson, though it took some years to reverse the policy shifts initiated by Buchanan.

Logistical problems also confronted the SSHA after 1945. The determination of many local authorities to develop their own housing departments and building workforces affected both labour and materials supplies. Thus councils' competitive bidding for skilled labour constrained the volume of work the SSHA could undertake; the materials shortages for cement, electric conduits, glass, timber, steel and cast iron products, and plaster board exacerbated the shortfall on housing targets. Management reorganisation and shortages of administrative personnel compounded the organisational problems of the SSHA. Accordingly, the drive to introduce new system building techniques of poured concrete and prefabrication was impeded by the problems of labour recruitment, and intensified by a local authorities' commencement of their own housebuilding programmes. As a result approximately half the SSHA housebuilding of the 1940s was with traditional materials.

SSHA post-war housing was initially of two types: miners' housing, and general housing provision (see Figure 7.2). The newly created National Coal Board reorganised mining operations after 1947 and accounted for over 10,500 houses or 30 per cent of SSHA housebuilding in the years 1945–50, and as much as 50 per cent in certain years. During the 1950s the NCB actively opened new pits throughout the central belt and remained an important source of demand for SSHA housing. The general housing needs programme produced over 23,000 houses during 1945–50, mainly concentrated in Kilmarnock (636), Clydebank (614),[23] Coatbridge (524), Kirkcaldy (436), Greenock (400), Ayr (392) and Aberdeen (330), but it assiduously avoided Glasgow where only 398 houses were built.[24] Originally, the SSHA had identified a severe shortage in Glasgow and planned 4,000 new houses there. It

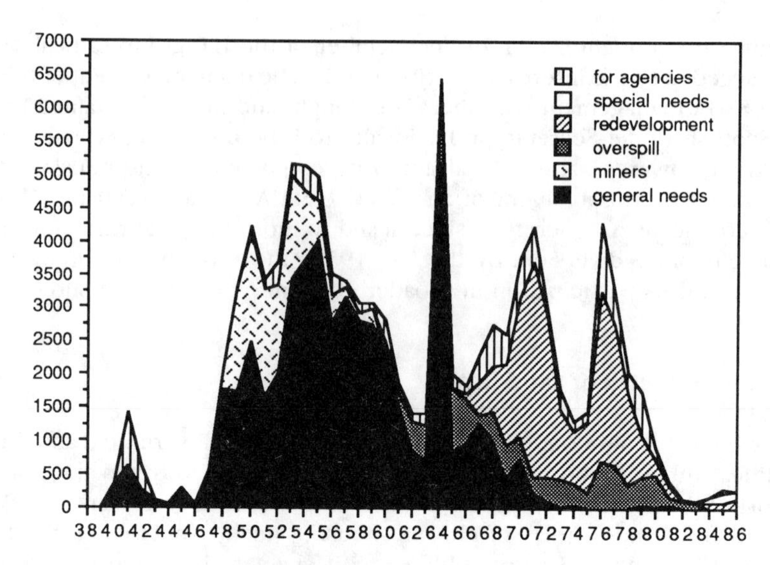

Figure 7.2 SSHA houses completed 1938–86

was a measure of Glasgow Corporation's hostility to the SSHA that so few houses were built.

As a result of the terms of reference set in 1945, SSHA housing efforts were so difffused that by 1950 houses had been built in 136 different locations, many of them in rural settings or small burghs, and frequently in small numbers. It was a reflection of the power of the Labour controlled burghs, principally Glasgow, to derail regional planning. Indeed, the SSHA was frequently involved merely in a site servicing capacity, laying drains and roads for other authorities.

Greater political sympathy for the aims and objectives of the SSHA were crucial to its subsequent activities. It had been marginalised under Labour in the Scottish Office. In the 1950s former SSHA priorities were reinvoked. The search for non-traditional techniques reinvigorated the no-fines method in the later 1950s, some prototype high-rise flats were constructed for Glasgow Corporation, design standards were reassessed as a consequence of public expenditure restrictions, though pre-fabrication methods were in retreat in view of structural weaknesses. Expanded output meant increased employment and a higher profile for the SSHA during the 1950s. However, just as building had brought the SSHA into conflict with municipalities, so too did an enlarged housing stock, since the SSHA then assumed the role of landlord with rental and management policies of deep significance to local councils.

Redefining priorities: special housing since the late 1950s

At its inception twin responsibilities were given to the SSHA—to provide employment for unskilled workers and to build houses for the working classes.

From the late-1950s, while fulfilling its dual baptismal obligations, the SSHA undertook more selective housing initiatives—housing support for specific industrial projects, the decongestion of inner city housing areas and the relocation of residents (the Glasgow overspill campaign), and progressively from 1977, a decisive move towards modernisation and rehabilitation of existing property in the light of opposition to high-rise council (and SSHA) building, inner city refurbishment programmes sponsored in Westminster, and tenants' opposition to satellite estates. By redefining housing needs, the SSHA permitted overlapping responsibilities to coexist, and provided a degree of continuity for itself. The late-1950s thus heralded the return of the SSHA to the central political arena in Scotland, to consultation and policy formation, and to a status akin to those years before 1945 when it was so abruptly redirected.

Between 1957 and 1959 the SSHA, and Scottish housing generally, changed direction. It was the combined product of five influences: first, the agreement on an overspill programme for Glasgow in 1957; secondly, the completion of the initial phase of SSHA high-rise flats between 1956–9; thirdly, discussions between the Department of Health for Scotland and the SSHA—the Joint Development Group—formed in 1959, which signalled the reconstruction of central Glasgow; fourthly, the introduction in 1959 of housing programmes in targeted areas of unemployment; and finally, the emergence of the SSHA in the wake of a rent dispute as a major housing agency managing its own properties.

Overspill policy focused on twin principles: the relief of congestion and overcrowding in inner city areas, and, the simultaneous containment of the suburban expansion of the city. They were principles enshrined in the *Clyde Valley Regional Plan* published in 1946 and in which was embedded the seed of bitter dispute between the Scottish Office and Glasgow Corporation. The contentious area was over the status of the green belt, the city council anxious to develop into such an area to rehouse its population, and the Scottish Office resistant to such proposals in its advocacy of integrated planning. By stubborn defence of the green belt, by its continued if more muted embrace of regional planning by the Clyde Valley Advisory Committee in 1953, and by the designation of a second new town, Cumbernauld, in 1956, the Scottish Office signalled a determination to sustain a policy which, in view of its urgent need to improve its housing stock, the city council could not resist indefinitely. By the mid-1950s grudging agreement existed between Glasgow and the Scottish Office that overcrowding and substandard houses were to be tackled by reducing the population of the city.[25] Two approaches were employed: the development of new towns, and, the implementation of an inner city slum clearance and comprehensive redevelopment programme. Thus the New Towns Acts empowered Development Corporations to build houses financed by Treasury loans, and under the second approach, the Housing and Town Development Act 1957 enabled houses to be built under the joint auspices of the SSHA and the local authorities receiving relocated Glaswegians.

Overspill housing sponsored by the SSHA totalled 9,954 houses, equivalent to about 10 per cent of its entire building programme 1937–77 and for about 40 per cent of SSHA housebuilding in the 1960s. Housing estates were geographically scattered around the east coast, the Highlands and Strathclyde

Figure 7.3 Overspill housing, Erskine, 1970's

region, and required delicate diplomatic discussions with local authorities who were politically sensitive to SSHA incursions into their perceived functions and the implications of such encroachments for council rents, rates and housing policies.[26]

If the joint overspill initiative—SSHA and Glasgow Corporation—literally cemented better practical relations between the two authorities, it nevertheless represented an attempt by the Scottish Office, through the SSHA, to intervene in the heartland of Scottish labour and in housing politics by reducing the size and influence of Glasgow, by boosting the power of adjacent burghs, and by obtaining a say in the redevelopment programme. SSHA policies, therefore, had a direct bearing upon the municipal housing of Glasgow Corporation. Given the immensity of the problems with which it was confronted, Glasgow had to cede some sovereignty to the Scottish Office through SSHA involvement. While flexible in its approach and responsive to housing needs, the SSHA was by no means wholly neutral in effect. By providing labour, materials, financial resources, green field sites and recreation, the SSHA did cooperate in practical terms with the Glasgow authority in the assault on housing deficiencies. Even the reluctant development by the SSHA of the 'no-fines' technique for high-rise blocks of flats seemed to signal a degree of cooperation with Glasgow Corporation's emphatic preference in the 1950s and 1960s for multi-storey housing, though in time both the maintenance and environmental implications of multi-storey block dwellings were discredited, and produced a vehement reaction in favour of refurbishment, in which policy both the SSHA and the local authority again collaborated.

Even while the overspill campaign was gathering momentum, the SSHA was evolving a policy of infrastructural support in the form of housing estates in areas with potential for economic development. To an extent this strategy built on the pre-existing agency housing which the SSHA had consistently undertaken on behalf of government departments. But this had always been on a limited scale (see Figure 7.2). The SSHA perceived expanded possibilities in this direction, and for its own position, at time when more coherent economic and regional planning as typified by the newly formed Scottish Development Department (SDD), formed in 1962, was in favour. The 1963 White Paper *Central Scotland: a Programme for Development and Growth*[27] therefore, represented the bold new policy underpinning to the next wave of SSHA involvement. The logic of the policy document was to anticipate the housing requirements of future economic expansion in the central belt of Scotland and to build approximately 3,000 houses annually for this purpose by a combination of New Town Development Corporation and SSHA activities.[28]

In supporting these new economic initiatives, the contribution of the SSHA was valuable for two reasons. First, the introduction of new industry to Scotland might be jeopardised by a shortage of reasonable quality rented accommodation. The continuing Scottish emphasis on basic local authority housing, as in the inter-war years, was unattractive to both young and senior business and professional groups,[29] and polarisation of the housing stock with its peculiarly Scottish form was considered an off-putting factor to potential incoming English ventures. Second, and more practically, local authorities were already overburdened with their own building work and with extensive commitments to local residents on lengthy waiting lists. So the SSHA was tactically deployed as an agency to relieve pressure on local authorities and to sweeten infrastructural conditions which at the margin might attract English and foreign capital.

The strategy was finely judged. Indeed Rootes (Chrysler UK) agreed to develop car production at Linwood, Renfrewshire, only on condition that 1,000 houses were conveniently provided for their workforce. The SSHA built these in two years, and in a second phase added a further 800 houses. Paper and pulp-milling activities in association with Scottish forestry were supported by SSHA design, contractual and planning staffs so that 300 homes were provided for the workforce in environmentally sensitive areas around Fort William. Tweedbank between Melrose and Galashiels was established to reverse a century of population decline in the borders and to regenerate the previously vigorous woollen knitwear industry by ensuring sufficient housing existed so as to attract potential employers to the area. The Erskine development fulfilled the overlap between overspill and economic expansion initiatives supported by the SSHA. In a sense it fused the dominant housing themes of the 1970s and defused the political dynamite which local councils faced were they to rehouse incomers ahead of local residents. This strategic local and regional housing contribution made by the SSHA was recognised in 1973

A Early SSHA modernization work: Rosyth Garden City housing 1960's

Figure 7.4 Renovation and redevelopment

B and **C** Modernized tenements at John Street, Forfar 1973: Before and after

Figure 7.4 cont'd

D Orbit Housing Leighstonehall, Hamilton: built 1947–53 modernized 1978–84
Figure 7.4 cont'd

in a further government policy statement:

> ... in some areas the number of houses that may be needed for new industry will be beyond the resources of the local authorities and the SSHA are prepared in these circumstances to build houses for incoming workers wherever this need arises.[30]

This infrastructural back-up produced nearly 20,000 SSHA houses between 1965 and 1986 with a surge of completions in the 1975–77 years to support oil related economic development. The previous SSHA geographical focus on the central belt and mining communities was redirected towards Aberdeenshire, the Moray Firth and the Shetlands,[31] one consequence of which was the diffusion of poured concrete housebuilding techniques throughout northern Scotland. To sustain housing production in line with targets the SSHA accumulated new powers, first of compulsory purchase (1966) to counter the dearth of suitable building land, and secondly, to purchase privately built houses to supplement housing stocks in conjunction with economic development (see Figure 7.2). Related to this, and perhaps of wider significance, was the assistance available from the SSHA library and technical support department to firms like Wimpey and Cruden in areas such as technical specifications, no-fines and pre-cast concrete information, bills of quantities, and access to a variety of designs which the private firms then used to secure further contracts with local authorities. Undoubtedly this contributed both to improved housing supply from such major contractors, and to the consolidation of output in fewer firms, but while it accelerated the production of non-traditional housing it also undermined municipal building departments.

Rehabilitation and renewal: the SSHA contribution

Just as in each previous decade the SSHA had encouraged or been assigned a new strand of housing responsibilities, so the 1970s was no exception. While the infrastructural support to economic expansion was in full swing major redevelopment work in inner city areas became expedient for central and local government, and fashionable for planners and newly-formed private housing associations. The SSHA was also involved.

As early as the mid-1950s SSHA renovation activities were underway in Dunkeld and Culross, and by the 1960s Saltire and Civic Trust commendations were increasingly awarded to new SSHA houses on the basis of their differentiation of design, preservation of historic detail, and the layout and conception of new estates. In the early 1960s housing in Rosyth again played a formative role in Scottish housing as the WWI properties of the National Housing Companies, then forty years old, were in urgent need of repair. With this, and a contract on behalf of Rutherglen town council, the SSHA gained early experience of conversion and upgrading work, and the SSHA management was prompt in seeking, and in 1962 obtaining, SDD approval for extending this type of work.

To begin with the SSHA upgraded properties under contract to local authorities in the 1960s. To do so under its own initiative was a logical development and did not constitute an enormous step in view of the available technical staff, accumulated library of information, and experience of town centre renovation. Not only did the SSHA positively embrace the prevailing current of housing opinion, increasingly based on qualitative improvement rather than quantitative additions, as before it had become an instrument for the diffusion of contemporary housing thought. To a certain extent an expanded SSHA involvement in renovation was inevitable for three reasons. First, apart from the transparently urgent need for local authority refurbishment of its housing stock, in some instances approaching fifty years old, the SSHA itself was experiencing heavier maintenance and upgrading requirements on its own ageing properties.[32] A second stimulus towards intervention in this field was a growing awareness and acceptance of the special housing requirements of the disabled, elderly, single and young people. This new focus on housing demand reflected wider societal acknowledgement of such priorities, sensitised by ginger groups, and a more subtle appreciation of housing needs than simple quantitative provision of floor space.[33] For such 'special' housing requirements one obvious participant was the Scottish Special Housing Association. Thirdly, deteriorating national economic performance imposed a brake on demand for new housing and the SSHA economic expansion programme was slowed and deferred as a result.[34] Inner city housing rehabilitation and modernisation of the SSHA's own stock filled the gap and perpetuated a role for the SSHA on the central stage of Scottish housing policy.

In redefining and developing its sphere of operations the SSHA drew on a period of stability in senior managerial staffing to adapt and reorientate policy. During the 1960s, with susbtantial overspill and economic expansion work in progress, the rehabilitation element remained modest, but with expanded powers from the SDD in 1970, renovation assumed significant proportions. A further boost to the renovations programme was the participation (see Figure 7.2) of the SSHA in the Redevelopment Housing Assistance Programme (RAP) to supplement Scottish local authority work.[35] New building and modernisation of existing housing was involved and in both respects the SSHA made important contributions to GEAR, the Glasgow Eastern Area Renewal project. This housing scheme involved cooperative participation by the SSHA with the SDD (finance), Scottish Development Agency (coordination, environmental, recreational works), Strathclyde Regional Council (roads, social work, schools, water, sewerage, police), Glasgow District Council (parks, planning, housing allocation), Greater Glasgow Health Board, Manpower Services Commission and the Housing Corporation. Such a multiplicity of official and political interests involved complex negotiation and liaison.[36] The main objective of this integrated project was to reverse the legacy of poor quality housing in eastern Glasgow through comprehensive redevelopment. The SSHA contribution to GEAR was 1,500 new houses and flats, rehabilitation of 800 others dating from the inter-war period, temporary housing and conversions, landscaping, restoration of eighteenth century tenement housing, and the comprehensive upgrading of 474 steel houses in Shettleston which the SSHA had itself inherited from the former Second Scottish National Housing Company. The SSHA also stimulated private sector investment by renovating tenement flats for sale to achieve a broader social and tenurial mix, and consistent with wider trends, integrated tenants' cooperatives and residents' associations as well as the special requirements of the elderly, disabled and young into the design decisions of the SSHA properties.[37] Community regeneration, therefore, was not simply imposed from above; involvement was solicited from below.

Though GEAR represented the most expansive, and expensive, of its refurbishment programmes, the SSHA was involved in many others. Indeed its own modernisation efforts extended in 1977 to 12,000 houses built by non-traditional methods, and included improvements such as re-wiring, replacing kitchen and bathroom facilities, improving heating, and upgrading roof and wall insulation. While the Glasgow council housing problems were most urgent and of daunting proportions, Leith, Dundee, Arbroath and numerous other locations were targeted for SSHA upgrading. Not the least of the initiatives was an SSHA programme of planned maintenance introduced in 1970 and a harbinger of redefined policy objectives.

The sale of SSHA houses: housing policy in the 1980s

The Conservative Government elected in May 1979 gave those who had been tenants for at least three years the right to purchase their local authority or SSHA houses. The Tenants Rights, etc (Scotland) Act 1980 laid down tenants' entitlement and in the fiscal year 1979–80 the SSHA sold eighty properties. From the peak housing stock of just over 100,000 houses a further 11,600 were sold between 1980 and 1985 to reduce SSHA housing stock to around 89,000 properties. Even though the visible reduction of public housing stocks was opposed within the SSHA, it had itself anticipated government strategy by initiating just such a scheme in the very month the Conservatives were elected.

The programme of house sales, whatever its ideological parenthood, was consistent with other constraints on housing imposed by the Conservative Government. The combined effects of economic recession, attendant changes in expenditure policies, and difficulties connected with the implementation of the redevelopment programme (RAP) slowed SSHA achievements. The RAP scheme projected refurbishment of 11,636 houses but achieved only 81 per cent of this (9,450 houses). Cash limits on public expenditure became the dominant doctrine in the search to combat inflation and regenerate the economy,[38] and curtailing housing programmes and selling houses, like other asset sales, was a consistent government attempt both to limit expenditure and to generate revenue.[39]

For the SSHA the new constraints axed 40 per cent of capital spending between 1981 and 1984. The SDD, again acting as government agent in the implementation of this policy, redirected SSHA activities principally to GEAR from 1984. The capital constraints and the consultative procedures inherent in the central city as opposed to green field housing resulted in much slower progress than formerly.[40] For example, only 4,200 houses were built and 1,660 modernised under RAP between 1977 and 1984 compared to a planned programme of 10,290, a shortfall of 43 per cent.[41] So national economic and financial considerations pruned the SSHA budget and forced changes in housing policy. From the late 1970s the primary SSHA role shifted from new house construction to the modernisation, maintenance and management of existing housing stocks. This tendency is reflected in a gradual increase in SSHA recurrent spending, ie expenditure on loan charges, minor modernisation, repairs, and administration compared to a plateau in capital spending on new building. As a result SSHA contributions to local authority housing have, since 1983, been virtually confined to 'special needs' housing for the elderly, disabled and other targeted groups.

As public expenditure cuts impose caretaker rather than housebuilder functions upon the SSHA in the 1980s, it would appear that the SSHA is in danger of retreating to a passive or static, rather than creative or dynamic, role as employer and supporter of economic initiatives. To some extent current government public expenditure and industrial regeneration objectives may therefore be in conflict, and appear to run counter to historical experience.

Agent or double agent? The SSHA, the Scottish Office and relations with local authorities

The nature of the inter-organisational relationships between the SSHA, Scottish Office, and local authorities reveals certain strategies behind housing policy. To some extent the SSHA is an organisational hybrid. It combines characteristics of the mandated agency[42] undertaking specific duties upon the instruction of another organisation—the Scottish Office. Externally imposed responsibilities for both new housebuilding and factoring placed the SSHA in such a mandated position. Yet in the SSHA–Scottish Office relationship there were also traces of resource dependency[43] and power dependency,[44] that is, the SSHA relied upon both the authority and budget allocations of the Scottish Office to secure its position of influence over local councils. As one SSHA chairman stated:

> . . . the facts are that we are a governmental agency, our funds come from government and it is laid down that the government can direct our policy. In this sense we cannot refuse to follow government policy.[45]

Such weapons as finance for building programmes and the force of executive orders, while enhancing the power of the Scottish Office over the SSHA and thus over local authorities, was not one way. There was an element of mutual cooperation and benefit[46] between the Scottish Office and its offspring, the SSHA, since without Scottish Office support SSHA initiatives would have been seriously damaged, and yet without SSHA cooperation, the Scottish Office would have encountered greater intransigence from local councils opposed to national intervention. Local councils ceded some autonomy, but gained as result of accretions to the local housing, shortened waiting lists, and reduced political fall-out.

No simple theory of administrative relations adequately describes the role of the SSHA. Complex, composite relationships emerged. For example, SSHA dependency on the power of the Scottish Office was painfully obvious when in 1945 carefully constructed alliances and friendships were abruptly torpedoed by the Scottish Office Under-Secretary's (Buchanan) curtailment of SSHA building plans in deference to his own political allies at local council level. So, too, was Scottish Office support crucial for the SSHA stance on rent increases in 1958. For different reasons, reductions in the financial base for the SSHA during World War II and in the 1980s contributed to a virtual cessation of new housebuilding and therefore demonstrated SSHA resource dependency. Cooperative overspill, rehabilitation and GEAR projects offered mutual gains; the SSHA secured continuity, the SDD obtained policy implementation by an agent able to deflect council resistance.

Perhaps most important in relation to housing policy implementation was the initial SSHA mandate—the 'special' housing terms of reference which enabled the SSHA itself to redefine and respond to what constituted 'special' housing needs—miners, agency, overspill, economic expansion, rehabilitation, disadvantaged. Pragmatic interpretation of the term 'special' thus offered a lifeline to the SSHA at a time when an escalating operational scale also imposed a policy imperative; to discover housing options which could legitimately be termed 'special' provided the SSHA with an insurance policy against dismemberment, and assurance of continued employment for SSHA staff. Consequently several national housing policy shifts were in fact reorientations partially as a result of SSHA pilot schemes; refurbishment, overspill, and sales to tenants were each introduced by the SSHA prior to general acceptance.

SSHA spheres of operations thus contributed to policy-making, and were not merely narrow technical implementations of housing directives. As an administrative appendage of the Scottish Office, subject to Civil Service procedures, pay scales, and recruitment, the SSHA was one of the bureaucratic progeny spawned by the Scottish Office and consequently under its largely protective wing.[47] Consequently it has enjoyed ease of access to the Scottish Office, and especially to the SDD, enabling the reformulation of housing policy and the enhancement of its own role.

In important, specific ways the SSHA has been deployed locally to implement national housing policy. Under such conditions the SSHA has assumed the role of Scottish Office agent, and its dependency upon the Scottish Office has then been most evident. Paradoxically, Labour dominated burgh councils in Scotland might have been expected to embrace a public housing agency which undertook multi-million pound capital projects financed by the Treasury for the benefit of their residents. But despite joint central and local involvement in housing schemes, local councils and the SSHA rarely coexisted comfortably as organisational equals in partnership.[48] Central–local tension continued.

The crux of the hostility to the SSHA revolved around the local power base, patronage, and council autonomy. Regional planning challenged municipal autonomy. Established relations between different administrative tiers were destabilised by proposals such as decentralised nodes of economic develop-

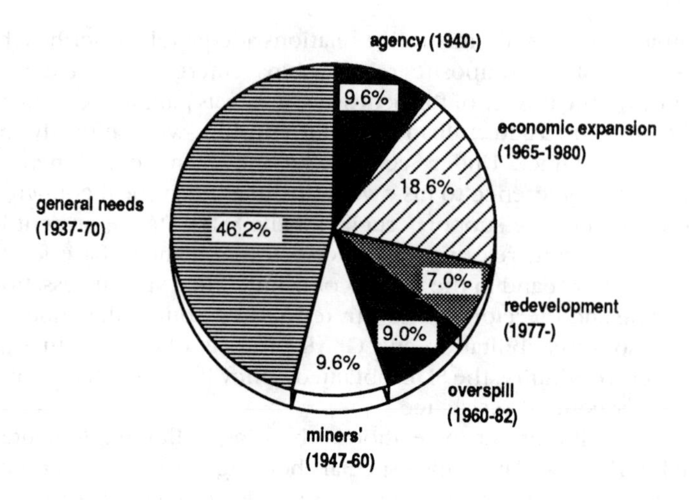

Figure 7.5 Completed SSHA housing 1937–87

ment, and overspill housing. Civic revenues were undermined by policies of decongestion, and political patronage in respect of council employment or contracts at ward level were severed or curtailed by policies which siphoned these off elsewhere. The SSHA therefore was perceived by councillors as an instrument of national infiltration into areas regarded as their terrain.

By what means did the Scottish Office, through the SSHA, assert itself? The determination of rents was one area where the SSHA proved instrumental as a Scottish Office agent. One consequence of the high proportion of council houses in Scotland compared to the remainder of the UK was that the rental issue assumed a political magnitude not matched elsewhere. Because so many voters were council tenants the political consequences of raising council rents was considerable, and as a result, by the 1950s the erosion of council rents meant they were less than half the pre-war levels in real terms. Since there was such a high ratio of council housing in Scotland, the proportion of owner occupiers was much lower and the revenue base for local councils was correspondingly very narrow. Raising rates was not possible indefinitely, nor was it desirable to increase business rates since this ran counter to regional economic policies geared to relocating business as a means of rejuvenating the Scottish economy. Indeed the low rent tradition was regarded by the Secretary of State as prejudicial to industrial recovery as it was indicative of 'an industrially and socially old-fashioned' area and off-putting to potential industrial newcomers.[49]

Low council revenues impaired local authority services; infrastructural decay impeded economic recovery. Thus, decontrolling rents in 1954 and revising the system of rateable values in 1956[50] were consistent with broader economic policies, and from 1957 policies geared to increasing council rents were a further element in that strategy, as well as a mechanism by which to limit Treasury advances to the SSHA and councils generally. Since rent covered only 29 per cent of the annual cost of a council house in 1957 the alternatives were to let ratepayers shoulder more of the burden, increase subsidies, or increase rents. In the vanguard to increase rents in 1958 was the SSHA, backed by the Secretary of State for Scotland, and further supported by a judicial enquiry[51] which found that Glasgow Corporation had not reviewed council rental levels. In the face of rent strikes, tenants' protests, and representations of local authorities to pressurise the SSHA, the backing of the Scottish Office was central to the stance and resolution of the SSHA to introduce increased rents for their properties. The contribution of the Association was recognised by the Minister of State, Lord Craigton, when in 1960:

> He wished to express thanks in particular to the Council of Management (of the SSHA) for their success in introducing the new level of rents ... the determined but fair actions (of the SSHA) had assured complete success and the government was very grateful.[52]

The SSHA used the accrued goodwill to secure further its position by repossessing houses which had been built by the SSHA but previously factored by local councils. By resuming the management function over such properties it strengthened its control over the housing stock.

Something of the imposition of government policy through the SSHA and intense conflict with local authorities in respect of regional versus city planning has already been considered, with the tensions between the Scottish Office and Glasgow Corporation laden with particular resentment. Alternative formulations were advanced to reduce housing problems: the overspill policies of the Scottish Office contrasting sharply with the peripheral estates strategy of Glasgow Corporation. That overspill housing built by the SSHA and New Town Development Corporations was so extensive may be presented as a victory for central Government, and the redefinition of local government in Scotland in 1975 based on regions rather than cities can be viewed as the culmination of an economic policy deliberate in its intent to undermine the dominance of Glasgow and to diffuse the power base in Scotland.

Region versus city thus has been the dynamic in SSHA activities. This theme was genetically imprinted at the birth of the SSHA in 1937, though the implications and resultant tensions could not have been anticipated. In its regional vision the SSHA has occasionally resisted the stance of the Scottish Office, as when civic interests held sway between 1945–48, and when administrative intervention at all levels receded in the name of consumers' choice after 1979 and SSHA and council housing stocks were sold. Whether the SSHA can survive the reductionist role presently afforded to it remains speculative, though there are few indicators of the organic policy renewal, technical innovation and design initiatives which have characterised previous decades and sustained new waves of SSHA activities.

It is difficult to escape the conclusion that the SSHA is a victim of its own success. What the SSHA achieved was the building and management of almost 111,000 houses—equivalent to about 10 per cent of new housebuilding in Scotland in the fifty years from 1937. For every two houses built in New Towns the SSHA built three throughout Scotland. This catapulted it from pre-1939 obscurity to national status, and as the second largest housing authority and landlord in Scotland it is hardly surprising that the SSHA was not a neutral agency in the implementation and successive reformulations of Scottish housing policy. But just as the SSHA was used to counter the power of the largest housing authority, Glasgow Corporation, so sales to tenants in effect have undermined its own position as a formidable policy making and executive housing agency.

Epitaph/Obituary
The SSHA: b. 8.11.1937 d. 1.4.1989

In keeping with the policy to extend choice, public housing has been reorganized in Scotland. The SSHA, along with the Housing Corporation in Scotland, has been abolished, and the 75,000 properties—at least a quarter of a million residents—have been transferred under the terms of the Housing (Scotland) Act 1988 to a new body—Scottish Homes. Ostensibly to extend tenants' choice of landlord, the move comes in the wake of tenants' right to buy their house from public authorities. Yet it is difficult to avoid the conclusion that the underlying intent is to diminish Scottish dependency on municipal landlords, and arguably to diminish the authority, employment and patronage associated with local government. SSHA tenants are now entitled to have their tenancies transferred to new, possibly private sector landlords who have also been accorded short assured tenancies which will guarantee landlords repossession after a fixed term. Apart from the controversy which surrounds the mechanism by which tenants decide to opt for a new landlord (much criticism has been levelled at the ballot arrangements and the fact that a majority of those voting is sufficient to determine the outcome for all tenants) the disappearance of the SSHA assumes that its function was primarily that of landlord. The lifespan of the SSHA demonstrated considerable vigour in the technological development of building materials, methods and designs, targeted support for economic initiatives, and a degree of forward planning in relation to the changing nature of housing priorities in Scotland. RIP.

Notes

1. This chapter is based on a detailed survey of SSHA documents, specifically, minutes of meetings of the Council of Management, annual and monthly reports, internal memoranda and other SSHA documents. Some material, including relevant statistics, is published in the Annual Housing Returns for Scotland. Though this chapter was written before the publication of T Begg, *50 Special Years: A Study in Scottish Housing* London, 1987, and an earlier version appeared as 'The implementation of housing policy; the Scottish Special Housing Association', *Public Administration*, **65**, 1987 pp.313–29, it has benefited from a reading of Tom Begg's book, and from his helpful comments. Participants at seminars in Gävle and Leicester also made observations from which the present chapter has benefited.
2. See chapter 2.

3. G E Cherry, 'The town planning movement and the late Victorian city', *Transactions of the Institute of British Geographers*, 4, 1979, p.307.
4. R H Campbell, 'Introductory essay', in Scottish History Society, *Scottish Industrial History: a Miscellany* Edinburgh, 1978, p.xxxix.
5. N K Buxton, 'Economic growth in Scotland between the wars: the role of production structure and rationalization', *Economic History Review*, **33**, 1980, pp.538–55; A D Campbell, 'Changes in Scottish incomes, 1924–49', *Economic Journal*, **65**, 1955, pp.225–40.
6. M Bowley, *Housing and the State 1919–44*, London, 1944, Appendix I.
7. R D Cramond, *Housing Policy in Scotland 1919–64: A Study in State Assistance*, Edinburgh, 1966, p.45.
8. J S Gibson, *The Thistle and the Crown: a History of the Scottish Office* Edinburgh, HMSO, 1985, 69–70. See also the excellent account of Scottish Office–London tensions in the 1920s in Begg, op.cit. (note 1), pp.51–3.
9. N von Tunzelman, 'Britain 1900–45: a survey', and I Drummond, 'Britain and the world economy 1900–45', both in R Floud and D McCloskey (eds) *The Economic History of Britain since 1700. Vol. 2. 1860 to the 1970s* Cambridge, 1981, pp.239–64 and 293.
10. House of Commons Debates, *332 HD Deb 5s* (1937–38 Session) and *325 HC Deb 5s* (1936–37 Session).
11. N Morgan, '"£8 cottages for Glasgow citizens": innovations in municipal house-building in Glasgow in the inter-war years', ch.5.
12. Further detailed references are available on request from the authors, or by reference to sources in H Al-Qaddo, 'An analysis of organizational change: a study of the Scottish Special Housing Association' unpublished PhD, CNAA, 1986. The authors wish to acknowledge the assistance of the SSHA and SDD for access to papers.
13. T Begg, op.cit. (note 1), pp.67–72 provides an account of the visit. See also the *Glasgow Herald*, 5 May 1938 and the *Motherwell Times*, 6 May 1938, quoted in Begg.
14. J S Gibson, op.cit. (note 8), pp.138–9.
15. P Dunleavy, *The Politics of Mass Housing in Britain 1945–75: A Study of Corporate Power and Professional Influence in the Welfare State* Oxford 1981, p.2.
16. D H Halley, *Scottish Special Housing Association: a Chronicle of Forty Years 1937–77* Edinburgh, 1977, p.12.
17. Quoted in T Begg, op.cit. (note 1), p.122.
18. SSHA, Second Annual Digest for year ended 31st March 1949, p.43.
19. R H Macintosh, 'The "No-Fines" Story'. (SSHA Public Relations Department, nd).
20. D H Halley, op.cit. (note 16), p.19.
21. We are grateful to Tom Begg for guidance on this point.
22. SSHA, *A Mirror of Scottish Housing: the History and Development of the Scottish Special Housing Association* 1984, p.8.
23. A Gibb, 'The redevelopment of the town' in J Hood (ed) *The History of Clydebank* Carnforth, 1988, pp.169–73 provides an account of the SSHA Clydebank initiatives.
24. T Begg, op.cit. (note 1), p.145; 100 houses were built at Balornock, 104 at Cadder Road, and 194 at Rosshall. There were a further 548 under construction at Toryglen.
25. There is an extensive literature on the Clyde Plan, see for example publications of and references in works by R Smith, 'The origins of Scottish New Towns policy and the founding of East Kilbride', *Public Administration*, **52**, 1974, pp.143–59;

'Multi-dwelling building in Scotland 1750–1970' in A Sutcliffe (ed) *Multi-Storey Living* London, 1974; 'The politics of an overspill policy: Glasgow, Cumbernauld and the Housing and Town Development (Scotland) Act', *Public Administration*, **5**, 1979, pp.79–94; and E Farmer and R Smith, 'Overspill theory: a metropolitan case study', *Urban Studies*, **12**, 1975, pp.151–68.

26. Scottish Development Department, *Rents of Houses Owned by Public Authorities in Scotland 1972* HMSO, Cmnd, 5260 1972–3, tables 5 and 6.
27. Scottish Development Department, *Central Scotland: a Programme for Development and Growth* HMSO, Cmnd 2188, 1963–4.
28. D H Halley, op.cit. (note 16), p.33.
29. *Glasgow Herald*, 22 and 23 November 1968.
30. Scottish Development Department, *Homes for People: Scottish Housing Policy in the 1970s*, Cmnd 5272, 1972–3, para 7.
31. SSHA, Annual Digest, year ended 31 March 1974, no 27, p.8.
32. D Niven, *The Development of Housing in Scotland*, London, 1979 p.84.
33. Scottish Office, *Scottish Housing: A Consultative Document* Cmnd 6582, 1976–7, p.xv.
34. SSHA, Annual Report 1976, p.3.
35. J J Hogan, and H Al-Qaddo, 'Policy succession in a Scottish quango: the Scottish Special Housing Association 1937–84', *The Scottish Government Yearbook*, 1984, 171–86. The SSHA began in 1975 to build and upgrade 2,650 houses (extended in 1979 to 10,290 houses).
36. SSHA, Annual Reports, 1978, 1979.
37. Scottish Development Department, *Scottish Housing Handbooks* Edinburgh, HMSO, No 5, Housing for the Elderly, 1980; No 6, Housing for the Disabled, 1979; No 7, Housing for Single People, Shared Accommodation and Hostels (1984).
38. G Bevan, 'Cash limits and public sector pay', *Public Administration*, **59**, 1981, pp.379–98.
39. L Pliatzky, 'Cash limits and pay policy', *Political Quarterly*, **53** 1982, pp.16–23.
40. *The Scotsman*, 1 April 1982.
41. J J Hogan and H Al-Qaddo, op.cit. (note 35).
42. R H Hall, *et al*, 'Patterns of interorganizational relationships', *Administrative Science Quarterly*, **22**, 1977, pp.457–74; J A Raelin, 'A mandated basis of interorganizational relations: the legal political network', *Human Relations*, **33** 1980, pp.57–68.
43. H Aldrich and S E Mindlin, 'Interorganizational dependence: a review of the concept and re-examination of the findings of the Aston Group', *Administrative Science Quarterly*, **20** 1975, pp.382–92; J Pfeffer and G R Salancik, *External Control of Organizations: a Resource Dependence Perspective* New York, 1978; K G Provan *et al*, 'Environmental linkages and power in resource dependence relations between organizations', *Administrative Science Quarterly*, **25** 1980, pp.200–23.
44. S M Schmidt and T A Kochan, 'Interorganizational relationships: patterns and motivations', *Administrative Science Quarterly*, **22** 1977, pp.220–34.
45. *The Scotsman*, 19 December 1980.
46. S Levine and P E White, 'Exchange as a conceptual framework for the study of interorganizational relationships', *Administrative Science Quarterly*, **5**, 1961, pp.583–601: M Tuite *et al*, *Interorganizational Decision Making*, Chicago 1972; K S Cook, 'Exchange and power in networks of interorganizational relations', *Sociological Quarterly* **18** 1977, pp.82–8.
47. B W Hogwood, 'The Tartan Fringe: Quangos and Other Assorted Animals in

Scotland', University of Strathclyde, Studies in Public Policy No 34, 1979, pp.1–14.

48. R A W Rhodes, 'Some myths in central-local relations', *Town Planning Review*, **51** 1980, pp.270–85.
49. Quoted in T Begg, op.cit. (note 1), p.181.
50. Housing (Repairs and Rents) (Scotland) Act 1954, and, Valuation and Rating (Scotland) Act 1956.
51. Department of Health for Scotland, *Rents of Corporation Houses in Glasgow.* Report by Mr C J D Shaw QC on the Local Enquiry in the matter of a review or rents of Corporation Houses in Glasgow', Edinburgh, HMSO, 1958.
52. Minutes of the Council of Management, 1960. Also quoted in Begg, op.cit. (note 1), p.186.

8 The decline of landlordism: property rights and relationships in Edinburgh

David McCrone and Brian Elliott

In the early years of this century, ninety out of every hundred dwellings in Scotland were owned by private landlords. Today, this figure is a mere six in every hundred. What has happened in a span of less than a century to effect this radical transformation in Scotland's housing tenure? The major shifts in Scotland, as in the rest of Britain are well established—the decline (almost the demise) of private rental housing, the rapid growth of council and other public housing since 1945, and especially in recent years, the massive increase in owner-occupation.

The stock of privately rented housing in Britain stood at 8 million dwellings in 1914, at 3 million in 1976, and by 1987, virtually at half that figure, a mere 1.7 million.[1] The rate of decline has been, in recent years, dramatic. Since the early 1970s, the stock of privately rented housing has been disappearing at a rate of 3 per cent per annum, rising in the 1980s to 4 per cent. This absolute decline is thrown into relief by the growth of the housing stock generally—at a rate of around 1 per cent per year—and especially of the owner-occupied sector which has risen from just under 11 million (56 per cent of the total stock) in 1976, to just under 14 million (63 per cent) in 1987. Given that the number of owner-occupied dwellings in the United Kingdom stood at 3.9 million in 1951, there has been a three-and-a-half-fold increase in 36 years. While the number of owner-occupied dwellings has increased at a rate of just under 300,000 a year in the last decade, those in the privately rented sector have fallen at a rate of over 100,000 annually.

Given these fairly consistent trends, we could be forgiven for thinking that the decline in private landlordism has been fairly continuous since the early years of this century, and especially since the 1915 Rent Restrictions Act which is conventionally taken as the political hammer-blow to the private landlord, controlling the level of rents for 'small dwelling houses' according to the Act, and thereby making the business uneconomic. In this respect, we would be mistaken, for it is only in recent post-war decades that the privately rented sector has declined significantly. As late as 1947, for example, as many as six out of ten households still rented from a private landlord. The inter-war years proved to be remarkably stable in this respect.[2] In England and Wales (no comparable data are available for Scotland), the stock of privately rented housing fell by a mere 7 per cent between 1919 and 1938, compared with 30 per cent between 1938 and 1960, 37 per cent between 1960 and 1975, rising to 42 per cent in the last decade. Why should the rate of decline have been less in the inter-war years? Simply put, owning and letting out property was an economic proposition. Property prices fell along with interest rates and building costs. In the general atmosphere of deflation, rental returns were of the order of 4 to 5 per cent in real terms. This favourable economic climate even encouraged builders to build for private rental, and some 60,000 new rented properties were added to the housing stock in England and Wales between 1933 and 1939, aided by government subsidies designed to help the housing problem. In Edinburgh, as in other Scottish and English cities, substantial tracts of, mainly suburban, housing were added in the 1930s. Much of this was specifically built by contractors (like MacTaggart and Mickel in Edinburgh's case) for rent.

Through the years of World War II, with few resources for new building or for maintenance, and with bomb damage and evacuations exacerbating the situation, pressure on the housing stock and the rental sector in particular increased. Together with the general conditions of a war economy, this meant the end of the inter-war 'Indian summer' for private landlords. There was rapid inflation of the order of 75 per cent in general prices between 1939 and 1948, and a further 45 per cent in the following decade. The trebling of prices for vacant properties between the late 1930s and 1945 meant that landlords were increasingly faced with a constant shortfall between the rents they could charge and the market value of the empty houses. Obviously, the economic answer was to obtain vacant possession and sell, and many did. The logic applied on both sides of the border. By 1964, in England and Wales (again, no such data are available for Scotland), some three-quarters of a million properties were transferred to the owner-occupied sector. In all, one and a half million rented homes found their way into owner-occupation between 1938 and 1960, and the stock was further depleted between 1960 and 1975 by further transfers of the order of 1.1 million dwellings. In this period, the demolition of rented property accelerated, so that one-sixth of the privately rented stock—some 800,000 dwellings—was destroyed. In the forty years from 1938, four million homes were lost to private letting. At this rate of decline, it looked as though the private landlord would be extinct by the end of the century. A combination of political controls dating from the 1915 Act restricting rent levels, and economic disincentives compared with owner-occupation and council letting appeared to be destroying the private rental market.

There are, however, dissenting opinions to this conventional view. One of the most telling was provided by David Eversley[3] who pointed out in 1975 that those who predicted the demise of the private landlord had failed to examine the data carefully enough. While the proportion of *dwellings* had fallen steeply (to 11.7 per cent in 1971), *households* living in privately rented accommodation had declined less sharply (12.9 per cent of all households). The 1981 census confirms this apparent discrepancy, for while there were 2.5 million households in privately rented accommodation, there were only 2.2 million dwellings in this sector in Britain. Eversley concluded:

> While the number of *dwellings* available for the (privately rented) sector is still being reduced, the number of *households* they must shelter is not. (p.120)

Why should this be? While according to the orthodox wisdom letting makes little economic sense, the social demand for it is higher than ever, a demand in particular from households who are either excluded from other sectors of housing, or who find private letting a more suitable form of tenure. For example, it is estimated[4] that over half of newly formed households start off in privately rented accommodation, and only a third in owner-occupation. Similarly, such accommodation often provides a last resort for those who cannot get or keep housing in the better established tenures.

In the major cities the private landlords have held sway, in the inner districts controlling on the one hand a good deal of expensive prestigious property for rent to the wealthy (particularly in areas of London), but also many more flats and houses of a contrasting character: the dilapidated, cramped and inadequate quarters of the poor. As recently as 1946, for example, over half of Edinburgh's housing stock was still owned by private landlords, while in the inner city wards virtually all property was privately rented.[5] In Dalry, for example, 93 per cent of dwellings were in the privately rented sector in the immediate post-war years, in the Old Town, 92 per cent, and in Leith, 76 per cent. By 1971, a number of these inner city areas were still dominated by the private landlord. St Giles ward had 52 per cent of its housing stock in the privately rented sector, St Andrews, 47 per cent, and Central Leith, 44 per cent. By the 1970s, most of the city's privately rented accommodation was to be found in these central districts. For the most part, it was poor property reflected in low rateable values, and lacking the proper amenities. And in the main, it was occupied by small housholds—the elderly, young married couples, and single people. In these respects, Edinburgh was not untypical, for we still find districts in our major cities in which the largest tenure is private renting, despite the fall in the national statistics to less than 10 per cent of all dwellings.

What these data suggest is that we need to look behind the broad aggregated set of national statistics on private renting—which point to the declining importance of the private landlord—and examine instead how landlordism has operated in localities, particularly the big cities. There we can chart the changing fortunes of the private landlord, and examine the social, political and economic processes surrounding property relations more carefully. Historical analysis is vital to such an understanding, and in this way we can obtain a more rounded and comprehensive view of private landlordism. This is what the study of landlords in Edinburgh tried to do.[6]

Explaining the declining fortunes of the private landlord might seem a straightforward task. Usually, the explanation[7] begins with the Rent Restriction Act of 1915, which marked the loss of political influence of the landlord.

Politicians 'interfered' with market processes by controlling rent levels for small dwellings, particularly in Scotland, and so began the slow decline of the privately rented sector. Once introduced, these restrictions on rents were renewed annually, reflecting the superior political power of tenants over landlords. Subsequently, no Government has been able to 'free' the privately rented market. True, there have been periodic attempts such as the 1957 Rent Act to do this, but their effects have been extremely limited, and critics dismissed these as half-hearted. The other and related explanation for the decline of the landlord has been a more overtly economic one. According to this view, private letting has been starved of investment because other forms of housing tenure are more attractive, notably owner-occupation. This form of tenure, the argument goes, has been subsidised in two ways—tax relief on mortgages, and the removal, in the early 1960s, of capital gains tax from profits made on house sales by the owner-occupier.

This account is premised on the assumption that private landlordism can only be revived if market forces are given their head. All political controls on rented accommodation should be abolished, according to this analysis, and the differential attractions of owner-occupation and council tenancy should be removed. On the face of it, the commitment of the Thatcher governments since 1979 to the 'market mechanism' seems consistent with this view, and might, therefore, suggest that the longstanding decline of private landlordism will be arrested and then reversed. In the new, entrepreneurial Britain there might once more be a bright future for landlords. But that is not a prospect to be accepted too readily. Nor should the general explanations of the changing fortunes of landlordism be adopted without further reflection, for though the economic and political processes identified are undoubtedly important, they really need to be put in a wider context.

Changes in the housing system are really part of a wider and more profound change which has taken place in the nature of *property* and *property relations* in Britain in the twentieth century.[8] Property refers to rights, not to things, and over the past seventy years or so the rights attaching to the ownership of housing have altered substantially. The stock of privately rented housing has been very largely in the hands of small, local investors. Typically, it was the shopkeepers, the owners of diverse modest businesses and some of the local professionals—the lawyers, doctors and others—or those closely associated with real estate—minor landowners, developers or building craftsmen—who held the bulk of the flats and houses for rent in British cities. In the nineteenth century and in the early years of the twentieth century, it was these people who put their money into 'stone and lime', who saw in the ownership of a few flats or cottages the opportunity for additional income or security. As the rights of landlords were progressively restricted—their rights to set rents or to evict tenants—so it was the local bourgeoisie that was most evidently affected. Changing these particular property rights contributed to broad shifts in the general condition of this petty bourgeois stratum and to the pattern of class relations in the cities and in the wider society.

The explanation for the decline of landlordism then must be set in context, must be appreciated as a feature of the broader decline in the fortunes of the small, local bourgeoisie in the twentieth century. It may be the intention of Mrs Thatcher and her ministers to revitalise the small business sector, but the prospects of reconstructing a stratum of small landlords as part of this is hardly likely to meet with success. The social and economic conditions out of which such a stratum originally developed were very different from those of the 1980s. Under recent Conservative Governments, the decline of petty landlordism has continued (from 2.4 million rented properties in 1979 to 1.7 million in 1987); the deregulation of rented housing has fallen far short of what free marketeers and landlords wanted; and where some expansion of the rented property market has occurred, this has been at the hands of large, corporate capital, not those of traditional, local property owners. To understand the changing fortunes and the likely developments of landlordism requires then a broad view of economic, political and social relationships. Above all, it demands some detailed attention to the history of this form of property holding. The history of landlordism in Edinburgh though, of course, contains features peculiar to that city, but reveals many of the most significant and general patterns.

The power of the landlord

In the nineteenth century, the power of landlords was expressed in different ways. It derived principally, of course, from the fact that they were the owners of a basic, scarce commodity which the vast majority of families—middle class as well as working class—sought from them. The landlords had real economic power, for except in periods when there were, briefly, oversupplies of particular kinds of housing, they could set the rent levels and fix conditions of tenure confident that the conditions of the market favoured them. It was true, of course, that landlords were in competition with one another for tenants, especially when the market had to cope with a significant number of vacant properties. The temptation to undercut one's competitors by reducing rents was certainly present, although it seems that landlords were in practice reluctant to do this.

The power of landlords, however, did not rest simply on their role as providers of housing, but from the social relationships they had with their tenants, and the basis of this relationship was the chronic indebtedness of a great many working class families. For many it was simply impossible to live each week without going into debt, a situation which stemmed not only from the level of wages, but from the nature of much work. Some of the skilled artisans with their relatively good levels of pay and job security, and with their diverse societies and associations through which they saved money, kept their domestic economies 'in the black', but for the largest number of workers unemployment and seasonal lay-offs and fluctuations in pay brought periodic indebtedness. Planning and thrift might be enjoined, but in practice setting money aside to cover periods of worklessness or illness was exceedingly difficult to do. And paying the rent was a formidable task in these circumstances, especially when, as was common, tenancies were set on a yearly or half-yearly basis. In his study of workers in nineteenth century Edinburgh, Gray[9] pointed to the ways in which systems of renting reflected important economic and status differences within the working class:

> According to the President of the Edinburgh Trades Council only 'the very poor class' paid weekly; yearly tenancies and half-yearly payment was the rule. It was no doubt fairly common for those who could manage it, to put money aside for the rent.

Despite important social and economic differences within the working class, all were dependent on the private landlord for accommodation until well into this century. All were tenants, locked into subordinate social relationships with house-capitalists. This was most obvious in the cases where tenants went into debt. Plainly, to be in debt, one had to be able to get credit, and to get credit, you had often to convince not only the landlord, but the grocer, the baker and others that you were able to pay, and that your 'character' was good. In this way, certain petty property owners became arbiters of the moral worth of the family.[10] The criteria for 'tick' were rigorous—not only financial standing, but also the abstemiousness and time-keeping of the breadwinner would be assessed, as well as the family's bad debts elsewhere. The tick book and the clean rent book became badges of integrity and probity. The very poor did not have these problems, for no-one allowed them any credit, and they had to 'pay their way' by buying minimal amounts of food and shelter. They would rent a room on a daily basis because that was all that they could afford.

The landlord did not give credit because he was a philanthropist. Partly, he realised the facts of working class life, for eviction was a poor way of recovering rent owed. He would press hard for his money in a manner likely to generate it. More importantly, credit gave the landlord a special hold over his tenant who was indebted and therefore dependent on him. Having a claim on a tenant was a useful means of social control, and correspondingly was often resented by the tenant. Neither could the tenant—at least the 'respectable' one—simply abscond and move on elsewhere. The moonlight flit must have appealed to many tenants, but it was not an answer in the longer term. As Englander[11] comments: 'The temporary escape from indebtedness gained by flitting had to be weighed against the loss of a credit connection'. Most tenants required a 'character', a reference, from the previous landlord before the new one took him on. Tenancy, then, was not simply a commercial arrangement, but a tacit recognition that the tenant was subordinated to a class which policed his life and that of his family at home and at work. And in Scotland, the law underpinned the landlord's position in a quite remarkable way. There existed the 'right of hypothec', by which, according to the Guthrie Report of 1907:[12]

> tenants' furniture and tools were liable to sequestration by a landlord immediately after they enter on possession of a house, as security for rent not then accrued, due or payable.

It is, perhaps, difficult to grasp what we read in this statement. It meant what it said, namely, that the landlord had security over what the tenant possessed *even before* the tenant went into rent arrears. Such a legal arrangement surely helps to explain just why landlordism became such a political issue north of the Border in the early decades of this century. These extraordinary powers meant effectively that nothing belonged to the tenant because of his potential indebtedness to the landlord who had the right to sequester his personal belongings. It is true that in England, the law of 'distraint' gave the landlord the right to seize, without legal process, what the tenant possessed, but for *non-payment* of rent.[13]

As political pressure was put on government to rescind this right, the representatives of the landlords and their factors or agents defended it on the grounds that, like eviction, it was rarely used. The evidence is to the contrary, for sequestration of property due to rent arrears amounted to one-sixth of the annual value of all small debt business in Scotland, and even 42 per cent in Glasgow in some years in the early twentieth century.[14] No doubt hiring and firing tenants occurred easily enough, although the Guthrie Committee seems to have accepted that 'the case for an 'obstreperous' landlord turning out a satisfactory tenant must have been a rare one.[15]

Much, of course, hinged on what was judged to be 'satisfactory', but landlords found the power to evict a useful shot to have in the locker. When, for example, the tenant refused to renew an annual lease because he felt it too long and unduly restrictive, the landlord would exercise his right to take on a new tenant. One Edinburgh landlord, a lawyer and politician who owned more than 1,000 properties in 1907, told the Guthrie Committee, somewhat disarmingly:[16] 'I never let a house over the head of a tenant without telling him that I have another tenant for it.' Perhaps fear of 'house-wrecking' and malicious revenge stopped more landlords from using their extensive powers of eviction and sequestration.

A tenancy, then, was really a lot more than a 'contract', a commercial transaction as we would understand it. It was a means whereby those with property could exert moral authority as well as material influence. The landlord could set the rent at any level he liked, given market conditions, and raise it at will. Before letting a property, he could demand evidence of probity and worth. The tenant had to bring his 'character' with him, and the landlord could grant or withhold similar documents if a tenant wished to leave or was evicted. The working class tenant was caught up in a complex of domination which lasted well into the twentieth century.

The politics of landlordism

This complex of domination found further expression in the local political system. Historically, the links between property ownership and local politics in Britain have been particularly strong because, as Peter Hennock[17] has pointed out, in contrast with most European countries, local authorities here were heavily or totally dependent for revenue on rates levied on property. In the absence of local taxes on income, trade or sales, the burden of local taxation fell on those who owned property. These were, in the main, not persons of great wealth, but the owners of small businesses, of a few flats or houses. Their property, the source of their political entitlement, being modest in extent, was often highly vulnerable. It was the source of their livelihood, the basis of their security, the foundation on which their status was built, and local politics was one important means of its protection. From time to time, the interests of these modest bourgeois conflicted with those of the larger manufacturers, retailers and builders, and separate 'economist' parties or ratepayers' associations were formed to give expression to their views. In many cities, it seems that the larger businessmen retreated from involvement in local politics, as many found the locus of their business activity shifting from the local to the national level.[18]

In the Edinburgh study,[19] the links between property and political power were examined for a hundred-year period, from 1875 to 1975, the choice of dates being dictated by the problem of data availability at the earlier end of the time-scale, and by the demise of the Town Council following local government reorganisation at the other. The composition of the council was explored at seven points over that time span: at 1875, 1905, 1925, 1935, 1955, 1965 and 1975. At each time period, data was collected on the property holdings of councillors; their occupations; their membership of committees; the holding of office such as Lord Provost, treasurer or bailie; and political affiliation.

The central purpose was to examine the connections between landlordism and political power, and in the early periods (1875 and 1905) these can best be summed up by two simple statistics: in 1875, 80 per cent of Edinburgh's town councillors were landlords, and in 1905, the figure stood at 72 per cent. While at the earlier date, councillors owned just under 1,000 properties, in 1905 it stood at over 1,300, overwhelmingly domestic properties rather than commercial premises or land. But the connection can be looked at in other ways too. Taking the composition of council committees, for example, reveals that on the Lord Provost's Committee—the most important one—no less than 95 per cent of members were landlords, on the Treasurer's Committee (which set the rates) 87 per cent, and on the influential Plans and Works Committee which gave official approval to new developments, 86 per cent. In 1905, the same committees figure again, but a new committee on improvements was also staffed by a large number of propertied councillors (83 per cent). In both periods, the Hospital Committee—at this time hospitals were a local government responsibility—also had very heavy concentrations of the 'property interests'.

In occupational terms, too, those with building interests played an active and disproportionate part in local political affairs. Combining the numbers of builders, house factors and building craftsmen shows that in 1875 almost one-fifth of the council were directly involved in the building trades. By 1905, this tendency was even more marked. Edinburgh, along with other cities, experienced periodic booms and slumps in its building industry, and at the turn of the century, the house-building market was generally buoyant. In 1905 23 per cent of councillors were working in building trades.

Edinburgh's local politics in the final quarter of the nineteenth century and the beginning of this gives an appearance of considerable confusion. The Liberals remained the largest faction, but the label was often qualified by terms like 'radical' or 'independent' or 'advanced'. For the most part, however, politics consisted of local men standing as individuals with only the loosest of affiliations to any known group or party. Certainly, there were few links to national politics, and many made a virtue of this political parochialism. This was not surprising, because local politics was judged to be about local issues for local people.

Tracing the local political history of this period, it is hard to find much evidence of vigorous debate structured along ideological lines. There seems, by today's standards, to be a remarkable lack of controversy. The major political issues in Edinburgh during these years were mostly concerned with attempts by the local administration to develop and control the supply of services which the citizens demanded. The debates in these years were taken up with discussing a new water supply from St Mary's Loch (in 1875), on the proposed purchase of the gas company (1887, and again in 1910), and the municipalisation of the tramways (1907). At the same time, housing and sanitary problems continued to be tackled largely under specific City Improvement Acts, a favourite device for forestalling central Government pressure and retaining local autonomy. The aim seems to have been to keep local affairs local, to avoid committing the ratepayers—the property owners—to 'excessive' expenditure, and to manage the political agenda so as to keep controversial issues out of the council chamber.

The power of the property interests, then, in 1875 and 1905 can scarcely be doubted. Given the overwhelming representation of domestic property owners on the council as a whole and the involvement of many in the building trades on the key committees, the interests of 'property' were surely well attended to. It is hard too to resist the idea that careers in property might well be advanced through membership of a corporation with such evident influence over urban real estate.

Putting the Edinburgh evidence alongside that from studies of other Scottish and English towns suggests that in the late Victorian and Edwardian periods, landlords enjoyed considerable political power at the local level.[20] Investing in one's town, being involved in local business and in local politics made sense to these local bourgeois. After all, local knowledge meant knowing the right people on whom one's business depended. Men of business and of the professions counted their knowledge of local networks as a key source of influence. Investing in rented property was attractive to them. Owning a tenement or two provided a steady if unspectacular income, a form of insurance against hard times in trade, and a means of supporting financially vulnerable members of the family, especially the womenfolk. These investors, says Gauldie,[21]

> were the very kind of people to have low expectations of returns from investment, to choose safety in the form of a small yearly income rather than greater possible profits over a long period of time.

Certainly, localism made good business sense. Knowledge of local conditions was vital, especially when over-building—much of this property was provided on a speculative basis—could have a drastic effect on demand. It seems that few landlords owned property outside their town. Much better, they thought, to own property locally, something they could go and look at. Providing housing was, then, a local affair, and the housing market was supported by small owners with small amounts of capital, and marshalled by local agents and lawyers. Working class housing remained the preserve of the small, local investor who could not risk his capital in some exotic foreign venture in Australia or the Americas.[22]

Tenants, especially working class tenants, quite often found themselves beholden to the landlord in much the same way that they were dependent on the local, small shopkeeper. From both they obtained credit; and to both they were subordinated by this debt relationship. It was, for the most part, the women in the families of tenants who managed these debt relationships. Through them they experienced the realities of class in a way different from, but no less significant than, that found in the workplace. Landlords used their economic superiority to assert a kind of moral or social power—'vetting' their tenants, providing or withholding references, certifying the moral worth of those who rented from them. Buttressing and extending these kinds of power, the property owners frequently entered, and indeed dominated, local politics.

The declining significance of landlordism

How, then, was it possible for landlords to lose such supremacy in Britain's towns and cities? What brought about this loss of domination which had given them such a hold over working class tenants? The conventional explanation is to focus on the deteriorating economic context for petty landlordism—the speculative nature of the working class housing market with its booms and slumps; the drying up of capital for builders and landlords; and the emergence of a new kind of housing tenure provided by local authorities. All these factors are important, but there are three somewhat different factors which seem to lie behind these deteriorating economic conditions for landlords.

First, the very strength of landlordism—its local base, its roots in the local community—contributed to its downfall. The localism of business interests is attested to by Offer,[23] who points out that by the turn of the century,

> House-capitalists were small men and women. Among investors, they were bound by the narrowest horizons, and the same reasons which made them prefer houses over other securities also prevented them from transcending the immediacies of their localities.

The problem for these house-capitalists was that they were, by and large, socially and economically marginal. They were a fraction of capital, and a not very important fraction at that on the national stage. Owning a few houses or flats was a sideline to some other trade, and few made a full-time living from landlordism. This marginality had political consequences too, as Daunton[24] points out:

> The ownership of housing was a widespread but marginal activity, a feature which was to have serious political consequences for landlords.

Landlords may have been successful in retaining power in their localities, but increasingly the localities, the urban corporations, were themselves subordinated to central political power, their rights and responsibilities defined by Westminster. And increasingly too their economic fortunes were shaped by national and international markets, and by the operations of large, national rather than local businesses.

The second factor which helps to account for the loss of landlords' influence was the politicisation of the housing question. This occurred partly through forms of collective action, popular, local resistance to the power of landlords, and partly through the growth of labour politics at a municipal and at a national level. By the late nineteenth century, a housing crisis was particularly severe in the major cities. In London, for example, the pressure on land and property, coupled with inadequate state regulation, placed heavy burdens on the existing housing stock. Urban redevelopment led to the systematic displacement of large sections of the working class.[25] The Scottish cities, too, had long had particular housing problems of overcrowding and dense building development. Political and philanthropic concern about the housing question in Scotland had grown in the last quarter of the nineteenth century, and the next fifty years saw a succession of Commissions, reports and Housing Acts. The most significant of these in Scotland were The Royal Commission into the Housing of the Working Classes in 1885; The Guthrie Report into House Letting Conditions of Working Men's Dwellings in 1907; and The Hunter Committee Report into the Alleged Increases in the Rental of Small Dwelling-Houses in Industrial Districts in Scotland in 1915. The Royal Commission into the Rent Restrictions Act of 1919 controlling the rents of 'small dwellings' (tenement flats) signalled the end of a phase of concern, agitation and inquiry into working class housing, and the Act undoubtedly marked a fundamental shift in landlord–tenant relations. The power of the landlord was never to be the same again. Behind this legislative activity lay widespread social unrest over housing conditions and rent levels. Glasgow's problems were of staggering proportions—70 per cent of its housing stock consisted of tenement flats of two rooms or less. The housing problems of the very poor—those who lived in the lodging houses or 'made down' houses—did not carry much weight, but the rents and living conditions of the largest section of the working class turned increasingly into a major political issue in the first decades of the century. Some indication of changing attitudes can be gauged from the reaction to housing problems in Edinburgh. Whereas in 1885, the president of the Trades Council rejected state intervention in housing—'I'm afraid it would strike at that industry and enterprise that lies at the very root of our national existence'[26]—, by 1907, labour and trades and tenants' organisations were lined up in opposition to year-long lets over against the landlords who wanted to retain them.[27]

While the letting issue was important, it was a sideshow compared with that of rents which helped to make housing the political issue in the first two decades of this century. World War I brought together political and industrial issues, especially on Clydeside.[28] Landlords found themselves on the receiving end of widespread moral indignation at 'profiteering'. At a time of war, landlords were enforcing rent increases on absent soldiers, and on essential munitions workers. Landlords were, of course, experiencing the effects of war, particularly the rise in interest rates which followed government attempts to generate war revenues, and as a consequence, found themselves starved of capital for investment. The rents issue was broadened into a wider class struggle, and began to involve groups usually excluded from political action, notably women. Women acted as 'street captains' in organising the defence of their territory, often with violent consequences for bailiffs and house factors who tried to carry out evictions. The Rent Act of 1915 was, in the first instance, an emergency measure in wartime to be rescinded following victory, but the Government found it was politically impossible to do this, and it was extended annually thereafter. Undoubtedly, the war acted as a watershed for the private landlord, and, as Englander[29] points out: 'Property owners still spoke fondly of the good old days before the war when the bailiffs could be put in without fuss.'

In the late nineteenth and early twentieth centuries, housing became a battleground for class struggles. Often there was greater likelihood that housing would generate class consciousness than periodic bouts of industrial conflict fought out behind factory gates. Although the Clydeside rent strikes are perhaps the best known, similar actions were taking place elsewhere—in Edinburgh, Aberdeen and Dundee, and farther afield in Birmingham, Belfast, Manchester and in the London boroughs of Woolwich, Tooting and Poplar. The redefinition of housing as a 'class' issue helps to explain why landlords found their hold on Britain's towns and cities draining away so quickly after 1915.

In Edinburgh between the wars, there were two principal developments in local politics. First, there was the rally of right-wing forces to meet the challenge from Trades Council and Socialist candidates at local elections. A loose alliance of erstwhile Liberals and Conservatives was formed—the Progressive Association—which united most of the anti-socialist members. This Association established control of the council, and held power from 1928 through to 1973. Second, there occurred the considerable extension of the role of the municipality as it took over from the Parochial Boards responsibility for education (in 1928), grappled with the problems of providing public housing, and extended its geographical boundaries by incorporating Leith (in 1920).

In this context, landlords found it more difficult to sustain their rather defensive-minded politics. The Progressive Association kept alive the belief that local government was essentially 'non-political', an enterprise in which *individuals* were elected on their merits, and owed no allegiance to national parties. Labour, they judged, were 'bringing politics into local government' in a quite illegitimate way. But the issues which dominated Edinburgh's politics in the inter-war period served to highlight the kind of pressures which were being placed on local government by Westminster. No fewer than eleven housing acts were passed between 1919 and 1938. Housing became a major issue at local elections, and directly threatened property and building interests, for landlords were faced with an increase in the supply of modern council houses at low rents, and local builders by plans to use direct labour to build them.

By 1925, the property interests on the council represented just over half (57 per cent) of those elected to office, and by 1935, this proportion had fallen to 45 per cent. Nevertheless, landlords were still considerably over-represented on the key committees—streets and buildings, burgh valuations, housing and planning, as well as the powerful all-purpose committees, the Lord Provost's and the Treasurer's committees. The hold of property on these committees can be gauged by the fact that in 1925 Housing and Town Planning Committee there were four builders (out of seven on the council that year). The Streets and Buildings Committee was chaired by a builder, and had another as a member. The property interests may have found their hold on the council diminishing, but they and their allies among other Progressive councillors (who were mainly small businessmen) retained power particularly on those committees that had to respond to the housing issues. Said the *Edinburgh Evening News* (3 November 1930):

> Housing has been the main topic; the effects of rent subsidies on tenants ... and the need to have sound businessmen on the Town Council.

Always there was fear of 'excessive' expenditure, and in 1935, we find one candidate complimenting the city on having 'the lowest rate of any burgh in Scotland'. The small businessmen on the council had practised 'sound economy'.

However, by the inter-war years, the character of this 'property interest' on the council was shifting—away from those concerned with the actual *production* of housing, towards those whose livelihood depended upon the *management* of property, the estate agents, house factors, and lawyers. For the first time too, owner-occupation was a prospect for a large number of people, and builders were encouraged to develop housing estates for artisans and white-collar workers instead of traditional tenement flats. Collecting rents and arranging sales became vastly more attractive for house factors. It was these managers of property who became, in the 1930s, important actors in local politics.

Since World War II, the representation of landlords on the council has continued: 13 per cent in 1955, 14 per cent in 1965, and in 1975, 20 per cent. But vastly enlarged public housing programmes, the sustained development of owner-occupation, along with a good deal of large-scale commercial and civic building gave many others an interest in political decision-making over urban land use. Many of the 'new men' in property were those servicing the construction industry rather than those owning some flats or factoring some property. These newcomers were much less directly involved in the building or the management of property, and more involved in providing technical expertise, knowledge of the local market, and legal or financial skills. Thus, as the property market has changed over the past hundred years, so has the character of property interests on the council.

The third reason for the decline of the private landlord can be traced to the state's role in changing the property market and in redefining property relations. As the housing question became more urgent, more contested, more politicised, so the State intervened to maintain social peace. It did so in two ways. First, in 1915, in the context of war and the threat of widespread labour unrest, it acted to head off the growing socialist challenge that was emerging in Glasgow. Industrial and consumption struggles, the term 'trenches', as Katznelson[30] has called them, from which the working class groups fought workplace and housing issues showed signs of running into each other, merging to form a more substantial redoubt from which the class war could be waged. The State addressed the more malleable of the two issues. It stepped in to restrain landlords from increasing working class rents. In doing so, it sacrificed (with the knowledge and complicity of other fractions of capital) the interests of the local petty bourgeois elements. It was a successful tactic. Along with other more overtly repressive measures, the prospect of serious challenge from the youthful socialist parties and movement was removed. Workplace grievances remained but the production of munitions and other goods vital to the war economy was maintained. But this action by the State proved to be more than an extraordinary and temporary expedient, for it altered once and for all the taken-for-granted traditional rights of the property owner, at least, the owner of domestic property. From that point on, the rights of landlords to set rents and to evict tenants have been substantially (though never totally) constrained by legislation. And in turn that has meant that the property relations surrounding private renting could not be restored.

The second way in which the State addressed the housing question was less dramatic and less readily located in a single piece of legislation, but over many years, and very evidently in the inter-war years, it began to alter the whole market for housing in Britain through measures that allowed, encouraged and ultimately required local authorities to provide public housing. This was part of the complex process of intervention in the working of a market economy which established new forms of public property, new rights which citizens could claim. In essence, these were rights not to be excluded from collective goods and resources. The right to decent housing was loudly proclaimed and, especially after 1945, loudly proclaimed by governments of both major parties. Municipalities and other state agencies provided housing on a very substantial scale, and nowhere more extensively than in Scotland. In Glasgow, for instance, nearly 60 per cent of the housing stock was 'corporation' housing by the time Mrs Thatcher came to power.

Taken together, these two major actions by the State totally altered the context in which private landlords operated. Thanks largely to the efforts of successive Labour governments, many tenants in private and public housing have come to enjoy rights to low levels of rents and a good deal of security of tenure. These are rights conferred upon them by the State even though they do not own the property. There is no doubt that those who received them welcomed these rights. But landlords, of course, did not. As they saw it, their legitimate rights were severely and unwarrantably curtailed. Landlords and tenants were recognising something that political philosophers had long told us; namely that property rights are conferred and guaranteed by the State.[31] They are contingent, not absolute. The rights we have can be taken away and given to others. It is this fact that helps to explain why landlords in the 1970s, when there was widespread apprehension that the privately rented sector was doomed, became so agitated; why landlords' associations contributed to the growing middle class discontent in 1974 and 1975, and why they welcomed a new Conservative leader who promised to 'restore' the rights of property. And since that time, although the legislative efforts to assist landlords have in fact been very modest, property and property rights have remained very much at the heart of political debate and the neo-conservative programme.

Over the past century or so, then, private landlordism has been subject to diverse pressures and outright attacks. Rent restrictions from 1915 onwards, large-scale provision of public housing, rapid inflation in domestic property prices from the 1950s, rising real incomes coupled with substantial tax advantages to owner-occupiers, all meant that by the 1960s most forms of private rental produced very poor returns. The time had come to sell out, and that landlords did. With that went more than simply a source of revenue. Landlords were severing a whole series of long-established property relationships. At the same time, their grip on local politics, which had been loosened by the 1930s, slipped. Local politics became more and more tightly enmeshed in a system of national struggles between the two main parties, Conservative and Labour. The social composition of councils and parties changed, the private landlord almost sinking from view.

The survival of petty landlordism

How, then, does landlordism survive? It does so partly because of inertia, and partly because it still provides some, albeit restricted, opportunities for up and coming entrepreneurs. In the mid 1970s, landlords in Edinburgh were studied using valuation roll data to provide a comprehensive profile of property ownership, data from the Register of Sasines to trace property histories, and survey material from a sample of 184 Edinburgh landlords. Overwhelmingly, landlords were individuals holding only one or two properties. While 70 per cent of them were private individuals, they owned between them only 34 per cent of all rented properties in the city. Clearly, many of these individuals were landlords in only the most modest way. Trusts—which represented 18 per cent of landlords—owed 19 per cent of Edinburgh's privately rented stock. These had been formed as legal devices mainly by Victorian and Edwardian owners who were anxious to leave some legacy to wives and families. As the Hunter Committee was informed in 1915, property owners were

> people of comparatively modest means, but there are a number of *trusts* which have come into operation by the death of people of comparatively modest capital.[32]

By the 1970s, private individuals and trusts represented 88 per cent of Edinburgh's landlords, and between them owned nearly 54 per cent of the city's rented property. Although there are no historic data for Edinburgh with which to assess over time profiles of ownership, the data provided by Daunton and Morgan for Glasgow in 1900 allow some comparison. And what is striking about their findings is the dominance of just such individuals and trusts at an earlier period. In Glasgow at this time, they represented 90 per cent of all landlords and held 82 per cent of the city's rented property. It seems that private landlordism, then, has not developed major corporate enterprises that dominate the market, but rather it is left to the same petit bourgeois interests who saw in such investment a safe and secure bank for their modest savings. There is evidence, nevertheless, that might suggest that property companies now play a more significant role in the market for rented accommodation—in Edinburgh they owned 24 per cent of the rented stock in the 1970s—but closer examination revealed that many of these companies were simply designed to take advantage of limited liability so that debts can be written off against marginal assets. Few could be described as corporate enterprises with the necessary capital and inclination to make major profits. The profile of Edinburgh's landlords is completed by a small number of public bodies like hospitals and universities that hold small stocks of rented housing, or diverse commercial or industrial firms that do likewise. Most landlords in Edinburgh by the 1970s were small, reluctant owners of very modest properties, properties which provided little by way of profit. Much of it was in the hand of house factors or family lawyers who took a fairly passive approach to these assets. And since the 1950s, many of these small owners and trusts had been selling off their holdings as the market for owner-occupation grew.

Some of the established individual owners and trusts recognised that if profits were to be made from their holdings, these would come not from rental but from sale of their properties. Blocks of property could be disposed of, a series of flats, say, sold with sitting tenants to a new landlord, often a factor or lawyer. Though the sums received for such properties were generally very modest, selling off the real estate in this way at least provided an escape from the responsibilities and the low—sometimes negative—returns from the rents. Capital was realised and could be invested in more rewarding ways. Those who acquired these properties typically sought to dispose of them fairly quickly, selling individual apartments in tenement blocks as soon as the tenant moved or died and vacant possession was obtained. A number of the new landlords became specialists in this 'break-up' process, as it was generally termed. In the 1970s it was not uncommon for someone to acquire a tenement of a dozen flats for a few thousand pounds and realise the total purchase price through the sale of only one or two apartments. The buoyancy of the property market and the rapid escalation of property prices provided a good many of these property entrepreneurs with a relatively quick profit if tenants could be persuaded to leave and the current market value of the vacant property traded. In some instances, of course, whole blocks could be sold for the site value rather than the value of the generally aged and dilapidated building.

A number of 'professionals' in the property business—lawyers, estate agents and factors—recognised the opportunities presented by the desire of many landlords to dispose of their holdings. Such professionals often managed trust property whose trustees had grown weary of property with controlled rents and rising repair bills that contributed more headaches than profits. These lawyers and factors were well placed to acquire cheaply, tenements and even whole streets to add to their portfolios, and dispose of as flats fell vacant. An elderly lawyer admitted that he bought up 'the rump end of executry estates' which he sold off in twos and threes for a couple of hundred pounds a year. One local house factor had sold 66 small flats—rooms and kitchens in the Scottish parlance—in five years for a quarter of a million pounds. Another had acquired two tenements of twelve and nine flats, costing a mere £2,000 in total (on average, a little over £90 each) and disposed of these for modest sums of £500 to £700 a piece, and realised a profit of 300 per cent in only five years. As long as they did not fall foul of closing orders and escalating repair bills, these 'break-up merchants' as they were called, could do very well.

All of this, though, did not mean that it was totally impossible to make a good living from rents. Petty property retained its appeal to those seeking to invest a little capital and a lot of personal effort as an alternative to more orthodox ways of making a living. A few achieved considerable profits by buying cheap property and letting it out to selected groups. Here we can see the paradox of contemporary landlordism. While the average owner made very little money, there were a few who were very successful. These landlords were 'traditional' insofar as they relied for income on rents, but they concentrated on furnished tenancies which at the time were not subject to the same legal controls as unfurnished properties. They achieved success and profit by careful letting and close personal involvement. And this is where they differed from the unsuccessful ones, who inherited property, were often reluctant owners, and who often were ashamed of what they owned. If, as was often the case, the property was factored, there was little incentive to take on personal responsibility for running the investment. Those who had taken a more active role were more likely to be those whose occupational skills would otherwise confine them to fairly modest livings. That is why in many cities, especially those with far more mobile populations than Edinburgh's, property ownership has been attractive to immigrant groups. Lacking social and occupational skills, newcomers have found in landlordism a way of making a better living. Thernstrom[33] noted it, for example, among the Irish in nineteenth century Boston, who indulged in 'ruthless under-consumption' to fund upward social mobility through property. In more recent times, Krohn[34] spotted the same phenomenon in the 'other economy' of Montreal in the 1970s. Studies of Asian and West Indian groups in English cities in the 1960s[35] also attest to the same phenomenon. In the course of the Edinburgh study, mentions were made of 'Poles' (in practice, Middle and East Europeans—Russians, Ukrainians, Lithuanians, Germans, as well as Poles) who had come to the city in this century, and who had bought their way into property because they lacked the educational and occupational skills of the native population. Old property was being put to new uses.

Given the legislative and fiscal constraints on private landlordism, it is tempting to predict the demise of the privately rented sector, but against this we have to set the fact that there are new recruits to the business of owning and renting out houses. True, the general profile is one of elderly and disengaged landlords, but in the Edinburgh study there was a small number—no more than a quarter—whose orientation to and involvement in property were quite unusual. Most of them were relatively young; they were in the main first generation landlords who had *chosen* to be involved in property. In many respects, they shared a perspective with the fathers and grandfathers of many who had inherited property—a personal commitment to the business, and a desire to make it pay. This new generation of landlords, operating in a quite different environment to that of a century ago, could be divided into those who were interested in acquiring blocks to sell—the break-up merchants—and those who were content to operate as rentiers, but who catered for a specialised clientele such as students and single people. Certainly, in the 1980s, profit-seeking landlords have been quick to identify special groups such as the single homeless and those in receipt of housing benefit as likely to generate big profits. Some of these younger and more active landlords were embarking on careers as professional landlords, developing expertise in all aspects of property purchase, control and maintenance.

The break-up merchants, on the other hand, garnered in the most spectacular profits in the 1960s and 1970s, as blocks of unwanted flats came on the market, for their interests did not lie in holding on to property once they had vacant possession, but to realise the profits quickly and invest them in another 'investment opportunity'. Around 20 per cent of landlords in the sample had bought property for this purpose, but the number of break-up merchants was probably closer to 10 per cent of the total. To these individuals, landlordism was incidental, for they considered themselves entrepreneurs rather than rentiers. They would act as the midwives of 'gentrification', buying up property in the inner city, carrying out some improvements, and selling it further up the market for owner-occupation.

The financial success of some landlords suggests that there are still considerable profits to be made from rented property, either by buying and selling—by trading property—or by selecting special categories of tenants. Maintaining close and careful supervision of tenancies seems to be the key to this success for those content to act as rentiers. Mixing one's own labour with a little capital—the classic petit bourgeois formula—can still give good returns on what is conventionally seen as a declining and unprofitable form of economic activity. The rate of decline in the private rented sector has continued over the past decade because the typical landlord does not have the commitment nor the expertise of those landlords who continue to make the running in this sector of the housing market. And it is because of their activities that the obituary for the landlord cannot yet be written.

Petty property and popular capitalism

Until very recently there was little concern in history or in sociology with the role of the small property owners in capitalist society. Even economists gave petty capital short shrift. In many ways this was understandable since plainly it could be argued that big capital or giant corporations or organised labour were the factors that did most to shape the development, particularly the recent development, of western societies. But in the last decade or so that has begun to change as historians, sociologists, economists and others have looked at the patterns of accumulation in the early phases of industrial take-off, at the development of class structures, the nature of local politics, the relations between central and local government, or the shaping of political institutions. And most recently, with a Conservative Government determined to promote entrepreneurial activity, the operation of the free market, popular capitalism and with all that, the role of the small businessman, there has been a considerable increase in studies of the minor capitalists.[36] What these diverse investigations tell us is that the petit bourgeoisie has played a more important part in shaping institutions, practices and values than has generally been recognised.

The legacy of the petit bourgeois in our towns and cities is certainly very clear. Most of our urban centres were shaped to a considerable extent during the phase of industrial capitalism by small capitalists whose transactions and investments laid down much of the urban ecology that survives today. Their role in local politics was, in many places, a major one. Not only were local councils often dominated by men (and later women) who were involved in local businesses (and as the Edinburgh case shows, local landlordism and property development or management), but a great many local institutions with control over education, health and welfare were largely in their hands until the post-1945 period. And in important ways too class relations in the cities were shaped by the material and, indeed, the moral preoccupations of those with modest property. The home and the shop no less than the workplace were permeated with bourgeois values. These were by no means uncontested, of course, especially in the working class districts, but their influence in structuring social relations can hardly be denied.

But by the 1960s and 1970s, the influence of the petty bourgeoisis was in decline.[37] This was particularly evident in Britain where the size of the small business stratum shrank remarkably. The fortunes of landlords, then, should be appreciated as part of the much broader decline of a once numerous section of the population. And it is this general loss of position, opportunity and influence that underlay the lamentations of landlords in the Edinburgh survey. Those who were interviewed constituted a residuum of that class of property owners who had, in earlier periods, controlled so much of the housing and, indeed, the social and political life of the city. Their comments on their own position and on the state of Britain in the mid-1970s were fearful, resentful, indignant. In a host of ways they expressed regret for a world they had lost. A few individuals gave vent to their disquiet through local associations or a (not very effective) national association of small landlords; others joined one or other of the small business groups that flourished in this period, and added their voice to the strident middle class discontent of these years. They inveighed against the unwarranted power of organised labour, against governments that were unsympathetic to them, against 'bureaucracy' that licensed, taxed and scrutinised their activities, against the new and, as they saw it, privileged class of professionals in a host of state agencies, against big business and against dominant moral precepts that were allegedly corrosive of bourgeois virtues. In the complaints of the Edinburgh landlords one could discern all the principal themes that were subsequently given such clear and powerful articulation by the 'new conservatism' of Margaret Thatcher and Sir Keith Joseph.

The new conservatism constructed a 'retrospect', an image of a time past, a golden age in which the former glories of nation and community were the justified rewards of a society ordered by specifically bourgeois values. Such a retrospect had enormous appeal to those, like the landlords, who felt themselves oppressed, unfairly treated, denigrated. And so too did the promise of legislative measures that would restore those bourgeois values and the economic conditions in which small business would once again prosper. The Conservative Government after 1979 made much of the need to defend the family, the primary source of authority, social order and accumulation.[38] That fitted nicely with many landlords' conceptions of their own biographies and histories, for much of the private rental stock consisted of flats and houses that had been acquired by and kept within families over several generations. The new, 'radical' conservatism, the emergent 'popular capitalism' held out the prospect of a remaking of the social world in Britain. It was to be a world in which the small property owners would be restored to their rightful place. And the place of landlords within that was clearly recognised. Measures would be taken to reconstruct the private rented sector.

But what has happened? When Mrs Thatcher came to power in 1979 there were 2.4 million rented properties in Britain; now there are less than 1.7 million, scarcely good evidence of a restoration of the landlords' fortunes. That is not to say that the Government made no efforts to ease the constraints on private renting. The 1980 Housing Act reformed the law relating to rented housing by introducing 'shorthold' tenancies of one or two years during which time the tenant had security of tenure. Thereafter the property would revert to its owner. A second measure, 'assured' tenancies allowed approved organisations—building societies, banks and major builders—to build for rent outside rent controls and security of tenure. There was a considerable gap between Government rhetoric ('freeing the landlord', and 'lifting the Rent Act curbs') and its practice. Shortly after its 1987 election victory, the Government introduced a radical Housing Bill with three relevant proposals for rented housing. Council tenants were to be given the right to transfer to landlords other than the Council; non-elected boards—Housing Action Trusts—could take over and manage run-down council estates; and assured tenancies were to be stimulated by scrapping 'fair' rents so that a 'reasonable return' would be given to the landlord. This deregulation falls far short of what free marketeers and landlords wanted, for 'market rents' were not to be the norm. Small, private landlords were particularly disappointed because preference was being given to institutional owners like building societies and banks to build property for letting.

What conclusions can be drawn from the recent rhetoric and legislation concerning private landlordism? There seem to be three principal points that can be made. First, much of the Conservative Government's interest in the plight of the small landlord should be seen as a device, part of a general objective to mobilise sectors of the small bourgeois stratum by expressing sympathy and understanding of their grievances. In this way they would be enlisted in the struggle to win and hold power and to reconstruct the 'market society' and forms of 'popular capitalism'. Secondly, the legislative changes that allow landlords to charge market rents will have some marginal effect on the small property owners and allow or encourage some of them to remain in the business. But the new practices and policies will likely have a much more substantial impact on big capital and corporate institutions. If there is any increase in the stock of privately rented accommodation, it will most probably be provided by them rather than the individual landlords. Thirdly, the persistence of the private rental sector will flow from the fact that in this as in other areas of the economy there will always be some economic niches that the small-time entrepreneur can fill. Providing shelter for the homeless, taking advantage of the payments from the Department of Social Security or the local council has proved to be the latest profitable venture for some landlords. Among the poor, the recent immigrants, the elderly and those excluded for whatever reason from private ownership or the public housing system, there will always be some who must turn to forms of private letting. Wherever such needs exist there will always be those with a little capital, a little property to provide for them. That, pre-eminently, is why the small landlord will survive, just.

Notes

1. HMSO *Housing and Construction Statistics in Great Britain* 1987, table 2.24.
2. For a useful account of this period, see Department of Environment *Housing Policy* (Technical Volume) HMSO 1977, part 3, ch.9.
3. D Eversley, 'Landlords' Slow Goodbye', *New Society*, 16 January 1975, pp.119–21.
4. Department of Environment *Housing Policy* op.cit. (note 2), 1977.
5. P Abercrombie and D Plumstead *A Civic Survey and Plan for the City and Royal Burgh of Edinburgh* Edinburgh, 1949, map 8 'Survey of Dwelling Ownership'.
6. D McCrone and B Elliott *Property and Power in a City: The Sociological Significance of Landlordism* (forthcoming), and 'Landlords in Edinburgh: Some Preliminary Findings', in *The Sociological Review*, 23 March 1975; 'Property and Political Power: Edinburgh 1875–1975', in J Garrard *et al* (eds) *The Middle Class in Politics* 1978; 'Urban development in Edinburgh: a contribution to the political economy of place', *Scottish J Sociology* 4 1980; 'The social relations of petty property', in P Hollowell (ed) *Property and Social Relations* 1982.
7. See, for example, *Rent Act 1957: Report of an Inquiry (The Social Survey)* Cmnd 1246, HMSO 1960; and more recently, *The Private Rented Housing Sector* House of Commons, First Report from the Environment Committee HC40, HMSO 1981–82.
8. E Gauldie, *Cruel Habitations: A History of Working Class Housing, 1780–1918* 1974; M J Daunton, *House and Home in the Victorian City. Working Class Housing, 1850–1914* 1983.
9. R Q Gray, *The Labour Aristocracy in Victorian Edinburgh* 1976.
10. R Roberts, *The Classic Slum* 1973, p.81; G Stedman Jones, *Outcast London* 1971, p.88.
11. D Englander, *Landlord and Tenant in Urban Britain, 1838–1918* 1983, p.110.
12. *The Guthrie Report into House Letting Conditions of Working Men's Dwellings* 1907, HMSO, Cd 3715, 2, para 774–5.
13. Ibid., p.30.
14. D Englander, op.cit. (note 11) 1983, p.31.

15. *The Guthrie Report*, op.cit. (note 12), 1907, **1**, p.13.
16. Ibid., **2**, para 6784.
17. E P Hennock, *Fit and Proper Persons* 1973; 'Finance and politics in urban local government', *Historical Journal* **6** 1963.
18. See E P Hennock, op.cit. 1973; D S Morris and K Newton, 'Profile of local political elites: businessmen as community decision-makers in Birmingham, 1836–1966', *The New Atlantis* **2** 1970.
19. The results of this research are fully described in 'Property and political power: Edinburgh 1875–1975' (note 6), 1978.
20. See, for example, D Fraser *Urban Politics in Victorian England: the Structure of Politics in Victorian Cities* 1976; E P Hennock op.cit. (note 17), 1973.
21. E Gauldie op.cit. (note 8), 1974, p.182.
22. See J P Lewis, *Building Cycles and Britain's Economic Growth* 1965; J R Kellett 'Property speculators and the building of Glasgow', *Scottish J Political Economy* **8** 1961; R Rodger, Scottish Urban Housebuilding, 1870–1914, unpublished PhD Edinburgh thesis 1975.
23. A Offer, *Property and Politics, 1870–1914: Landownership, Law, Ideology and Urban Development in England* 1981, p.297.
24. M J Daunton, op.cit. (note 8), 1983, p.117.
25. G Stedman Jones, op.cit. (note 10), 1971.
26. *Second Report of Her Majesty's Commissioners for Enquiring into The Housing of the Working Classes: Scotland* 1885 Cd 4409, evidence of Mr A C Telfer, president of Trades Council, para 19, p.188.
27. *Guthrie Report*, op.cit. (note 12), 1907, **1**, p.7.
28. J Melling, *Rent Strikes: Peoples' Struggle for Housing in West Scotland, 1890–1916* 1983; J Melling (ed) *Housing, Social Policy and the State* 1980,.especially chapters by Melling and by Damer; I McLean, *The Legend of Red Clydeside* 1983.
29. D Englander, op.cit. (note 11), 1983, p.310.
30. I Katznelson, *City Trenches: Urban Politics and the Patterning of Class in the U.S.* University of Chicago Press, 1981.
31. C B Macpherson, 'Capitalism and the changing face of property', in E Kamenka and R S Neale (eds) *Feudalism, Capitalism and Beyond* 1975; C Reich, 'The new property' *Yale Law Review* **73** 1964.
32. Hunter Committee, *Report of the Committee to Enquire into the Circumstances connected with the Alleged Recent Increases in the Rental of Small Dwelling Houses in Industrial Districts in Scotland* cd 8111, 1915, para 1093.
33. S Thernstrom, *Poverty and Progress: Social Mobility in a Nineteenth Century City* Harvard University Press, 1974.
34. R Krohn *The Other Economy: the Internal Logic of Local Rental Housing* Peter Martin Associates Ltd, Toronto, 1977.
35. J Rex and R Moore, *Race, Community and Conflict: a study of Sparkbrook* 1967; J G Davies, *The Evangelistic Bureaucrat* 1972.
36. See, for example, F Bechhofer and B Elliott (eds) *The Petite Bourgeoisie* 1981; G Bannock, *The Economics of Small Firms: Return from the Wilderness* 1981; H Newby, et al, *Property, Paternalism and Progress* 1978; R Scase and L Goffe, *The Entrepreneurial Middle Class* 1982.
37. J E Bolton, *Small Firms: Report of the Commission of Enquiry on Small Firms* 1971; Eurostat, *Employment and Unemployment* 1970–1982 (1983).
38. B Elliott, *et al*, 'Bourgeois social movements in Britain: repertoires and responses' in *Sociological Review* **30** 1982; and B Elliott and D McCrone, 'Class, culture and morality: a sociological analysis of New Conservatism', in *Sociological Review* **35** 1987.

APPENDIX A: COMPLETED HOUSES—SCOTLAND

	Local Authority	*New Town*	*Scottish Special Housing Association*	*Other Housing Associations*	*Government Departments*	*Total Public Sector*	*Private Sector*	*Total All Agencies*
1919	–	—	—	—	—	—	—	—
1920	—	—	—	—	—	817	1,140	1,957
1921	—	—	—	—	—	4,342	2,237	6,379
1922	—	—	—	—	—	9,523	2,527	12,030
1923	—	—	—	—	—	6,462	1,667	8,129
1924	—	—	—	—	—	2,993	3,274	6,267
1925	—	—	—	—	—	4,822	5,227	10,049
1926	—	—	—	—	—	9,501	5,906	13,407
1927	—	—	—	—	—	16,923	5,484	22,407
1928	—	—	—	—	—	15,071	5,172	20,243
1929	—	—	—	—	—	14,316	5,199	19,515
1930	—	—	—	—	—	7,918	4,546	12,464
1931	—	—	—	—	—	8,315	4,153	12,468
1932	—	—	—	—	—	11,631	5,913	17,544
1933	—	—	—	—	—	15,808	8,155	23,963
1934	—	—	—	—	—	15,216	9,684	24,900
1935	—	—	—	—	—	18,814	7,086	25,900
1936	—	—	—	—	—	16,044	7,757	23,801
1937	—	—	—	—	—	13,341	8,187	21,328
1938	—	—	—	—	—	19,162	7,311	26,473
1939	—	—	—	—	—	19,118	6,411	23,329
1940	—	—	—	—	—	10,474	3,732	14,206
1941	—	—	—	—	—	4,714	692	5,406
1942	—	—	—	—	—	3,072	224	3,296
1943	—	—	—	—	—	2,717	92	2,809
1944	—	—	—	—	—	2,383	170	2,553
1945	1,351	—	77	—	—	1,428	141	1,569
1946	3,321	—	490	—	—	3,811	499	4,310
1947	8,919	—	1,854	20	2	10,795	1,354	12,149
1948	16,615	—	2,932	14	109	19,670	1,541	21,211
1949	20,004	60	4,116	72	493	24,745	1,102	25,847

1950	20,989	158	3,167	91	624	25,029	782	25,811
1951	17,971	120	2,906	139	647	21,783	1,145	22,928
1952	22,393	485	4,745	285	797	28,705	2,242	30,947
1953	29,719	1,316	4,957	217	946	37,155	2,393	39,548
1954	29,748	1,466	4,117	115	799	36,245	2,608	38,853
1955	24,210	1,323	3,745	131	1,137	30,546	3,523	34,069
1956	22,084	1,073	3,133	148	887	27,325	4,576	31,901
1957	24,239	951	3,136	105	493	28,924	3,513	32,437
1958	22,622	1,474	3,277	93	643	28,109	4,061	32,170
1959	18,665	1,551	2,493	4	348	23,061	4,232	27,293
1960	17,913	1,519	2,071	127	433	22,063	6,529	28,592
1961	16,823	1,265	1,453	53	489	20,083	7,147	27,230
1962	16,245	1,576	967	65	124	18,977	7,784	26,761
1963	17,699	1,649	1,816	32	399	21,595	6,622	28,217
1964	24,814	2,608	1,734	12	341	29,509	7,662	37,171
1965	21,823	2,996	1,765	154	825	27,563	7,553	35,116
1966	21,343	3,870	2,302	118	526	28,159	7,780	36,029
1967	27,092	3,941	2,189	181	557	33,960	7,498	41,458
1968	26,756	3,207	2,048	288	970	33,269	8,720	41,989
1969	27,497	3,656	2,779	183	187	34,302	8,327	42,629
1970	28,045	2,790	3,525	244	302	34,906	8,220	43,126
1971	23,125	2,394	3,058	332	260	29,169	11,614	40,783
1972	16,335	1,519	1,739	413	151	20,157	11,835	31,992
1973	14,432	1,589	1,328	245	224	17,818	12,215	30,033
1974	13,016	2,099	1,067	480	435	17,097	11,239	28,336
1975	16,086	3,636	3,062	766	402	23,952	10,371	34,323
1976	14,361	3,980	2,813	1,152	517	22,823	13,704	36,527
1977	9,119	3,167	2,042	546	314	15,188	12,132	27,320
1978	6,686	1,510	1,711	1,127	282	11,316	14,443	25,759
1979	4,755	2,018	1,084	544	206	8,607	15,175	23,782
1980	5,048	1,288	1,119	881	33	8,369	12,242	20,611
1981	3,770	1,516	1,779	1,928	1	8,994	11,021	20,015
1982	2,342	729	645	1,167	17	4,900	11,529	16,429
1983	2,311	667	508	1,271	6	4,763	13,178	17,941
1984	2,120	233	280	2,076	14	4,723	14,118	18,841
1985	1,989	201	621	1,099	17	3,927	14,445	18,374
1986	1,733	157	297	1,466	114	3,767	14,843	18,610
1987	1,790	107	678	1,119	139	3,833	13,794	17,627

Sources: Annual and quarterly Housing Returns

APPENDIX B
PRINCIPAL SCOTTISH HOUSING LEGISLATION SINCE 1890

It is now widely accepted that state subsidised council housing was not simply the product of an electoral slogan or an inevitable consequence of pre-war municipal intervention.[1] 'Homes for Heroes' was a useful political device by which Treasury money for improved housing was made available to local authorities. But the deeper, short term purpose of government funded house-building should be set against the background of mounting labour unrest, not the least disturbing aspect of which to the Government was a police strike in 1919. Broad social reforms and an early intimation of a housing programme was vital, Lloyd George told the Cabinet in March 1919, since, 'Even if it cost a hundred million pounds, what was that compared to the stability of the state' and the threat posed by Bolshevism?[2] The Parliamentary Secretary to the Local Government Board took this theme further: 'the money we are going to spend on housing is an insurance against Bolshevism and Revolution.' Once the immediate threat of instability had passed in 1921, that particular premium was no longer paid. The 1919 housing programmes was suspended within 2 years, and though and subsequent housebuilding proposals transpired, these were curtailed as was public expenditure generally, by deflationary monetary policies of the 1920s associated with the return to the gold standard.

Though the principle of state subsidised housing was never wholly reversed, many changse subsequently were introduced. What follows is intended only as a selective outline guide[3], and as the contributors themselves explain, these legislative changes should not be treated as fixed points of historical departure, but rather as the product of societal forces. Housing legislation was, thus, the result of composite political, social and economic forces, a dependent rather than an independent variable. The danger of mentioning the legislation at all is that it then assumes a dynamic of its own.

Housing of the Working Classes Act 1890 *53 & 54 Vict c.70*
Parts I and II consolidated earlier demolition or clearance powers concerned with insanitary properties either as individual houses or small areas. Part III enabled local authorities to initiate building of new houses.

Burgh Police (Scotland) Act 1892 *55 & 56 Vict. c.55*
Schedule IV required building regulations for all towns (extended to county councils in 1897) and *Burgh Police (Scotland) Act 1903 (3 Edw 7 c.33)* required municipalities to compile a register of streets so as to regulate activities, uses and parks.

Industrial and Provident Societies Act 1893 *56 & 57 Vict. c.39*
Government loans available to limited dividend housing societies.

Small Dwellings Acquisition Act 1899 *62 & 63 Vict. c.44*
Local authorities could lend money to assist house purchase. Effectively a 'dead letter' in Scotland.

Housing, Town Planning etc. Act 1909 *9 Edw 7 c.44*
Allowed urban local authorities to extend their municipal boundaries for the purpose of housing, and enabled town planning schemes to be drawn up. Third Schedule and sections 52 and 53 applied the act to Scotland.

House Letting and Rating (Scotland) Act 1911 *1 & 2 Geo 5 c.53*
Strengthened landlords' powers of eviction. This was balanced by requiring further collections of local rates by landlords, and by encouraging shorter house-letting periods, which tenants preferred.

Rent and Mortgage Interest (War Restrictions) Act 1915 *5 & 6 Geo 5 c.97*
Rents were fixed for the duration of the war plus a further 6 months at 1914 levels for properties with a certain rateable value. Mortgate recall and interest increases were disallowed.

Housing, Town Planning, etc (Scotland) Act 1919 (Addison) *9 & 10 Geo 5 c.60*
Local authorities obliged to conduct a survey of housing needs, and to submit plans to Whitehall (Dept of Health) to eliminate shortages. Financial cost of housebuilding limited to the equivalent of 0.8d on the rates (elsewhere in the UK it was 1d), with the Treasury paying any further costs. About 25,000 houses built under this act ie 10 per cent of needs.

Increase of Rent and Mortgage Interest (War Restrictions) Act 1919 *9 & 10 Geo 5 c.67*
Renewed and extended rent controls. Limited rent increases approved.

Housing (Additional Powers) Act 1919 *9 & 10 Geo 5 c.99*
Private builders eligible for Treasury lump sum subsidy.

Housing (Scotland) Act 1920 *10 & 11 Geo 5 c.71*
Councils able to 'hire' (compulsorily take over) private properties for working class housing.

Housing (Scotland) Act 1921 *11 & 12 Geo 5 c.33*
Limited exchequer grants under 1919 legislation to £1.65 million.

Housing etc., Act 1923 (Chamberlain) *13 & 14 Geo 5 c.24*
Lump sum payments to private builders from councils, who were then

compensated by a fixed £6 per house payment from the Treasury for 20 years. Council housebuilding approved only if Scottish Board of Health agreed that this was 'more appropriate' than private enterprise building. A reaction to the limited acheivements of the 1919 scheme. A 50 per cent subsidy was available for rehousing cost resulting from slum clearance.

Housing (Financial Provisions) Act 1924 (Wheatley) *14 & 15 Geo 5 c.35*
Eligibility for subsidy extended, raised to £9 (for rural houses and those for letting), and burden of proof on councils to prove the inadequacy of private enterprise removed. A reaction to the failure of the 1923 act to generate much enthusiasm in private sector.

Housing (Scotland) Act 1925 *15 & 16 Geo 5 c.40*
Consolidating act. Gave local authorities powers to fix rents independently, though in practice laid down firm guidelines.

Housing (Rural Workers) Acts 1926 *16 & 17 Geo 5 c.56*
Grants and loans to workers from local authorities (up to maximum £100, half of which payable by Treasury) to reconstruct houses for agricultural workers. (34,000 improved rural houses 1926–45.)

Housing (Revision of Contributions) Act 1929 *20 & 21 Geo 5 c.6*
Part of process to revise 1923 subsidies downwardly in line with reductions in building costs.

Housing (Scotland) Act 1930 *20 & 21 Geo 5 c.40*
Slum clearance programme which made £2.50 available to local authorities for 40 years for each *person* rehoused. (To replace condemned properties, 15,800 houses were built in 1933 and 1934 compared to 19,700 during the entire period 1919–32.)

Housing (Financial Provisions) (Scotland) Act 1933 *23 & 24 Geo 5 c.16*
Decisions in 1929 to limit subsidies taken further by suspending payments to private enterprise under the 1923 and 1924 acts; contributions to local authorities reduced from £9 to £3, and then discontinued from 1935. Maximum rents specified to local authorities.

Housing (Scotland) Act 1935 *25 & 26 Geo 5 c.41*
Fixed, for the first time, a national minimum standard of overcrowding. Councils obliged to survey needs to conform to this standard. Subsidy of £6.75 for 40 years for each house built to relieve overcrowding. Consolidated local authority housing finance into one housing revenue account. Less categorical rent policy from central government.

Housing (Agricultural Population) (Scotland) Act 1938 *1 & 2 Geo 6 c.38*
Higher rates for replacement of unfit farm housing.

Housing (Financial Provisions) (Scotland) Act 1938 *2 & 3 Geo 6 c.3*
Revised subsidies on a sliding scale according to house size in response to 38 per cent increase in building costs 1934–38.

Housing (Temporary Accommodation) Act 1944 *7 & 8 Geo 6 c.36*
Treasury to finance the manufacture of temporary pre-fabricated houses, leased to local authorities who were responsible for site preparation. 32,000 built (20 per cent of entire programme) in Scotland.

Housing (Scotland) Act 1944 *7 & 8 Geo 6 c.39*
Financial assistance under the 1938 act extended for a further two years to assist the general supply of new houses. (Acknowledgement in a report in 1944 that housing stocks and economic growth points did not exactly coincide.)

Housing (Financial Provisions) (Scotland) Act 1946 *9 & 10 Geo 6 c.54*
More than doubled the subsidies available under the 1938 act and fixed local authority contributions at a low level. Increments available for flats in blocks of four or more storeys, and for miners' housing.

Town and Country Planning (Scotland) Act 1947 *10 & 11 Geo 6 c.6*
Extended land use planning and development control.

Housing (Scotland) Act 1949 *12 & 13 Geo 6 c.61*
Grants of 75 per cent (87.5 per cent in the highlands and islands) towards modernisation costs payable by Treasury to local authorities. Improvement grants recognised for the first time as an intermediate policy stage between new building and demolition. Gave local authorities greater discretionary powers in relation to fixing rents. References to the 'working classes' removed.'

Housing (Scotland) Act 1950 *13 & 14 Geo 6 c.34*
Purely consolidating measure. No changes to financial arrangements.

Housing (Scotland) Act 1952 *15 & 16 Geo 6 and 1 Eliz 2 c.63*
Almost doubled exchequer and local authority financial contributions. (Higher subsidies for rural housebuilding.)

Housing (Repairs and Rents) (Scotland) Act 1954 *2 & 3 Eliz 2 c.50*
Substantial rental increases tied to qualitative improvement of private rented property, which could more easily qualify for modernisation grants. 'Patching' grant available to local authorities to make properties habitable in the short term prior to demolition and replacement. Policy redirected towards maintenance.

Valuation and Rating (Scotland) Act 1956 *4 & 5 Eliz 2 c.60*
Introduced 'revolutionary changes to valuation and rating' in Scotland (resulting from the Sorn Committee report 1954 Cmd. 9244) by abolishing owners' rates and abandonment of the principle of valuation (introduced in 1854)). Rateable values to be determined by estimates of reasonable rental value of property. Since tenants paid rent only from 1957, the real amount was not clouded as before by a rates element. This revealed the drastic reduction in real rents and prompted central government to change subsidies and policies to recoup more of housing costs from council tenants. Reactions prompted rent strikes in 1957.

Housing and Town Development (Scotland) Act 1957 *5 & 6 Eliz 2 c.38*
Marks the first post-war reduction in subsidies as a response to growing deficits on local authority housing revenue accounts. Trend of rising housing costs matched by increasing Treasury subsidies reversed, throwing burden more on to tenants. Flat rate payments (£24 per house over 60 years) reintroduced. Higher subsidies for overspill houses (£42), incoming industrial workers (£30), and high rise flats.

House Purchase and Housing Act 1959 *7 & 8 Eliz 2 c.33*
Extended improvement grants and encouraged building societies to ease the terms of mortgages on older properties.

Building (Scotland) Act 1959 *7 & 8 Eliz 2 c.24*
Redefined building regulations, inspection procedures, and safety standards, and replaced historic building byelaws administered by Dean of Guild courts by building standards regulations superintended by local council building control departments.

Housing (Scotland) Act 1962 *10 & 11 Eliz II c.28*
Gave discretionary power to the Secretary of State for Scotland to reduce subsidies. Further changes in the rate of subsidy. Introduced a 'resources test' ie authorities most in need of financial assistance would receive more from the Treasury.

Housing Act 1964 *12 & 13 Eliz 2 c.56*
Established the Housing Corporation in Great Britain (responsible in Scotland to the Secretary of State) to promote co-ownership and cost-rent housing. Also loaned money to housing associations. The Housing Act 1974 re-routed considerable government finance directly to housing associations, thereby giving them a stimulus.

Housing (Scotland) Act 1966 *14 & 15 Eliz 2 c.49*
The act itself proclaimed that it was 'purely codifying the housing legislation ...

Housing Subsidies Act 1967 *15 & 16 Eliz 2 c.29*
Introduced option mortgages and more generous council mortgage terms. (Option mortgages offered reduced home loan repayments in return for forgoing mortgage interest relief entitlements.)

New Towns (Scotland) Act 1968 *16 & 17 Eliz 2 c.16*
Designated five development corporations—Cumbernauld, East Kilbride, Glenrothes, Irvine and Livingstone (Stonehouse was designated in 1973 but decommissioned in 1977)—to have powers to provide housing for sale and rent within their areas.

Housing (Scotland) Act 1969 *17 & 18 Eliz 2 c.34*
Improvement grants raised, and definitions widened. 'Tolerable standard' specified, replacing vague definition of 'fitness for human habitation'.

Rent (Scotland) Act 1971 *19 & 20 Eliz 2 c.28*
The 1920 Act consolidated wartime rent acts 1915–19 (which had limited rent increases) and introduced a system of rent control and security of tenure applicable to the majority of let property. This system remained largely intact until 1971, despite some decontrol of higher rented accommodation in 1923, 1933 and 1938. Further controls were introduced in 1939. A distinction between properties controlled under essentially WWI and WWII emergencies continued into the 1950s. The Rent Act 1957 (5 & 6 Eliz 2 c.25) decontrolled many rentals, exempted new property from controls, and prescribed a minimum 4 weeks notice to quit. This meant protection to tenants was diminished in decontrolled property, though this was reinstated under the Rent Act 1965 (13 & 14 Eliz 2 c.75). Tenancies protected under the 1919–39 rent acts were known as 'controlled tenancies' and those protected under the 1965 act as 'regulated tenancies'. The 1971 act, while retaining the different terms, attempted to standardise tenants rights.

Housing Financial Provisions (Scotland) Act 1972 *20 & 21 Eliz 2 c.46*
Fair rents procedures widened to include council tenancies and controlled sector. Rent rebate system and rent allowances, administered locally but subsidised by 90 per cent Treasury grants, designed to take account of low incomes and family housing needs.

Housing (Scotland) Act 1974 *22 & 23 Eliz 2 c.45*
Increased improvement grants. Set up and improved financial assistance for housing action areas (earlier formulations of HAAs in the 1966 and 1969 acts). Housing Associations and their supervisory body, the Housing Corporation, boosted by significant sums and borrowing powers available to them. Local authorities required to provide housing to a specified minimum standard or otherwise to close or demolish houses which do not meet it.

Housing Rents and Subsidies (Scotland) Act 1975 *23 & 24 Eliz 2 c.28*
Rent determination returned to local authority. Councils' freedom to set rents was restricted by retention of subsidies by Scottish Office if rents set too low. Rent rebate system retained. Additional subsidies to local authorities.

Housing (Homeless Persons) Act 1977 *25 & 26 Eliz 2 c.48*
Elaborate procedures imposed on new regional and district councils to provide accommodation for the homeless.

Housing (Financial Provisions) (Scotland) Act 1978 *26 & 27 Eliz 2 c.14*
Local authorities empowered to lend and award grants to housing associations and voluntary organisations to repair and improve property. 'Improvement orders' enabled councils to compel owners not in housing action areas to upgrade their property to minimum standards.

Tenants Rights, etc. (Scotland) Act 1980 *28 & 29 Eliz 2 c.52* and *c.61*
Defined terms on which tenants could buy public sector housing. Valuation procedures established, and tenants entitled to buy at 32–60 per cent discount according to duration of previous tenancy. Tenants rights enhanced by publication of councils' housing allocation procedures, by rules governing admission to the housing list, and by security of tenure procedures akin to those of the private sector.

Rent (Scotland) Act 1984 *32 & 33 Eliz 2 c.58*
Converted 'controlled' and furnished tenancies to 'regulated' tenancy status, thus standardising procedures on eviction and landlords' redress.

Housing (Scotland) Act 1986 *34 & 35 Eliz 2 c.65*
Extended tenants' rights to purchase to properties owned by housing association, regional councils, fire and other government departments. Available discount price raised to 70 per cent for tenants purchasing a flat from such agencies.

Housing (Scotland) Act 1987 *35 & 36 Eliz 2 c.26*
Major codification of housing law in Scotland.

Housing (Scotland) Act 1988 *36 & 37 Eliz 2 c.43*
Replaced the Scottish Special Housing Association and the Housing Corporation in Scotland by a new agency 'Scottish Homes' (full powers assumed 1.4.1989) to give public sector tenants the right to have their tenancies transferred to new landlords which could include private companies, housing associations and cooperatives. Introduced short 'assured tenancies' by which landlords are guaranteed repossession at the end of a fixed period.

Notes

1. M Swenarton, *Homes Fit for Heroes: The Politics and Architecture of Early State Housing in Britain* (London 1981); M Daunton, *A Property Owning Democracy? Housing in Britain* (London 1987).
2. M Swenarton, op.cit. 78–9.
3. C Himsworth, *Public Sector Housing Law in Scotland* (Glasgow 1982) provides a synopsis of modern housing law.

Index